Business Enviro

Managing in a strategic context

Second edition

John Kew and John Stredwick

The CIPD would like to thank the following members of the CIPD Publishing editorial board for their help and advice:

- Pauline Dibben, Sheffield University
- Edwina Hollings, Staffordshire University Business School
- Caroline Hook, Huddersfield University Business School
- Vincenza Priola, Keele University
- John Sinclair, Napier University Business School

The Chartered Institute of Personnel and Development is the leading publisher of books and reports for personnel and training professionals, students, and all those concerned with the effective management and development of people at work. For details of all our titles, please contact the publishing department:

tel: 020-8612 6204

e-mail publish@cipd.co.uk

The catalogue of all CIPD titles can be viewed on the CIPD website:

www.cipd.co.uk/bookstore

Business Environment

Managing in a strategic context

Second edition

John Kew and John Stredwick

Published by the Chartered Institute of Personnel and Development,
151, The Broadway, London, SW19 1JQ

First published 2005
Second edition published 2008

Typeset by Curran Publishing Services
Printed in Spain by Graphycems

British Library Cataloguing in Publication Data
A catalogue of this publication is available from the British Library

ISBN 978 18398 204 3

Chartered Institute of Personnel and Development, CIPD House, 151, The Broadway,
London, SW19 1JQ

Tel: 020 8612 6200
E-mail: cipd@cipd.co.uk Website: www.cipd.co.uk

Incorporated by Royal Charter. Registered Charity No. 1079797.

Contents

List of figures xiii

List of tables xv

Preface to the second edition xvii

1. Organisations and their environments 1
   Learning outcomes 1
   What is the environment? 4
   Analysing the environment 5
   Why do we need to understand and manage the environment? 7
   Tools for analysing the environment 11
   SWOT and strategy 13
   Criticisms of SWOT 13
       E-V-R congruence 14
   Managing the environment 19
   Conclusions 21
   Key learning points 21
   Questions 21
   Seminar activity: Activity holidays 22

2. The competitive environment 25
   Learning outcomes 25
   Economic systems 25
       The market economy 26
       Mixed economies 27
   Market structures 27
       Perfect competition 28
       Monopolistic competition 34
       Monopoly 34
       Oligopoly 36
       Monopsony and bilateral monopoly 40
   Competitive structure 40
       Michael Porter's five forces model 40
       Criticisms of five forces 44
       Portfolio analysis 45
       Boston matrix 45
       Shell directional policy matrix 47

The public and voluntary sectors   48
HR implications of response to changes in the environment   50
Strategic responses   51
Conclusions   52
Key learning points   52
Questions   53
Trends to watch   53
Explore further   53
Seminar activity: Supermarkets: an oligopolistic industry   54

3.   The world economy   57
Learning outcomes   57
The European Union   58
    The historical background to the European Union   58
    The aims of the European Union   58
    The institutions of the European Union   60
    EU enlargement   64
    The EU Constitution   67
The European Union and other regional blocs   69
International financial institutions   70
    The Bretton Woods conference   70
    The IMF   70
    The World Bank   72
International trade and comparative advantage   74
The World Trade Organization (WTO)   75
    The working of the WTO   76
Debt relief   78
Globalisation   80
    Drivers of globalisation   82
    Multinational and transnational corporations   84
    The globalisation debate   89
    Globalisation, growth and poverty   90
    Multinationals and brands   91
    Globalisation and the labour market   94
Conclusions   97
Key learning points   98
Questions   99
Trends to watch   99
Explore further   99
Seminar activity: Polish plumbers   100

4.   Government policy   103
Learning outcomes   103
Introduction   103
The legislative process in the United Kingdom and the
European Union   104
    The United Kingdom   104
    The European Union   105

Informal influences on policy	106
Political parties	106
Pressure groups	106
The government and the economy	108
Some key definitions	108
Economic objectives	110
The tools of government policy	111
The link between unemployment and inflation	114
Interest rates	115
Central banks and interest rates	116
Public ownership, privatisation and PFI/PPP	120
Public ownership	120
Privatisation	121
Public interest companies	123
The Private Finance Initiative and public-private partnerships	125
Competitiveness	129
Productivity	130
Conclusions	136
Key learning points	137
Questions	137
Trends to watch	138
Explore further	138
Seminar activity: Economic development in India and China	138
5. Regulation	**143**
Learning outcomes	143
Introduction	143
Legal contours	144
Legal concepts	144
Types of law	145
From where does the law originate?	147
The courts system	147
Law of contract	151
Regulating business and protecting the consumer	153
Controlling and enhancing competition	154
Consumer protection	157
Employment law	159
Sources of the employment contract	160
Employee rights	161
Benefits	164
Regulation of contracts through collective bargaining	164
Regulating health and safety	168
Introduction	168
Health and Safety at Work Act 1974 (HASAWA)	168
The Health and Safety Commission and Health and Safety Executive	170

Control of Substances Hazardous to Health
Regulations (COSHH) 1988   170
Regulations arising from European Union Directives   171
Reporting of Diseases and Dangerous Occurrences
Regulations (RIDDOR) 1995   171
Enforcing the law   171
Risk assessment   172
Occupational stress   173
Role of Human Resources   175
Implications of regulation   177
Industry regulators - privatised utilities   177
Industry regulation - financial services (FSA) and
communications (Ofcom)   179
Regulation and the public sector   180
Regulation and other sectors   181
Codes of practice   181
Key learning points   182
Questions   182
Trends to watch   183

6.   Demography   185
Learning outcomes   185
Introduction   185
Demography: the facts   186
Population growth   186
Drivers of population change   187
Ethnicity of the population   195
Other demographic changes   197
Trends to watch – and the future?   204
Implications of demographic predictions   205
Implications for organisations   206
Implications for governments, especially the UK
government   209
Implications for international society   213
The world's resources   215
Key learning points   216
Questions   216

7.   Social trends   217
Learning outcomes   217
Introduction   217
Class   218
Karl Marx   218
Max Weber   218
Socioeconomic classifications   219
Social mobility   220
Inequality   223
Poverty   225

Trends in employment   228
    Changes in the industrial structure   228
    The feminisation of the workforce   229
Work organisation   232
    The flexible organisation   232
    The future of the workplace   234
    The psychological contract   234
    Work-life balance   236
    Equal opportunities and diversity   238
    Trade unions   240
Conclusions   242
Key learning points   243
Questions   243
Trends to watch   244
Explore further   244
Seminar activity: Social mobility, education and the meritocracy   245

8. Technology   247
Learning outcomes   247
Introduction   247
What's happening in technology   248
    Patterns of technological development   248
    Types of technological change   249
    Information technology   250
    Communication technologies   250
    Transportation technologies   251
    The Internet   252
    Biotechnology and medical technologies   252
    Artificial intelligence (AI) and robotics   253
The impact on business strategy, goods and services   254
    Effects on business strategies and operations 255
    Specific products   257
Effects on labour markets and Human Resources   258
    Increase in temporary labour   258
    Recruitment/selection processes   259
    Teleworking   260
    Call centres   263
    Effect on the structure of HR operations   263
Knowledge management   265
Technology - the darker side   268
    Gene therapy   268
    Lettuce leaves   269
    Shared HR services   269
    The darker side of employment   269
Trends to watch – what of the future?   271
Key learning points   272
Questions   272

9.   Ethics, social responsibility and sustainability   273
      Learning outcomes   273
      Introduction   273
      Ethics   274
      Ethical principles   274
      Ethical dilemmas   276
      Whistleblowing   278
            The Public Interest Disclosure Act 1998   279
      Professional ethics   279
      Business ethics   281
      Stakeholders   282
      Values   286
      Codes of ethics   287
      Corporate governance   289
      Corporate social responsibility   293
      Sustainability   298
      Corporate social responsibility and HR   300
      Corporate social responsibility and the government   302
      The bottom line   304
      Conclusions   306
      Key learning points   307
      Questions   307
      Trends to watch   308
      Explore further   308
      Seminar activity: Responsible tourism   308

10.   Strategic management   311
      Learning outcomes   311
      Introduction   311
      What is strategic management?   312
      Models of strategy   313
            Corporate planning   313
            Strategic management   314
      The elements of strategic management   317
            Strategic analysis   318
      Gap analysis   319
            Strategic choice   320
            Strategic implementation   320
      Strategic analysis   320
            Vision, mission, values and objectives   320
            The mission statement   323
            Resource analysis   324
      Strategic choice   330
            Generic strategies   330
            Selection of strategies   337
      Evaluation of strategies   338
            Suitability   338
            Acceptability   339

Feasibility 340
Strategic option screening 340
Strategic implementation 343
Incremental and transformational change 343
Models of change 343
Managing change 344
Resistance to change 346
The role of HR in change management 346
Change leadership 351
Conclusions 352
Key learning points 353
Questions 354
Trends to watch 354
Explore further 354
Seminar activity: The Second World War 355

11. Managing in a strategic business context – integrative
case studies 357
Learning outcomes 357
Introduction 357
Strategy in the beer industry 369

Bibliography 371
Index 395

Figures

Chapter 1

1.1   A systems model of the organisation and its environment   5
1.2   Opportunity analysis   12
1.3   Threat analysis   12
1.4   A congruent organisation   15
1.5   The unconsciously competent organisation   15
1.6   The consciously incompetent organisation   16
1.7   Strategic drift   17
1.8   The lost organisation   17

Chapter 2

2.1   Flows in the market economy   27
2.2   A typical demand curve   29
2.3   An increase in demand   29
2.4   The supply curve   29
2.5   Supply, demand and equilibrium   30
2.6   easyJet's dynamic pricing   31
2.7   The Boston matrix   45
2.8   The Shell directional policy matrix   47

Chapter 3

3.1   Clark's patterns of industry internationalisation   85

Chapter 5

5.1   The court system in England and Wales   148

Chapter 6

6.1   Marriages in the United Kingdom   204
6.2   UK dependency: the ratio of 16-64 year-olds to over-65s   210

Chapter 9

9.1   Stakeholder mapping   283

Chapter 10

10.1 Gap analysis   320

Tables

Chapter 2

2.1   UK concentration ratios 1992   37

Chapter 3

3.1   Enthusiastic and cautious approaches to globalisation   91

Chapter 5

5.1   Employee benefits introduced through legislation   165
5.2   Aims of the FSA   180

Chapter 6

6.1   World population 1800 to 2005   186
6.2   UK population   187
6.3   Birth statistics, United Kingdom   187
6.4   World fertility rates   188
6.5   UK life expectancy   191
6.6   Average annual migration into and out of the United Kingdom,
        1989 to 2005   193
6.7   The UK labour market 2006   198
6.8   UK population age distribution, 1901 to 2026   198
6.9   Sectoral employment 1993 to 2006   202
6.10   Public pension expenditure as a percentage of GDP   211

Chapter 7

7.1   A class stratification system   219
7.2   Distribution of wealth in the United Kingdom   224
7.3   Distribution of income (United Kingdom) (before housing
        costs)   224
7.4   Gini coefficient (before housing costs)   225
7.5   The most common flexible working arrangements   237
7.6   Differences between equal opportunities and diversity   238

Chapter 8

8.1   The K-waves   249

Chapter 9

9.1	Carroll's ethical guidelines	275
9.2	Sources of dilemmas	276
9.3	Example of scoring a dilemma using Carroll's guidelines	278
9.4	Responses to a survey on codes of ethics	288
9.5	Strengths and weaknesses of different corporate governance models	290
9.6	Why organisations are involved in community activities	295

Preface to the second edition

The worldwide interest in business continues to grow at an extraordinary pace, fuelled by the burgeoning power and influence of Far Eastern economies and especially by the growth of China. This revised edition provides a number of updates on crucial political, economic and legal areas, including the European Union, international institutions and regulatory developments.

An understanding of the business environment continues to be vital for students who wish to gain a fuller understanding of both the context in which business decisions are taken and the major influences on those decisions. As the context becomes more turbulent and unpredictable, the more important it becomes to grasp the complexity of the many issues presented and the strategic options that can be followed.

This publication follows closely the CIPD standards for Managing in a Strategic Business context but is suitable for students at all levels whose syllabus includes a module on Business Environment, as it covers all the standard subjects normally included in such modules. The emphasis is very much on developing the knowledge and understanding of students, while the main aim has been to make the text accessible and encourage students to follow up key issues by linking the text with up-to-date cases, activities and associated reading.

The distinctive feature of this book is the large number of practical activities and case studies which apply the theory to real life situations. A large number of new case studies have been written for this second edition, and there is now a seminar activity for each chapter, as well as a number of self-assessment questions. Feedback for all the activities, along with a large number of additional activities, is provided on the companion website at www.cipd.co.uk/tss which supports the book.

The information contained on this site is available free of charge to tutors, but tutors will need to register to gain access to the material. Visit www.cipd.co.uk/tss to complete the online registration form. The site contains links to general business sites and advice to lecturers who adopt the text on how to use the book as part of a planned series of lectures. PowerPoint presentations will be available to accompany each chapter and there will be suggested feedback for activities, as well as additional activities.

A summary of the book's contents is as follows.

Chapter 1 sets the scene for business in its environment, explaining how the environment influences business decisions while, in turn, decisions by business help to shape the contexts within which businesses operate. The STEEPLE model is utilised to illustrate this process.

Chapter 2 introduces students to the principles of market economies, reveals theories on sources of competitive advantage, discusses the roles of players in the economic and ethical scene, such as trade unions and professional associations and illustrates how different competitive strategies have implications for human resource activity.

Chapter 3 discusses the role and function of the European Union and debates major issues around integration and enlargement. The causes, extent and desirability of the globalisation process then follow, together with the range of responses by governments, and their impact on the markets for goods, services and labour. The attempts by international bodies to support and regulate trading behaviour are also examined.

Chapter 4 analyses the roles and functions of government in the fields of economics, industry, education and social policy with their implications for employment markets. International variations in government policy are set out with particular reference to the European Union. The chapter ends with an examination of the ways that organisations seek to influence the development of government policy through the operation of variants of pressure groups.

Chapter 5 examines a wide range of legal and regulatory aspects, starting with an essential summary of the UK legal system and the way that the regulation has developed in the fields of employment, health and safety, consumer and commercial law. The impact of regulation on particular sectors is discussed and the direction of regulation is debated.

Chapter 6 summarises the startling changes in demography in recent years both in the United Kingdom and worldwide, discussing the major implications of an ageing population in the advanced economies and a still rapidly rising population in the developing countries. There is a debate about the natural flow of migrants from one grouping to the other. The influence on markets for goods and services, and the challenges and opportunities in the employment field, are considered in detail, together with government initiatives in key areas, such as pensions and migration.

Chapter 7 focuses on the major social trends and attitudes alongside the changing social structure. The causes of major social problems, such as the increase in criminal behaviour, are debated and the implications for employment and labour markets are examined. How organisations can react to the changes and the options available are considered.

Chapter 8 presents an analysis on technological change and its substantial influence on the business environment, especially in the fields of information and communication technology. The opportunities in the labour markets that technology offers, such as teleworking and online recruitment, are discussed together with the benefits and difficulties associated with such techniques. The reasons that there is considerable resistance to technology in certain quarters are examined.

Chapter 9 focuses on the application of social responsibility and ethics to the business community, examining stakeholder models and issues of accountability and professionalism. The nature and extent of corporate social responsibility and the systems of ethical responses to developments in the competitive environment are debated, together with issues arising from environmental developments, such as global warming and sustainability. The role of human resources in these issues is examined.

Chapter 10 brings together all the major strands covered earlier to examine the effects upon constructing and developing business strategy. This includes the major tools and techniques in environmental analysis, the various approaches to strategy-making and the constraints that the environment imposes upon strategy formation and implementation. The chapter includes debates on project and risk management and the major principles in effective strategic leadership, change formulation and management.

Chapter 11 concludes the book with extended business case studies.

We would like to acknowledge the help and encouragement we have received from colleagues and friends in writing the text, and special thanks are extended to our families for their support and forbearance over an extended period.

For those tutors and students using this text to support the CIPD Leadership and Management module 'Managing in a Strategic Business Context', a table is provided on the next page detailing how the content of the text fits with the indicative content of the CIPD module.

CIPD Leadership and Management Standards: Managing in a Strategic Business Context

The indicative content of the standards is covered as follows:

CIPD Leadership and Management Standards	Business Environment chapters	
1 The Competitive Environment	Chapter 2	The competitive environment
2 The Technological Context	Chapter 8	Technology
3 Globalisation	Chapter 3	The world economy
4 Demographic Trends	Chapter 6	Demography
5 Social Trends	Chapter 7	Social trends
6 Government Policy	Chapter 4	Government policy
7 Regulation	Chapter 5	Regulation
8 Developing Strategy	Chapter 10	Strategic management
9 Social Responsibility and Ethics	Chapter 9	Ethics, social responsibility and sustainability

National Occupational Standards: Management and Leadership Standards

The knowledge and understanding of the standards are covered as follows:

B2 *Map the environment in which your organisation operates*
> Chapter 1   Organisations and their environments
> Chapter 2   The competitive environment
> Chapter 3   The world economy
> Chapter 4   Government policy
> Chapter 6   Demography
> Chapter 7   Social trends
> Chapter 8   Technology

B3 *Develop a strategic business plan for your organisation*
> Chapter 10 Strategic management
> Chapter 11 Managing in a strategic business context – integrative case studies

B4 *Put the strategic business plan into action*
> Chapter 10 Strategic management

B8 *Ensure compliance with legal, regulatory, ethical and social requirements*
> Chapter 5   Regulation
> Chapter 7   Social trends
> Chapter 9   Ethics, social responsibility and sustainability

C4 *Lead change (part)*
> Chapter 10 Strategic management

C5 *Plan change (part)*
> Chapter 10 Strategic management

C6 *Implement change (part)*
> Chapter 10 Strategic management

CHAPTER 1

Organisations and their environments

LEARNING OUTCOMES

By the end of this chapter, readers should be able to understand, explain and critically evaluate:

- the distinction between the general and the task environment

- the STEEPLE model of environmental analysis

- the difference between placid, dynamic and turbulent environments, and their impact on organisations

- the identification of key environmental factors

- the use of SWOT analysis

- the E-V-R congruence model

- the Miles and Snow classification of environmental responses.

VIETNAM AND IRAQ

CASE STUDY 1.1

In the early 1960s, the United States intervened in the civil war in Vietnam. The North Vietnamese, under the political leadership of Ho Chi Minh, and the military leadership of Vo Nguyen Giap, had driven the French colonial government out of Vietnam in the 1950s, and the country had been divided in two – North Vietnam, under communist control, and South Vietnam, with a pro-western government. The Northerners and their South Vietnamese communist allies, the Vietcong, had started a guerrilla civil war in the south against the South Vietnamese government.

The Americans had overwhelming military superiority, and won every pitched battle between the two sides, including the North's biggest attack, the Tet Offensive in 1968, when Vietcong soldiers infiltrated the South Vietnamese capital, Saigon, and even penetrated the US embassy.

Even so, in the end it was the North Vietnamese and the Vietcong who won the war. The Americans lost over 50,000 dead (compared with more than a million Vietnamese dead), and in 1975 they finally pulled out of Saigon. The next day, 30 April 1975, the North Vietnamese army took the presidential palace in Saigon, and the unified communist republic of Vietnam was born.

Why did the Americans lose? Firstly, the North Vietnamese understood that ultimately the war was political, not military. If they could pin down the Americans for long enough, public opinion in the United States would turn against the war, and the loss of American life, and political pressure at home would force the Americans to pull out. Ho also had a clear aim, to unify Vietnam under the communist banner. The Americans did not. Were they supporting the South Vietnamese government, fighting the Vietcong, seeking to defeat North Vietnam, or to stop the advance of world communism? An example of their ambivalence was the decision not to invade North Vietnam with a ground force, but bomb the country, including its capital, Hanoi.

Secondly, the Americans had no clear strategy for fighting a guerrilla war. Their strategy was based on their overwhelming advantage in firepower, but this was of little use when every Vietnamese could be a potential guerrilla fighter. Typical was the way the Americans could do nothing to prevent the infiltration of fighters and equipment into Saigon in 1968. The 'overkill' approach used by the Americans also caused hundreds of thousands of civilian casualties, which helped to turn public opinion in the United States, and throughout the West, against the war.

In 2003, a US-led coalition invaded Iraq. Again, there was a backdrop to the action. In 1990, Iraq, under Saddam Hussein, had invaded and occupied its neighbour Kuwait. A massive widely based but US-led coalition had expelled him from Kuwait in a brilliant military campaign. This operation had clear limited objectives – to liberate Kuwait – and commanded a high level of world support. The 2003 war was different. This time, the Americans had much less world support, did not have the clear endorsement of the United Nations, and were unable to make it clear to the world exactly why the invasion was happening. Was it to depose Saddam Hussein? Was it because Saddam was alleged (incorrectly) to possess chemical and biological weapons (the so-called 'weapons of mass destruction')? Was it to protect ethnic and religious elements in the Iraqi population who had been persecuted by Saddam – the Kurds in the north, and the Shi'ites in the south? Was it to fight world terrorism and in particular al-Qaeda? Was it a desire on the part of the US president, George Bush Jr, to complete the job his father George Bush Sr had started as president in 1991? Or, as many observers cynically suggested, was it to seize control of Iraq's huge reserves of oil?

The Americans believed that they would be welcomed as liberators, and for a brief period here was relief among many Iraqis at the overthrow of Saddam, particularly among the Kurds, but also to some extent among the Shia in the British-occupied southern part of the country. However, the Americans had underestimated the underlying religious and political divisions in the country. Iraq was an artificial country, invented after the First World War from the wreckage of the Turkish empire. The Shia had close links with their co-religionists in Iran, while the Kurds had much more in common with the Kurdish minority in eastern Turkey than with the rest of Iraq.

Although the Shia were the majority in the country, the Saddam government had been dominated by the minority Sunni, who were strong in Baghdad and central Iraq. The Sunni population was generally hostile to the Americans because they had overthrown Saddam, and they quickly started a guerrilla campaign against the Americans. The Shia sought revenge on the Sunni, while al-Qaeda, which had previously had no influence in Iraq, took advantage of the chaos to move into the country.

The Americans were again involved in a guerrilla war, just as in Vietnam, and again they reacted in a heavy-handed fashion, launching punitive operations against insurgent-controlled towns, and making little effort to reconstruct the country or to win hearts and minds. American casualties rose into the thousands, and Iraqi casualties into the hundreds of thousands. Again, just as in Vietnam, the war was increasingly unpopular in the United States, and the guerrillas realised that in order to win, all they had to do was to outlast the Americans. Eventually public opinion would force an American withdrawal.

What has an account of wars in Vietnam and Iraq to do with business? What lessons can we learn from the wars that are relevant to business environment and strategy? A surprising amount.

- The need for clear objectives. If a business does not know what it wants to achieve, any amount of strategic planning is irrelevant. There is a clear contrast between the totally clear objectives of Ho and Giap, and the confused objectives of the Americans in both Vietnam and Iraq.

- An understanding of the environment. The guerrillas in both Iraq and Vietnam were totally at ease in their local environments. The Americans, on the other hand, did not understand the motivation of their enemies in Vietnam, or the complex political environment in Iraq. The Vietnamese also understood and exploited the political environment in the United States.

- An understanding of the competition. The Americans did not understand the strengths and motivations of their enemies in either Vietnam or Iraq.

- An understanding of one's own resources. The Vietnamese made the most of their limited military resources, while the Americans were hamstrung when the enemy in both Vietnam and Iraq neutralised their key resource, their overwhelming firepower.

- The importance of values and culture. The communist beliefs of the Vietnamese gave them a motivation and a will to win that the Americans could not match. At a tactical level, the gung-ho, macho culture of the US Marine Corps made them ideal for spearheading the invasion of Iraq, but totally unsuitable for any campaign to win hearts and minds.

- The importance of ethics. In both wars the Americans were accused of committing atrocities (as were their opponents), and British participation in the Gulf War without an explicit UN resolution was the subject of massive protest on ethical grounds.

- The importance of stakeholders. Businesses, like countries, have external stakeholders – third parties who can affect their actions. In Iraq, the key stakeholders are Iran, with considerable influence over the Iraqi Shi'ites, and Turkey, the sworn enemy of the Kurds. The views of stakeholders must be taken into account in strategic management.

- The importance of an exit strategy. Businesses, like armies, need to know how to abandon a strategy at minimum cost. The Americans in Vietnam were forced to make a humiliating exit, while they have been heavily criticised over Iraq for their seeming failure to have a clear exit strategy.

All these themes will be explored later in this book.

WHAT IS THE ENVIRONMENT?

At its simplest, the environment is anything outside an organisation that may affect an organisation's present or future activities. Thus the environment is situational – it is unique to each organisation. As a result, we must always bear in mind the interaction between a particular organisation, and its particular environment.

It is useful to think of the environment on two levels. One is the general environment (also known as the societal environment, the far environment or the macro environment). The other is the task environment (or the specific environment, the near environment or the micro environment).

Forces in the general environment have a major impact at the level of the industry. These forces include national culture, including historical background, ideologies and values; scientific and technological developments; the level of education; legal and political processes; demographic factors; available resources; the international environment; and the general economic, social and industrial structure of the country.

The task environment covers the forces relevant to an individual organisation within an industry. These include customers, suppliers, competitors, regulators, the local labour market and specific technologies.

The distinction between general and task environments is not a static one. Elements in the general environment are continually breaking through to the task environment, and impacting on individual organisations.

A different but complementary approach is to see the organisation as an open system, which interacts in two main ways with its task environment. It takes in resources from the environment, converts them into goods and/or services, and returns outputs to the environment in order to satisfy some need (see Figure 1.1).

In order to function effectively in such a system, the organisation must fully understand both its input and its output environments.

A more complex variation is to add a third element – that of regulations that

Figure 1.1 A systems model of the organisation and its environment

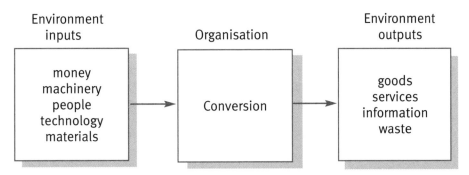

control the conversion process. The three elements (inputs, outputs and regulations) provide the organisation with both opportunities and constraints. All three elements are also subject to the influences of the general environment.

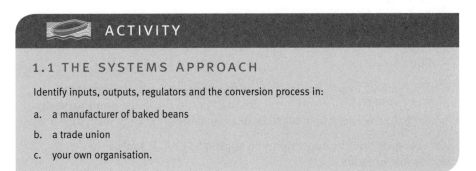

ACTIVITY

1.1 THE SYSTEMS APPROACH

Identify inputs, outputs, regulators and the conversion process in:

a. a manufacturer of baked beans

b. a trade union

c. your own organisation.

ANALYSING THE ENVIRONMENT

Most organisations will not have a great deal of problems in analysing their task environment. They know who their customers, suppliers, competitors and so on are. Analysing the general environment is rather more complex. The first step will probably be to brainstorm a list of various environmental factors which seem to impact on the organisation. This is a start, but to progress further, it will be necessary to classify these influences.

One widely used tool for classification is PEST analysis and its derivatives. PEST analysis breaks down environmental influences into four categories:

Political/legal Taxation policy, EU directives, trade regulations, geopolitical factors like the 'war on terror', government stability, employment law, contract law, competition law, etc.

Economic Business cycles, economic growth, interest rates, supply and demand factors, competition factors, public spending, money supply, inflation, unemployment, disposable income.

Sociocultural Demographic trends, income distribution. Social mobility, lifestyle, attitudes to work and leisure, levels of education.

Technological Research and development, new inventions or innovations, speed of technology transfer, rates of obsolescence, development of systems.

PEST analysis was widely used during the 1980s and early 1990s. By the mid-1990s, it was becoming more common to talk of PESTLE analysis. Political and Legal were split from each other, and an extra factor, Environment, was added. This reflected a growing awareness of environmental factors, and the first concerns about global warming.

By the early 2000s, PESTLE had evolved into STEEPLE, with the addition of Ethics, reflecting the development of concern for corporate social responsibility and business ethics. The classification currently used is thus:

S   Social
T   Technological
E   Economic
E   Environmental
P   Political
L   Legal
E   Ethical

The STEEPLE model forms the structure of this book. We shall be examining each of the STEEPLE elements in turn (although not in this order), and we shall conclude by bringing everything together in an analysis of strategy formation.

The next case gives you the opportunity to apply a STEEPLE analysis to a relatively simple situation.

THE FLETCHERS

CASE STUDY 1.2

Mr and Mrs Fletcher have owned the sub-post office and only shop in a medium-sized village (600 inhabitants) in central Wales for two years. The village is 60 per cent Welsh-speaking, but the Fletchers, who originally came from Birmingham, do not speak Welsh. The sub-post office is operated under licence from the Post Office. The post office business has shown a slow rate of increase over the last 10 years, but this now seems to be levelling off. They also sell basic groceries, sweets, tobacco, soft drinks, children's' toys, and stationery. The village still has an agricultural sector in farming and food processing, although this was hard hit by foot-and-mouth disease in 2001. The population of the village has declined by about 100 in the past 20 years, and a number of houses are now weekend holiday cottages, mainly owned by people from the West Midlands. About a third of the village population are retired.

There are three small towns (population 5–10,000) within 20 miles. There are weekly bus services from the village to each of these towns. Some inhabitants of the village work in light industry in these towns, each of which has at least one small supermarket. There is a local farmer with a milk round in the village. He has recently started carrying groceries on his round.

The village is on a holiday route to the Welsh coastal resorts, and there is a certain amount of passing trade. There is also a well-known pub and a stately home in the village. When the Fletchers bought the shop, they found that the business was about breaking even, but that its turnover had declined in the previous three years as their predecessors had deliberately cut down on their range of groceries, partly because of their own increasing age, and partly because of difficulties they had encountered with efficient stock-keeping.

The Fletchers manage all the work themselves, except for employing one part-time assistant for two mornings a week – Saturday to cope with the passing trade, and Tuesday, when George Fletcher goes to the cash and carry for supplies.

Using the STEEPLE model, analyse the general environmental factors that could impinge on the shop.

There are obviously a wide range of factors you might identify. Our preliminary list is below, but it is far from definitive:

Social:	Ageing population
	Declining population
	Car ownership levels (shopping in supermarkets)
	Holiday cottage owners (where do they shop?)
	Holiday/passing trade seasonal?
	Welsh hostility to English incomers?
Technological:	Payment of pensions and benefits by direct debit
Economic:	Unemployment
	Interest rates
	Level of pensions
	Reliability/future of bus service
	Cost of petrol
Environmental:	More extreme climate – more rain? – impact on Welsh holiday trade
Political:	Impact of the Welsh Assembly
	Changes to agricultural subsidies – impact on hill farmers?
	Rural post office closures
	Possible privatisation of the Post Office
Legal:	Licensing regulations – opening an off-licence
	Working Time regulations
Ethical:	Social responsibility to pensioners dependent on shop/post office

The analysis in the Fletcher case is the first stage in a STEEPLE analysis. The next stage is to identify what impact each identified factor would have on the organisation.

WHY DO WE NEED TO UNDERSTAND AND MANAGE THE ENVIRONMENT?

Organisations have a choice in how they manage their relationships with their environment. They can sit back and wait for the environment to change, without attempting to predict its behaviour, and then react to changes as they happen. Here they are being reactive – constantly fire-fighting immediate problems. Or they can identify and foresee changes in the environment, and plan their responses before these changes happen. They are being proactive – planning for the future. A few organisations are in the fortunate position of being able to go even further and manage the environment in their own interests – at different times since 1900, Ford, IBM, Sony, McDonald's and Microsoft have done this.

The nature of the environment is also significant. Some organisations have static or placid environments, where it is reasonable to suppose that the future will be a continuation of the past. For example, this was true of many UK nationalised industries before privatisation. An organisation in this happy situation can afford to limit its analysis of its environment to past history. However, such an organisation is likely to be caught totally unawares if the nature of its environment does change rapidly. For example, many airlines in continental Europe were either owned by, or heavily protected by, their home governments. This cosy relationship was totally disrupted by the events of 11 September 2001, with the resultant rapid collapse of two national airlines, Swissair and Sabena, while to add insult to injury, American Airlines received massive subsidies from the US government.

Other organisations face turbulent environments, either because the environment is dynamic or in a state of rapid change, for example the pharmaceutical industry or the defence industry; or because the environment is complex, and thus difficult to analyse: for example a multinational company with interests in many countries or industries. Turbulent environments are uncertain.

Igor Ansoff (1987) argued that the extent to which an environment is turbulent depends on:

- changeability of the market environment
- speed of change
- intensity of competition
- fertility of technology
- discrimination by customers
- pressure from government and influence groups.

In order to cope with a turbulent environment, the organisation must be aggressively ready to change.

If the environment facing an organisation is dynamic, the organisation will need procedures for sensing future environmental changes, and contingency plans for dealing with a range of possible changes. This involves the technique known as scenario building. This increases managerial awareness by examining what-if situations – if x happens, what will its impact be on us, and what can we do about it? The technique was first developed by Shell in the early 1970s, when it correctly forecast the 1973 oil crisis, and so was ready to deal with it. Schwartz (2003) argues that although most scenarios will be wrong, the mere fact of having been through the scenario-building process will make managers more able to cope with change.

VIDEO BLUES — A TURBULENT ENVIRONMENT

CASE STUDY 1.3

On 18 June 2007 the BBC2 business programme *Working Lunch* highlighted the plight of Peter Citrine, owner of a video rental store on the Wirral. His turnover had fallen by 70 per cent in the last five years, even though several rival stores in his area had gone out of business. He was not alone. In June 2007, the rental chain Global DVD, with 47 stores, went into liquidation, following the third largest retail group, Apollo Video Film Hire, which failed in April, with the closure of 100 stores. In five years, the number of stores nationally halved to less than 1,000.

The retail video rental market has been the victim of a whole series of hammer blows from changes in its turbulent environment.

- Nobody rents or buys videos any more. The VHS format has been totally superseded by DVD, which means that store owners have had to replace a lot of worthless VHS stock.

- DVDs are one of many markets in which supermarkets fight their price wars. The typical price of a DVD in a supermarket is £11, while some DVDs are imported from Jersey, and sold for as little as £3.93, virtually the same as a rental fee. Since 2000, DVD sales have grown from 16 million to 227 million a year, while rentals have fallen from 200 million to 116 million.

- Small stores like Peter Citrine's are hit by the dual pricing policy of the major film studios. DVDs for rental are charged a much higher price – £25 rather than the £11 in a supermarket. This is permitted under the EU's Rental Rights Directive of 1992.

- Until 2002, video stores benefited from a rental window of up to a year, during which the only sales allowed were to rental stores. This gave the rental stores the opportunity to recoup the higher price that they were charged before they faced competition from supermarkets. In 2002, Warner Home Video abolished the rental window, but still kept its dual pricing, and it was followed by other suppliers.

- The structure of the industry has changed. The Amazon model of orders placed through the Internet being met centrally from a enormous backlist of titles has been applied to the DVD market, by Amazon itself, by Blockbuster, and most successfully by LOVEFILM. LOVEFILM has 400,000 subscribers, who in 2006 rented 2 million DVDs each month, 20 per cent of the UK market. The company owns 1.5 million DVDs, covering 75,000 titles, far more than a local store could stock. Through analysis of orders and customer feedback, it has a huge database of customers' hirings and preferences.

- The online rental sector also has a different pricing structure. Customers pay a monthly fee, typically £9.99 a month, for which they can rent one DVD at a time, up to £14.99 for three DVDs at a time. Orders are placed by Internet and delivered by post. There are no limits on the total number that can be rented each month, and no late fees. The online suppliers also have the opportunity to earn more revenue by including junk mail in the post with the DVDs.

- As broadband speeds improve, it becomes easier to download films over the Internet. In May 2007, Tiscali started to offer legal downloads, charging between 99p and £3.49.

- DVD rentals are also being hit by social changes. With the proliferation of TV channels available via satellite or Freeview, many showing films, competition for the DVD rental industry is constantly increasing, and the market is also being hit by the increasing range and sophistication of games consoles.

In April 2007, Choices, the second biggest rental chain, issued a profits warning, and its CEO, Anthony Skitt, said that it was unlikely that any retail video/DVD rental stores would survive the next five years.

CASE STUDY 1.4

WILD GARDENS

In the mid-1990s, British Airways carried out a scenario planning exercise for 2005. Two scenarios were developed. One (called Wild Gardens) predicted:

1   rapid growth in Asia

2   a US recession

3   EU enlargement into eastern Europe

4   no single currency

5   a Tory election win in 1997

6   an EU–US open skies agreement, which partially opened up European routes to US competition, and vice versa.

They were right on three of the six – numbers 1, 3 and 6 – partially right on one (number 2), and wrong on the other two. However, what is more important is what they didn't foresee – the two most traumatic events to hit world aviation for many years, namely 9/11 and the Iraq war.

An organisation with a complex environment may need to break down the complexity, so that environmental analysis is decentralised to product groups or countries within the organisation.

The most difficult situation of all, of course, is where the environment is both dynamic and complex. Here the organisation may have to recognise that it cannot predict its environment, and what is important is to foster a culture in the organisation that welcomes and is able to cope with radical change. The organisation must learn to live with chaos. One definition of a learning organisation is an organisation which has developed systematic procedures to ensure that it can learn from its environment.

 ## ACTIVITY

1.2 TURBULENT ENVIRONMENTS

In what ways have the environments of local authorities become more turbulent in recent years?

TOOLS FOR ANALYSING THE ENVIRONMENT

Johnson, Scholes and Whittington (2004) propose a five-stage model in analysing the environment, as follows:

Stage 1 Audit of environmental influences

Stage 2 Assessment of nature of the environment

Stage 3 Identification of key environmental factors

Stage 4 Identification of the competitive position

Stage 5 Identification of the principal opportunities and threats

Stage 1 involves the preparation of a STEEPLE analysis. Stage 2 builds on the placid/dynamic/turbulent classification of environments discussed above. Stage 3 involves a more sophisticated analysis which may include:

- Identifying a smaller number of key environmental influences. For example, for the NHS these might be demographic trends (ageing population), technological developments in healthcare, and implementation of government policy (public–private partnerships).
- Identifying long-term drivers of change: for example, the increasing globalisation of markets for some products, eg consumer electronics, cars and pharmaceuticals.

The key principle here is that not all environmental influences are equally important. The analysis in Stage 3 involves identifying those that are most important.

Stage 4 (identifying the organisation's competitive position) will be tackled in the next chapter, using techniques such as Porter's Five Forces (Porter 1980).

Stage 5 (identifying principal opportunities and threats) involves another well-known technique, SWOT analysis.

SWOT stands for:

Strengths

Weaknesses

Opportunities

Threats

Strengths and weaknesses are inward-looking, and particularly concerned with the resources of the organisation. Opportunities and threats are outward-looking and involve the analysis of environmental factors. The organisation should ensure that its strengths (or core competencies) are appropriate ones to exploit opportunities or to counter threats.

Both opportunities and threats can be analysed using matrices. Opportunities can be assessed according to their attractiveness and the organisation's probability of success (see Figure 1.2).

Figure 1.2 Opportunity analysis

Probability of success

	High	Low
High	1	2
Low	3	4

Attractiveness

Opportunities in cell 1 offer the greatest scope, and organisations should concentrate on these. Cell 4 represents opportunities which in practice can be ignored. Cells 2 and 3 may be worth investigating further.

Threats can be assessed on the basis of their seriousness and their probability of occurrence (see Figure 1.3).

Figure 1.3 Threat analysis

Impact

	High	Low
High	1	2
Low	3	4

Probability of occurrence

A threat that has a high probability of happening, and the likelihood of a considerable impact on the organisation (cell 1), will be a key factor which must be a driver of the organisation's strategy, and for which detailed contingency plans must be prepared. At the other extreme (cell 4), a threat that has little likelihood of happening, and little impact if it does happen, can be largely ignored. The threats in cells 2 and 3 should be monitored carefully in case they become critical.

It should be remembered that opportunities and threats are rarely mutually exclusive. Many factors can be both – indeed, the Chinese characters for 'threat' and 'opportunity' are identical (Nathan 2000). For example, the technological development of EFTPOS (electronic funds transfer at point of sale) money transfer systems (using debit and credit cards) can be a threat to small retailers, as their use by competitors may give the latter a competitive edge, but can also be an opportunity, because they lessen the amount of cash likely to be in tills, and so make the shop less attractive to thieves.

 ACTIVITY

1.3 THE HOSPITAL

How would you classify the following factors on a probability/seriousness matrix for a hospital trust? What contingency planning should the trust make?

a. a serious accident on the local railway line, causing scores of deaths and injuries

b. an ageing local population

c. a leakage of radioactive material at a nuclear power station 200 miles away downwind.

SWOT AND STRATEGY

Weihrich (1982) argues that SWOT is misnamed. He suggests renaming it TOWS. His argument is that SWOT implies that strengths and weaknesses come first, but that this is mistaken. The only logical starting point for analysis is with opportunities and threats. They are outside the organisation, largely beyond its control, and must be managed using the organisation's strengths and weaknesses.

Four combinations of opportunities, threats, strengths and weaknesses are possible, and each suggests a possible strategy.

- Strengths–opportunities (maxi–maxi). The organisation should pursue strategies that make most use of its strengths to capitalise on opportunities.

- Strengths–threats (maxi–mini). The organisation should use its strengths to minimise or neutralise threats.

- Weaknesses–opportunities (mini–maxi). Make the most of any new opportunities to overcome weaknesses.

- Weaknesses–threats (mini–mini). This combination calls for a defensive strategy, to minimise internal weaknesses and avoid external threats.

CRITICISMS OF SWOT

As an analytical technique, SWOT has many strengths. It is simple, easy to understand and (at least at a superficial level) easy to use, and it does encourage managers to think about both the internal and external aspects of their business.

However, it does have a number of weaknesses. It runs the risk of being subjective, particularly if it is done primarily by one person. It encourages generalisations. It has a tendency to be backward rather than forward-looking, and it often leads to a feeling of 'So what?' when faced with a long list of factors.

In order to be a useful tool, SWOT (or TOWS) must be used intelligently.

- Don't give it as a job to one person. It is an ideal technique for use in a focus group, which could usefully include customers and suppliers as well as internal managers.

- Use the probability/attractiveness and probability/seriousness matrices discussed earlier to identify which opportunities and threats are most important.

- Identify why they are important.

- Be specific. For example, don't just list 'overseas expansion' as an opportunity. Identify which markets represent the best opportunity, and why: 'opportunities for expansion in France, because the major producers of our product in France are very weak'.

- Similarly, identify why weaknesses are important. You may think something is a weakness, but this is only so if it affects your competitiveness. For example, you may identify 'authoritarian management style' as a weakness, but if this does not affect your competitiveness, it is not really a weakness.

- Don't put down the same factor as both an opportunity and a threat. Decide which is more important. For example, earlier we looked at the impact of EFTPOS on small retailers. On balance, this is clearly an opportunity rather than a threat, because it provides the chance to give a better service to customers.

In essence, SWOT is a simple framework and a potentially valuable tool which is often badly used by managers as an alternative to undertaking the grind of detailed internal and external analysis.

E-V-R CONGRUENCE

Thompson (2005) developed the concept of E-V-R congruence as a measure of how well an organisation is attuned to its environment. He develops the idea of SWOT analysis to incorporate values. In his model E represents the environment (the opportunities and threats part of a SWOT analysis), while R represents resources and V values, both of which are traditionally subsumed within the strengths and weaknesses sections of a SWOT. To Thompson resources would be physical, while values represent the human strengths and weaknesses of the organisation, specifically its leadership and culture, as well as the underlying values which it holds.

More important than the mere idea of E-V-R is the concept of congruence. An organisation will achieve congruence when its environment, resources and values are mutually reinforcing. Its strategic position will be strong. A congruent organisation is shown in Figure 1.4.

Thompson then identifies types of organisations where the three elements are not congruent. The first is the unconsciously competent organisation (Figure 1.5).

Figure 1.4 A congruent organisation

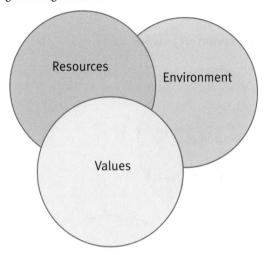

Figure 1.5 The unconsciously competent organisation

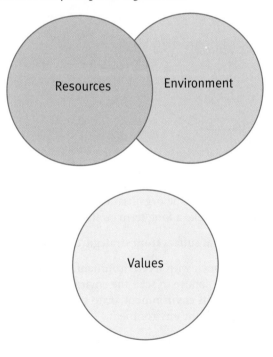

Here the values of the organisation are out of line with its environment and resources, but because environment and resources are still aligned, the organisation still works, at least on a superficial level. This type of organisation is likely to be complacent, and runs the risk of serious trouble if its environment and resources start to drift out of line. The strategic imperative here is for a change in leadership style and a redefinition of values and culture.

The second is the consciously incompetent organisation (Figure 1.6).

Figure 1.6 The consciously incompetent organisation

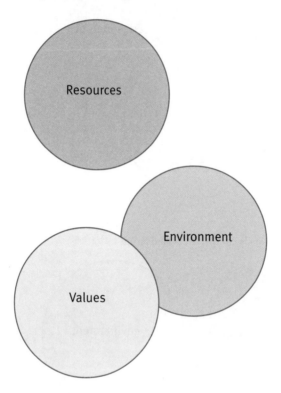

Here the organisation is aware that there is a resource mismatch, but tends to see it as a series of short-term problems. The organisation will tend to be reactive and to fight fires, while unable to take a long term strategic view of resources.

Next, there is the organisation that suffers from strategic drift (Figure 1.7).

Here the organisation has lost touch with its environment, perhaps because of complacency, perhaps because of failure to scan the environment effectively. It must either find a way to change its environment, or to bring its resources and values back in line with changes in the environment.

Finally, Thompson identifies what he calls the lost organisation (Figure 1.8).

Unless this organisation takes swift and drastic action to reachieve congruence, in the long run it is doomed.

Figure 1.7 Strategic drift

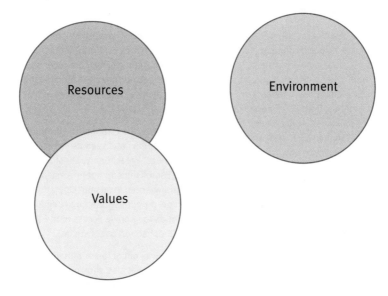

Figure 1.8 The lost organisation

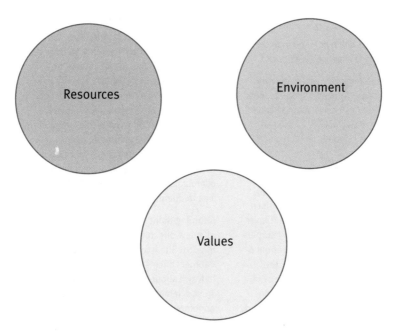

THE NATIONAL TRUST AND E-V-R

The National Trust has as its core aim to 'look after special places, for ever, for everyone'. It is the largest private landowner in Britain, owning 640,000 acres, mostly rented out to tenants on commercial terms. It also owns 600 miles of Britain's coastlines, guaranteeing free public access to the coast, and around 300 houses and gardens, which are open free to members, and at a small charge to others. In 2005–6, there were 13.7 million visits to NT properties, of which 2.9 million, or around 20 per cent, were paying visits, while the rest were visits by members (National Trust 2006).

Clearly the National Trust estate is a hugely valuable asset, which on an open market valuation would be worth billions of pounds. However, remember the words 'for ever' in the core purpose. The Trust is legally prohibited from selling property, and the result is that in many ways the estate must be seen as a liability rather than an asset, which must be maintained at ever-growing expense (Legg 2005).

More conventional physical resources include National Trust gift shops at most sites, and also extensive catering facilities (which earned £25 million in 2005–6, twice as much as admissions).

A key resource of the Trust is its membership. This has increased from 152,000 in 1971 to 3.4 million in 2006. Over the same period income has risen from £2.4 million to £337 million (Clover 2003). The Trust makes a healthy surplus of around £20 million a year, or about 6 per cent of turnover. In addition, the National Trust has 6,000 staff, many of them highly qualified in conservation, property management or gardening, and tens of thousands of active volunteers.

However, the membership is overwhelmingly white, middle-aged and middle-class, with little penetration in the inner cities, and it is thought that most members join solely to get free access to Trust properties. The activists, the volunteers, who to visitors are the public face of the National Trust, are older and more middle-class than the membership – seen by many as representatives of the 'green welly' county set.

By the 1990s, the National Trust, though growing rapidly, was seen as increasingly out of touch – reactionary, elitist and part of the Establishment, not interested in promoting social inclusion. Operation Neptune, a populist campaign begun in the 1960s to improve access to the coastline, had run out of steam.

Just as it was out of touch with modern urban society, it also antagonised many of its county-based members by getting involved in the hunting dispute. In 1997 it banned stag hunting on its property, and was split over fox hunting, with each side accusing the other of dirty tricks. Part of the problem was the Trust's system of governance. It was controlled by a 52-member council, mostly nominated by interest groups like the RSPB and the Open Space Society, which met only four times a year. The council was widely seen as a self-perpetuating old boy network (Houlder 2003). The system also gave great power to the chairman, who controlled proxy votes which he could use at his discretion. The pro-hunting lobby complained that the proxy voting system was frequently used against them.

A turning point came with the appointment of a new director-general, Fiona Reynolds, in 2001. She had previously headed the Cabinet Office's women's unit, was close to New Labour, and talked of shedding the Trust's 'remote and elitist' image. She appointed Lord Blakenham, sometime chairman of the *Financial Times* and the RSPB, to review the National Trust's system of governance.

Blakenham reported in April 2003. He recommended that in future the governing body should be a 12-member board of trustees (effectively a board of directors). The council would remain and would in effect become a supervisory board on the German model. The proxy voting system should be replaced by postal voting. The board of trustees formally took control in 2005. The Blakenham report seems to have turned the tide. The national ban on foxhunting has also helped, defusing the main internal bone of contention. Reynolds has increased the educational role of the Trust, expanded family memberships, bringing younger people into membership, and has spearheaded a move into the inner cities, preserving back-to-back working-class houses in Birmingham, and John Lennon and Paul McCartney's boyhood homes in Liverpool (Proby 2005).

How does the National Trust rate in terms of E-V-R convergence? In the late 1990s the organisation was at best unconsciously competent. Its values were clearly out of line with resources and environment. At worst, it was at severe risk of becoming a lost organisation, with resources and environment slipping apart. Reynolds' leadership since 2001 seems to have pulled it back into congruence, with environment, resources and values back in line.

There are still tensions, of course. When the National Trust outsourced its membership administration, the result in the short term was chaos. In 2005, the Trust ran into trouble when it imposed charges at its car parks on the South Downs, seemingly in contradiction to the free access principles of Operation Neptune (Payne 2005), and again when it decided to split up one of the Lake District hill farms which it had inherited from Beatrix Potter of Peter Rabbit fame (Page 2005). There are also possibly worrying signs in the Trust's own Annual Report. Visitor ratings for customer service (67 per cent) and for a 'very enjoyable visit' (62 per cent) are both low, and both are below target.

In 2007 the National Trust published a new strategy document, covering the period to 2012 and beyond. This demonstrates an extension of the new thinking in the Trust. The key future role of the Trust was to be an environmental education group, engaging with government and society in a quest to find ways of tacking climate change. Fiona Reynolds stressed that this represented a return to the original aims of the Trust's founders, which emphasised social philanthropy and mutual benefit. As Reynolds said, 'This is going back to our roots. We are a cause. It's a profound moment of recognition' (Vidal 2007). Whether she can carry the more diehard and reactionary elements among the Trust's volunteers is anther issue.

MANAGING THE ENVIRONMENT

Miles and Snow (1978) suggest four main ways in which organisations can cope with and manage their environments. These involve an interaction between the organisation's strategy, its culture and its environment. They can be:

Defenders   They operate in generally placid environments. They do not actively search for new opportunities, but concentrate on maximising the efficiency of their existing operations. They are very vulnerable to a sudden shift in their environment.

Prospectors They are attracted to turbulent environments. They are constantly experimenting with novel responses to the environment. They thrive on change and uncertainty, but pay little attention to efficiency. They are decentralised and promote creativity and innovation. They are thus vulnerable if the environment settles down.

Analysers   They are successful poachers. They watch competitors for new ideas, and adopt the successful ones. Their approach to the environment is therefore second-hand, and they let the prospectors make the mistakes. A classic example of the analyser strategy is the video recorder war. Sony pioneered the industry with the Betamax format, but was eventually defeated by Matsushita and its VHS format. Analysers are seeking at the same time to maintain their shares in existing markets, and to exploit new opportunities. They can be seen as a hybrid between defenders and prospectors.

Reactors   They make adjustments to their strategy when forced to do so by environmental pressures. Unlike the defenders, they are prepared to change, but they are even more market followers than the analysers. They are not prepared for change, and do little planning. Miles and Snow see this strategy (or lack of it) as basically a failure mode.

Organisations must recognise that a strategy which suited them very well in the past may no longer be appropriate if the nature of the environment which faces them has changed. For example, big national airlines, which were highly bureaucratic and cost-efficient, were highly successful in the tightly regulated environments of the 1960s and 1970s, but were hard hit by more agile budget airlines (Southwest in the United States, Ryanair and easyJet in the United Kingdom) as the airline market was deregulated and became more turbulent.

In appropriate types of environment, each of the defender, prospector and analyser strategies can be successful, but the reactor strategy is unlikely to be successful in the long term.

Many later scholars have tested the validity of Miles and Snow's model, and generally have confirmed their findings. For example:

- Shortell and Zajac (1990) found that defenders are the first type of organisation to adopt new production technologies; analysers the first to adopt new management systems, and prospectors the first to develop new products.

- Gimenez (1999) found that among Brazilian small and medium-sized enterprises, reactors were the least successful in terms of increasing their turnovers.

- Peng, Tan and Tong (2004) found that in China, state-owned firms followed defender strategies, privately owned firms prospector strategies and foreign-owned firms analyser strategies.

CONCLUSIONS

This chapter has analysed the nature of environments, ways in which they can be analysed, and responses that organisations can make to them.

ACTIVITY

1.4 MECHANISTIC AND ORGANIC ORGANISATIONS

Mary Jo Hatch (1997) distinguishes between mechanistic and organic organisations. Mechanistic organisations specialise in routine activities, with strictly demarcated lines of authority and responsibility. Tasks are highly specialised. Organic organisations have less specialisation. They are less

formalised and hierarchical than mechanistic organisations, and use lateral communication.

What parallels can you see between the analyses of Hatch and Miles and Snow?

KEY LEARNING POINTS

- The general environment consists of factors that impact at an industry-wide level, while the task environment is primarily concerned with the immediate environment that impacts on an individual organisation within an industry.

- Organisations can be seen as open systems which interact with their environments.

- The STEEPLE model lists and classifies the major general environmental factors that impact on organisations.

- The main point of STEEPLE analysis is to identify key environmental drivers.

- Opportunities and Threats to the organisation can be classified according to probability of success and attractiveness, and probability of occurrence and impact respectively.

- The E-V-R congruence model is an extension of SWOT.

- Miles and Snow have identified four different ways in which organisations react to their environments.

QUESTIONS

1. What do you think are the main differences between the general and the task environments?

2. Why has the PEST model evolved into the STEEPLE model?

3. What are the main differences between placid and turbulent environments?

4. Why did Weihrich suggest that SWOT analysis should be renamed TOWS analysis?

5. What criticisms have been made of the SWOT/TOWS approach?

6. In E-V-R analysis, what are the main differences between an unconsciously competent and a consciously incompetent organisation?

7. In Miles and Snow's analysis, what are the main differences between defenders, prospectors, analysers and reactors?

8. What are the main differences between mechanistic and organic organisations?

SEMINAR ACTIVITY

ACTIVITY HOLIDAYS

The holiday industry

The holiday industry is in a state of flux. The mainstay of the industry, the foreign package holiday – two weeks in the sun, with everything (flight, accommodation, food, transfers and so on) provided by the tour operator – is in slow decline. In the 1980s, package holidays had 60 per cent of the market, but in 2005 this had fallen to 45 per cent (*Daily Telegraph* 2006). In 2001 20.6 million package holidays were sold, and this had fallen to 19 million in 2006.

Looking more closely at market segments, the bottom of the package holiday market is relatively stable, although not very profitable. The top end is growing rapidly, and has better profit margins. The segment that is really coming under pressure is the mainstream mid-market sector, which is in the most rapid decline, and where the competition is fiercest, with wafer-thin margins.

The package holiday market as a whole is coming under increasing threat from the short break market, built around the budget airlines, particularly Ryanair and easyJet. Increasingly people take a number of short, often city-based, breaks, booking both their flight and their accommodation through the Internet. The other major growth area is the specialist package holiday segment, loosely described as activity holidays, about which more later.

At the same time as the traditional package holiday has been declining, the method of selling them has been changing. In 1999, 61 per cent of package holidays were booked through a high street travel agent, but by 2003 this had fallen to 49 per cent. At the same time, the numbers of bookings made direct with a tour operator and through the Internet both rose.

The trend is even more stark when we look at all holidays, rather than just package holidays. In 2004, travel agents and the Internet each had a one-third share of bookings, with the other third shared between family and friends and direct booking with a tour operator (*Marketing* 2004).

Until 2007, there were four major players in the UK overseas travel industry. All are vertically integrated, operating retail travel agents as well as tour operations and an airline. The market leader, Thomson, is owned by the German company, TUI, while Thomas Cook is also German-owned. First Choice and the weakest company, My Travel, are UK plcs.

Different companies have adopted different strategies to cope with changes in the market. Thomson has concentrated on marketing different segments of its packages, rather than the complete traditional package holiday. If the customer wants to buy just a flight, or just accommodation, that is fine with Thomson. First Choice has gone for market segmentation. It is concentrating on two major segments, the bottom of the package market, and the much more upmarket specialist (particularly activity) segment. In early 2007, it put its mainstream package operations up for sale, with both My Travel and Thomas Cook interested. However, these two companies decided to merge instead, leaving First Choice out in the cold. In response, in the spring of 2007, First Choice and Thomson/TUI agreed to merge.

The activity holiday market

An activity holiday is broadly defined as a holiday in which some form of physical exertion is the main reason for the holiday. It covers a wide range of activities, including skiing, boating, golf, walking, cycling, fishing and birdwatching, as well as multi-activity, which combines two or more activities.

Unlike mainstream package holidays, activity holidays are growing rapidly. Twenty-four per cent of the population claim to have taken an overseas activity holiday in the past five years, and a further 20 per cent say they are likely to in the future. Numbers of holidays sold (including UK holidays) are expected almost to double between 2001 and 2010, from around 5 million a year to around 10 million, with the value of holidays sold also doubling from around £4.5 billion to around £9 billion, or around 17 per cent of all holidays (Keynote 2006). At an average cost of nearly £1,000, activity holidays are also significantly more expensive than other packages, and much more profitable. In 2006 the operating profit of First Choice's activity holiday division made up half of all group profits (First Choice 2007).

This seminar activity will concentrate on two types of activity holiday, walking/trekking and multi-activity. Walking holidays are the most popular activity holiday, with 10 per cent of the population claiming to have taken a walking holiday in the past five years, while 9.5 per cent claim to have taken a multi-activity holiday.

However, the consumer profiles for the two types of holiday are different. Walking holidays are almost exactly split between male and female, and are more popular with the ABC1 social groups (broadly the middle class), people who live in the South, the Midlands and Wales, and single people. People are more likely to take a walking holiday as they get older, with penetration among the 45–54 age-group (11.4 per cent) and 55–64 (10.8 pr cent) higher than the penetration for the population as a whole (10 per cent). Multi-activity holidays are favoured by men (70 per cent) and the under-35s, but again have a bias towards ABC1s, the South and the single. Perhaps people who enjoy multi-activity holidays when they are young switch towards walking holidays as they get older.

Companies

This activity will look at five companies in the walking/multi-activity segments of the market. Two (Exodus and Waymark) are owned by First Choice, one (Explore) is owned by the holiday group Holidaybreak plc, and two by member organisations (HF

Holidays by the Holiday Fellowship and Ramblers Holidays by the Ramblers Association).

Exodus

Exodus is one of two leading companies in the 'soft adventure' sector. It provides walking-trekking holidays combined with sightseeing, white water rafting, sailing and other activities. Founded in 1973, it was taken over by First Choice in 2002. The number of bookings is unknown, but is believed to be in the region of 30,000 a year. Most holidays are outside Europe, including many in exotic locations, operated in liaison with indigenous specialist companies/guides.

Waymark

Waymark is a specialist walking company. The company is small, with around 4,500 bookings a year, but a loyal clientele. Like Exodus, it was taken over by First Choice in 2002, with the remit to grow volumes and margins. In 2004, its managing director Stuart Montgomery admitted that clients 'have a problem' with being part of First Choice (although First Choice ownership is very much played down in the Waymark advertising material) (*Travel Weekly* 2004). Most holidays are in Europe, often using local agents. In 2006–7 Exodus and Waymark started to cross-promote each other.

Explore Worldwide

Founded in 1981, Explore uses a similar business model to Exodus. The average price of holidays is around £1,000, often including a local payment at the start of the holiday. Holidays are usually offered on a bed and breakfast basis, with extensive use of local agents to guide tours. Explore was taken over by Holidaybreak in 2000, and forms about half of Holidaybreak's Adventure Travel division. The division had a turnover of £76 million in 2006, and operating profit of £5.6 million (Holidaybreak 2007). The average age of Explore clients is in their early 40s. About 30,000 holidays are sold each year, and 45 per cent are repeat bookings. Like Exodus, most bookings are made direct, but the company also sells through local travel agents in Australia, Canada and the United States.

HF Holidays

This is the oldest of the companies surveyed, and also the biggest. Founded in 1913, and owned by the Holiday Fellowship, it has over 50,000 guests, over half in the United Kingdom. The company runs 17 country house hotels. It is noted for its 'English House party style of warm hospitality' (HF Holidays 2007), and has a very high degree of client loyalty. It claims that at least 80 per cent of customers come back again the next year. It explicitly aims at the 'grey' market, and has the oldest client base of the companies surveyed.

Ramblers Holidays

Ramblers Holidays was founded by the Ramblers Association in 1946, and covenants its net profits to a charitable trust which supports environmental projects. Originally purely a walking company, in recent years it

has expanded the proportion of sightseeing on many of its holidays, and also runs a range of holidays concentrating on birds or flowers. More than half of holidays are in Europe, but the proportion of long-haul (and more expensive) holidays has been increasing. In 2006 it introduced 'cruise and walk' holidays. It recently acquired Countrywide Holidays to increase its UK holiday coverage, and also offers a range of holidays aimed at the under-40s. Holidays are led by a volunteer leader from the United Kingdom, but on long-haul holidays a local agency/guide is also used. In 2001 17,000 holidays were sold, and in 2004 turnover was £14 million, giving a pre-tax profit of £1.1 million. Details are not available of the average age of clients, but from personal experience this seems to be mid-50s.

Questions

1. Compile a STEEPLE analysis for the activity holiday industry.

2. Compile a SWOT analysis for Ramblers Holidays.

CHAPTER 2

The competitive environment

LEARNING OUTCOMES

By the end of this chapter, readers should be able to understand, explain and critically evaluate:

- the fundamental economic problem of scarcity and choice, and the ways in which this problem is tackled by market and mixed economies

- determinants of supply and demand

- the main types of market structure, including perfect and monopolistic competition, monopoly and oligopoly, and their implications for price and output

- Michael Porter's five forces model of competitive structure

- portfolio approaches to SBU analysis, including the Boston matrix and the Shell directional policy matrix

- the effect of environmental pressures on the public and voluntary sectors

- HR implications of responses to environmental change

- strategic responses to environmental change.

ECONOMIC SYSTEMS

Different types of societies have organised their economies in different ways, but all have to produce answers to the same questions, whatever their economic system.

 ACTIVITY

2.1 SCARCITY AND CHOICE

Economists often say that economics is about scarcity and choice. What do you think they mean by this? What problems are caused by the conflict of scarcity and choice?

Three main models have emerged:

- the command economy
- the market economy
- the mixed economy.

Of these we shall consider the market and mixed economies in some depth. The pure command economy we can dismiss quite quickly, as it no longer exists in any real sense, except perhaps in North Korea. Here all economic decisions are made by the state, or rather by a central planning authority acting on the state's behalf, which decides what will be produced, by whom and who gets it. However, a command mentality was powerful in western economies at least until the 1970s. In the United Kingdom, large sectors of the economy were controlled by the state through nationalised industries. For example, the Labour government of the 1960s decided that the way to meet the country's future energy requirements was through nuclear power, and in particular the development of untested advanced gas-cooled reactors (AGRs). The decision was disastrous. Each reactor took up to 20 years to build, and they did not reach their planned output until the 1990s. In 1996 prices they cost over £50 billion to build (Kay 2003 pp91–93). When British Energy was privatised in 1996, the AGRs were sold for £1.9 billion, but only after the state agreed to underwrite liabilities for future decommissioning costs.

Nor was the private sector much different. The 1960s and 1970s were the heyday of detailed quantitative corporate planning, which in many companies bore a close resemblance to the Soviet Union's five-year plans. A classic example, also discussed by Kay, was General Electric. When Jack Welch took over as CEO in 1981, he inherited what the US Defense Department described as 'the world's most effective strategic planning system'. Welch promptly dismantled the whole elaborate planning system, and in its place brought in systematic decentralisation of decision making (Kay 2003, pp96–97).

THE MARKET ECONOMY

Here economic decisions are taken on the basis of prices. There are no central planners, and decisions are taken by millions of individual consumers and producers. Producers produce only what they can sell to consumers, and workers sell their services to producers and receive income, which they use to buy goods and services from the producers. In the last resort it is thus the consumers who decide what is produced (consumer sovereignty), and the economy is a closed two-player system (see Figure 2.1).

Our core economic problems are thus answered as follows:

- What is going to be produced? Anything which consumers are prepared to buy (demand in the jargon).
- How is it going to be produced? In the most efficient way. If a producer is not efficient, it will be driven out of business by an efficient one.
- Who is going to get it? Anyone who is prepared to pay for it.

Figure 2.1 Flows in the market economy

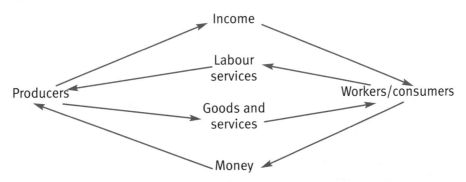

ACTIVITY

2.2 MARKET ECONOMIES

● What would you say are the strengths and weaknesses of the market system?

● Can you think of any examples of pure market economies?

MIXED ECONOMIES

In practice all economies are mixed to a greater or lesser extent. Command elements commonly include:

● a framework of law – the law of contract, company law

● publicly provided social goods like defence, police, education, welfare and health

● publicly owned industries – the BBC in the United Kingdom, Amtrak in the United States, Electricité de France in France

● state regulation of the level of economic activity

● control of economic behaviour – employment law, anti-trust law, anti-discrimination law etc

● often the use of taxation to redistribute income as well as to raise revenue for public services.

Throughout the rest of this chapter we shall be analysing the working of the mixed economy, with particular reference to the United Kingdom.

MARKET STRUCTURES

Economists classify market structures by the number of firms within the market (and to a lesser extent the number of purchasers). The main classifications are:

CASE STUDY 2.1

MARKETS IN THE NHS

In an article in the *Guardian*, a Sheffield GP, Paul Hodgkin, discussed the different types of market operating in the NHS.

- **The market economy.** This is the model which underpins the concept of patient choice, where informed consumers choose between different providers, thus driving up quality. Unfortunately, there are at least two snags. First, in the public sector, markets are zero sum. As spending is capped, more spent on one procedure means less on another. Second, consumers (patients) are not informed, and they are not attempting to 'buy' a desirable good. No one in their right mind would positively desire a major operation! The patient is by definition anxious, and frequently not in a fit state to take an informed decision.

- **The barter economy.** This most clearly operates between the NHS and social services. Partnerships here are only possible given local give and take and mutual obligations – do me a favour today with patient X, and next month I'll do the same for you.

- **The centrally planned economy.** This includes evidence-based medicine, treatment dictated by the National Institute for Health and Clinical Excellence, targets, star ratings, inspections and so on.

- **The gift economy.** This has always existed throughout the public sector, and is part of the public service ethos – giving more than is strictly required under contract, for the good of the patient. Hodgkin sees this as being eroded in the NHS, as new contracts become much more restrictive and time-based. A classic example of the gift economy which Hodgkin does not mention was identified in the NHS many decades ago – the totally free and voluntary UK blood donor scheme.

Source: Hodgkin (2007).

- perfect competition
- monopolistic competition
- monopoly
- oligopoly.

There are also two less commonly found firms

- monopsony
- bilateral monopoly.

PERFECT COMPETITION

This is a market where no one producer has an advantage over any other producer. There are many producers, none of which has a sufficient share of the market to be able to influence the market price. They are known as price takers. Similarly, there are a large number of buyers, who are also price takers. The price in the market is set by supply and demand.

Demand measures the amount of the good or service which buyers are willing to buy at a given price (note not the amount they need – demand is based on willingness to pay). Broadly speaking, the lower the price, the greater the quantity that buyers will demand. This enables us to plot a demand curve – in practice plotted as a straight line (see Figure 2.2).

Figure 2.2 A typical demand curve

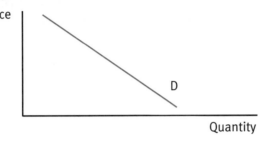

If the price rises, the quantity buyers are prepared to buy will fall. This is known as a fall in quantity demanded. On the other hand, some external event may mean that buyers are prepared to buy more of the product at all prices – perhaps their incomes have increased. This is known as a rise in demand, and is illustrated on our diagram by a shift of the demand curve to the right (see Figure 2.3). Similarly, a fall in demand is shown by a shift of the curve to the left.

Figure 2.3 An increase in demand

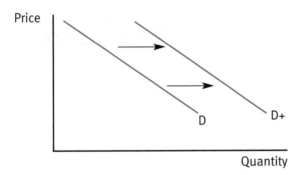

The same principles apply to supply. Broadly speaking, the quantity of a good that producers are prepared to supply is higher the higher the price, producing a supply curve. Again a movement along this line is known as a change in quantity

Figure 2.4 The supply curve

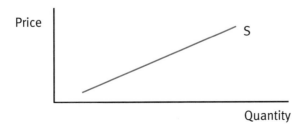

supplied, and a shift of the curve rightwards or leftwards is known as an increase or decrease in supply.

If we put together the supply curve and the demand curve, we get Figure 2.5. This shows that there is one unique combination of price and quantity where the two lines intersect (equilibrium, point E). This sets the price that will be charged in that market, and the quantity that will be bought and sold, and crucially this is an outcome that is equally acceptable to both buyers and sellers.

Figure 2.5 Supply, demand and equilibrium

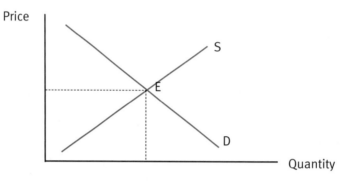

ACTIVITY

2.3 OIL PRICES

In 1973, OPEC quadrupled the world price of oil overnight. The result was a severe bout of stagflation for the world economy – simultaneous rising inflation and unemployment. In 1990–1, the oil price again rose rapidly in the build-up to the first Gulf War. However, after the war, oil prices quickly fell back, and by the late 1990s were at their lowest level for many years. In 2003, oil prices again rose rapidly in the build-up to the second Gulf War, but this time, after a brief fall in the immediate aftermath of the war, they have continued to rise, and on 2 January 2008 reached US$100 a barrel, five times their low in the late 1990s. Despite this, world inflation has stayed relatively low, and economic growth has stayed high.

Questions

1. Why have oil prices been so high since the war in 2003?

2. Why did the increase in the price of oil after 2003 not lead to stagflation, as in the mid-1970s?

EASYJET AND DYNAMIC PRICING

The classic way to price a product is to charge each consumer exactly the same price. Tesco and Sainsbury do not haggle with their customers – a price is published and the customer takes it or leaves it. However, supermarkets do reduce prices as goods approach their sell-by date, or if perishable goods are unlikely to keep until the next day. This is an example of dynamic pricing or yield management – if the alternative is to throw the good away, any price for it is better than nothing.

A much more sophisticated use of the dynamic pricing model is common in the airline industry. Taking advantage of its computerised reservations system, and the deregulation of airlines in the United States in the late 1970s, American Airlines introduced dynamic pricing in the early 1980s, charging different customers different fares, depending on when they booked their flight. This is much easier to do online than in the physical market, as the costs involved in changing prices are much lower. American is alleged to make up to US$500 million a year through its dynamic pricing system. It changes half a million prices each day, an enormous number, as it only carries 50,000 passengers a day (McAfee and te Velde 2005). The model is widely used by low-cost airlines in the United Kingdom, and has been copied by

full-cost carriers such as British Airways. The result is that theoretically each passenger on a particular flight might have paid a different fare, although they are all consuming the same product – a flight from A to B.

The economic theory underlying dynamic pricing is price discrimination – the idea that different consumers will place a different value on the same product, and that if possible the seller will strive to extract as much of this value as possible from each customer (Weiss and Mehrotra 2001).

The classic model for dynamic airline pricing is that the price will start low for a flight which is several weeks or even months ahead. This will attract the tourist or leisure market, where customers are not prepared to pay a premium price, but are prepared to book some time ahead of the flight. As the date of the flight approaches, the price will rise, attracting business travellers, who are less price sensitive, and who may well have to fly at relatively short notice. As the date of the flight approaches, the price will fall if there are still large number of seats unsold, or will rise if the plane is nearly full.

To test the model, we plotted the prices charged by easyJet on one particular flight, flight 211 from London Stansted to

Figure 2.6
easyJet's dynamic pricing

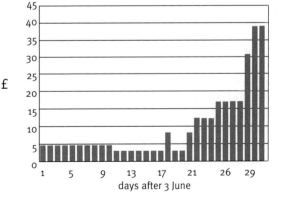

Glasgow, departing on 3 July 2007 at 11.25 am. We checked the price being charged on the easyJet website once a day from 3 June 2007 until the day of takeoff on 3 July (easyJet 2007).

The results confirmed the classic model. The price on 3 June was £4.99, and remained at this level until 13 June, when easyJet started its summer sale, and the price fell to £2.99. It stayed at that price until 20 June, when it rose to £7.99, but it was back to £2.99 on the next two days. It then started a steady rise – £7.99 on 23 June, £11.99 on 24 June, and £16.99 on 27 June. The price remained at £16.99 until 1 July, when it rose to £30.99, and then to £38.99 on 2 and 3 July.

Stelios Haji-Ioannou, the founder of easyJet, is a passionate advocate of dynamic pricing, and he has applied the concept in at least two other of his many ventures, easyCinema and easyInternetcafe. However, both of these projects were failures. Part of the problem was a general lack of demand for the products, but there was also a fundamental flaw in the dynamic pricing model as applied to these products. Although the supply conditions were appropriate for value management, this was not true of demand conditions. In the case of the airline, price discrimination is possible, because different customers do value a flight differently, but this does not really apply to a cinema seat or an hour in an internet café (*Economist* 2005).

The products sold in a perfectly competitive market are assumed to be identical, thus there is no reason to favour one seller over another on grounds of quality or special features or service. It is also assumed that all players in the market are extremely well informed, and capable of reacting very quickly to any changes. There is thus no point in advertising – all products are identical and buyers know them to be identical. Buyers will react very quickly to any change in price, while sellers will very rapidly copy any innovation introduced by one of their rivals. Entry to the market is also completely free – anyone can enter or leave the market at any time.

Because of the nature of the market, there is no incentive for any one seller to cut its price – remember it can sell as much as it likes at the current market price. Conversely, if it raises its price even a fraction above the market level, it will sell nothing, because there is no incentive for its customers to stay loyal.

Economists freely admit that perfect competition is extremely unlikely to exist in the real world – its assumptions are too restrictive. Why spend so much space describing it, you may ask? The reason is that it is a classic example of an economic model – it is a stylised attempt to explain behaviour, rather than a prescription for managers who want to make sound decisions. Models simplify the real world, and cut it down to its bare essentials, and on the basis of these bare essentials they make logical predictions. Thus the essence of the perfect competition model is that if the real world were like this, certain predictions would logically follow from it.

One consequence of the model is that it would lead to an efficient use of resources in the economy. Market forces would push production costs down to the minimum, and ensure that the most efficient production methods were used.

Any firm that did not use them would be forced out of business. Profits would also be forced down to the minimum level required to keep firms in business. Any firm that made more profits than the minimum in the short term would be unable to sustain this position in the long term. Unfortunately this also writes economic progress out of the model. There is no incentive to innovate or develop new products, because any advantage will be immediately wiped out through perfect knowledge.

 ACTIVITY

2.4 THE LEMON

In 1970 the economist George Akerlof discussed the case of the used car market as an example of imperfect information (Akerlof 1970). In the used car market, sellers have much better information than buyers. In particular, sellers know whether there is something wrong with the car they selling – whether it is a lemon. Because the buyer knows that some cars being sold are lemons, but not which ones, the price in the market will be an average of the values of good cars and of lemons. If particular car is a good one, the buyer will get a better deal than the seller. The opposite happens with a lemon. As a result, owners of lemons will be willing to sell, but owners of good cars won't. The proportion of lemons in the market will increase, buyers will be even more suspicious, and prices will be pushed down more. The whole used car market will spiral downwards.

It is in the interests of potential sellers of good cars to do something to improve information in the market, and so to get better prices. There are many ways of doing this. One is to offer warranties on used cars, as is done by Ford through its dealers, for example. Another is to encourage buyers to get the car checked by an independent third party, like the AA.

From the point of view of the buyer, it is essential to know the reputation of the seller. Large, established main dealers of the major car brands are likely to have a better reputation than back-street garages or cars sold through small ads in newspapers.

The lemon problem is really a modern application of Gresham's law, which dates from the sixteenth century. This law, 'bad money drives out good', was invented by Sir Thomas Gresham, treasurer to Queen Elizabeth I. Governments at the time were notorious for debasing the currency – mixing cheaper material into the gold and silver used to make coins. The government made a profit on this, as the coin cost less to make than its face value. If people had two coins, one of which they knew to be good (of full gold content), and the other to be debased, they would hoard the good one, and spend the bad one – bad money drives out good. Unfortunately, everyone else would know that only bad coins stayed in circulation, and as a result prices would go up. Gresham advised Elizabeth to avoid inflation by resisting the temptation to debase the currency.

Questions

1. In the eighteenth and nineteenth centuries, farm labourers were frequently hired for the year at hiring fairs, like those described by novelist Thomas Hardy. Would the lemon problem have applied here?

2. Find out how eBay, the online auction site, gets round the problem that buyers know very little about the reputation of sellers on the site.

It is also possible to apply the perfect competition model to labour markets. The lower the wage, the higher the number of workers that will be demanded by employers, while the higher the wage, the greater the incentive to work in that industry. The only difference is that people's labour services are being sold, rather than, say, apples. Again, the result will be a market equilibrium – exactly the number of workers who are prepared to work for the equilibrium wage will be employed.

 ACTIVITY

2.5 PERFECT COMPETITION

How far do you think that the market for Tesco shares on the Stock Exchange meets the requirements of perfect competition?

MONOPOLISTIC COMPETITION

Rather more likely is that many firms will compete in a market, but each will sell a slightly different product. This type of market is classified as monopolistic competition. As the product is differentiated, the firms in the market have slightly more freedom in setting their prices. They can decide to charge a slightly higher price and sell a slightly lower volume of goods, and vice versa. To a small extent they are price-makers. They can build up customer loyalty, and loyal customers will be prepared to pay a higher price for what they perceive as higher quality, or a closer match with their precise requirements, either in the product itself, or in the services which surround its delivery. Each firm is thus seeking to obtain a mini-monopoly for its product.

Note that a real different in product is not necessary – what is required is that consumers perceive there to be a difference. Firms in monopolistic competition frequently advertise in order to differentiate their product, while firms in perfect competition do not, as they can sell all they wish anyway.

 ACTIVITY

2.6 MONOPOLISTIC COMPETITION

Can you identify any real-world examples of monopolistic competition?

MONOPOLY

Theoretically, a firm has a monopoly if it is the only firm supplying a market – ie, it has 100 per cent of the market. This is very rare in practice, particularly if one defines a market widely. The Post Office has a monopoly in the United Kingdom for delivery of letters of a certain weight, but we also need to include close substitutes for letters in our definition of this market. Once we do this, it is clear that the Post Office faces competition in information transfer from a host of organisations and services, including e-mail, faxes and courier services. Virtually the only organisation with anything approaching a world-wide monopoly is Microsoft, whose operating systems have about 90 per cent of the PC market. Even here, in practice the monopoly is weakened by software piracy, with some estimates saying that half of all software in the United Kingdom is illegally copied.

In practice economists tend to define monopoly functionally – a firm is in a monopoly position if it is able to control the market price of the product it produces. This depends on the size of the firm relative to that of other firms in the industry. If firms in the industry tend to be large, the market leader may need to have perhaps half the market in order to dominate, but in an industry characterised by very small firms, 20 per cent of the market may be enough.

Because it has some control over price, a monopolist can manipulate the price and the quantity which it produces in order to maximise its own profit. Thus price will tend to be higher and quantity produced lower than in a competitive market. This does not necessarily mean that a monopolist will make an excessive profit. If no one wants to buy the product sold by the monopolist, there will be no excessive profit. Being the only producer of horse-drawn hansom cabs is not the best short-cut to a fortune!

However, monopoly does have a tendency to excess profit, as well as other disadvantages. It encourages inefficiency in management and production, as there is no competition to force efficiency, and most crucially, monopoly leads to a misallocation of resources in the economy as a whole. This suggests that monopoly is not in best interests of consumers, and therefore should be at worst controlled, at best banned. This is broadly the approach taken by anti-trust legislation in the United States.

In practice things are not so simple. Often monopolists can gain significant cost advantages (economies of scale) purely because they are big, and the end result might be both higher profits for the monopolist, and a lower price for the consumer. As we shall see later, this argument is put forward by supermarkets in the United Kingdom. This argument (the natural monopoly argument) was put forward to oppose the break-up of British Rail at privatisation. Similarly, it may be judged desirable for a company to have a monopoly in the UK market, if the result is that it is big enough to compete efficiently on the world market. As a an example, the Monopolies Commission in the 1970s and 1980s was prepared to tolerate both British Airways' dominant position in the UK market, and its takeover of competitors like British Caledonian and Dan-Air.

There is also a view that monopolies and monopoly profits may well be a necessary part of the competitive process (Schumpeter 1950). Entrepreneurs are continually trying to exploit new opportunities. If they do so, they will achieve a temporary monopoly. Unless this monopoly arises from the sole ownership of a resource for which there is no substitute, the monopoly will be temporary because other firms will recognise the opportunity and enter the market, or they will devise substitute products. Schumpeter called this process 'creative destruction'.

Profits may thus be true monopoly profits, based on ability to restrict entry to the industry; windfall profits, based on short-term fluctuations in the environment and which in different circumstances could be windfall losses; and entrepreneurial profits, based on superior foresight or management, exploiting opportunities which are open to all. This view is supported by the law on patents. Anyone may invent a new process or product, but the reward for doing so is to be granted a temporary monopoly by the state, in return for the entrepreneurial risk and research and development expenses which have been incurred. Patent protection is the driving force behind industries like pharmaceuticals.

Following this view, the key element in assessing monopoly power is not market share but barriers to entry. This has led to the development of the concept of contestable markets (Lipsey and Chrystal 1999). Markets are contestable if entry is easy, entrants can compete on equal terms with incumbents, and they are not deterred by the threat of retaliatory price-cutting by incumbents. The threat of entry to the market can be as effective as actual entry.

OLIGOPOLY

An oligopoly exists when a few large producers control a market between them. The number of firms may vary between two (a duopoly) and about a dozen, and the products can be homogeneous or diversified. Oligopolies are also known as complex monopolies, and it is the latter term that is used by the UK competition authorities. In all cases, the firms in the industry are interdependent. The performance of each firm depends not only on its own actions, but also on the actions of the other firms in the industry. Thus, for example, before an oligopolist takes the decision to raise its prices, it must decide whether the other firms are likely to follow, or to keep their prices down and aggressively push to increase their market shares.

Oligopoly is extremely common in the United Kingdom. Indeed, think of any major consumer good or service, and it will almost certainly be supplied by oligopoly firms – cars, petrol, banks, cigarettes, soap powder, instant coffee, chocolate, baked beans etc.

One way of measuring oligopoly is by calculation of the five-firm concentration ratio. This is simply the share of the market in percentage terms held by the five largest firms. The higher this figure, the higher the degree of oligopoly (see Table 2.1).

Remember that these figures only cover UK producers. As a result of globalisation, all manufacturers are subject to greater and greater international competition, and only in tobacco and pharmaceuticals of the industries listed in Table 2.1 can the United Kingdom be considered world class. Real oligopoly power is higher in services, where there is less chance of competition from imports. The five-firm ratio in food retailing in 2003 was 75, and this has become a four-firm ratio since the takeover of firm number 4 (Safeway) by Morrison (number 5). In the case of food production and retailing there is a bilateral oligopoly. Many branded goods are produced by oligopolies, and then sold through oligopolies.

Table 2.1 UK concentration ratios 1992

Industry	Concentration ratio
Tobacco	99.3
Motor vehicles	87.7
Ice-cream and sweets	58.8
Pharmaceuticals	55.8
Toys and sports goods	24.7
Leather goods	12.4

Source: Census of Production 1992; Business Monitor PA 1002 1992.

Firms in an oligopoly market have a choice between a number of broad types of behaviour:

- Collusion. One possible outcome is that the firms in the industry join together and collectively behave as if they were a monopolist. They can then collectively exploit any monopoly profits which are available. An extreme form of this type of behaviour is a cartel or price ring like OPEC (the Organization of Petroleum Exporting Countries). Unfortunately from the point of view of potential cartel members, in most countries cartels and other forms of collusive behaviour are illegal. Cartels also tend to be unstable. They must have some mechanism for dividing up production and market quotas among their members, and this is fraught with difficulty. There is also a great temptation for individual members to cheat on their quotas. The cartel may be undercut by new producers (like UK oil in the 1970s), or new substitutes may be developed (as happened to a limited extent after the oil price hikes of 1973 and 1979).

- Price war. An opposite possibility is a price war, with the aim of driving the competition out of business, and eventually emerging with a single-firm monopoly, which can then be exploited. The enormous risk, of course, is that the players might lose, and themselves be forced out of business. In nearly all cases the stakes are simply too high, and the risks too great. Indeed, in many cases it is only the market leader that can afford the risk of a price war, and it is the market leader that has the least need of one. In practice, most apparent price wars are extremely limited, and are used by the market leader as a sharp shock to the rest of the industry to stay in line. There are also risks in winning a price war. Driving a weak competitor out of business may just create a vacuum which can be filled by a much more formidable rival. A parallel is the decision taken by the United States to disband the Iraqi army after victory in the Iraq War in 2003. This left a military and political power vacuum which was quickly filled by sectarian militia groups and by al-Qaeda.

- Non-price competition. Rather than risk an all-out price war, firms will frequently engage in non-price competition – they will compete on everything except price. This might include competitions, quality, individual features, BOGOF (buy one get one free – for a limited period). The aim is not to drive the competition out of business, but to gain a marginal increase in market share. All participants understand the rules of the game, and know very well that the war is limited, not total. Another possible form of non-price competition is complexity. In the old days, there was one mortgage rate, charged by all mortgage lenders on all mortgages. Now there are a multiplicity of different types of mortgage, each with its own terms and conditions, with the result that it is almost impossible to compare rates. The same thing has happened with utility pricing.

CASE STUDY 2.3

OLIGOPOLY AND THE CUT-PRICE AIRLINE INDUSTRY

The cut-price airline industry has developed in the United Kingdom since the mid-1990s, on the lines pioneered in the United States by Southwest Airlines. It is based on providing a no-frills service at low cost. It is dominated by two firms, Ryanair and easyJet, which between them control half the total European low-cost market. Both Ryanair and easyJet are constantly engaged in sniping at each other, with each claiming that it has the lowest fares, and that the other is inefficient, incompetent or worse. There appears to be every sign of a constant price war, with both companies sometimes in effect offering free flights, and offers of twice the fare back if a customer can find the same flight cheaper elsewhere. However, appearances can be deceptive. Until 2003, the main target of Ryanair's knocking copy was its bête noire, the Irish

state airline Aer Lingus (which it unsuccessfully tried to take over in 2007), while easyJet's prime target was British Airways, and particularly its low-cost subsidiary Go. Neither has the serious intention of driving the other out of business. Direct competition between them (in the sense of flights to and from the same airport) is limited. On a strict definition, Ryanair and easyJet are direct competitors on only one route, London Stansted to Rome Ciampino. As a result, the 'price guarantee' is almost meaningless. The price war is aimed much more at deterring new entrants to the industry (both Ryanair and easyJet have taken over one of their main competitors, Buzz in the case of Ryanair and Go in the case of easyJet), and to squeeze better terms out of airports (which gain from a big throughput of passengers).

- Price leadership. Here one firm within the industry is regarded unofficially as the price leader. If the leader changes its prices, the other firms in the industry are likely to follow suit. In order to be legal, it is essential that there is no collusion between the firms.

- Game theory. Here the firm makes assumptions about the nature of the environment and the behaviour of competitors. Game theory is a huge area, but two simple strategies which can be followed are *maximax*, where the firm assumes that the best possible combination of circumstances will happen, and chooses the strategy that will maximise its position in this favourable set of circumstances, and *maximin*, where the firm assumes that the worst will happen, and chooses the best (or least bad) strategy on these pessimistic assumptions.

THE EASTER EGG PRICE WAR OF 2007

CASE STUDY 2.4

The seasonal chocolate market is a vital sector of the confectionery market. It is estimated to be worth £420 million a year, 14 per cent of the total chocolate market. It is defined as chocolate confectionery that is manufactured for specific events – Easter eggs, Advent calendars, and lines produced for other events like Mother's Day or Halloween.

Easter takes a 64 per cent share of this seasonal market, although an early Easter cuts sales, as people are still on a health kick following Christmas. Shell eggs account for two-thirds of all Easter sales (the single best-selling brand, the Cadbury Crème Egg, has all-year sales (*Marketing* 2006). Easter sales are thus important for both retailers and manufacturers, particularly as most sales are made in the week before Easter.

People buy Easter eggs for children, and for loved ones. These two segments are marketed in different ways, children's eggs on price, loved ones' eggs on quality (Chomka 2006).

This trend into two almost unrelated market segments moved to a new level at Easter 2007. At the premium end of the market, consumers are increasingly turning to organic and fair-trade eggs. Green & Black's sold 1 million organic eggs in 2006. In 2001 the company's turnover was £4 million, but this had risen to £40 million by 2006. In 2005 Green & Black's was purchased by Cadbury for £20 million, but continued to trade under its own brand name. This is part of a trend of ethical companies being taken over by mainstream ones, which includes the Body Shop takeover by l'Oréal, and Ben & Jerry's by Unilever. The leading fair-trade chocolate producer, Divine Chocolate,

increased its egg sales by 17 per cent in 2006. Its sales and marketing director was quoted as saying, 'all the big supermarkets stock us and we must be one of the few brands … on sale at Liberty and Oxfam' (Walsh 2006).

At the bottom end of the market, prices have collapsed. In 2002, the typical hollow egg with two bars of chocolate sold at £2.99. In 2007, these eggs were sold by Tesco on a BOGOF (buy one get one free) promotion at two for £1.49 (Finch 2007). At these prices, Easter eggs were being sold as loss leaders, purely to increase footfall in stores.

Who gained and who lost from this price war? Clearly consumers gained. Schoolchildren were reported to be buying supermarket eggs as they were cheaper than standard countlines like Kit-Kats or Mars bars. Tesco almost certainly gained. It had the cheapest eggs, and was the supermarket brand leader anyway. The other supermarkets probably broke even. They were not making any money on eggs, and probably did not significantly increase their footfall.

There were clear losers. One is the mid-price egg, typically retailing at £4.99, which has been squeezed out of the market by cut-price and premium eggs. Another is Woolworths, traditionally the biggest single seller of Easter eggs, but which cannot compete with the bottomless purses of the big supermarkets. The third is the mainstream manufacturers – Cadbury, Nestlé and Mars – which have lost control over their pricing, and run the risk of their brands being devalued. As always with the big supermarkets, they are also being asked to share in the cost of discounting.

The last loser is the Easter egg market itself. The long-term prospects for the market are not good. Children are the key consumers, and the number of 5–11-year-olds is expected to drop by 10 per cent between 2000 and 2010. By 2010, Mintel forecasts that the seasonal confectionery market will be worth £332 million (at 2006 prices), a fall of 21 per cent (*Marketing* 2006). Perhaps discounting is a rational strategy in a declining market.

MONOPSONY AND BILATERAL MONOPOLY

Monopsony is a market form where there is a monopoly buyer. Normally the monopsonist is the government or one of its agencies. For example, for all practical purposes the NHS is a monopsony buyer of pharmaceuticals in the United Kingdom. When there is a market where a monopoly is selling to a monopsony, it is known as a bilateral monopoly. This applies where the NHS buys a particular patented drug from one pharmaceutical company.

COMPETITIVE STRUCTURE

MICHAEL PORTER'S FIVE FORCES MODEL

The economic theory of market structure, distinguishing perfect and monopolistic competition, monopoly and oligopoly, provides a powerful but inevitably simplified model. The real industrial world is much more complex. One important model which attempts to match this complexity is Michael Porter's five forces model of competitive rivalry (Porter 1980).

According to the model, the structure of competition in an industry can be described in terms of five major forces. These are:

- the threat of entry of new firms
- the power of buyers
- the power of suppliers
- the power of substitutes
- the intensity of rivalry among existing forms.

Each of the five forces is itself determined by a number of different factors. When the five forces are analysed completely, this determines how attractive the industry is to firms within it, and those that might wish to enter it.

Unlike economic models, the value of this model lies not in its predictive ability, but in the way in which it provides a checklist whereby particular firms can clearly analyse and define their own position in relation to their own industry. It is a tool which can be used as the first stage of strategic analysis.

The threat of entry

The threat of entry of new firms to an industry depends on the extent of barriers to entry. These include:

- Economies of scale. Some industries have very high economies of scale – unit costs of output fall considerably as output increases, as in the car industry or the aircraft industry. Others have very low economies of scale, for example estate agency. A new firm seeking to enter an industry with big economies of scale must either buy a high market share on entry or suffer a cost disadvantage. Economies of scale are measured by the concept of minimum efficient scale (MES), or the market share that is necessary to compete at minimum unit cost. It is also possible to calculate the cost penalty incurred by producing at below this volume. However, note first that globalisation has meant increasingly that what is significant is not share of the UK market, but share of a world market, and second, that lean production and flexible manufacturing techniques like just-in-time (JIT) have somewhat reduced the importance of economies of scale.

CASE STUDY 2.5

ECONOMIES OF SCALE IN THE AIRCRAFT INDUSTRY

The aircraft industry is an extreme example of economies of scale. The MES for the aircraft industry is more than 100 per cent of the UK market, and there is a considerable increase in cost for a firm operating below MES. This means that it is not economic for a UK company to compete on its own in the mass-market airliner industry. BAe Systems, the UK's only mainstream aircraft producer, has put its airliner manufacturing activities into joint ventures, particularly with the European-based Airbus Industrie, in order to keep a foothold in a world market which can only accommodate two manufacturers, Boeing of the United States and Airbus.

- Capital requirements. Capital-intensive industries like the car industry have a very high cost of entry, while an online consultancy operating from home has a very low cost of entry.

- Access to distribution channels. A new entrant must establish its own distribution channels. For example, it is difficult to persuade supermarkets to stock new products in competition with existing brands. Reforms in the tied house system, and the spread of the concept of guest beers, have made it easier for small real-ale brewers to gain a foothold in the beer market.

- Absolute cost advantages. Established firms in an industry frequently gain from a learning curve effect, which gives them a cost advantage over new entrants. In other cases incumbents may use a technology or process that is protected by patents.

- Expected retaliation. The likely reaction of existing firms is key. If incumbents are expected to retaliate to defend their markets, entry becomes more difficult.

- Government policy. In some cases, the government might restrict entry (commercial television and radio). In other cases, government policy might open up a market to competition (the telephone directory enquiries service).

- Differentiation. If existing operators have established a strong brand image for their products or services, this effectively deters new entrants. Existing operators often produce a wide range of brands to plug all possible niches in the market.

- Switching costs for buyers. If it is very expensive for buyers to switch to a new supplier, this will deter new entrants to the market. For example, if you have a gas central heating system, it is very expensive for you to switch to electricity, but very cheap to switch to a new gas supplier.

The power of buyers

Buyer power will depend on:

- Concentration of buyers. If there is only a small number of buyers, buyer power will be high, particularly if the volume purchases of the buyers are high. For example, although cola drinks are sold through a multiplicity of outlets, high volume sales are dependent on the big supermarket chains, and even Coca-Cola does not have the muscle to dictate terms to them.

- Alternative sources of supply. If buyers are able to shop around, this will increase their power. This may come about because deregulation of markets has produced new competitors. For example, when the gas industry was privatised and deregulated, consumers became able to buy gas from a large number of possible suppliers, not just British Gas. Similarly, the ending of pre-entry trade union closed shops has helped buyers of labour such as the newspaper industry.

- Component cost as a percentage of total cost. If materials form a high percentage of the total cost of a finished product, there is a greater incentive for buyers to shop around. Thus the provision of power to a steel works forms a high percentage of cost, while the provision of paper clips to a management consultancy forms a very low percentage.

- Possibility of backward integration. If there is a risk that the buyer may be in a position to set up its own supply operation, this increase the buyer's power.

Power relationships between buyers and suppliers can be changed as a result of deliberate strategic decisions. For example, car manufacturers since the 1980s have followed a deliberate strategy of reducing the number of their suppliers. Suppliers have gained bigger orders and greater security, but at the cost of strict adherence to quality and JIT requirements.

The power of sellers

Seller power will depend on:

- Number of suppliers. The smaller the number of suppliers, the greater their power, as in any other monopoly or oligopoly situation.

- Switching costs. If switching costs to another supplier are high, this will increase seller power, particularly in a situation where the product supplied is highly specialised, and the supplier is integrated into the production process, for example in a JIT environment.

- Brand power. If the supplier's brand is powerful, this will give it more bargaining power. For example, Heinz and Kellogg's, which do not produce own brands, can exercise influence over supermarkets, which have to stock the brand leader.

- Possibility of forward integration. If there is a risk that the seller may be in a position to set up its own distribution operation, this increases the seller's power.

- Dependence on customer. If the supplier is not dependent on selling a high volume of output to a particular customer, and its individual customers are generally small, this will increase seller power.

Threat of substitutes

The threat of substitution can take many forms. There could be technological substitution of one product for another – the fax for the letter, then the e-mail for the fax. In the last resort all goods are substitutes for each other, because they are all competing for consumer spending. This is particularly true of non-essential goods, where there is the ultimate substitute of doing without.

Key questions that need to be addressed are:

- Relative price and performance of substitutes. If substitutes are available that offer similar performance at comparable prices, the threat of substitution is very strong and limits are put on the ability to charge high prices – for example brands of pet food.

- Switching costs. The cheaper it is for consumers to switch to other products, the higher the threat of substitutes. Switching costs for pet food appear to be zero, as long as the pet is prepared to eat the substitute!

- Buyers' willingness to substitute. If an article is both low-cost and an infrequent purchase, little effort is likely to be put into shopping around. No one shops around for the best-value box of matches.

Competitive rivalry

Competitive rivalry is to some extent a function of the other factors. However, there are other special aspects:

- Industry growth. If the industry is growing rapidly, there is plenty in the cake for everyone so competition does not need to be intense. As an industry moves into the maturity phase of its life cycle, competition will become more intense.

- High fixed costs. This is likely to lead to a high break-even point, and the likelihood of price wars in times of depression to maintain turnover. See for example the steel wars of the late 1990s, when the United States and the European Union each accused the other of dumping steel on export markets.

- Volatile demand. This is likely to lead to intermittent over-capacity, with resultant price wars – steel again.

- Product differentiation. The more homogeneous the product, the more intense the rivalry – steel yet again.

- Extra capacity in large increments. The competitor making such an addition is likely to create at least short-term over-capacity. For example in the late 1980s, the Japanese car firms Nissan, Toyota and Honda all built new car assembly plants in the United Kingdom.

- Balance of firms. If the number of firms is large and/or firms are of a similar size, the risks of aggression may appear acceptable, and rivalry will be intense, although probably not lethal. Conversely, a clear market leader can enforce discipline in the industry.

- High exit barriers. If there are high exit barriers, excess capacity is likely to persist and rivalry to be intense. This would apply, for example, if there were high pollution clean-up costs associated with decommissioning a plant.

Bear in mind when using five forces that it is an analytical technique, which can tell you where the organisation is now, probably why it is there, but not how to get where it wants to get. There is also a danger is carrying out more and more detailed analysis – paralysis by analysis!

CRITICISMS OF FIVE FORCES

It must be remembered that Porter takes an economist's approach to his analysis. As a result, his model is over-simplified, and makes some basic assumptions. In particular, it is a static analysis. It assumes that change will be slow, and that as a result, the firm can take a planned approach to strategy once it has carried out its five forces analysis. This view is challenged by more recent writers on strategic management, who advocate a much more experimental emergent approach to strategic management (see Chapter 10).

There are also some serious gaps in the five forces analysis. It ignores the influence of government, and of regulation, which restricts the freedom of organisations to act as they might like. It is very much a private-sector model, and much less relevant to the public or not-for-profit sectors. It also assumes that competition is a zero-sum game – if one organisation wins, then another must lose. However, it does not take account of co-operation-based strategies like strategic alliances or joint ventures (Lynch 2006). Sumantra Ghoshal (2000) developed this point. He argued that an excessive preoccupation with competition and market forces, by stressing efficiency at the cost of effectiveness, will discourage innovation.

The five forces analysis was a product of its time. Porter was writing before the economy was transformed by mass computerisation and the Internet. In a comprehensive critique of five forces, Larry Downes (1997) identified three new forces which had to be taken into account:

- Digitisation. The development of the Internet means that all players now have instant access to enormous amounts of information. As a result, change has become much more rapid than in the late 1970s, and the environment much more unpredictable. As a result, new competitors can appear extremely quickly, and from outside the conventional definition of an industry. Examples are the way in which the bookselling industry has been transformed by the rise of Amazon, and the travel agency industry by the rise of online bookings.

- Globalisation. Businesses now operate on a global scale, and customers, using the Internet, can shop around and compare prices on a global scale. A five forces analysis must now take account of global as well as of national trends.

- Deregulation. In the United Kingdom, the United States and the European Union, many industries have been radically deregulated since Porter wrote about the five forces. Again, the effect is to make the environment more dynamic, complex and unpredictable. An example is the explosive growth of low-cost airlines like Ryanair and easyJet, and the effect they have had on the environment facing full-cost airlines like British Airways.

Remember, though, that just as Porter was a product of his time, so was Downes. He was writing in 1997, approaching the peak of the dot.com boom. Since the dot.com crash in 2000, views on the future of the Internet are perhaps less gung ho than in 1997.

PORTFOLIO ANALYSIS

In the 1970s and early 1980s, strategic emphasis was on organisations building up a balanced portfolio of activities, or strategic business units (SBUs). Several techniques were developed to assist with analysis of portfolios of SBUs.

BOSTON MATRIX

This technique was developed in the 1970s by the Boston Consulting Group, and plots SBUs according to their rate of market growth and their market share (see Figure 2.7).

Figure 2.7 The Boston matrix

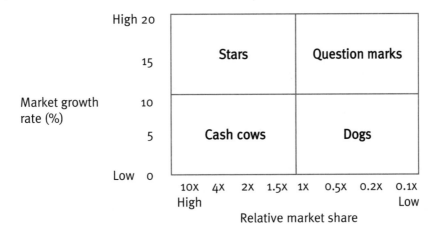

Market growth rate is arbitrarily divided into high growth and low growth, ranging between 0 and 20 per cent per annum. Market share is assessed as share relative to that of the largest competitor, with a high of 10 times the nearest rival, and a low of one-tenth. SBUs are plotted on the matrix, with their precise position within a cell depending on their exact market share and market growth rate.

The significance of the Boston matrix is that an SBU's position on the matrix has an impact in its profits and its cashflow. One of the main selling points of the technique is the colourful names attached to the various cells (Joyce and Woods 1996).

Dogs: They have a weak market share in a low-growth market. They generate a very low profit or even a loss, and also may well have negative cashflow. They absorb management resources, and the organisation must decide whether they are worth being kept in the long term, closed down or sold off.

Stars: They have a high market share in a high-growth market. Production will be at relatively low cost because of economies of scale, and profits are likely to be sound. However, because the market is growing rapidly, heavy investment will be needed to sustain market share. Cashflow is therefore likely to be at best neutral.

Question marks: They have a low market share in a high-growth market. This means that like the stars they need heavy investment, but as they are not the market leader they cannot fully exploit economies of scale. Cashflow is likely to be negative, but profits may well be positive. Management has to take hard decisions – either close down (on the assumption that the question mark may turn into a dog) or sit it out (on the assumption that it will turn into a cash cow).

Cash cows: They have high market share in a low-growth mature market. In the short and medium term this is an ideal position. Because the product is a market leader, it will be low-cost, and it does not need heavy investment to cope with market growth. It is therefore likely to produce both profits and positive cash flow, which can be milked.

Two further types have also been identified off the bottom of the matrix. These are war horses (high market share and negative growth – a cash cow on its last legs), and dodos (low market share and negative growth – dead dogs!).

The strategic implications are that an organisation should aim for a balanced portfolio of SBUs, which should include products which can evolve through the sequence of question mark–star–cash cow Some organisations, particularly at the height of the popularity of conglomerates in the 1980s, became extremely successful by identifying and exploiting cash cows.

One such was Hanson Group, whose strategy was to purchase cash cow products/companies (Imperial Tobacco in cigarettes, London Brick in bricks,

EverReady in batteries), put in the minimum level of new investment, and exploit the cash-generating potential of the products.

There are however some weaknesses in the Boston matrix approach. One is that there is no clear-cut way to define markets. If the market is defined too narrowly, the organisation will overstate its market strength, and so tend to ignore 'over the horizon' competitors, which may be quietly building up their strength in a related market. Possibly more serious is that the matrix ignores any synergy factors. Synergy is defined as the way in which the whole organisation is greater than the sum of its parts. SBUs are not totally self-contained – they often provide each other with benefits, such as sharing production processes or distribution channels, or being part of a balanced catalogue of products. As a result, if an organisation decides to kill off a dog product, this may have adverse impacts on its other products. A final weakness is that it assumes a simple relationship between market leadership and profitability. This ignores the way in which many organisations have prospered long-term by exploiting small niche markets. Despite these weaknesses, however, the Boston matrix has been used successfully by a number of companies, including Black and Decker Europe, although alongside other techniques (Walker 1990).

SHELL DIRECTIONAL POLICY MATRIX

This technique, developed by the Shell Chemical Company, meets some of the criticisms of the Boston matrix. Rather than using market share as a variable, it uses the enterprise's competitive capabilities, assessed as weak, average or strong. This can take into account factors such as managerial skill and possession of appropriate technology and competencies as well as market share. Market growth rate is replaced by prospects for sector profitability, which again can include other factors. Finally, the analysis is made more discriminating by being based on a 3x3 matrix rather than the Boston matrix's 2x2 (see Figure 2.8).

Figure 2.8 The Shell directional policy matrix

	Prospects for sector profitability		
	Unattractive	Average	Attractive
Weak	Disinvest	Phased withdrawal	Double or quits
Enterprise's competitive Average capabilities	Phased withdrawal	Custodial growth	Try harder
Strong	Cash generation	Growth leader	Leader

ACTIVITY

2.7 KILLING THE DOG

The board at Gamma Manufacturing was deeply divided. Under discussion was Product X, which had been a source of argument within the company for years past. The finance director wanted Product X dropped. He argued that it had absorbed considerable development funds over the years, but had never fulfilled its original promise. It tied up valuable production capacity in the factory, and wasted a lot of management time. 'It's a dog,' he said. 'We should put it out of its misery now.'

The marketing director disagreed. She argued that a lot of time, energy and money had been put into the product, and it would be a shame to waste all this just at the point when it might be about to take off. She also made the point that it filled a hole in the product mix. With some customers, it was important to be able to offer a complete product line, including Product X. 'If we haven't got X, I can name at least two big customers who will go straight to the competition,' she said.

If you were the managing director, how would you evaluate the arguments put forward by the finance and marketing directors?

THE PUBLIC AND VOLUNTARY SECTORS

Broadly speaking, three types of organisation operate in the United Kingdom today. The first is businesses, which produce goods and services with the aim of making a profit. The second is the public sector, which supplies goods and services that cannot be supplied at a profit, public goods (where the whole of society benefits from a service such as public health, whether they pay for it or not) and natural monopolies. Finally there is the voluntary sector, which meets the needs of its members (clubs, mutual organisations or professions), its clients (charities), or campaigns on issues (Greenpeace, RSPB).

Unfortunately, these distinctions are not as watertight as they were 30 years ago. Some public goods and natural monopolies are now supplied by privatised businesses, and the private and voluntary sectors provide some services, such as refuse collection and welfare services, on behalf of the public sector. Many public-sector and voluntary bodies have commercial arms (like BBC Enterprises and CIPD Enterprises) which operate in competition with the private sector. One organisation, Railtrack, has changed in a five-year period from being part of a nationalised industry (British Rail), to being a privately-owned company on privatisation, and then to a non-profit-making trust (Network Rail), when Railtrack collapsed in 2001.

The three sectors also have more similarities than differences in how they are managed. They all:

- spend money
- need income to carry out their activities
- produce a product or service

- have consumers for their good or service (whether or not the consumers directly pay for this)
- need people to staff their operations
- use the same range of management services – accounting, IT, personnel etc.

This all suggests a convergence. This view would be supported by the former prime minister, Tony Blair. His Third Way philosophy argues that what is important is not ownership (public or private), but how efficiently services are delivered, along with accountability.

Lawton and Rose (1994) distinguish four different cultures which they see as prevalent in the public sector:

- Political culture. Particularly prevalent in local government, where council officers are in almost day-to-day contact with the politicians to whom they are answerable. Also true in the sense that the whole of the public sector is ultimately politically directed.
- Legal culture. Public bodies are only permitted to do what is specifically allowed to them by statute. Any other action is *ultra vires* (beyond their powers), and is subject to judicial review. Private-sector companies are in theory limited in their activities by their Articles and Memorandum of Association, but the control is much less strict.
- Administrative culture. Concerned with rules, roles, and authority – the 1960s and 1970s caricature of the local authority 'jobsworth'.
- Market culture. Where public-sector organisations are exposed to the market through competitive tendering, best value, contracting out, internal markets etc.

They argue that the last of these, the market culture, is becoming predominant, and that as a result, running the public sector is becoming much more an issue of management, and much less an issue of administration.

The distinction between the sectors is becoming more and more blurred:

- Many local authority services which had previously been free are now charged for, and often contracted out to the private sector (leisure centres, for example). This has involved the development and application of legal systems such as TUPE (the transfer of undertakings legislation).
- Much of the long-term finance for the public sector is now provided by the public sector, through the Private Finance Initiative and public–private partnerships. The biggest of these is London Underground, where train services continue to be provided by the public sector, but where all the maintenance of and investment in improving the lines is carried out by three private-sector consortia.
- There is a growing realisation that the private sector, almost as much as the public sector, operates in a political environment, and that the activities of the private sector are heavily constrained by the legal environment.
- The government is keen to increase the involvement of the voluntary sector

in the delivery of public services, partly to move the debate away from a head-to-head clash between the public and private sectors (Ward 2001). Not-for-profit trusts are the government's preferred option for failing public services. They can borrow private cash without this counting as public borrowing, and they can also reinvest any surpluses into service improvement (Weaver 2001).

CASE STUDY 2.6

👁 THE TWO-TIER WORKFORCE

Under the EU Acquired Rights Directive, implemented in the United Kingdom through the Transfer of Undertakings (Protection of Employment) Regulations (TUPE), from 1981 onwards, workers who are transferred from the public to the private sector as a result of the contracting-out of a public service to the private sector have their wage level and terms and conditions of employment protected (although not their pension arrangements). However, no protection was afforded to new recruits who were subsequently taken on by the transferee. This resulted in a two-tier workforce, where two workers could be doing exactly the same job, but under different wages, terms and conditions.

The trade unions have long campaigned against this, and in 2002 it was agreed that the two-tier workforce in local government would be abolished. The agreement, which came into effect in 2003, was originally proposed by the CBI, and involved detailed negotiation over the precise wording of the protection to be offered. The unions called for 'no less favourable terms and conditions' for new recruits, while the CBI offered 'broadly comparable' terms and conditions. In the first year of the agreement, the unions raised no disputes, which suggests either that workers are broadly satisfied with the deal, or that companies are in practice simply replicating local authority employment conditions.

In July 2004, the CBI agreed to end the two-tier workforce across the public sector, an offer which was taken up by the Labour Party and the unions in late-night negotiations to agree the terms of the Labour manifesto for the next election. The unions and Labour also agreed that pensions should be protected on transfer (Wintour 2004a, 2004b).

HR IMPLICATIONS OF RESPONSE TO CHANGES IN THE ENVIRONMENT

We illustrate this section with an activity which analyses several examples where environmental change had to be met with HR responses.

ACTIVITY

2.8 HR IMPLICATIONS

After privatisation in the 1980s, British Airways (BA) was extremely successful under the leadership of Sir Colin (later Lord) Marshall. Marshall's strategy was to emphasise customer care and employee empowerment in a (largely successful) attempt to build the 'world's favourite airline'. He shed the airline's previous quasi-RAF culture, and ensured that the old nickname of 'Bloody Awful' became a thing of the past.

In 1996 Marshall became chairman, and was replaced as chief executive by Bob Ayling, who had a very different vision. He saw BA as over-staffed and bloated, with an excessive cost base. Although profits were still high, as a result of the airline boom which followed the recovery from the first Gulf War in 1991, he initiated an ambitious cost-cutting programme, which inevitably involved redundancies.

In practice, few redundancies were actually carried through, but the result was labour unrest in 1997 which cost BA £130 million. By 2000 BA had slumped into a loss, and morale was at rock bottom. In March 2000 Ayling was sacked, and replaced by the Australian Rod Eddington, who had previously run Quantas.

Before Eddington could impose his own personality on the company, BA, like other world airlines, was hit by the hammer blow of the 11 September 2001 attacks. BA reacted very quickly, and announced 12,000 redundancies (about 20 per cent of staff). Twenty per cent of all Heathrow flights were scrapped.

The recovery from 11 September was slow, but by 2004, BA was back in profit. It was then hit by the side-effects of the redundancy programme. It found itself under-staffed, particularly among check-in staff. The result was long waits for check-in, rising tempers among customers, stress for staff, and a soaring absenteeism rate. Over the August bank holiday BA was forced to cancel many flights, leading to furious travellers and much adverse publicity (Harper 2000, Gillan 2001, Kim and Mauborgne 2001).

Questions

1. Given that the cost-cutting programme was necessary, what steps should BA have taken to ensure that it was carried out more effectively? Could the crisis in 2004 have been avoided?

2. What do you feel are the HR implications of the introduction of a more market-oriented culture in the public services?

STRATEGIC RESPONSES

A later chapter on developing and implementing strategy will consider this issue in greater depth, but here we shall consider strategic response in general terms. Basically, an organisation can make only two responses if it is in an industry where it does not have monopoly or oligopoly power, and so is not in a position to manage its competition and its environment. It can opt for low price, or it can opt for differentiation. In the supermarket industry, Aldi and Netto have opted for low price, albeit at the cost of low perceived quality, and have seized a somewhat precarious niche by doing so. Differentiation could include high quality, innovation or specialisation. The next activity examines other strategies adopted in the supermarket industry

A firm in an oligopoly market has more freedom of manoeuvre, but it is constrained by the need to consider how its competitors will react to a change in its tactics. If it increases its price, and its competitors follow, the chances are that all firms in the industry will increase their profits, although if there is a suspicion of collusion, the competition authorities may intervene. However, if the firm increases its price, and the competition does not follow, it will lose sales, and almost certainly lose profit, while the competition will gain.

A monopoly has a simpler decision to make. In principle it can choose whatever combination of price and quantity produced and sold which will maximise its profits, although in practice its ability to do this is constrained by the ability of new firms to enter the market (contestability).

CONCLUSIONS

This chapter has analysed the nature of the competitive environment, explored various models which can be used, and examined the responses which organisations can make to the competitive environment. A different approach to the competitive environment is given in Chapter 5 on Regulation.

KEY LEARNING POINTS

- The fundamental economic problem is how to reconcile scarcity and choice. Market and mixed economies tackle these problems in slightly different ways.

- Market economies are underpinned by the concepts of supply and demand, and their interaction to create equilibrium.

- Perfect competition is an unrealistic but ideal model. Other models of the market are measured by their deviation from perfect competition.

- The extent of monopoly power can be measured either by market share or by the degree of contestability of the market in which firms operate.

- Performance in oligopoly markets depends on an interaction between the firms operating in the market.

- Porter's five forces model is a powerful way of analysing the competitive forces operating in an industry.

- Portfolio analyses, including the Boston matrix and the Shell directional policy matrix, are valuable but must be used with care.

- There is growing convergence between the market, public and voluntary sectors.

- A variety of strategic responses can be made to changes in the competitive environment, and these have implications for HR.react to their environments.

QUESTIONS

1. What would you say are the differences between a pure command economy and an economy with a command mentality?

2. What are the major command elements in any mixed economy?

3. What is the difference between an increase in demand and an increase in quantity demanded?

4. What are the main theoretical requirements for perfect competition?

5. What do you understand by the concept of dynamic pricing?

6. What are the differences between oligopoly and monopolistic competition?

7. Why is non-price competition a favoured strategy in an oligopolistic market?

8. What are the five forces identified by Porter in his model?

9. What criticisms have been made of the five forces model?

10. Why might a firm decide not to drop a dog product, as identified in the Boston matrix?

11. In what ways have differences between the public and private sectors lessened in the last quarter century?

TRENDS TO WATCH

- Watch out for changes in the oil price. How far can supply and demand analysis explain any changes which occur?

- Does convergence between the market, public and voluntary sectors continue, particularly if there is a change of government in the UK?

- Is there an increase in regulation of the supermarket industry?

EXPLORE FURTHER

The theoretical background to this chapter is covered in any good economics textbook, such as Lipsey and Chrystal's *Principles of economics* (1999). However, as a manager you need to be able to apply the theory to contemporary examples and situations. The best way to do this is to make sure that you regularly read the *Economist*, and at least one of the quality broadsheet newspapers – preferably two, one broadly liberal, like the *Guardian* or the *Independent*, and one broadly conservative, like *The Times* or the *Daily Telegraph*.

SEMINAR ACTIVITY

SUPERMARKETS: AN OLIGOPOLISTIC INDUSTRY

Introduction

The supermarket industry has come a long way since Sainsbury opened the first self-service supermarket in the United Kingdom in 1951. Until the 1970s, the industry was fragmented, with a large number of supermarket groups mostly operating small stores, and over 100,000 independent grocery outlets of various types. Economies of scale were low, with deliveries being made direct by wholesalers or manufacturers to individual stores. Supermarkets were in town centres, and most people shopped regularly several times a week.

By the late 1970s, two leaders had emerged from the pack – Sainsbury and Tesco. Sainsbury was a private family company until 1973. It was concentrated in London and the south-east, with a mainly middle-class clientele. Tesco was a much younger company, founded by Jack (later Lord) Cohen, who was responsible for the notorious slogan 'pile 'em high, sell 'em cheap'. In the late 1970s, Tesco began the slow and at times painful move upmarket that has continued ever since. The two firms were neck and neck in the market until 1995, when Tesco took the lead for the first time.

Tesco is now way out in front, with a market share of 30.4 per cent in 2006 (Competition Commission 2007). Sainsbury, with 15.9 per cent, is neck and neck with Asda (16.5 per cent), which was a northern-based also-ran until it was taken over by the biggest grocer in the world, Wal-Mart of the United States, in June 1999. In fourth place is Morrison's, which again was a long-established northern chain which came from nowhere to take over the struggling but larger Safeway group in 2004. It had 10.3 per cent of the market in 2006, but is having trouble in digesting its prey. Its market share was significantly higher immediately after the takeover.

Between 2000 and 2006, total supermarket grocery sales rose by 26 per cent in real terms, although there was a small fall in the total number of stores. Supermarkets increased their share of grocery sales over this period from 67 to 72 per cent. Convenience stores held their market share at 20 per cent, while other grocery outlets, including specialist grocery stores, fell from 13 to 8 per cent (Competition Commission 2007).

Superstores

In the late 1970s, the UK supermarket groups started to adopt the French concept of hypermarkets, huge out-of-town stores. In the United Kingdom they became known as superstores. A superstore was defined as a store with at least 25,000 square feet of selling space, at least 20 checkouts and selling at least 16,000 lines. In theory a superstore can be located anywhere, but increasingly they came to be purpose-built buildings on green or brownfield sites either on the edge of towns or out of town, with their own extensive and normally free car parking. Increasingly, they also included a petrol station selling cut-price petrol, rapidly making the supermarket chains the biggest retailers of petrol in the United Kingdom. Evidence suggested that people were prepared to drive up to 10 miles to visit a superstore. By 1993 there were 750 superstores, taking half of all grocery sales.

Superstores yielded very high economies of scale. They were supplied from huge centralised depots, which minimised distribution costs, and the huge superstore buildings were very cheap to maintain. Increasingly the big groups used new technology to improve efficiency and lower costs. Electronic point of sale (EPOS) was used by all the big groups. This enabled the store to reorder automatically from the till, to minimise on warehousing, to maximise use of shelf space as less stock needed to be on the shelves, and to react almost instantaneously to changed circumstances. Combined with EFTPOS (electronic funds transfer at point of sale), this meant transaction costs were lower. Both EPOS and EFTPOS, although very cost-effective, were extremely expensive to install, and stretched the financial resources of the smaller groups.

By the mid-1990s, the explosive growth period of superstores was over. Most of the best sites had gone, and the government was tightening up the planning controls on new development. The response of the supermarkets, particularly Tesco, was fourfold:

- Extended opening hours. Many of the larger stores are now open 24 hours a day, and only close (very reluctantly) on Christmas Day.

- A move into e-commerce, with grocery deliveries co-ordinated from the local store.

- A move back into town centres. Tesco started to develop its Tesco Metro chain, and Sainsbury started Sainsbury's Central. Both aimed particularly at lunchtime and commuter shoppers, selling a more restricted range of convenience goods.

- Introduction of new services, like pharmacies, film processing and in some cases dry cleaning.

Diversification

Another growth route for the supermarkets was diversification. Both Tesco and Sainsbury accelerated their movement into the convenience store market through takeovers. Tesco took over T&S Stores in 2004, acquiring 850 stores, and Sainsbury took over Jacksons Stores (110 stores) (Wheatcroft 2004). Even the Co-op got into the act, taking over Alldays, doubling its number of convenience stores to over 2,300. At the end of 2006 Tesco owned 1,150 convenience stores, and Sainsbury's 287, together making up 3 per cent of the national convenience stores total (Competition Commission 2007). The big groups also moved heavily into non-food sales, which now make up more than 10 per cent of their total sales (Hiscott 2004). One pound in every eight spent

in the United Kingdom goes to Tesco. It sells more DVDs than HMV and more shampoo than Boots (Purvis 2004). In the summer of 2004 it was reported that Asda had become the United Kingdom's biggest clothing retailer, overtaking Marks & Spencer. Sainsbury for a long time owned the DIY store Homebase.

Diversification has also been global, particularly by Tesco. It has moved into France, Hungary, Poland and Thailand, and is poised to move into China. It was thus excellently positioned to exploit the expansion of EU membership into central Europe in May 2004. Sainsbury made less good strategic decisions by opting for expansion in the United States, a saturated market. Asda went the other way. It was expanded into by Wal-Mart, with its huge purchasing power, which gives Asda a bigger influence on the market than its market share would suggest.

Price wars

Supermarkets are notorious for their price wars. These are launched by all the groups at regular intervals with a fanfare of publicity. The reaction of customers to price wars tends, probably rightly, to be cynical. Market research in the summer of 1993, during a particularly intense period of price cutting, showed that more than half of shoppers regarded price cuts as gimmicks, 20 per cent said they took no notice, and only 22 per cent believed they were genuine. Price cuts always tend to be concentrated on known value items (KVIs) – the 200 or so items, like tea, butter and coffee, where customers remember prices. The great bulk of the 20,000 lines stocked by the average superstore are not affected by price cuts. The analysts Smith New Court estimated that the 1993–4 price war would have saved on average 1.5p on a £100 shopping trolley. Remember also that in the main it is not the supermarkets who pay for the price cuts – it is the suppliers.

All the major supermarkets engage in below-cost selling (selling goods below their cost price), representing up to 3 per cent of total revenue. Below-cost selling is concentrated on dry groceries, alcohol, and CDs, DVDs and books. Two case study examples, of Easter eggs (this chapter) and Harry Potter books (Chapter 10), are discussed elsewhere in this book. The Competition Commission does not think that below-cost selling is part of a predatory policy aimed at excluding rivals, but does think that it could unintentionally harm smaller grocery retailers and specialist stores (book shops in the case of Harry Potter). If it leads to these shops exiting the market, this could harm consumers (Competition Commission 2007).

After an investigation of the industry, the Office of Fair Trading in 2002 brought in a 'voluntary' code of practice governing how supermarkets treat their suppliers, particularly farmers. A review of the working of the Code of Practice in 2005 found that on the whole the supermarkets had complied with its terms (Competition Commission 2007).

Competition

In the mid-1990s, supermarkets appeared for the first time to be facing serious new competition. On the one hand this came from the American warehouse club operation Costco, a giant cash and carry, which opened its first store in the United Kingdom in 1993. Tesco, Sainsbury and the then number three in the market, Argyll, brought a joint High Court action, claiming that Costco was really a retailer not a wholesaler, and so should have been subject to the tougher retail planning controls. They lost, in a welter of bad publicity (Cohen 1993). However, the warehouse club concept failed to take off in the United Kingdom.

The other new competition came from the entry into the market of discount stores from the continent, particularly Aldi and Netto, which had been very successful in Germany and the Netherlands. They stocked a very limited range, mainly of tertiary brands (brands no one had ever heard of), and at rock-bottom prices. Although much feared at the time, they seem only to have affected the bottom end of the market, particularly Kwik Save (see the Kwik Save case study in Chapter 10).

Questions

1. Why do you think the competition authorities allowed Tesco to take over T&S Stores, even though Tesco had a market share over the 25 per cent which would make it a monopoly under UK law?

2. In what ways does the behaviour of the supermarkets fit with the theory of oligopoly?

3. Carry out a five forces analysis of the UK supermarket industry.

CHAPTER 3

The world economy

LEARNING OUTCOMES

By the end of this chapter, readers should be able to understand, explain and critically evaluate:

- the role and functions of the European Union and its major institutions

- debates about the evolution of the European Union (integration and enlargement)

- major international bodies that impact on the business environment of organisations (IMF, World Bank, WTO)

- the causes and extent of globalisation processes

- major debates about the significance and desirability of globalisation

- the response of governmental organisations to globalisation processes

- the impact of globalisation on markets for goods and services

- the impact of globalisation on employment and labour markets.

Should the United Kingdom ratify the new European Union Reform Treaty? Is globalisation good or bad for the developing world? These are the kinds of issues which will be explored in this chapter on the international economy.

Since the end of the Second World War, the world economy has become more and more integrated. Partly this has been a deliberate, planned development. The International Monetary Fund, the World Bank and the General Agreement on Tariffs and Trade were set up to regulate the world economy, and to ensure that the world did not suffer from a recurrence of the Great Depression of the 1930s. The European Economic Community, the predecessor of the European Union, was set up partly to ensure that France and Germany could never again go to war with each other. Other developments were only made possible as a result of technological developments in communication and transport which enabled the growth of globalisation.

THE EUROPEAN UNION

THE HISTORICAL BACKGROUND TO THE EUROPEAN UNION

The origins of the European Union go back to the period just after the Second World War, when there was a strong desire in Continental Europe (particularly France and West Germany) to ensure that a further war would be impossible. One way to achieve this was to integrate the economies of Europe, thereby limiting the ability of an individual country to wage war. The result was the European Coal and Steel Community, set up by the Treaty of Paris in 1951. The European Economic Community and Euratom followed with the signing of the Treaty of Rome on 25 March 1957.

The founding states of the three Communities were France, West Germany, Italy, Belgium, the Netherlands and Luxembourg. Britain declined an invitation to join, seeing its economic interests as lying much more with the United States and the Commonwealth.

The United Kingdom, Ireland and Denmark joined on 1 January 1973, Greece on 1 January 1981, Spain and Portugal on 1 January 1986, and Sweden, Austria and Finland on 1 January 1995. The former East Germany automatically joined on German reunification in 1990. Norway twice negotiated entry, but on each occasion that was rejected by a referendum. Switzerland did not apply to join, citing its long-standing policy of strict neutrality (it is not even a member of the United Nations), but it has close economic relations with the European Union.

In 1976, the three Communities were merged, and were designated the European Community, and the Maastricht Treaty of 1992 adopted the name European Union from 1 January 1993.

Up to the end of the twentieth century, the European Union was very much a Western European club. With the exception of Greece, Spain and Portugal, which had recent histories of Fascist rule, all the members were long-standing stable, prosperous, democratic countries. This changed fundamentally with the next enlargement, from 15 to 25 members on 1 May 2004. This came about with the accession of five post-Communist central European states (Poland, Hungary, the Czech Republic, Slovakia and Slovenia), the three Baltic states of Estonia, Latvia and Lithuania, which had previously been republics within the USSR, and two small Mediterranean islands (Malta and Cyprus). Romania and Bulgaria followed in 2007. The implications of this expansion for the European Union are considered below.

THE AIMS OF THE EUROPEAN UNION

The European Union has a number of general aims. These include:

- upholding peace in Europe by integrating national economies
- increasing prosperity by developing a single market
- easing inequalities between people and regions
- pooling the energies of Member States for technological and industrial development

- developing an effective means of resolving political disputes
- implementing a Union-wide social policy
- implementing European Monetary Union
- assisting people of the Third World.

These aims reflect a number of different perceptions concerning the future development of the Union (Morris and Willey 1996).

Single market ('European single market')

This sees the European Union in economic terms, and concentrates on removal of national restrictions which limit the free movement of labour, capital, goods and services. In effect, the European Union is seen as solely a free trade area, without a political dimension. Common political institutions should be minimal, and so should the structure of EU law, which should be limited to that necessary to ensuring that the single market functions effectively. The single market concept underpinned the early development of the European Community, and reached its fullest expression in the Single European Act 1986, which led to the setting-up of the Single European Market in 1993. At least in theory, this ensured the free movement of labour, capital, goods and services. However, this does not fully work in practice. For example, the Schengen Agreement in 1990 eliminated internal border controls within the European Union, meaning that travel within the European Union was possible without a passport, but the agreement has never been implemented by the United Kingdom and Ireland.

Federalist ('United States of Europe')

Here the European Union is seen as having the structure of a federal state like the United States or Germany – a central or federal government which sets the general direction of policy, and local governments (states in the United States, *Länder* in Germany, nation-states in the European Union) which are responsible for the practical administration of policy. Some political mechanism is needed at the centre to decide on overall policy, but this should be kept to a minimum,. The function of EU law is to settle disputes between the central authority and the Member States. Central to this perspective is the concept of subsidiarity, which says that as a matter of principle, decision-making in the European Union should be taken at the lowest possible level.

Integrationist ('Europe')

The aim here is ultimately a long-term shift of power from member states to EU-wide institutions. The classic example of this is economic and monetary union (discussed in detail in a later chapter), which led to a single currency, the euro, and to control of EU monetary policy passing from Member States to the European Central Bank. Subsidiarity may still apply, but the Member States would only have those powers specifically delegated to them by the central government. EU law would not only settle disputes between Member States and the centre, but would also directly impinge on EU citizens.

The issue of how far to move towards the integrationist model underpins the

ACTIVITY

3.1 MODELS OF THE EUROPEAN UNION

1. Which of the models of EU organisation (single market, federalist, integrationist) would best describe the view of the following political parties in the UK?

    a. New Labour

    b. Conservative

    c. Liberal Democrat

    d. UK Independence Party.

2. Why do the other members of the European Union feel that true implementation of the single market also requires harmonisation of taxation, and why does the United Kingdom oppose this?

ongoing argument about an EU constitution, which has occupied much of the European Union's efforts since the Nice Summit in 2000, and is discussed in detail below.

THE INSTITUTIONS OF THE EUROPEAN UNION

In this section, we examine the institutions of the European Union as they were just before the massive changes made in mid-2004 – the EU enlargement of May 2004, from 15 to 25 members, and the agreement on the EU Constitution, in June 2004. In later sections, we shall look at the impact of the enlargement and of the Constitution.

Responsibility for achieving the aims of the institutions of the European Union rests with four institutions:

-   the Commission
-   the Council of Ministers
-   the European Parliament
-   the Court of Justice

and two auxiliary bodies:

-   the Economic and Social Committee
-   the European Central Bank.

The Commission

The Commission is the executive of the European Union. It is responsible both for proposing policy and legislation, and for implementing policy after it has been agreed. It is completely independent of Member States, even though its members are appointed by the Member States.

Before the 2004 enlargement, the Commission had 20 members, two each from France, Germany, the United Kingdom, Italy and Spain, and one from each of the other Member States. Each Commissioner is responsible for an area of EU policy. This was already causing some problems, as it was generally felt that there were not enough real areas of policy available to keep every Commissioner fully occupied. The Commission is headed by a president, appointed by the Council of Ministers. The president is usually a powerful figure in his own right. The president until October 2004 was Romano Prodi, ex-prime minister of Italy, and from late 2004 to the time of writing it has been Jose Manuel Durao Barroso, ex-prime minister of Portugal.

The Treaty of Nice in 2002 made provision for reform of the Commission after enlargement. Each Member State was to have one commissioner, a major concession by the large Member States, which lost one of their two commissioners.

The responsibilities of the Commission are laid down by the various EU treaties (Rome, Maastricht, Amsterdam, Nice etc). They include:

- Initiating legislation. The Commission tables proposals to the Council of Ministers after wide-ranging consultation with interested parties.

- Guardian of the treaties. The Commission has to ensure that the treaties and EU legislation are properly implemented.

- Implementing policy. The Commission either directly implements policy itself, or supervises programmes administered by Member States under the principle of subsidiarity, which we looked at earlier.

The Commission is collectively answerable to the European Parliament, and can be removed by a vote of censure carried by a two-thirds majority – although there is no procedure for removing individual commissioners. In early 1999, after a report which criticised the then president, Jacques Santer, and several individual commissioners, and a series of debates in the European Parliament, the whole Commission resigned, and Santer was replaced by Romano Prodi.

The Council of Ministers

The Council is the final decision-making body of the European Union. It consists of representatives of the governments of the Member States. In practice, the Council is really a series of specialist bodies, dealing with particular areas of policy, and attended by the appropriate ministers from the Member States. When the heads of state or government meet, the Council is referred to as the European Council, which meets twice a year. Each Member State in turn acts as president of the Council for six months. Council meetings are attended by the president of the Commission, who has a full right to take part in discussions, but who does not have a vote.

Until 1986, decisions in the Council of Ministers were taken by unanimity, which meant that each Member State had an absolute veto. This was becoming unworkable, and would clearly become more so as more countries joined the European Union. The Single European Act in 1986 introduced the concept of

QUALIFIED MAJORITY VOTING

With a simple majority voting system, decisions are taken on the basis of half the votes cast plus one. With a QMV system, as used by the European Union, additional conditions are introduced into the decision process. Prior to the EU enlargement of 2004, following the Treaty of Nice, votes of Member States were weighted roughly according to population, with Germany, France, Italy and the United Kingdom having 10 votes each, down to Luxembourg with 2 votes. A qualified majority was 62 votes out of an available 87. The Treaty of Nice made provision for QMV after enlargement. When Romania and Bulgaria joined in 2007, taking membership to 27, a qualified majority became 255 votes out of 345, or 73.91 per cent. In addition, a qualified majority must represent at least 62 per cent of the total EU population, and also a majority of Member States.

qualified majority voting (QMV), under which decisions in clearly specified areas could be taken by a majority vote. In practice, this gave the Big Four states a collective veto, but meant that they could not force a proposal through unless they obtained the support of several of the smaller states.

The European Parliament

This is directly elected by voters in all Member States for five years. The most recent elections were in June 2004. Its powers are mainly budgetary. It has the final say on all 'non-compulsory' spending (any spending that is not the inevitable consequence of EU legislation, making up 25 per cent of the budget). It can also reject the budget in total, and did so in 1979 and 1984.

The Parliament has a right to debate all EU issues, and the Council can reject its views only by a unanimous vote. It cannot initiate legislation (the responsibility of the Commission), not does it have the final say in passing law (the responsibility of the Council of Ministers), but it can reject measures which were passed by the Council of Ministers through QMV. In October 2004, it came very close to rejecting the whole of the new Commission proposed by the new President, Jose Manuel Barosso, because of the illiberal views held by the Italian nominee. The crisis was only defused at the last minute when Barosso withdrew his whole Commission for reconsideration, and the Italian government withdrew its nominee.

The European Court of Justice (ECJ)

The ECJ rules on the interpretation and application of EU rules, and on disputes between the Commission and Member States. Its decisions apply directly in the Member States. It consists of judges appointed by the Member States.

The Economic and Social Committee

This is a consultative body made up of representatives of employers (UNICE – the Union of Industrial and Employers' Confederations of Europe – and CEEP – The European Centre of Enterprises with Public Participation), trade unions

(ETUC – the European Trade Union Confederation), and special interest groups (collectively known as the 'social partners'). It must be formally consulted by the Commission on economic and social proposals.

The European Central Bank (ECB)

The ECB was set up in 1999 to administer economic and monetary union (EMU) (which is discussed in detail in a later chapter). It has sole responsibility for setting interest rates in the eurozone. It is headed by a president appointed by the Council of Ministers, and representatives from each member of EMU (which does not include the United Kingdom).

ACTIVITY

3.2 EU INSTITUTIONS AND POWER

1. Why do you think that ultimate power in the European Union lies with the Council of Ministers rather than the Commission?

2. You work for a FTSE-100 company. Your company is concerned about a possible change in EU social policy which could lead to legislation in the next few years. How can your company influence forthcoming EU decisions on this change?

CASE STUDY 3.2

THE STABILITY AND GROWTH PACT

In 1996, as part of the preparations for the launch of the single currency, Germany called for a Stability and Growth Pact which would impose financial discipline on members of the eurozone. One crucial element of this was that no member of the eurozone would be permitted a budget deficit greater than 3 per cent of its GDP. Any member which breached this limit would be subject to a fine of up to 0.5 per cent of GDP (ie billions of euros). The Stability and Growth Pact was agreed as part of the Amsterdam summit in June 1997, and incorporated in the Amsterdam Treaty. This gave it the force of EU law. There was a let-out clause, but only if the Member State's GDP fell by 0.75 per cent.

By 2003, both France and Germany were in breach of the 3 per cent limit. The Commission therefore called on the Council of Ministers (technically ECOFIN,

the Council of Economic and Finance Ministers) to impose the financial sanctions. Despite opposition from countries such as the Netherlands and Portugal, ECOFIN refused to do so. The Commission took ECOFIN to the ECJ.

The ECJ produced its judgement in July 2004. The judgement was not completely clear-cut, but its key point was that ECOFIN was acting illegally in refusing to apply sanctions. EU law, as expressed in the treaties, was binding not only on Member States but also on the Council of Ministers.

This case throws some interesting light on who has the final say in the European Union. It is not the Commission, nor the Council of Ministers, but the law, as expressed in the treaties and interpreted by the ECJ. The treaties, right back to the Treaty of Rome, have in effect always been the EU's written Constitution.

EU ENLARGEMENT

The enlargement of the European Union that took place on 1 May 2004, from 15 to 25 members, increased the population of the European Union by 74 million, ranging from 38 million in Poland to 400,000 in Malta. This enlargement was qualitatively different from any which had gone before:

- The sheer number of new entrants was larger than any before. This in itself put new strains on the European Union's institutions, and increased pressure for speedy agreement on the new Constitution.

- Some of the new entrants – Latvia, Lithuania and Slovakia for example – were far poorer than any previous entrant. GDP per head of the new entrants was about 15 per cent of the old EU average.

- The biggest new entrant, Poland, had a massive and under-developed agricultural sector.

- There were fears in some quarters that enlargement would release a flood of immigrants from the new to the old EU states.

- Eight of the new entrants were ex-communist, and three, the Baltic states, were once part of the USSR. Russia inevitably felt threatened by this, particularly as an outlying part of its territory, Kaliningrad, was now completely surrounded by EU territory (Poland and Lithuania).

- One new entrant, Cyprus, was divided between an officially recognised Greek state, which is in the European Union, and a non-recognised Turkish state, which is not.

- Further expansion was inevitable. The accession of Bulgaria and Romania had been agreed in principle. These countries were even poorer than the 2004 entrants.

Bulgaria and Romania both formally joined the European Union in 1 January 2007, bringing the membership to 27.

 ACTIVITY

3.3 EU EXPANSION

What do you think is the likely impact of EU expansion on your own organisation or sector?

TURKEY AND THE EUROPEAN UNION

CASE STUDY 3.3

Turkey has been an associate member of the European Union since 1963, and has sought full membership since that date. It was formally recognised as a candidate in 1999 (Lungesen 2004), and formal accession talks started in October 2005 (Akcapar and Chaibi 2006). However, accession talks were 'part-suspended' in December 2006 following a dispute about Turkish recognition of Cyprus (Tisdall 2007).

Should Turkey join the European Union?

There are four requirements for new entrants to the European Union, known as the Copenhagen criteria:

● Each applicant must show that it is in sympathy with the fundamental ethos of the European Union, by demonstrating that it practises liberty, democracy, respect for human rights and fundamental freedoms, and the rule of law.

● Each applicant must create a functioning market economy.

● Each applicant must comply with the body of EU laws and standards (the *acquis communitaire*) – which is 100,000 pages long!

● The applicant must be part of Europe.

Turkey does have a history of military coups, and a dubious human rights record in relation to its treatment of its Kurdish minority, but the country argues that it meets the criteria. It is a long-standing democratic country, and since the present government came to power in 2002, it has taken a number of steps to improve its human rights record. It has abolished the death penalty, released some Kurdish activists, and started television broadcasts in Kurdish. Few dispute that it has a functioning market economy. Only a small part of Turkey (Thrace) is technically within geographical Europe, with the rest (Anatolia) being in Asia, but Turkey has always seen itself as part of Europe. The geographical position of Turkey could be a problem, as it has frontiers with Iraq, Iran and Syria, but the former EU enlargement commissioner, Guenter Verheugen, saw this as an asset not a drawback. Membership would demonstrate to the Middle East that the European Union could work with a Muslim country (Lungesen 2004). As the Portuguese foreign minister said about the negotiations with Turkey, this was a victory for Europe and a bitter defeat for Osama bin Laden. Turkish membership should increase Turkish prosperity and so, paradoxically, decrease rather than increase immigration from Turkey (Kirisci 2007).

There is some opposition to Turkish entry on the grounds that its 70 million predominantly Muslim population would upset the religious and cultural balance of the European Union, but Turkey is a fiercely secular state, not an Islamic one, and to say that we do not want Muslims in Europe is an insult to the Muslim minorities in the United Kingdom, France, Germany and Spain. However, in April–May 2007 there was considerable unrest in Turkey over the election of a known Islamist as president, with the threat of a military coup to preserve secularism.

One argument against Turkish entry is that Turkey was too poor. However, this is difficult to support, as Turkey's GDP per head on a purchasing power parity basis is almost identical to that of Romania, which joined the European Union in 2007 (CIA 2007). Another fear is an increased influx of Turkish workers into the European Union, which already has 3 million Turkish-born workers. However, Turkey claims that by 2015 its economic growth will have reached a point where it will itself be a net importer of labour.

The strongest argument against Turkish entry is its sheer size. Its population is just smaller than that of Germany, but it is rising at 1 per cent per annum, and will soon overtake Germany. The population of the EU 27 is probably already falling. By 2050, Turkey could make up between a fifth and a quarter of the total EU population. This is of particular concern to France and Germany, which see their power base being eroded.

In surveys in 2005, 35 per cent of EU citizens supported Turkish entry, while 52 per cent opposed it. If Turkish entry were approved, Austria would hold a referendum on the issue before agreeing to ratify the accession. Only 10 per cent of Austrians

support Turkish entry, which may be a historical folk memory of two sieges of Vienna by the Turkish Empire (Akcapar and Chaibi 2006).

Until recently, Turkish public opinion has been firmly in support of EU membership, but this is now waning, because of what the Turks see as the patronising approach of the European Union. One Turkish commentator recently said, 'The EU is off the radar. It has confirmed Turkey's worst expectations. At present, it is an irrelevancy,' while another said, 'Europe is not ready for Turkish membership' (Tisdall 2007).

THE COMMON AGRICULTURAL POLICY

CASE STUDY 3.4

The Common Agricultural Policy (CAP) has been a key element of European policy since the Treaty of Rome set up the European Economic Community in the 1950s. The Treaty set out the objectives of the CAP which are still in place today:

- to increase productivity

- to ensure fair living standards for the agricultural community

- to stabilise markets

- to ensure availability of food

- to provide food at reasonable prices.

In the early days the CAP was the price Germany paid for French support for industrial free trade. The policy guaranteed farmers prices well above world prices, while imports were restricted by high tariffs. When farmers could not sell all their produce, surpluses were bought by the Community. The result was the infamous stockpiles of the 1970s and 1980s – the butter mountain, the wine lake and so on. These were dumped on the world market at subsidised prices, infuriating other agricultural producers.

In the conditions of the 1950s and 1960s,

the CAP made sense. In 1958 25 per cent of the EEC's workforce worked in agriculture, and farmers and farmworkers were a key political constituency, particularly in France. The members of the EEC also had painful memories of near-starvation during the war, and were desperate to be self-sufficient in food.

Despite its obvious benefits for EEC farmers, the CAP had serious costs. Even by 2005, the European Union spent €49 billion on the CAP, 46 per cent of the budget, and the relative cost was much higher in the 1970s and 1980s. Costs were also borne by EU consumers, who were estimated in 2003 to pay €55 billion more for food than world prices would have justified. The third major group of losers were farmers elsewhere in the world, who were denied access to the European Union by high tariffs, and who saw their markets elsewhere threatened by EU dumping. This was particularly contentious in the case of sugar, the only commodity where the European Union competed directly with Third World producers. Subsidised EU beet sugar kept much cheaper Third World cane sugar out of the European Union. The biggest recipient of CAP funds in the

United Kingdom in 2005 was the sugar company Tate & Lyle, which received €186 million (BBC 2005b).

Most of the CAP's spending goes to large landowners and agribusinesses. It is estimated that 80 per cent of funds go to 20 per cent of EU farmers, with the smallest 40 per cent of farmers sharing just 8 per cent of funds.

By the early 1990s it was clear that the CAP was in urgent need of reform. The lakes and mountains were a political embarrassment, the share of agriculture in EU employment had fallen to around 5 per cent, and the need for self-sufficiency had passed. Agriculture was included in the Uruguay Round free trade negotiations of the General Agreement of Tariffs and Trade, the forerunner of the World Trade Organization (WTO), and the European Union found itself under attack from the rest of the world.

The result was the McSharry reform of 1992. Gradually the system of price support was replaced with direct payments to farmers. The idea of set-aside, that farmers would be paid to take selected fields out of cultivation, was also introduced. Intervention prices were reduced to levels that merely represented a safety net against price collapses. However, import tariffs were maintained, to protect EU farmers from world competition.

During the 1990s and 2000s other considerations started to come to the fore. As concerns for the environment increased, the potential of farmers as protectors of the countryside was increasingly recognised. Less emphasis was placed on highly intensive farming, and more on environmental protection, rural development and food safety. Payments were based primarily on acreage, subject to environmental criteria, which meant that the largest landowners and farmers continued to receive the biggest payments.

The other major issue for the CAP in the 2000s was EU enlargement in 2004 and 2007, from 15 to 27 members. The EU 15 agreed two principles in 2002:

- Expenditure on agricultural support (but not rural development) was to be held constant in real terms between 2006 and 2013, despite the accession of 12 new members. As a result, CAP payments to the EU 15 would fall by 8–9 per cent in real terms by 2013.

- CAP subsidies would initially be paid to the new members at 25 per cent of the full rate, gradually increasing to parity by 2013. In the long run, this would particularly benefit Poland, which had more farmers than any other EU member, but in the short run it would accelerate the movement of farmers away from the land in the accession countries.

THE EU CONSTITUTION

By the late 1990s, it was clear that the European Union was about to undergo a dramatic enlargement, and equally clear that the existing structure of EU institutions would not be able to cope with a greatly increased membership. Hence the move towards an EU Constitution to modernise the European Union's structure. A first attempt at modernisation was made at the Nice Summit in 2000, but the arrangements agreed there really satisfied no one. A Convention under the former French president, Giscard d'Estaing, produced a draft Constitution, and eventually, after much haggling and amendment, a new Constitution was provisionally agreed in outline in June 2004.

The main points of the Constitution were:

The Council president. The European Council (the heads of state or government of Member States) would elect a president of the Council, by qualified majority, for a term of two and a half years, renewable once. The president would have to be approved by the European Parliament. The idea here was to give greater continuity. Previously the Presidency rotated through the Member States every six months.

The foreign minister. The European Council would appoint a foreign minister, by qualified majority. That individual would speak for the European Union on foreign policy. This new post effectively combined two existing posts. However, the foreign minister would not decide policy, and would only be able to speak for the European Union where the European Council had decided on policy. Most importantly, foreign policy was one of the three areas (the others being defence and taxation) where each Member State still had a veto.

The Commission. From November 2004, each Member State was to appoint one commissioner. This meant that the big powers (Germany, France, United Kingdom and Italy) would lose one of their commissioners, as already agreed at Nice. However, it was agreed that by 2014 the size of the Commission would be reduced to two-thirds of the number of Member States, although the precise mechanism for doing this had yet to be negotiated.

The Parliament. The powers of the Parliament were to be significantly increased. It would have powers of 'co-decision' with the Council of Ministers for those policies requiring a decision by qualified majority. This meant that the Parliament would effectively have the right to veto proposed legislation, a very real increase in power.

Qualified majority voting. There were two significant changes to the system of QMV in the Council of Ministers. First, more areas were to be subject to majority voting. These included asylum and immigration policy, and cross-border crime. As we saw above, only foreign affairs, defence and taxation were still subject to veto. Second, the procedure of QMV was to change. Gone was the system where Member States had different numbers of votes. Now all were to have one vote, but a qualified majority was defined as 'at least 55 per cent of the members of the Council, comprising at least 15 of them and representing Member States comprising at least 65 per cent of the population of the Union'.

Several points are of interest here:

- The Constitution already made provision for some limited expansion (presumably the accession of Bulgaria and Romania). At present, 15 members represent 60 per cent of membership, not 55 per cent.

- By setting a population threshold, the Constitution gave considerable power to the big states, particularly to Germany, which on its own has 18 per cent of the European Union's population. Together, Germany, France and either Italy or the United Kingdom would have a blocking minority.

Charter of Fundamental Rights. This sets out key 'rights, freedoms and principles'. These include the right to life and liberty, and the right to strike. This could affect existing UK industrial relations law, but the UK government feels that national laws on industrial relations will not be affected. This has yet to be tested by the ECJ.

The fact that the Member States had agreed on the Constitution did not mean that it immediately came into force. The Constitution had to be ratified by each of the (then) 25 Member States. Along with several other states, including Spain, France, the Netherlands and Ireland, in the United Kingdom it was agreed that it would only be ratified after a referendum.

The key referenda were those in France and the Netherlands, held in May and June 2005. Both campaigns were very difficult for the national governments and the European Union. France voted 54.9 per cent no on 29 May, and in the Netherlands, 61.7 per cent voted against on 1 June (Nugent 2006). In each case, non-EU issues muddied the picture. In polls held by the Commission after the referenda, a third of Dutch people who voted no said it was because of lack of information, and 14 per cent said it was because they opposed the ruling party. A third voted no on specifically constitution-related issues – 19 per cent because of a fear of loss of national sovereignty, and 13 per cent because they felt Europe was too expensive (the Netherlands is the largest per-head contributor to the EU budget). In France, reasons for voting no were predominantly economic – either a fear of negative effects on employment (31 per cent) or that the economic situation was too weak (25 per cent). Another third thought that the Constitution represented an unacceptable move towards Anglo-Saxon models of capitalism, or a weakening of the European social model (Church and Phinnemore 2007).

As a result of these rejections, no further referenda were held in the United Kingdom or elsewhere. The Constitution was renegotiated in June 2007 and significant changes were made:

- The name 'Constitution' was dropped, and replaced by 'Reform Treaty'.

- The Constitution proposal for a 'double majority' system of QMV (55 per cent of Member States representing 65 per cent of the European Union's population) was maintained, but to meet Polish objections that this gave too much weight to Germany, it was not to be phased in until 2014–17.

- The national veto was to be maintained for social security and culture, as well as for defence, foreign policy and taxation.

- The post of EU Council president remained, but the EU foreign minister's title was changed to 'high representative'.

- The UK obtained an opt-out from the Charter of Fundamental Rights (BBC 2007).

Like the Constitution, the Reform Treaty still has to be ratified. The UK government has announced that it is happy with the Treaty, and will not hold a referendum, but that the decision will be taken by Parliament. Ireland will definitely hold a referendum, and so may Denmark and the Netherlands (which voted against the Constitution in 2005) (Mulvey 2007).

THE EUROPEAN UNION AND OTHER REGIONAL BLOCS

The European Union is not the only major regional trading group in the world. The North American Free Trade Agreement (NAFTA) covers the United States,

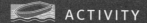

ACTIVITY

3.4 THE EU CONSTITUTION

The opinion polls after the announcement of agreement on the Constitution suggested that there would have been a two to one majority against it in a UK referendum. Why do you think this was so?

Canada and Mexico, while the Association of South East Asian Nations (ASEAN) includes the Asian Tiger states of Indonesia, Malaysia, the Philippines, Singapore and Thailand, as well as states including Vietnam and Myanmar, with China, India, Japan and Australia as Dialogue Partners. Both NAFTA and ASEAN are primarily free trade area agreements, and as such, of much narrower scope than the European Union.

All three encourage trade within their own area, and thus may indirectly discourage trade between the three blocs. If you have read George Orwell's *Nineteen Eighty-Four,* you might see parallels with his three competing blocs of Eurasia, Eastasia and Oceania, which divided up the world between them!

In 2000, the so-called Triad of the United States, the European Union and Japan received 71 per cent of total world inward direct investment, and were responsible for 82 per cent of outward direct investment (Williams 2001).

INTERNATIONAL FINANCIAL INSTITUTIONS

THE BRETTON WOODS CONFERENCE

In 1944, the wartime Western allies held a conference at Bretton Woods in New Hampshire which was to shape the economic future of the international economy. Their prime aim was to prevent a repetition of the competitive devaluations and protectionism which had followed the Wall Street crash in 1929, and which had made the ensuing Great Depression even more severe in its impact. The idea was to impose strict controls on the ability of each country to follow beggar-my-neighbour policies, and to force international economic co-operation.

Out of Bretton Woods came three great international institutions, the International Monetary Fund (IMF), the International Bank for Reconstruction and Development (the World Bank), and the General Agreement on Tariffs and Trade (GATT).

THE IMF

The main plank of the IMF regime was a system of fixed exchange rates, which all member countries agreed to maintain. In practice this meant that each member state fixed the value of its currency in terms of the US dollar, while the

US dollar itself was linked to gold. It was recognised that members might experience problems with their balance of payments in the short term (an excess of imports over exports). In such a situation, the IMF agreed to make hard currency available to them on a short-term basis, to allow the member a breathing space to adjust its economy. Only if the balance of payments problem was long-term was the member state permitted to devalue its currency. The system was financed by subscriptions from member countries, with by far the largest contribution coming from the United States.

The system worked reasonably smoothly for nearly 30 years, although there were still balance of payments crises, and occasional devaluations (most notably in the United Kingdom, France, and Italy). Most lending was to developed countries, and the IMF had little involvement with the Third World. However, the world economic structure changed fundamentally in the early 1970s. Now it was the United States which experienced a balance of payments crisis. The IMF system could not cope with this – the absolute stability of the dollar was fundamental. Eventually, President Nixon abandoned the fixed price link between the US dollar and gold – in effect devaluing the dollar. As a result, fixed exchange rates were abandoned, and have never been restored on a world level.

The floating exchange rate regime immediately removed the IMF's major role. It still carries out its role of alleviating short-term financial crises, but almost always with developing rather than developed economies – the Asian Tiger economies (Thailand, South Korea, Indonesia) in 1997, Russia in 1998, Brazil in 1999 and Argentina in 2001 – but the IMF also started to develop a wider role of encouraging structural reform in member states (often known as 'mission creep' – a typical example of an organisation broadening its original aims beyond all recognition). An early example of this was the loan to the United Kingdom in 1976, which was made conditional on the (Labour) government cutting public spending and adopting monetarist policies. This process has now gone much further, and from the 1980s onwards the IMF has followed a policy of imposing Thatcherite, free-market neo-liberal conditions (particularly privatisation) on its support, particularly to Third World countries:

- Tanzania was forced to charge for hospital visits and school meals.
- Ecuador was forced to sell its water system to foreigners and to increase the price of cooking oil by 80 per cent.
- Malawi was told to sell off its strategic reserves of maize, two years before the country was hit by famine.
- Guyana was told to privatise its sugar industry.
- Zambia was told to private its banks (Mathiason 2003).

Should the IMF try to impose long-term neo-liberal reform in the Third World, rather than concentrating on lending money to countries in short-term financial difficulties? There are three main arguments in favour of this policy:

- State-run sectors in Third World countries tend to be inefficient, corrupt, devourers of resources, and they discourage foreign investment. The state may also spend wastefully and not in the best long-term interests of its population – for instance by excess spending on arms.

- Moral hazard – the concept that because countries expect to be bailed out if they get into difficulties, they will be reckless in their behaviour, because they know they will never really be called to account for their actions. For example, Brazil has defaulted on its debts five times, and Venezuela nine times. In essence, this is the same argument that says that insurance companies should carry out very strict checks before they pay out on policies, in order to discourage fraudulent claims.

- Short-term intervention tends by definition to treat short-term symptoms rather than the long-term illness. The only way to tackle long-term problems is through long-term reform.

There are two counter-arguments:

- While the above may be true in the long run, the short-term effect of privatisation and liberalisation is to increase poverty and inequality in the Third World.

- By concentrating on the long term rather than the short term, the IMF is moving into areas which should more appropriately be the responsibility of the World Bank (Stiglitz 2003).

The current consensus seems to be that the IMF should concentrate on macroeconomic factors such as budget deficits and inflation, rather than trying to micro-manage the economies of clients. Charles Wyplosz, professor of economics at the Institute of International Studies in Geneva was quoted in the *Financial Times* in May 2004 as saying, 'when firemen come to your house to put out a blaze, you would not expect them to meddle in your marriage' (Swann 2004).

Ngaire Woods suggests three changes:

- The IMF should be the cornerstone of global monetary co-operation.
- The IMF should help countries mitigate or cushion shocks from the global economy.
- The IMF must command the confidence of all its members (Woods 2007).

THE WORLD BANK

Like the IMF, the World Bank was set up at Bretton Woods, and nearly all countries in the world are members. Unlike the IMF, its main role is to provide access to capital for long-term development, particularly in the Third World. It does this partly through direct lending through a number of its own agencies, some of it interest-free, and partly by leveraging investment from the private sector.

It also has a wider social remit than the IMF. It emphasises social services, the environment and gender equality as well as economic growth. However, like the IMF it has been criticised for the neo-liberal conditions that it tends to attach to its loans, and also for over-lending to relatively advanced developing countries like Brazil and particularly China, which have sufficient clout to be able to borrow to finance their development on a commercial basis. The Bank is also a key component in the so-called Washington Consensus, not least because of the convention that its President is nominated by the United States (Woods 2007).

One proposal that has been put forward is that the IMF and the World Bank should merge. There is clear overlap – in practice if not in theory – between the activities of the IMF and World Bank, although in principle their functions are distinct. A merger might therefore seem logical, and it might help to prevent mission creep. However, if the IMF had a dominant role in the merged organisation, its neo-liberal agenda might swamp the wider social and environmental principles of the World Bank.

 MALAWI, THE IMF AND EDUCATION

CASE STUDY 3.5

Education is key to economic and social development in the Third World. Education has become a higher priority for the IMF and the World Bank. The IMF no longer insists on fees for primary education, while the World Bank is striving to achieve its Millennium Development Goal (MDG) of all children receiving primary education by 2015.

However, the example of Malawi, quoted by the development charity ActionAid in a research report in 2006 (ActionAid 2006), shows how difficult this is to achieve in practice. Malawi made primary education free in 1994, and as expected this led to a boom in enrolments. The enrolment rate for primary education in Malawi is now 95 per cent. So far, so good. But the primary pupil–teacher ratio in Malawi is 72:1, way above the MDG target level of 40:1. The increase in enrolment inevitably led to an acute shortage of teachers, so in 1994 the Malawi government recruited 22,000 untrained teachers, who later received a token six weeks' training. From 1995 to 2005, no pre-service teacher training at all was carried out in Malawi. A teacher is paid the equivalent of US$55 a month, while the official subsistence-level wage is US$107. About 500 teachers each year die of AIDS. Not surprisingly, the drop-out rate from primary education is high. The completion

rate is only 32 per cent for boys, and an even worse 27 per cent for girls.

ActionAid discussed the role of the IMF in this situation. As part of its loan arrangement with Malawi, the IMF imposed a ceiling on public sector wages of 7.2 per cent of GDP. Teachers' wages are 2.7 per cent of GDP. To stay within the wage ceiling, there is thus very little scope for either recruiting more teachers or increasing their pay.

In an article in the *Guardian* in April 2007, George Monbiot examined this situation (Monbiot 2007), and placed all the blame on the IMF for preventing the government from employing more teachers. In a memorable phrase, he says, 'Except for the district commissioners in pith helmets, little has changed since the country was called Nyasaland.'

However, Monbiot's source, the ActionAid analysis, is more balanced. It reports that the IMF claims that the wage ceiling is flexible, and that as long as it stays within the overall ceiling, there is nothing to stop the Malawi government from giving priority to teacher recruitment. The educational sector is specifically exempted from the recruitment freeze. The IMF also says that there are other reasons for the lack of teachers: skewed staff deployment, 'ghost' teachers (dead teachers officially kept on the payroll, with someone corruptly receiving their salary), failure to train, and lack of predictable donor aid.

ActionAid does blame the IMF for not insisting on higher education spending, citing the IMF's policy horizon of two to three years, unlike the 10–15 year horizon needed to see a pay-off from education spending. It says that the 'IMF approach encourages nations to believe that there is just one truth, one concept of macroeconomic stability'. But it also blames the Malawi Ministry of Finance, which does not involve the Ministry of Education in the negotiations with the IMF.

ActionAid proposes three reforms:

- The IMF should stop attaching specific policy conditions to its aid – it should not try to micromanage.

- The Malawi government should place education and development goals at the centre of its macroeconomic planning.

- Donors should provide increased and more predictable aid.

ActionAid does not feel the situation is hopeless. If Malawi grows at the target rate of 6 per cent for the next 10 years, even within the wage ceiling this would lead to an increase in the education budget of 70 per cent over the 10 years, giving scope to bring the pupil–teacher ratio to 40:1, fund the necessary teacher training and slightly increase teacher pay.

Two main lessons can be drawn from this case study. One is that IMF restrictions can act to frustrate World Bank goals. The other is that newspaper comment must be handled with care. It is often the truth, but not necessarily the whole truth.

INTERNATIONAL TRADE AND COMPARATIVE ADVANTAGE

Very few countries are self-sufficient, in the sense that they produce everything they need within their own boundaries. Ever since the Stone Age, societies have traded with each other. The most obvious reason for a country to trade is to obtain something it is incapable of producing for itself. For example, until the discovery of North Sea oil, the United Kingdom had to import oil. However, strictly speaking this only applies to extractive industries. Anything else could be made or grown, at a price. There is nothing to stop the United Kingdom growing its own bananas in greenhouses (except common sense!). It is a much more efficient use of resources for countries to concentrate on what they are best at producing, and to import other goods. For example, if we compare the United Kingdom and the Windward Islands, the United Kingdom has an absolute advantage in the production of pharmaceuticals, while the Windwards have an absolute advantage in the production of bananas. It therefore makes sense for the United Kingdom to specialise in pharmaceuticals, and to export these to the Windwards, while the Windwards should export bananas to the United Kingdom. (As we shall see later when we look at the banana war, the real world is a lot more complicated than this simple example suggests.)

Even if one country is better at producing everything than another country, international trade will still benefit both sides. For example, let's stretch our banana example even further. Assume that the United Kingdom is four times as efficient as the Windwards at producing pharmaceuticals, but twice as efficient at producing bananas. In this case, the United Kingdom has a comparative advantage in the production of pharmaceuticals, and the Windwards a comparative advantage in bananas. Both sides would benefit if the United Kingdom specialised in pharmaceuticals, and the Windwards in bananas. The mathematics to prove this can be found in any textbook on international economics.

For comparative advantage to work, however, it is essential that there are no restrictions on trade between the countries involved, ie that there is free trade. For example, assume that the United Kingdom has a banana industry which is struggling to cope with competition from Windwards bananas, and then assume that the UK banana industry persuades the UK government to place either quotas (restrictions on quantity) or tariffs (taxation) on imports of Windwards bananas. People working in the UK banana industry would benefit, but everyone else in both economies would lose.

If you think that this example seems totally unrealistic, you are probably right, but bear in mind that Japan, for example, protects its rice growers with a 500 per cent tariff on imported rice.

ACTIVITY

3.5 IS COMPARATIVE ADVANTAGE GOOD FOR YOU?

The theory of comparative advantage suggests that everyone gains from free trade. Why then do so many countries protect their own domestic industries?

THE WORLD TRADE ORGANIZATION (WTO)

After the Second World War, the Allies set up GATT, whose remit was to encourage free trade, and prevent the destructive protectionism that had blighted the world economy in the 1930s. Its objectives were to:

- eliminate existing trade barriers
- deter the formation of new barriers
- eliminate all forms of trade discrimination.

In 1995 GATT was absorbed into a new body, the WTO, with wider objectives. Its membership now includes virtually the whole world, following the accession of China and Taiwan in the early 2000s. The WTO continues the process of liberalising world trade, but its powers also extend to trade in services as well as goods, and also the regulation of international property rights like patents and copyright. It also has the power to adjudicate on disputes between members, with the right to impose financial penalties.

THE BANANA WAR

The banana war was one of the most bitter trade disputes of the 1990s, and one of a number of disputes between the two dominant trading blocs, the European Union and the United States. The key to the dispute was the preference that the European Union gave to bananas from ex-British and French colonies in Africa, the Pacific and the Caribbean (the APC countries). The EU argument was that without protection, the banana industries in these areas, particularly in the Caribbean, would collapse, devastating the local economies, and perhaps pushing producers to alternative less desirable crops like cannabis or coca. They pointed out that the WTO had an objective to assist developing and transition economies.

The United States responded that the EU action was a gross breach of WTO rules. Three US companies – Chiquita, Dole and Del Monte – control two-thirds of world trade in bananas from their huge plantations in Central America (the APC has 4 per cent of the world market).

Legally, the United States had an unanswerable case, but it weakened its moral position by imposing punitive import tariffs in 1998 on a range of EU exports to the United States in retaliation, before the WTO delivered its judgement. Worse, this was announced shortly after Chiquita gave a big donation to the ruling US Democratic Party.

The WTO ruled in favour of the United States, and ordered the European Union to abolish its protective quotas on APC bananas by 2005. The effects on the Caribbean have been predictably devastating. Between 1993 and 2000, two-thirds of the banana growers in the Windward Islands went out of business, while exports of bananas from St Vincent and the Grenadines fell from US$120 million to US$50 million (Ryle 2002).

THE WORKING OF THE WTO

The WTO (and its predecessor GATT) works in a series of long trade rounds, initiated at a major conference, and then negotiated and implemented over a long period. The Uruguay Round in the 1990s was primarily concerned with textiles, where the developing world had a comparative advantage, but where the developed countries maintained protection of their own textile industries. The developed Western countries agreed to eliminate protection, but only over a 10-year period, with most of the concessions coming in the last year! This tends to be the pattern – the West speaks the language of free trade, is keen to impose free trade on the developing world, but drags its heels when it comes to its own concessions.

Larry Elliott in the *Guardian* in 2004 drew a telling parallel with medieval Europe, where in theory all states owed spiritual allegiance to the papacy and the universal values of the Church, but in practice spent most of their time at war with each other (Elliott 2004).

THE FAILURE OF DOHA: FROM 9/11 TO THE IRAQ WAR

The Doha Round of trade negotiations was launched by the WTO in 2001, in the wake of the 9/11 terrorist attacks on New York and Washington. The negotiations were specifically designated as a 'development round', aimed at improving the economic position of developing countries, as a symbol of world solidarity against terrorism (*Economist* 2003).

WTO negotiations are always difficult, as all agreements have to be unanimous. Unlike the IMF, rich countries do not have disproportionate power. Three main issues of particular interest to developing countries dominated the negotiations: special trade treatment for developing countries, supply of cheap generic medicines for poor countries, and liberalisation of agriculture (De Jonquieres 2003).

The deadlines for special trade treatment and generic medicines were missed at the end of 2002. In the case of generic medicines the only country voting against agreement was the United States.

Agricultural liberalisation was a much more crucial issue. When the first Doha meeting was called, it produced a pledge to improve market access for Third World countries, to reduce trade-distorting domestic support, and to reduce export subsidies.

Reform was urgently needed. In 2001, assistance to rich country farmers amounted to US$311 billion, compared with US$50 billion in development aid. The European Union paid subsidies of US$913 a year to each EU cow, and US$8 in aid to each sub-Saharan African. Comparable figures for Japan were US$2,700 and US$1.47 (Wolf 2005, p215). The European Union was the world's largest exporter of skimmed milk powder, sold at half its cost of production, and of white sugar, sold at a quarter the cost of production (Wolf 2005, p216).

Stuart Harbinson, the WTO chairman for agriculture, proposed a package that would:

- end export subsidies in nine years
- reduce tariffs by 40–60 per cent
- cut trade-distorting farm support by 60 per cent.

It was calculated that these proposals would increase annual global income by US$100 billion, with 20 per cent of the gain going to developing countries and 80 per cent to rich countries through lower prices (De Jonquieres 2003).

The United States and the Cairns Group of major agricultural exporters (including Australia and Canada) argued that the Harbinson proposals did not go far enough, while the European Union and Japan claimed that they were too ambitious. India wanted to maintain its own tariffs to protect its farmers. The ACP group of developing countries sided with the European Union, worried about losing their preferential access to EU markets (see the banana war case study).

The key to the negotiations was the attitude of the European Union. The European Commission proposed reform of the CAP which, by phasing out incentives for over-production and switching to support based on rural development and protection of the environment, would reduce export subsidies, but would not make EU markets more open to imports. Meanwhile France and Germany had reached an agreement to maintain spending on the CAP until 2013.

Under the terms of the negotiations, agreement was required by 31 March 2003, by which time the Iraq war had just broken out, relations between the United States and France were at an all-time low and, ironically, Doha was the military headquarters for the war.

The 31 March deadline was missed. The day after this, Franz Fischler, the EU agriculture commissioner, and Pascal Lamy, the trade commissioner, wrote an article in the *Financial Times* justifying the EU position (Fischler and Lamy 2003). They criticised the Cairns Group, arguing that it wanted nothing more than 'an unlimited right to exploit its members' undeniable comparative advantages'. They also pointed out that the European Union is the largest importer of agricultural products and the main importer of food from developing countries, taking in more food imports than the United States, Japan, Canada and Australia put together. Lamy is now (2007) the head of the WTO – a classic case of poacher turned gamekeeper!

Negotiations staggered on for another three years. In Geneva in August 2004, the WTO agreed that export subsidies should be abolished, but no starting date or timetable has been agreed. The final breakdown came over fundamental disagreement between the European Union and the United States. The United States argued that the European Union was not offering big enough reductions in tariffs, while the European Union claimed that the United States was not proposing a big enough reduction in subsidies. Eventually the United States decided that no deal was better than a weak deal – 'Doha lite', as the US trade representative, Susan Schwab, put it. On 24 July 2006, the Doha Round was formally suspended, with no date set for a resumption. (*Economist* 2006a).

What does the failure of Doha tell us? It shows:

- the hypocrisy of the developed world, which is ready to impose trade liberalisation on the developing world, but not to make meaningful concessions itself

- the strength of the farm lobby in both the European Union and the United States, which prevented any agreement

- divisions among the developing countries and agricultural exports, with diametrically opposing stances being taken by India, the Cairns Group and the ACP.

DEBT RELIEF

One of the most pressing problems of the world economy is the crushing burden of Third World debt. The 52 most indebted countries, mostly in Africa, have debts of US$375 billion, most of it unpayable, but on which interest still has to be paid. In 1998, it cost these countries US$23.4 billion to service their debt, mostly owed to Western governments, the IMF or the World Bank. In many countries, debt repayment dwarfs welfare budgets. Mauritania pays US$63 million to service its debt, but only US $51 million on education, and US $17 million on health (Madeley 2001).

Much of the debt is a product of the cold war period, when the West was keen to tie the Third World to its side, and much of the money was wasted, either going on armaments, or disappearing through corruption, by the likes of the late unlamented presidents Amin and Mobutu.

Many arguments can be advanced for relieving at least some of this burden of debt. These include the moral – that debt is denying the inhabitants of these countries the human rights of decent education and health – the economic – that money being spent on debt repayment is not being spent on imports from the West – and the geopolitical – that poverty and discontent create an environment conducive to terrorism.

A international campaign for debt relief was launched in 1996 by the pressure group Jubilee 2000, which has produced some results. The IMF and the World Bank have set up the Heavily Indebted Poor Countries (HIPC) initiative to administer debt relief to the 52 poorest states, the G7 promised the cancellation of US$110 billion of debt, while the UK government agreed to hold debt repayments in a trust for poverty relief, to be released when each country agreed a poverty reduction plan (Madeley 2001).

However, progress has been limited. By the end of the Jubilee 2000 campaign in December 2000, only one country, Uganda, had debt cancelled, with reductions agreed for another 21, and in line with normal IMF/World Bank policy, stringent conditions were attached. HIPCs are still expected to pay 20–25 per cent of their export earnings towards debt service (Sassen 2001) However, some progress has been made. In a sample of 10 HIPC countries, education spending rose by 50 per cent between 1998 and 2002, from less than the 10 states were spending on debt relief in 1998, to almost double the amount in 2002 (Stewart 2002).

The Jubilee 2000 campaign was followed by the Make Poverty History campaign, which seemed to have reached success at the Gleneagles conference of the G8 in July 2005, chaired by Tony Blair. This pledged to double development assistance to Africa, including debt relief and aid, to US$100 billion a year by 2010. However, in April 2007 the Africa Progress Panel (APP), set up to review progress on the pledge, headed by Kofi Annan, the former UN secretary-general, reported that the G8 was only 10 per cent of the way to reaching its target. The United Kingdom alone of the G8 had met its commitments in full, but Bob Geldof, who is also a member of the APP, singled out Germany and Italy as countries which were significantly failing to meet their commitments. At the same time the OECD reported that after one-off packages of debt relief for Iraq and Nigeria were taken into account, aid flows from the West fell for the first time in a decade in 2006 (Elliott and Connolly 2007).

However, the issue of debt relief and aid is not straightforward. Boone (2005) argues that much aid is ineffective. Countries that received large aid flows did not do better at reducing child mortality than those that received small amounts of aid. Indeed, contrary to popular belief, little aid goes to finance social reform. Only 4 per cent went to health, 12 per cent to education and 6 per cent to deal with emergencies. Countries or regions that were most successful at reducing

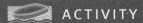

ACTIVITY

3.6 DEBT RELIEF

Can you put forward any arguments against either the principle or the practice of debt relief for the Third World?

VULTURE FUNDS

Vulture funds, like their namesakes, pick on the carcases of poor countries. They are companies that buy up debt of Third World countries from lender nations or banks. The sellers are willing to sell this debt at a fraction of its face value, as they think it is highly unlikely that it will ever be paid. The vulture fund then sues the debtor country for recovery of the face value of the debt.

One example of a vulture fund is the US company Donegal International. It purchased Zambian sovereign debt with a face value of US$44 million from Romania in 1999 for US$3.2 million. It then claimed the full face value of the debt from Zambia, but agreed in 2003 to accept US$16 million, with a provision that any default meant that full value of the debt would become payable. Zambia paid US$2.5 million in 2003, but then ceased payment. Interest since 2003 took the amount that

Donegal now claimed through the High Court to US$55 million. However, Mr Justice Andrew Smith ruled in April 2007 that although the 2003 agreement was legal, the amount payable in the event of default was penal. He awarded Donegal US$15.5 million, the original amount outstanding plus US$2 million interest, and heavily criticised Donegal's behaviour, saying, 'I do regard the dishonesty with which I was confronted to be rather serious' (Seager 2007).

This case illustrates the rapacious nature of the claims made on developing countries, and the urgent need for debt relief. It also illustrates the potential profit that can be made by vulture funds. Donegal has already received all but US$0.7 million of the money it paid for the debt in 1999. Virtually anything further which it recovers from Zambia will be pure profit.

child mortality were Cuba, Sri Lanka and the Indian state of Kerala. These had very different political systems, but all had put a lot of effort into developing their infrastructure. As a result, aid was spent where it was needed, rather than being wasted on bureaucracy or corruption.

GLOBALISATION

Globalisation is an emotive word. It has inspired violent demonstrations all over the world, and also vehement defence. But what is globalisation? This is no single clear definition.

First, it is useful to look at what globalisation is not (Scholte 2000):

- Internationalisation. The world has always been international. There were trade links between the Roman and Chinese empires, for example.

- Free trade. Trade was at least as free in the late nineteenth century as it is now.

- Westernisation. Western culture was exported to much of the world as a result of the dominance of Western empires in the late nineteenth and early twentieth centuries.

- Universalisation. Global lifestyles and ideas are nothing new. Islam spread across half the known western world in 50 years in the sixth century, and later spread to countries as far apart as Nigeria and Indonesia.

John Gray sees its key features as free mobility of capital and free trade (Gray 1995). Ngaire Woods sees globalisation as much wider, and political and social as well as economic. She distinguishes three elements (Woods 2000):

- The expansion of markets. Technological changes like the mobile phone and above all the Internet have speeded up communications to the extent that both financial and physical transactions can be carried out instantaneously, while improvements in transport permit goods to be shipped quickly and relatively cheaply anywhere in the world. (Think of the universal availability in the United Kingdom of asparagus from Peru and French beans from Kenya.) At the same time, governments throughout the world have been deregulating, and reducing their control over their economies, at the same time as the growth of e-commerce has started to erode their control of their tax base. The result has been the spread of transnational enterprises and global brands, leading to what Kenichi Ohmae, the Japanese management guru and one of the early proponents of globalisation, called *The borderless world* (Ohmae 1990).

  The knowledge economy also creates a borderless world. Knowledge is not dependent on possession of natural resources, and can instantaneously be transmitted via the Internet. As Lester Thurow says, 'knowledge is the new basis for wealth' (Thurow 1999). Hence then outflow of call centre and data handling jobs from the United Kingdom to India.

- The transformation of politics. Free movement of capital has produced a world financial market which has the potential to swamp any single economy. At the same time, transnational issues have become of increasing importance – global warming, human rights, drugs, world poverty, immigration and terrorism. Increasingly, in order to have any influence, nation-states have to join together in regional groupings. The European Union is the best known, but there are other important groupings like NAFTA and ASEAN. Just as nation-states are handing over power to regional groupings, they are also devolving power internally to regional entities – Scotland and Wales in the United Kingdom, Catalonia in Spain.

- The emergence of new social and political movements. A global (or American) culture has developed, with US corporations like McDonald's, CNN, Disney and Nike setting trends across the world. At the same time, counter-movements have developed, ranging from the anti-globalisation movement to militant Islam.

Globalisation is nothing new. An early example came with the Opium Wars in the 1840s, when Great Britain forced China to open its borders to imports of opium in order to finance the early Victorians' obsession with China tea. It has often been argued that the golden age of globalisation was the period from 1880 to 1914, when the world economy was regulated by the universal use of the gold standard, there was almost universal free trade, and free movement of capital. Indeed, this period had one element of globalisation which does not apply today – free movement of people. Not only could an individual travel without a passport, there was also free movement of labour, and very little control on international migration. This is the period when the Statue of Liberty was erected in New York. One commentator even said in 1911 that a major war was now impossible, as the world had become so interdependent (Micklethwait and Wooldridge 2000).

Two dates mark the development of modern globalisation. One is 1973, and the first oil crisis. This led to two things – a realisation that the world economy was inextricably linked through its dependence on oil, and the collapse of the Bretton Woods system of fixed exchange rates, which ushered in a period when world financial markets became much more dominant.

The other is 1989. One factor here was the collapse of communism as a world ideology, and the triumph of the United States in the cold war – what the US political scientist Francis Fukuyama (1992) called *The end of history*. The other, much less noted at the time, but equally important, was the final bursting of the Japanese 'bubble economy'. Throughout the 1980s, it seems that globalisation was likely to be Japanese rather than US-dominated. Japanese industrial techniques were sweeping the world, and most of the world's biggest corporations were Japanese rather than American. The economic collapse of Japan ensured that globalisation would be US-dominated economically, as well as politically and culturally.

DRIVERS OF GLOBALISATION

A number of drivers of globalisation have intensified in the last 20 years or so:

- Technology. The most important developments here are in information and communication technology (ICT), particularly the mobile phone and the Internet. These have transformed the way in which particular industries operate. An example is the insurance industry, which traditionally was staid and conservative, but has been transformed by the application of new technology, which has led to a wave of mergers.

- Cultural homogenisation. The universal availability of television, and the global audiences for international sporting events like the World Cup and the Olympic Games, combined with the explosion in overseas travel, have led to a homogenisation of international culture, which permits the development of global brands. However, global brands like McDonald's still have to be responsive to local cultural differences – no traditional beef Big Macs in India, for example.

- Economies of scale. Developments in manufacturing techniques have meant that the minimum efficient scale of operations in many industries has become a significant percentage of the available world market. The most extreme example is the aircraft industry, where the total world market is barely big enough to support two firms (Boeing and Airbus).

- Deregulation. Deregulation has been driven by bodies such as the WTO and the European Union. It reduces the costs of cross-border trade, and so promotes the development of global companies.

- Competition. If one firm in an industry globalises, it will gain a competitive advantage. In order to stay in touch, its competitors will also be forced to globalise (Segal-Horn 2002).

TWO GLOBAL COMPANIES

CASE STUDY 3.9

Siemens

Siemens was founded in Germany in the mid-nineteenth century, and by 1865 was already operating in the United Kingdom and Russia. In 1872 it supplied China with its first telegraph. It is now Europe's largest engineering company, operating in 190 countries. Eighty per cent of its sales, 70 per cent of its factories and 66 per cent of its workforce are outside Germany.

Its workforce in China is 36,000, and its annual Chinese sales are €4.4 billion. Like most globalised companies, it uses low-cost countries to manufacture components. But unlike most, it also does a lot of its R&D abroad. For example, a tailor-made low-cost body scanner for use in poorer countries was developed and is manufactured solely in China. Customers are happy to buy the product because they know that they can trade up at a later date to a more sophisticated German-made product using the same software. The company's Medical Solutions Group is investing over €30 million in its Asia Center of Excellence in Shanghai.

In non-medical areas, the company is building 60 high-speed trains in China with its local partner Tangshan Locomotive Rolling Stock Work, in a contract worth €670 million to Siemens. In 2005, Siemens filed over 1,000 patents in China. The company also sees India as key to its world development. It exports railway locomotives to the Middle East, but does so through India, where it employs 15,000 people.

Philips

Philips is smaller than Siemens, employing only 122,000 people in 60 countries. It has also had a much more chequered recent history. It started as a light bulb manufacturer in Holland in 1891. It then moved into X-ray machines and radio equipment. In the 1970s it moved into the record business, and also expanded in electronics, including mobile phones and semiconductors.

By 2000, Philips had run into trouble. In most of its markets it was number three, four or worse, and so very vulnerable to competition. In 2001–2 it lost over €3 billion, and shed 55,000 jobs. It cut its 30 separate divisions to five – domestic appliances, lighting, medical, consumer electronics and semiconductors. This turned the company around, but downsizing continued. Philips exited the mobile phone business, and sold a majority stake in its semiconductor business to the private equity company KKR.

The company's strategy now is to develop advanced products that are well designed and easy to use. China is key to this. Philips has long had links with China. In the 1920s it sold an X-ray machine for the personal use of the last Chinese emperor. It now has 20,000 employees in China, with production there worth €6 billion, half of which is exported. Like Siemens, it carries out R&D in China, at 15 centres employing 900 staff. The CEO, Gerard Kleisterlee, recently said, 'for us China is not just a workshop or a marketplace – it is a centre of innovation for new products and services with global applications'.

The lessons

- Globalisation leads to constant and rapid change. It makes the environment more turbulent. Both companies, but particularly Philips, are continually restructuring, developing new product ranges and dropping old ones.

- It is an old-fashioned view of globalisation to see India and China solely as low-cost manufacturing production lines. They are huge, rapidly growing and increasingly sophisticated markets in their own right. Successful globalisers design products for China, in China (and India).

MULTINATIONAL AND TRANSNATIONAL CORPORATIONS

Multinational corporations (MNCs) are companies producing or distributing goods or services in two or more countries. A transnational corporation (TNC) is an MNC with more than two-thirds of its activities outside its home country. Such companies can locate different activities in parts of the world where they reap the biggest comparative advantage. Thus Rupert Murdoch's News Corporation is controlled through holding companies in the Cayman Islands, a notorious tax haven. The result is that News Corporation pays an average tax rate of 10 per cent.

In another example, the fall in the costs of air transport has led to the centralisation of the world flower industry in the Netherlands. Flowers are flown in from Kenya or India one day, sold at auction and then flown to customers on Europe or the United States the next day.

The best-known example of local advantage is low labour costs. This is most obvious in low-wage industries like textiles, but a high-tech example is the Brazilian manufacturer of regional jet airliners, Embraer. Its employment costs in 2002 were US$26,000 per employee, as against US$63,000 in the regional jet business of its major Canadian competitor, Bombardier (Ghemawat 2003).

In 2001 there were estimated to be 63,000 TNCs, which had 800,000 foreign affiliates, and which controlled two-thirds of world trade. Of the top 100 non-financial TNCs, 91 were based in the United States, the European Union or Japan (UNCTAD 2001). Of the companies in the 2006 Fortune Global 500 (measured by turnover), 172 were based in the European Union, 114 in the United States, 70 in Japan and 20 in China (*Fortune* 2006).

Interbrand identifies its Best Global Brands each year. To qualify as a global brand, the brand must achieve more than a third of its sales outside its home country (which excludes Wal-Mart, most of whose sales are in the United States). Interbrand's valuation is based on expected future earnings, rather than on current turnover or profit (Interbrand 2006). It is interesting that only one company (Toyota) appears in the top 10 of both the Fortune and Interbrand lists. Whereas there are five oil companies in the *Fortune* top 10, there are none in Interbrand's.

Not all industries can be globalised. Clark (2005, p413) distinguishes four patterns of industry internationalisation, based on level of international trade in the industry's products, and degree of foreign direct investment (see Figure 3.1).

- Sheltered industries supply a domestic market, and are not attractive to foreign investment. Typical examples are hairdressing and railways.

- Multidomestic industries supply domestic markets, but may do this in a number of countries. Typical examples are hotels and management consulting.

- International industries supply a world market, but are tied to one country by availability of raw materials (diamond mining or agriculture) or by economies of scale (aerospace).

Figure 3.1 Clark's patterns of industry internationalisation

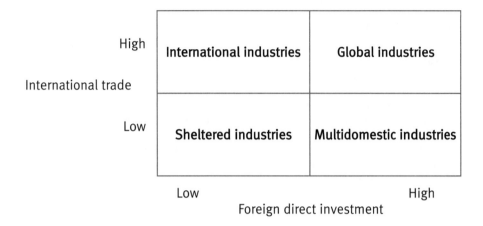

Source: adapted from Clark (2005, p413).

- Global industries have no national restrictions, and can truly be globalised – cars, oil, consumer electronics.

However, even global industries may still be forced to differentiate between national markets. This may be because:

- of laws and regulations: cars must be made either left or right-hand drive, depending on local regulations
- distribution channels may differ between national markets
- some markets are lead markets – they have a higher level of sophistication and acceptance of innovation
- differences in national culture may affect acceptability of products (Clark 2005, p429).

 ACTIVITY

3.7 WHY DO PEOPLE HATE THE WTO AND GLOBALISATION?

Throughout the West, there is deep suspicion, on many cases verging on hatred, of the progress of globalisation in general, and the activities of the WTO in particular. Why do you think this is?

EXAMPLES OF GLOBALISATION

CASE STUDY 3.10

The Java furniture industry

The furniture industry in the Jepara region of central Java, Indonesia, is often cited as one of the success stories of globalisation. An article by Lienda Loebis and Hubert Schmitz, for the Institute of Development Studies at the University of Sussex, examined the extent of this success (Loebis and Schmitz 2003) In particular, they examined two questions – are the furniture companies and their workers winners from globalisation, and is their success sustainable?

There are two main ways in which local enterprises can compete in a global market. One is the race to the bottom – to aim to be the cheapest by paying low wages, disregarding environmental and employment standards, and avoiding taxes. The other is to compete by upgrading processes and standards. Loebis and Schmitz found examples of both in Java. Some big firms had long-standing contracts with Western customers. For example Suwastama, employing 650 workers, supplied rattan furniture to IKEA. It had 350 subcontractors, and supported a total of 7,000 workers. Working with both IKEA and its own suppliers, Suwastama had improved quality, and could guarantee timely delivery.

At the other extreme there were hundreds of small businesses employing a few workers, without direct access to Western buyers or Western know-how. The only way in which they could remain competitive was to use illegally logged timber, especially teak, which is considerably cheaper than legal timber.

Loebis and Schmitz concluded that the furniture industry was successful, and that on balance companies and workers were benefiting from globalisation. Part of their evidence for this was the motorcycle test – in the Jepara region the number of motorbikes registered increased by 50 per cent between 1998 and 2001, which they saw as clear evidence of growing prosperity.

As to the second question, they concluded that the success of the industry was probably not sustainable in the long term. Indonesia is running out of hardwood, a problem made worse by illegal felling, which tends to take immature trees. The industry had also received a short-term boost from the collapse of the Indonesian rupiah after the Asian financial crisis of 1997, and this may not last. Finally, the focus of the furniture industry was already starting to move to Vietnam and China, which could beat Indonesia on price.

This case illustrates several general points about globalisation:

- Western buyers, often portrayed as one of the villains of globalisation, can often play a positive role by providing technical advice and long-term contracts.

- Third World gainers from globalisation are frequently large companies and their employees, who can take a value-added approach.

- In the race to the bottom, there are no long-term winners.

The Mozambique sugar industry

Mozambique was ranked as the poorest country in the world in the 1990s. It is slowly recovering from a ruinous civil war. Under the Portuguese colonial administration, sugar had been one of the country's key industries, but the infrastructure was devastated during the civil war. After peace was signed in 1992, the government saw sugar as a way of creating thousands of new jobs (Macmullan 2004).

The world sugar trade is heavily distorted. Sugar can be produced either from beet, grown in rich northern hemisphere countries and expensive to produce, or from cane, grown in the poor south, and cheap to produce. To protect their own industries, wealthy countries, especially the European Union, heavily subsidise their sugar beet production and protect their markets from imports. The world price is thus held artificially low. In addition, surpluses are generally dumped anywhere where there is a market, frequently at prices below that of the most efficient producers.

Mozambique thus faced a problem in developing its sugar industry – how to protect its own market? It decided to impose import duties, based on a complex reference price. Unfortunately, this fell foul of the IMF, which in 2000 argued that Mozambique should open its market to international competition, thus reducing prices for consumers.

The Mozambican government admitted that it was true that in theory liberalisation should mean lower prices for consumers. However, there was no guarantee traders would pass on low import prices to their customers, and Mozambique's huge size and poor communications would make it difficult for imported sugar to reach consumers. On the other hand, liberalisation would destroy many jobs in a very poor country, and imports would also cost foreign exchange which Mozambique did not have.

After pressure from European donors and aid agencies, and, it is believed, the World Bank, the IMF was persuaded to change its mind, and the Mozambican sugar industry was saved. By 2004 it employed 20,000 workers, and produced a foreign exchange benefit for Mozambique of US$25 million.

The lessons of this case seem to focus on:

- The hypocritical approach of the West, including the European Union, to globalisation. Liberalisation is fine for a country like Mozambique, but not for its own protected sugar beet farmers.

- The hard-line approach of the IMF to liberalisation, and the more pragmatic approach of the World Bank.

- The law of comparative advantage. Under the logic of free trade, Mozambique should be exporting sugar to the West.

Retail globalisation in Thailand

Retailers in the developed world are increasingly facing saturated markets. Companies like Tesco and Wal-Mart already dominate their home markets, and prospects for further growth are limited. An obvious solution is to expand overseas.

However, retailing is much less globalised than other major industries. Of the world's top 250 retailers in 2006, 104 have no international operations at all. The most globalised retailer, the French supermarket group Carrefour, has stores in 29 countries (*Economist* 2006b). Turn this on its head, and Carrefour has no presence in over 80 per cent of the world's countries.

Many retailers have had spectacular failures overseas. Wal-Mart pulled out of Germany in 2006, having previously failed in Indonesia, Marks & Spencer pulled out of continental Europe in 2001, while IKEA abandoned Japan as early as the 1980s (Emmott, Crook and Micklethwait 2002, *Economist* 2006b).

So what is the secret of success as a global retailer? The contrasting experiences of Tesco and Boots in Thailand provide some clues.

To most people in the West, Thailand is little more than an exotic holiday location, but it is actually a significant player on the world stage, and is one of the 20 biggest world economies. Its population is 64 million, and its GDP per head (on a purchasing power parity (PPP) basis) is slightly higher than that of Brazil or Turkey. The Thai economy on a PPP basis is one-third the size of the United Kingdom's.

In the 1980s and 1990s it was one of the Asian Tiger economies, which enjoyed the kind of explosive growth experienced by China today. It received a severe setback in the late 1990s (the Asian financial crisis started in Thailand in 1997), but by 2000 it was back on the growth path, and in 2003 its growth rate of GDP was 6.9 per cent. Literacy is high at well over 90 per cent, which encourages the rapid dissemination of new ideas, inflation and unemployment is low, and its capital, Bangkok, is one of the major world conurbations (CIA 2007).

The Asian financial crisis provided an ideal opportunity for Western retailers to enter Thailand. During the crisis, the Thai baht collapsed in value by 25 per cent against the dollar, making inward investment much cheaper. Among those retailers taking advantage of the opportunity were Boots and Tesco.

Boots opened its first store in Thailand in 1997, and by 2001 operated 67 stores throughout the country. The stores were very similar to those operated in the United Kingdom. Boots own brands represented 60 per cent of the product range, while only 18 per cent, or about 400 lines, were produced in Thailand (Jitpleecheep 2002a). As most lines were imported, they were too expensive for the price-conscious Thais, even though the typical Boots Thai customer was affluent by Thai standards, with average earnings of 17,000 baht a month (about £280).

The stand-alone Boots operation was not a success. Between 1997 and 2001, it had accumulated losses of 700 million baht (about £11 million). In 2001 alone, it lost 388 million baht (about £6 million) on turnover of 1.5 billion baht (about £25 million) (Jitpleecheep 2002b).

Boots ceased new store openings in 2001, and decided instead to sell through dedicated sections in supermarkets. Its chosen partner was the Tops supermarket chain, operated by CRC Ahold, the Thai arm of the Dutch retailer Royal Ahold. For Boots this lowered risk, while it gave Ahold the opportunity to attract more up-market customers (Jitpleecheep 2001). Meanwhile, Boots closed 12 non-performing stores in 2002 (Jitpleecheep 2002a). In 2002, Boots had 20 outlets in Tops stores, with a

turnover of around 100 million baht (about £1.6 million) (Jitpleecheep 2002c).

Tesco took a different route. It entered Thailand in 1998 by purchasing the Thai retailer Lotus. Expansion has been rapid. In February 2007, Tesco Lotus had 366 stores open – 57 hypermarkets, 17 Value stores, 23 Talad Lotus stores, and 269 Express stores. By 2008, it expects to have up to 500 Express stores opened (Tesco Lotus 2007).

By 2006, Thailand had the third highest sales in the Tesco group (after the United Kingdom and South Korea), at just under £1 billion a year (Fletcher 2006). Group sales in Asia grew by over 60 per cent in 2006 (Datamonitor 2006). Information on profits from the Thai operation is not available, but as Tesco Lotus paid over 1 billion baht (about £16 million) in corporation tax in 2006, profits must be substantial.

Why has Tesco done so well in Thailand and Boots so badly? Boots seemed to have cloned a UK operation in Thailand, with little consideration for local conditions or sensibilities. Its style of operation seems to have been aimed at expatriates, tourists and wealthy cosmopolitan Thais. This could have led to a profitable niche operation, but Boots' prices were too high for a mass Thai market.

The company predominantly imported Boots own-brand products from the United Kingdom. While these had a high reputation for quality in the United Kingdom, they were virtually unknown in Thailand. The joint venture with CRC Ahold promised access to a bigger market with lower risk, but still did not tap local Thai expertise. In short, the Boots operation was a typical example of Western-centric globalisation.

The Tesco expansion was different in almost every way. It is a classic example of glocalisation (Swyngedouw 2004). Throughout the process, Tesco was extremely sensitive to Thai conditions. Rather than starting with a greenfield operation like Boots, it took over Lotus, but was careful to retain the Lotus brand name and logo, which were well known in Thailand. It tailored its scale of operations by opening hypermarkets, supermarkets (Value stores) or convenience stores (Express stores) as appropriate to local demand. It even supported small 'Mom and Pop' competitors by selling them 'Club packs' for resale (Tesco Lotus 2007).

Whereas Boots imported 82 per cent of its products, Tesco sourced 97 per cent in Thailand, and it also facilitated the export of Thai products worth over £100 million a year to Tesco UK. The company also set up a charitable foundation, Tesco for Thais, which although small-scale, was valuable in securing goodwill in Thailand.

Both Boots and Tesco have gained from the open market policies espoused by the Thai prime minister Thaksin Shinawatra between 2001 and 2006. However, there are always losers in globalisation, and Thailand has been no exception. Between 1996 and 2001, the share of retail food sales in Thailand made through traditional markets fell from 75 to 50 per cent, which has severely damaged the earnings of thousands of Thai market traders.

Before he was overthrown by a military coup late in 2006, Thaksin was seriously considering placing curbs on foreign-owned retailers and giving greater support to small shopkeepers. These policies have been taken further by the military government, and this may clip even Tesco's wings in the future (*Economist* 2007a).

THE GLOBALISATION DEBATE

Aisbett (2003) identifies four main areas of concern over globalisation:

- An objection not to globalisation in principle, but to the way in which it is skewed in favour of developed countries. This is exemplified by the protectionist agricultural policies of the United States and the European Union.

- Loss of sovereignty, to transnational corporations and to institutions like the IMF and the WTO.

- Neo-liberal or 'Washington consensus' policies, as imposed by the IMF on debtor countries – privatisation, welfare cut-backs etc.

- The rise of big corporations. Of the 100 biggest economic units in the world, 52 are corporations. They can expand or contract their activities in particular countries in order to maximise their overall profit.

However, Aisbett points out that the debate is no longer between supporters and opponents of globalisation. The anti-capitalist protest movements of the late 1990s have run out of steam, and the main arguments are now between enthusiastic and cautious globalisers. Even Oxfam has recognised that globalisation can have some benefits. A similar point is made by Jacobs (2001).

Aisbett identifies areas of agreement between the enthusiastic and cautious globalisers. These include:

- Trade is often a source of economic growth, and growth is good for the poor (although the Green Party argues that local production may be more efficient – see the Mozambique sugar case study above) (Lucas 2001).

- The United States and the European Union should open their markets to the developing world.

- Safety nets should be provided for the losers from globalisation, and education, health and welfare in developing countries should be safeguarded.

- Income is an inadequate measure of poverty, and social factors should be taken into consideration.

- Excessive corporate power is a problem.

- Political reform is needed in many developing countries.

There are also still important areas of difference. These include those summarised in Table 3.1.

GLOBALISATION, GROWTH AND POVERTY

The evidence appears to be indisputable that globalisation has led to higher growth in most of the developing world, particularly in China and East Asia. The Asian Tigers, particularly South Korea and Thailand, were early to liberalise their trade, and have experienced rapid growth. So has China following its market reforms in the 1980s, and India, where Manmohan Singh, then finance minister, now prime minister, reduced protectionism.

Wolf (2005, p142), quotes World Bank figures from 2002 which suggest that the gains from globalisation have been widespread. In 1980s less globalised countries had higher GDP per head than more globalised ones, while by 1997 the situation was reversed. Annual growth rates per head in the more globalised countries were 3.1 per cent, in the less globalised ones only 0.5 per cent. Further evidence came from growth of a global middle class (defined as an annual income of between US$3,650 and US$14,600 a year, at PPP and 1993 prices). In 1960, 64 per cent of the global middle class lived in high-income Western countries (not including middle-income countries such as those of Eastern Europe and Latin America), and only 6 per cent in Asia, the Middle East and North Africa. By 2000, only 17 per cent lived in developed countries, and 51 per cent in Asia, the Middle East and North Africa (Wolf 2005, p170).

There is some evidence that MNCs in developing countries pay higher wages than local manufacturing employers, although the evidence is rather old, dating from 1994 (Emmott, Crook and Micklethwait, 2002). Multinationals in low-income countries paid an average wage of US$3,400, while local employers paid US$1,700. The ratio of 2:1 between multinational and local wages was higher than that in high-income countries, where the ratio was 1.4:1.

Strong as the evidence seems, there are some caveats. GDP per head is not the same as standard of living, and there were losers as well as winners in the globalising countries. Winners tended to work in manufacturing, losers in agriculture and extractive industries (see the banana war case study). Workers in developing countries tend to be non-unionised, capital inflows are unstable, MNCs can move out very quickly, and the risk of financial crisis increases, as in Thailand in 1997.

Table 3.1 Enthusiastic and cautious approaches to globalisation

Issue	Enthusiastic view	Cautious view
Attitudes to poverty	Globalisation in all its forms is good for the poor, and reducing poverty is what matters, even at the cost of	Reducing inequality is equally important, and globalisation frequently increases it
Trade liberalisation	Trade liberalisation is always beneficial	Totally free trade will often have adverse social or environmental side-effects. Decisions should be taken on a case-by-case basis – see Mozambican sugar again.
Transnational corporations	Their activities should be encouraged as they provide jobs and bring in new	Big corporations destroy indigenous producers, and the net effect may be negative
Privatisation	Government provision of essential services in developing countries is invariably corrupt and/or inefficient, and therefore these services should be privatised	Only government provision of essential services can ensure that they are available to the poor
Competitiveness	Opening developing economies to foreign trade and investment improves competitiveness by destroying local monopolies	Opening developing economies to foreign trade destroys indigenous producers whether or not they were monopolies and further increases the power of the transnational

There is also evidence that inequality has increased in globalising countries (Legrain 2003). As Legrain points out, globalisation is no guarantee of economic success. It won't help war-torn countries like Somalia or the Democratic Republic of Congo, it won't cure AIDS (particularly after the collapse of the Doha trade round – see the case study p77–78), and it won't stop crooked rulers salting money away in Switzerland (Legrain 2003, p52). But although globalisation is not a sufficient cause for economic growth, it seems to be a necessary one.

MULTINATIONALS AND BRANDS

Are MNCs and their brands too powerful? Foreign-owned MNCs employ one worker in every five in European manufacturing, and sell one euro in every four of manufactured goods in Europe (Venables 2005). Aisbett (2003) quoted the claim that 52 of the world's largest economic units are corporations, not states. However, supporters of globalisation like Legrain dispute this. They point out that this figure compares the turnover of corporations with the GDP of states. This leads to double or triple counting in the case of corporations. The correct comparison is with company value added (after deducting the cost of inputs). On this measure, there are only two corporations in the top 50 (Wal-Mart and Exxon), and 37 in the top 100. The US economy is 200 times bigger than Wal-Mart, Japan 100 times bigger, China 20 times bigger (Legrain 2003, pp139–140).

Corporations are also less powerful than nation-states. They cannot impose taxes or regulations, they cannot go to war, they cannot force people to buy their products, and unlike states, they can go bust.

There are also limits to their mobility, although this tends to benefit their home country rather than the developing world. It is very rare for companies to move their headquarters from one country to another (although Ericsson did it in 1999, when it moved its corporate HQ from Sweden to London to avoid high Swedish taxes) (Legrain 2003, p159). Nokia is happy to stay in very high-cost Finland, and Lego in Denmark. On the other hand, the 'branch factory syndrome' seems to apply. When companies downsize, it always seems to be the branch factories rather than those near the headquarters that are closed down first.

Foreign direct investment (FDI) (which creates multinationals) originates predominantly from developed countries (93 per cent in 1998–2000), and also goes to other developed countries (78 per cent). Of the FDI that goes to developing countries, the great bulk goes to China (the 2005 takeover of Rover by China's Nanjing Automotive, and the 2007 takeover of Corus by India's Tata Steel are very much the exceptions – for now). Inward investment creates jobs in the host country, but can also force up wages there, which in the long run makes the host less competitive. One country that has avoided this vicious circle is Ireland, which has used the additional wealth brought in by high-tech multinationals to invest in its infrastructure and education, which makes it still attractive even at higher wage levels (Venables 2005).

One clear counterweight to global corporations is global trade unions. On 1 May 2007, the TGWU and Amicus merged to form the United Kingdom's biggest union, Unite, with 2 million members. Its joint general secretaries, Derek Simpson and Tony Woodley, writing in the *Guardian*, said 'the challenges presented by world capitalism … cannot be met by any union that confines its operations within one country alone'. They announced an agreement to seek a merger with the United Steel Workers of the United States and Canada, to form the first transatlantic union. 'Only a worldwide organising agenda has any long-term hope of levelling the playing field' (Simpson and Woodley 2007).

The high point of globalisation came in the 1990s, in the euphoria which followed the collapse of communism, and 'the end of history'. This era of full-blooded, red in tooth and claw globalisation may have already passed. The onward march of e-commerce, and the idea that the world had entered a 'new economic paradigm' of endless economic growth, were shattered by the dot.com crash in 2000, and the collapse of giant new-economy corporations like Enron

SPORT AND GLOBALISATION

CASE STUDY 3.11

Much has been written about the homogenisation and Americanisation of world culture. Sport provides an interesting test of how far this generalisation is true.

Only four sports can be seen as truly global in their impact, coverage and following – football, tennis, golf and motor racing. Of these, only tennis and golf can really be seen as predominantly US-based. Both football and motor racing, while followed globally, are essentially European, Latin American and Asian-based.

Thus it is too simple to equate sport globalisation with Americanisation. What is undoubtedly true, however, is that sport has been globalised, in that it is seen as a homogenised global commodity, promoted by global media, particularly television. Advertising plays a key role in this. Nike, although a relatively small company by world standards, has promoted itself as a world brand through its promotion of the US basketball player Michael Johnson and the Real Madrid and Brazil footballer Ronaldo. Similarly, it is popularly thought that the main reason that Real Madrid agreed to buy David Beckham from Manchester United was not his footballing ability, but his fan base and brand value in East Asia, an area in which Real Madrid saw its own brand as weak (Millers 2006).

Like Real Madrid, Manchester United promotes itself as a world brand, with much more of its income stream coming from sponsorship, television rights and merchandising than from match receipts. Much the same is true of Chelsea, Arsenal and Liverpool. All four have attracted international capital, in the case of Manchester United from the US entrepreneur Malcolm Glazer, and at Chelsea from the Russian oil billionaire Roman Abramovich. Millers sees the future of football in Europe as the equivalent of medieval city states, down to the employment of well-paid foreign mercenaries. Power will rest with city-based teams, playing in a European super league, rather than with national teams.

Football in the United Kingdom, at least at Premier League level, is highly commercialised, partly because of the influence of huge television contracts. Kick-off times are scheduled for the convenience of television rather than of fans watching live, and seat prices have rocketed. An Arsenal season ticket in 2005–6 cost up to £1,825. In a recent survey, nearly half of fans said that their club was not protecting their interests as fans. The same pressures operate in Italy, made worse by the Italian football corruption scandal of 2006. Spain is different, however. Both Real Madrid and Barcelona are member-owned, democratic, non-profit organisations. A season ticket for Barcelona costs just €250! (Crane and Matten 2007).

Football is also truly globalised in the sense that it recruits from a world talent pool. Of the big four British football clubs discussed above, three have coaches from Europe, and all have squads drawn from throughout the world. Indeed, Arsenal have frequently fielded a first XI without a British-born player in it.

A classic example of the globalisation of football talent is Brazil. In the 1999–2000 season, 658 football players were exported from Brazil to 61 countries worldwide, including 137 to Germany and 136 to Portugal. Of these, 41 played in the 1999–2000 European Champions League. When one considers that 98 per cent of football players in Brazil were paid the monthly minimum salary of £90, such an exodus is not surprising (Garvie 2006). When Brazil played England at Wembley in June 2007, every member of the team played for a European club. The same is true of players from African nations such as Senegal and Egypt. Even American football players prefer to play in Europe rather than in the United States!

and WorldCom. Just as the economic confidence of the United States was shaken, its sense of political and military invulnerability was shattered by the attacks of 11 September 2001.

Coupled with the US military response to 'the war on terror', there is a growing though implicit feeling that the war on terror will be lost unless the West wins the hearts and minds of the Third World. Hence the criticisms from both left and right of the aggressive neo-liberal policies of the IMF and the World Bank, and the move to possibly a more caring approach to debt relief and aid.

At the same time there is a growing realisation that globalisation has not made the nation-state redundant. The role of the nation-state is to provide good governance. In an article previewing his new book, *State building*, Francis Fukuyama of 'the end of history' quotes from the doyen of free-market economists, Milton Friedman, as saying that his advice to former communist countries 10 years ago had been to concentrate on privatisation. Now he feels that he was wrong. 'It turns out that the rule of law is probably more basic than privatisation' (Fukuyama 2004).

 ACTIVITY

3.8 WHY IS AFRICA POOR?

The UN Development Programme has two main approaches to the definition of national poverty. One approach calculates a Human Development Index for member states, based on a equation incorporating life expectancy, educational attainment and real income per head. The other categorises countries on the basis of their stage of economic and social development. The poorest of these are labelled as Least Developed Countries (or, popularly, the Fourth World). These countries are characterised by extreme poverty, civil war or ethnic clashes, political corruption, and government based on dictatorship,

warlordism or kleptocracy ('rule by thieves'). On both measures, Africa, particularly sub-Saharan Africa, does extremely badly (UNDP 2006). Of the bottom 30 countries on the Human Development Index, all except Yemen are in Africa. Of the 50 countries defined as Least Developed, 34 are in Africa.

Question

Why do you think that Africa has not shared in the growing prosperity of the rest of the world?

GLOBALISATION AND THE LABOUR MARKET

Does globalisation help or harm workers in developed countries? As always, the evidence is mixed. Legrain (2003) argued that it is very hard to separate out the impact of globalisation from the impact of higher technology. Manufacturing has been declining for many years in all developed countries, while at the same time manufacturing jobs have been outsourced to Third World countries. He suggests that most of the impact comes from technology rather than globalisation. He cites the example of Bethlehem Steel in the United States, where the Sparrows Point plant in Maryland produces the same amount of steel as it did in the 1960s, but with 3,500 workers rather than 30,000 (Legrain 2003, p37). As he says 'producing more with less is what economic growth is all about'.

Legrain makes an attempt to quantify the relative effects of globalisation and technology. Between 1990 and 2000, manufacturing's share of GDP fell by around 6 per cent, while the manufacturing trade deficit worsened by only 0.4 per cent of GDP (Legrain 2003, p40).

The impact on jobs has been disproportionately on unskilled workers. Third World countries have an abundance of unskilled workers, which suggests that it is jobs using unskilled workers that will be offshored from rich countries.

However, more recent work suggests that the impact of globalisation on rich country workers may be greater than previously realised. Globalisation is becoming more complex. Increasingly parts of production processes are being offshored, rather than the whole process. This is known as 'high-resolution globalisation', 'trade in tasks' (Economist 2007a) or vertical disintegration (*International Labour Review* 2006). A good example is the Barbie doll. The raw material (plastic and hair) comes from Taiwan and Japan. Assembly takes place in the Philippines, Indonesia and China. Moulds come from the United States, as does the last coat of paint. Marketing and R&D is centred in the United States.

The rich world's comparative advantage in high-tech sectors is falling, as education levels in countries like China and India are rising rapidly. China and India produce as many graduate scientists and engineers as the United States, the European Union and Japan combined (*Economist* 2006b). Increasingly, higher-skilled jobs are being offshored – in software, medical diagnostics, finance and business consulting.

These finding are supported by a CIPD report on *Offshoring and the role of HR* in January 2006 (CIPD 2006). A total of 589 organisations responded to a survey, covering 2.4 million employees. Of these, 14 per cent had offshored at least one activity in the previous five years, 7 per cent were currently considering it, and 4 per cent had decided against it. The most popular offshoring locations were India (53 per cent) followed by China (27 per cent) and Poland (18 per cent). A wide range of functions were offshored:

Manufacturing and production	34 per cent of those who had offshored
IT support	24 per cent
IT development	22 per cent
Call centres/customer services	22 per cent
Financial, back office support	19 per cent
Product development	18 per cent
Accounts	16 per cent

Fifteen per cent had brought back activities that had previously been outsourced. The most common motives for outsourcing were cost reduction (86 per cent), UK skill shortages (27 per cent), to improve processes (21 per cent) and involvement in a joint venture (21 per cent). The biggest disadvantages were seen as: managerial control is more difficult (48 per cent), associated job losses in the

United Kingdom (44 per cent), language problems (30 per cent) and risk of disruption to supply (24 per cent).

Most interesting was the type of job lost:

Skilled	29 per cent
Semi-skilled	25 per cent
Managerial	19 per cent
Unskilled	15 per cent
Graduate	8 per cent

The report included a case study of a telecommunications firm, which offshored 500 jobs to Delhi in 2004–5. It decided to employ these staff directly, rather than to outsource the operation, because it was felt that outsourcing might compromise quality of service and managerial control. Activities offshored included transactional processing for all operational areas, including order handling, part of engineering and sales support; processing of company payments and credit control; and IT support and development.

Motives for offshoring were to reduce costs, to take advantage of skilled Indian graduates, to exploit the differences in time zone, and to take advantage of less restrictive Indian employment law. The company employed 4,100 staff across Europe, including 1,200 in the United Kingdom. Of these a total of 400 were made compulsorily redundant, with 100 of these redundancies in the United Kingdom. (CIPD 2006, pp7–8).

The threat of globalisation seems to be increasingly to wages, rather than jobs. Real wages in the United States, Germany and Japan are all falling. The share of wages in GDP is the lowest for three decades, while profits are at all-time highs. In the United States, the share of profits in GDP rose from 7 per cent in 2001 to 13 per cent in 2006 (*Economist* 2006b).

Globalisation has boosted profits in several ways. Firms have reduced their costs by offshoring, while the bargaining power of workers in developed countries has been weakened, as firms can always threaten to offshore. The global capital–labour ratio has shifted massively against workers. In the last 20 years, China, India and the former Soviet Union have effectively joined the world market economy, doubling the world supply of workers from 1.5 billion to 3 billion. Economic theory says that this will raise the return to capital and lower that to labour, which is exactly what has happened. At the same time, incomes have become more unequal. The top 1 per cent of workers in the United States now receive 16 per cent of GDP, rather than 8 per cent in 1980.

Case study 3.12 and Activity 3.9 examine some of the impacts of globalisation on the UK labour market.

CASE STUDY 3.12

THE OUTSOURCING OF CALL CENTRES

The call centre industry in the United Kingdom is large, employing 867,000 people, or 3 per cent of the workforce, in 2004 (Shah 2004). It is also a new industry, having grown from almost nothing over the past 15 years. As a result, there has been considerable concern about the steady movement of call centre jobs, particularly in the financial services industry, to India, particularly to Mumbai and Bangalore. Opponents of globalisation see this as an example of the detrimental effect of globalisation on UK employment, while supporters see it as a positive development, lowering costs for UK industry, and so increasing national prosperity.

Both are right. The short-term effect is that the United Kingdom is losing jobs. Call centres in the United Kingdom were frequently set up in areas of high unemployment, and the loss of these jobs is felt disproportionately. On the other hand, if outsourcing increases the profits of UK companies, this should free up resources for future investment. A short-term loss must thus be set against a long-term gain.

The typical Indian call centre goes to great lengths to make its operators acceptable to UK consumers. The call centres operate on UK rather than Indian time, and operators are expected to keep themselves informed about the English weather, and the latest plot twists in *Eastenders* (Warren 2007). However, there is some evidence that Indian call centres are less efficient than UK ones. One study claimed that UK operators answered 25 per cent more calls per hour, resolved 17 per cent more calls first time, and stayed with their company three times as long, although this is offset by average Indian salaries that are only 12 per cent of the UK level (Clennell 2004). This would suggest that UK companies that are more concerned with the quality of their customer service than with minimising their short-term costs should think very seriously before they outsource to India.

The long-run future of the call centre industry in the United Kingdom must lie with developing a more sophisticated knowledge-based, value-added service. Basic information-giving services can be better performed in India, or over the Internet.

ACTIVITY

3.9 GLOBALISATION AND YOUR ORGANISATION

What impact, if any, has globalisation had on your own organisation?

CONCLUSIONS

Both Europeanisation and globalisation are intensifying, and their impact on the UK's economy, society and organisations is increasing. This will affect all of us, as consumers, citizens, workers and professionals.

- The European Union's key aims have always been to maintain peace in Europe (particularly between France and Germany) and to enhance prosperity.

- Although there is general agreement on these overriding aims, there are considerable differences of opinion about the future direction of the European Union, epitomised by the single market, federalist and integrationist perspectives.

- The Commission is the executive of the European Union, initiating and implementing policy; the Council of Ministers is the political decision-making body; the Parliament is mainly consultative; the European Court of Justice rules on the legal interpretation of the EU treaties and legislation.

- The European Union expanded from 15 to 25 members in 2004, with the accession of mainly ex-communist countries from central Europe, and to 27 in 2007, with the accession of Bulgaria and Romania. This has necessitated the drafting of a new Constitution, published in 2004, which was rejected by referenda in France and the Netherlands in 2005.

- The expansion in 2004 led to very large but initially unexpected immigration from the new members, particularly from Poland.

- Since the mid-1940s, the world economic system has been regulated by three major international institutions: the IMF, the World Bank and GATT (now the World Trade Organization, WTO). All have been criticised by the left as imposing capitalist norms on the developing world.

- Globalisation has been characterised as having three main elements: the expansion of markets, the transformation of politics and the emergence of new social and political movements.

- The theory of comparative advantage and international specialisation underpins the concept of globalisation. Globalisation has also become more feasible with modern developments in communications, particularly air transport and the Internet.

- Aisbett (2003) identified four main areas of concern over globalisation: an objection not to globalisation in principle but to the way in which it is skewed in favour of developed countries; loss of sovereignty to transnational corporations and to institutions like the IMF and the WTO; neo-liberal or 'Washington consensus' policies; and the rise of big corporations.

- Globalisation has almost certainly raised GDP in developing countries, while in developed countries it has held down inflation, but also real wages.

- Offshoring of jobs to developing countries increasingly affects skilled and professional jobs as well as the traditional call centre jobs.

QUESTIONS

1. What are the key elements of the Single Market, Federalist and Integrationist approaches to the European Union?

2. What are the main roles of the European Parliament?

3. What are the three criteria for accession to the European Union?

4. Why was there such a high level of immigration from Poland to the United Kingdom after 2004?

5. What are the main roles of the IMF, the World Bank and the WTO?

6. What were the main reasons for the collapse of the Doha Round?

7. Do you agree that transnational corporations have too much power?

8. In what ways does globalisation (a) help and (b) damage the Third World?

TRENDS TO WATCH

- Progress on the EU reform treaty (the 'Constitution'), signed in Lisbon in December 2007. Is it ratified? Does the United Kingdom decide to hold a referendum on it?

- Are there any further movements to grant Turkey EU membership? What about Croatia?

- Is there a replacement for the WTO's Doha Round, and if so, what form does it take?

- How does the debate on globalisation evolve?

EXPLORE FURTHER

Books on the European Union tend to be dry and fact-ridden, but two which are relatively readable are Neill Nugent, *The government and politics of the European Union* (2006), and Michelle Cini (ed), *European Union politics* (2007).

Micklethwait and Wooldridge's *A future perfect: the challenge and hidden promise of globalisation* (2000) is an easily readable (but positive) introduction to globalisation. More recent pro-globalisation books are Martin Wolf's *Why globalisation works* (2005) and Philippe Legrain's *Open world: the truth about globalisation* (2003). Joseph Stiglitz's *Globalisation and its discontents* (2003) is fiercely critical of the role of the IMF. For a generally anti-globalisation perspective, check out websites like Oxfam or ActionAid. For both the European Union and globalisation, the way to keep up to date is to read good-quality newspapers regularly. The same general advice applies as to Chapter 2 – make sure you get a balance of left and right-wing views.

SEMINAR ACTIVITY

POLISH PLUMBERS

On 1 May 2004, 10 new members joined the European Union. Eight of these, known as the A8, came from Central and Eastern Europe, the biggest of these being Poland, with a population of about 38.5 million. The United Kingdom already had a significant Polish minority, the descendants of the Free Poles who had fought on the Allied side in the Second World War, and who had decided not to go back to a Communist Poland. In the 2001 census, there were nearly 61,000 people who had been born in Poland, with a third of these living in London (BBC nd). With their descendants, they made up a population of Polish ancestry of about a quarter of a million.

Under the EU rules on free movement, people from the A8 countries had the right to come to other EU countries, but this did not necessarily extend to the right to work. As part of the accession arrangements, the 15 'old' EU countries had the right to impose restrictions on work for A8 citizens for up to seven years. Only Sweden allowed A8 citizens an unrestricted right to work. The United Kingdom and Ireland granted them the right to work, but no right to unemployment benefit until they had worked continuously for a year.

It was forecast at the time of accession that 13,000 A8 workers a year would come to the United Kingdom. However, this has proven to be a gross under-estimate. Denis MacShane, who was Europe minister at the time, claimed that the original figure was based on all 15 old EU members opening their doors to A8 workers (MacShane 2006).

Although it is clear that many more A8 workers, particularly Poles, are working in the United Kingdom than originally thought, nobody really knows how many. As Poles and other A8 citizens can enter other EU countries without visas, there is no way of telling how many of those who enter the country intend to work, and how many are just passing through. The Office for National Statistics carries out random interviews on arrivals to the United Kingdom, and on this basis estimates that 56,000 Poles entered the United Kingdom to work in 2005. However, the Department of Work and Pensions says that 170,000 Poles applied for National Insurance numbers in 2005 (Doward and McKenna 2007).

The other main source of information on numbers is the Worker Registration Scheme (WRS), under which A8 workers are encouraged to register. This is not compulsory, is not required for the self-employed, and costs £75. There is also no requirement to deregister if a worker leaves the United Kingdom. In May 2005, the BBC reported that 176,000 had registered by March 2005. Of these 82 per cent were aged between 18 and 34, 96 per cent were working full-time and a third may have been working illegally in the United Kingdom before accession and merely regularising their position. Poland was the biggest provider, with 56 per cent of the total, followed by Lithuania with 15 per cent, and Slovakia with 11 per cent (BBC 2005a). This is not surprising, as Poland had by far the biggest population of the A8 countries, it had 20 per cent unemployment, wages one-sixth of those in the United Kingdom, and a well-educated population, many of whom spoke English.

By January 2007 579,000 had registered under the WRS, of whom 63 per cent were from Poland. The anti-immigration pressure group Migration Watch claimed that this was an under-estimate, and that the true figure was nearer 600,000, although they admitted that many of these will have left the country (Migration Watch 2007).

Some figures are also available from the Polish end of the migration. In 2004, the year of accession, there were fewer movements of Poles out of the country than in 2003 (population 27.2 million compared with 38.6 million) (Iglicka 2005). However, there is no way of telling how many of these were going out of Poland to work, or perhaps on day trips to Germany or the Czech Republic. What may be significant, however, is that the number of those leaving by air increased by 37 per cent in 2004 to 1.89 million. Official emigration in 2004 was also lower than in 2003, and only 543 Poles officially emigrated to the United Kingdom, compared with 12,646 to Germany.

Rumours and urban myths abound of the number of Poles in the United Kingdom. There are said to be 10,000 in Slough, 15,000 in Boston, Lincolnshire, 3,000 in Crewe (Doward and McKenna 2007). According to some stories, every other plumber in the United Kingdom is now Polish, although according to WRS figures there are only about 100 Polish plumbers registered. Remember, though, that the self-employed do not have to register.

The plain truth is nobody really has any idea how many Poles are working in Britain. Latest estimates are that up to a million Poles may have left Poland, although they have not all come to the United Kingdom (Barrell, Guillemineau and Liadze 2006). If, say, a third have come to the United Kingdom, this makes about 400,000. It is thought that most Polish and other A8 workers come to the United Kingdom with every intention of going back to Poland, and, unlike other immigrant groups, going back is very easy and cheap – £10 on a Ryanair flight. When questioned by the Joseph Rowntree Foundation immediately after accession, only 6 per cent said they intended to stay in the United Kingdom permanently. A year later, this had risen to 29 per cent (Spencer et al 2007). The best estimate is probably that at any one time, there are about 200,000–250,000 Polish workers in the United Kingdom, which approximately doubles the figure of people of Polish descent in 2001. We shall not have any really accurate figures until the 2011 census.

Question

What do you think is the likely economic and social impact of the influx of Polish and other A8 workers into the United Kingdom?

CHAPTER 4

Government policy

By the end of this chapter, readers should be able to understand, explain and critically evaluate:

- the legislative process in the United Kingdom and the European Union

- informal influences on policy formation, including the role of political parties and pressure groups

- the key components of the UK economy

- the key objectives of UK economic policy

- the tools of economic policy including fiscal, monetary, competitiveness and exchange rate policy

- techniques for managing interest rates in the United Kingdom, and their impact on inflation and economic growth

- public ownership, privatisation and PFI/PPP

- factors that influence productivity and competitiveness.

INTRODUCTION

In this chapter we analyse the evolution of government policy in social, economic and industrial fields, and the impact of government policy on organisations. As developments in the United Kingdom are heavily influenced by the actions of the European Union, we shall be concerned with both UK and EU policy. We start with formal legislative procedures in the United Kingdom and the European Union, and then go on to consider informal influences on the evolution of policy. We then consider recent developments in policy in the United Kingdom.

THE LEGISLATIVE PROCESS IN THE UNITED KINGDOM AND THE EUROPEAN UNION

THE UNITED KINGDOM

Most legislation originates in government departments and is directly sponsored by the government. Some legislation, particularly on matters of conscience, starts as a private member's bill. Most of these fail. Normally they only pass with substantial cross-party support, and support, or at worst neutrality, from the government. Indeed, frequently the purpose of a private member's bill is not actually to pass a new law, but to bring public attention to an issue which is important to an individual MP and those pressure groups that support him or her. In this section, we are only going to look at government bills.

At least for bills published relatively early in the life of a parliament, the general subject matter of the bill will appear in the governing party's election manifesto – 'we intend to bring in legislation to put right the long-standing grievances concerning …'

The next (optional) stage is a Green Paper. This is a consultative document setting out the case for the forthcoming legislation, and the pros and cons of various approaches to legislation. This does not commit the government to anything, but forms a basis for discussion with interested parties and pressure groups. After consultation on the Green Paper, the government may choose to:

- follow it up with a White Paper
- go straight to legislation
- drop the proposal.

A White Paper firms up on the proposal, but again does not commit the government on detail. A lengthy period of consultation may then follow.

The parliamentary session normally starts in November, with the Queen's Speech, where the Queen sets out the programme of legislation for the coming year – 'My government intends to introduce legislation on …'. The government will then publish a bill, drafted by specialist parliamentary lawyers. The bill then goes through a number of formal stages:

- First Reading – a formal presentation of the bill to the Commons.
- Second Reading – a full debate on the principles of the bill rather than the details.
- Committee Stage – the bill is then scrutinised in detail by a standing committee of the Commons, consisting of between 15 and 20 MPs, with a government majority. The bill will be debated and voted on clause by clause, and some provisions may be amended.
- Report Stage – the amended bill goes back to the full Commons, where the government has an opportunity to reverse any amendments forced on it at the Committee Stage.
- Third Reading – this is formal, and not usually debated.

- The bill then goes to the House of Lords, and repeats the same stages as in the Commons. The Lords can amend the bill or reject it. If they reject it, this delays the bill for one parliamentary session. Having passed through the Lords, the bill goes back to the Commons, which can reject any amendments made by the Lords.

- Royal Assent – the Queen then agrees to the bill, which becomes an Act. In theory the Queen could reject the bill, but this has not been done for 300 years.

As a legal document, every word of an Act matters, and it is subject to interpretation by the courts.

THE EUROPEAN UNION

This is very different from the process in the United Kingdom. Initial proposals for legislation are drawn up by the European Commission, and must be based on one of the EU treaties (Rome, Maastricht, Amsterdam, Nice etc). Each treaty has to be unanimously ratified by the Member States. By contrast, in the United Kingdom the government has a free hand to legislate on anything that it chooses (including leaving the European Union).

At this stage, the proposal is known as a draft directive (or after the implementation of the new EU Constitution of 2004, a draft framework law). The draft then goes out for consultation to the Council of Ministers, the European Parliament, and the social partners (the two employers' bodies UNICE and CEEP, and the trade union body ETUC). The Commission then revises its proposals, which are then formally presented to the Council of Ministers, which will take a decision on unanimity or qualified majority voting, depending on the subject of the legislation. The European Parliament has the right to debate and to comment on the proposed directive, but until the new Constitution is adopted, no right to amend or reject it. Under the new Constitution, the European Parliament will have the right to reject or amend the proposal, but only by a majority of more than half of all MEPs (not just those who vote).

The law will be adopted under the new Constitution if:

- both the Parliament and the Council of Ministers approve it (by either unanimity or qualified majority, depending on the type of legislation)

- the Council of Ministers approves the Parliament's amendments (if the Commission opposes an amendment, it must be approved by a unanimous vote of the Council of Ministers).

 **ACTIVITY**

4.1 UK AND EU LEGISLATION

What are the differences in passing legislation between the United Kingdom and the European Union? Which system do you think is more democratic?

The directive then has to be implemented by Member States – ie EU directives become law in the United Kingdom through a UK Act of Parliament. At the end of 2003 there were about 2,500 EU directives, and the compliance rate by Member States ranged between 96 and 99 per cent (Mulvey 2003).

INFORMAL INFLUENCES ON POLICY

POLITICAL PARTIES

Traditionally the electoral system in the United Kingdom has ensured a predominantly two-party electoral system (plus regional and/or nationalist parties representing Scotland, Wales and Northern Ireland) – a broadly 'right-wing' party in favour of maintaining the status quo (the Tories in the early nineteenth century, the Conservatives from the late nineteenth century onwards), and a broadly 'left-wing' party in favour of change (the Whigs in the early nineteenth century, the Liberals in the late nineteenth century, Labour from the 1920s). The two wings broadly represented different class interests – the right wing the 'haves' who resisted change (the ruling class, and later the middle class), and the left wing the 'have-nots', those seeking change (the working class). Thus ideology and social class were seen as underpinning the UK party system. In Activity 4.2 you will explore how far this is still true.

The influence of members of political parties, even MPs, over government policy-making is small, and probably getting smaller. MPs are subject to party discipline, and although they can and do vote against their own government on occasions, every MP knows that if he or she votes to bring down his/her own government, his or her party career will be finished. Even massive revolts are unlikely to change government policy, as can be shown by the Labour revolt on university fees, and on the Iraq war, where even the resignation of a leading Cabinet member, Robin Cook, had no influence on policy.

Party conferences can pass resolutions critical of government policy, but governments have never had to take much notice of these. Policy is nowadays decided much more by focus groups and think tanks. MPs do have the power to force an election for the post of party leader, and when the Conservatives ousted Margaret Thatcher and replaced her with John Major, the decision was taken solely by Conservative MPs. However, the Conservative Party, like the Labour Party, now elects its leader through a complicated electoral college system, where MPs, peers, MEPs and party members all have a weighted vote.

PRESSURE GROUPS

A pressure group is 'any group in society which, through political action, seeks to achieve changes which it regards as desirable or to prevent changes which it regards as undesirable' (Forman and Baldwin 1999, p128). They can broadly be classified into two main types:

- interest or sectional groups
- attitude or cause groups.

ACTIVITY

4.2 POLITICAL PARTIES

1. What arguments would you put forward if asked to support the argument that ideology and class no longer underpin the present party system?

2. David Farnham argues that there are two crucial differences between a political party and a pressure group (Farnham 1999, p137):

   - Parties try to win political control to use political power. Pressure groups seek to influence political decisions, not to get in a position where they can make those decisions themselves.

   - The political programmes of parties are broad-based, while pressure groups tend to concentrate on a single issue.

   Given the above, would you say that the UK Independence Party (UKIP), which won several seats in the EU elections in 2004, is a political party or a pressure group?

Interest groups are those pressure groups that have a common interest, and they exist to promote the interests of that group. Classic examples are trade unions and employers' associations, but interest groups also include professional bodies, the Royal British Legion and the AA, the last of which started as a members' organisation but later became a public company.

Attitude groups are those pressure groups whose members have attitudes or beliefs rather than material interests, and they seek to advance particular causes. Examples include the National Trust, Oxfam, Greenpeace, Liberty and the RSPB. Some pressure groups appear to be hybrids. The Countryside Alliance, for example, would see itself as an attitude group, while its opponents would see it as an interest group.

Pressure groups have a number of important functions:

- **Intermediaries between the government and the public.** The prime role of a pressure group is obviously to apply pressure on the government (or sometimes on other political bodies like the European Union, the IMF or a foreign government). They channel and express public opinion on key issues. Some pressure groups use professional lobbying organisations to put forward their point of view to decision-makers. American gaming interests are alleged to have spent £100 million in 2004 in support of the Gambling Bill which would introduce Las Vegas-style 'super-casinos' to the United Kingdom (Mathiason 2004). For a detailed analysis of the tactics used by the lobbyists in this case see Hencke (2004).

- **Opponents and critics of government policy.** Party discipline prevents governing party MPs from opposing government policy, while criticism from opposition parties tends to be ignored because everyone expects the Opposition to oppose. Pressure groups can provide detailed and (one hopes) constructive criticism of policy. Indeed, on some occasions pressure groups in effect write government policy for it.

- Agents of government. This is controversial. Increasingly, pressure groups which themselves provide services – particularly charities – receive government grants towards providing those services, which some feel may compromise their independence.

- Publicists to promote an interest or defend a standpoint.

 ACTIVITY

4.3 A QUESTION OF INFLUENCE

Make a list of the ways in which pressure groups can influence the government.

THE GOVERNMENT AND THE ECONOMY

SOME KEY DEFINITIONS

Before we can examine ways in which the government can manage the economy, we need to define some key concepts.

Gross domestic product

The most common method of measuring the output of an economy is gross domestic product (GDP). This is the measure of the country's total annual output of goods and services. This is not the same as the sum of the outputs of all organisations in the economy, as this would involve double counting. For example, sales of cans of baked beans made by a supermarket are counted, but not sales of the tinplate for the cans made by a steelworks. When calculating GDP:

- indirect taxes and subsidies (like VAT) are normally ignored

- exports are included, because they form part of the output of the United Kingdom

- imports are excluded, because although they are consumed in the United Kingdom, they are part of the output of other countries.

An important distinction to make is between GDP and the standard of living or quality of life. Governments are concerned to achieve economic growth, defined as an increase in GDP over time. Individuals are much more concerned with their own standard of living.

 ACTIVITY

4.4 STANDARD OF LIVING

How might an individual's standard of living increase without there being an increase in GDP?

Business cycles

The economy tends to move in a series of ups and downs in the short term, although the long-term trend is for the size of GDP to grow. These fluctuations, over a 5–10-year period, are known as the business cycle. Governments attempt to dampen the effects of these cycles, but have not succeeded in abolishing them entirely. The top of a cycle is known as a peak, the bottom as a trough. In the period between a peak and a trough, economic growth may merely slow down, as in the period 2001–3, following the terrorist attacks of 11 September 2001, or GDP may actually fall. If GDP falls for two consecutive quarters, this is technically known as a recession, as the United Kingdom experienced in 1973–5, 1979–81 and 1990–2. If a recession is both deep and long-lasting, it is known as a depression, as with the Great Depression of 1929–33 following the Wall Street crash.

Unemployment

Unemployment is a surprisingly complex concept which has significant social as well as economic consequences. It is not even simple to define unemployment. A person can only be unemployed if he or she is out of work and seeking work. But what about someone who is:

- working part-time but would rather work full-time?
- apparently seeking work, but has totally unrealistic expectations about the sort of job he or she could obtain?

There are two main ways of measuring unemployment:

- To count those people who are claiming unemployment benefit (the claimant count). This means that those who do not have work, and are seeking work, but who do not qualify for benefit, are excluded. On the other hand, some people who are not genuinely seeking work may be included.
- To carry out a survey and ask people whether they are employed or unemployed. This is carried out through the Labour Force Survey, using internationally agreed definitions provided by the International Labour Organization (ILO). Here people are classified as unemployed if they:
  - are out of work
  - have been seeking work within the last four years
  - are available to start work within two weeks.

The ILO method is now the government's preferred measure, but both are regularly published in the United Kingdom. The ILO figure comes out higher than the claimant count measure, mainly because it includes large numbers of women who are ineligible for unemployment benefit.

Inflation

Inflation is a general rise in the level of prices. In the United Kingdom it is measured in three ways:

- RPI – the Retail Price Index. This is calculated by measuring monthly changes in the price of a basket of goods which is meant to represent the spending pattern of the average family. This is the measure used to assess yearly increases in pensions and other state benefits.

- RPIX – the Retail Price Index excluding mortgage interest. Until November 2003 this was the government's preferred target measure, as it represents the underlying rate of inflation in the economy (mortgage interest rates depend on the general level of interest rates, set by the Bank of England).

- CPI – the Consumer Price Index. This is the agreed measure of inflation used throughout the European Union, and was adopted as the official inflation target in the United Kingdom in November 2003 (when it was known as the Harmonised Index of Consumer Prices – inevitably called hiccup!).

Balance of payments

The balance of payments is a measure of flows of money into and out of the UK economy. It is extremely complex as it has a number of different components. The most commonly used elements are:

- The balance of trade. This measures imports and exports of goods.

- The balance of payments on current account. This measures imports and exports of goods and services.

ECONOMIC OBJECTIVES

All governments, whatever their political complexion, are basically trying to achieve four main economic objectives:

- Economic growth. Since the 1990s this has increased by an average of around 2–2.5 per cent, with some periods of falling GDP, and others when the growth rate in the short term has gone as high as 4 per cent.

- Full employment. This does not mean that nobody is unemployed, but that there are in theory jobs available for those seeking them, at current wage rates. In practice, this means that full employment is achieved if the number out of work is matched by the number of unfilled vacancies.

- Stable prices (or low inflation). Again there is some dispute about the optimum level of inflation, but most economists would agree that it is around the Labour government's target of 2.5 per cent on the RPI-X index in the late 1990s (restated as 2 per cent on the CPI index in November 2003).

- Equilibrium in the balance of payments. That is, that the value of goods and services exported should roughly equal the value imported. This has deteriorated in recent years, with the trade deficit around £60 billion in 2004, although this is offset to some extent by a strong surplus on the balance on services.

The New Labour government since 1997 has been more successful than most governments, achieving full success on economic growth and inflation, and considerable success on full employment. The only blot on its record is a worsening balance of payments.

In addition, governments will have policies on other economic objectives. These might include:

- Redistribution of income – this is seen as a social objective in its own right, but its prime economic function is as a means to achieve economic growth.

- Exchange rates – the exchange value of the pound is seen as a political virility symbol, but it is primarily important as a means of managing the balance of payments. UK entry to the euro is of course a long-running contentious political issue.

- The level of taxation and the level of government spending –in terms of both their absolute level in the economy, and the balance between them.

- Interest rates – these are seen either as a means of controlling inflation or of managing growth.

- Money supply – in the 1980s this was seen as an objective in its own right, but it is now seen as a means of achieving other objectives.

- Privatisation (or nationalisation). Linked with this is more general regulation or deregulation of the economy.

As you will see from the above list, economics is not value-free. Managing the economy inevitably has strong political and social, as well as economic elements.

THE TOOLS OF GOVERNMENT POLICY

A range of tools are available to the government in its objective of managing the economy.

Fiscal policy

This involves a manipulation of the level of taxation and/or government spending. The theory underpinning this was established by the economist John Maynard Keynes in the 1930s. If there is a persistent level of unemployment in the economy, he argued that this is fundamentally because of a lack of demand. In order to increase demand in the economy, the government can inject demand into it, either by increasing its own spending, which will directly lead to a higher demand for goods and services, or by cutting taxation, which will put more money into the hands of consumers, and so enable them to demand more goods and services. However, changes in taxation or public spending are subject to long time lags before they take effect, and increasingly chancellors of the Exchequer have not seen fiscal policy as an appropriate tool for short-term management of the economy. Instead, they have taken the view that the level of spending and taxation are much more issues of political rather than demand management policy. Gordon Brown has expressed this in his golden rule, which states that over an economic cycle, the government should aim for a balanced budget, ie, the revenue raised through taxation should equal the amount spent on current goods and services. This policy does allow for some flexibility, ie for expenditure to exceed taxation during the trough phase of the cycle, as long as this is balanced by a surplus at the peak.

Monetary policy

Monetary policy was strongly in vogue during the 1980s, at the height of the power of Margaret Thatcher, and under the influence of the American economist Milton Friedman, who argued a direct causal link between the supply of money and the level of inflation. Policies were therefore implemented directly to control the supply of money. However, as the leading monetarist economist Sir Alan Budd, who was chief economic adviser to the Treasury between 1991 and 1997, says, 'I hope I can say without offending anyone that the experiment in seeking to control inflation by setting quantitative monetary targets did not match the hopes of its most enthusiastic supporters (among whom I am willing to count myself)' (Keegan 2004a, p1). One of the main problems was not the existence of the link between money supply and inflation, but the difficulty in producing a watertight definition of money at a time of great technological change, including the explosive growth in the use of credit cards (which enable people to spend money that they do not possess, and which does not exist until they spend it).

Monetary policy is now much simpler. It consists of control over interest rates, set by the independent Bank of England. The way in which this works is explored in considerable detail below.

Competitiveness (supply-side) policy

Policy here is linked to the concept of NAIRU (non-accelerating inflation rate of unemployment, the rate of unemployment that ensures a stable level of inflation). If the economy can be made more competitive, the rate of NAIRU should fall, and the economy will be able to operate at lower levels of inflation and unemployment. This involves deregulating the markets both for goods and services and for labour, through policies including privatisation and rigorous control of monopolies and cartels. It also involves a concerted drive to increase the rate of growth of productivity in the economy, by encouraging investment in research and development, and in the enhancement of worker skills. Again, this policy is examined in depth below.

Exchange rate policy

It is possible to manipulate the exchange rate in order to achieve economic objectives. For example, if an exchange rate is set at a level below that justified by market forces, the currency will be under-valued. This will stimulate exports, which will be artificially lowered in price, and discourage imports, which will be artificially highly priced. An over-valued currency will have the opposite result. However, there are two major snags with this.

Manipulation of the exchange rate is only seriously possible if the exchange rate is fixed. However, since the 1970s most currencies have floated, ie been subject to market forces. Even in a fixed exchange rate system, it is very difficult in the long term to maintain an exchange rate markedly different from that implied by market forces.

The other key issue in exchange rate policy is of course the euro. Should the United Kingdom join, or not? At the moment, the United Kingdom has an opt-out from European economic and monetary union (EMU), and thus from the euro. However, the United Kingdom is qualified to join EMU if it chooses. In 1997, the Chancellor of the Exchequer postponed a decision on entry, saying that the United Kingdom would only consider joining if five economic tests were met. These were:

- Are business cycles and economic structures compatible so that the United Kingdom can live with euro interest rates?

- Is there sufficient flexibility to deal with any problems that might arise?

- Will joining EMU create better conditions for firms making long-term decisions to invest in the United Kingdom?

- What impact will entry have on the competitive position of the City?

- Will joining the euro promote higher growth, stability, and a lasting increase in jobs?

If the government decided that these tests were met, it would recommend entry to the euro, but the final decision would be taken by a referendum. Public opinion in the United Kingdom appears to be heavily against euro entry, and entry is opposed by the Conservative Party and by significant elements in industry. In the last resort any decision on entry is likely to be political rather than economic. Labour may be in favour in principle, but will only hold a referendum if it is sure it will win. Most voters will probably make their decision on gut feeling, rather than the detail of the economic arguments. To no one's surprise, the government decided in 2003 that the five tests had not been met, and as a result, any decision in favour of entry has been postponed until the late 2000s.

INFLATION AND INTEREST RATES

CASE STUDY 4.1

The impact of inflation

We have already defined inflation as a general increase in the level of prices in the economy, measured in various ways – RPI, RPIX or CPI. In the last resort this is caused by excess demand in the economy, basically when the amount of goods and services people want to buy is greater than the productive potential of the economy – 'too much money chasing too few goods'. The generally accepted view is that inflation is harmful, and it follows from this that low inflation is beneficial, for the following reasons:

- Increased price competitiveness for UK goods. The important factor here is relative inflation – in order for UK goods to be competitive, UK inflation must be rising at a slower rate than that of its international competitors. Of course, if UK inflation is very rapid, it is likely that the value of the pound will fall, but this itself could generate further inflation, as import prices will rise.

- Distribution of income will be less distorted. High inflation benefits borrowers, particularly those with outstanding mortgages, which fall in value in real terms as the value of their houses tend to rise. In addition, the gap in money terms between wage settlements obtained by strong unions as compared with weak ones tends to be greater in times of rapid inflation.

- Reduced uncertainty. The more rapid

the rate of inflation, and particularly the more variable it is, the more unpredictable the environment becomes for business and individuals. As a result, investment will be discouraged, as firms do not want to take risks, and the result could be falling output and rising unemployment.

- High inflation means high nominal interest rates. This puts pressure on the cash flows of borrowers if their main source of income is interrupted, for example by unemployment.

ACTIVITY

4.5 DEFLATION

If the effects of high inflation are adverse, would it be better to have falling prices (deflation)?

THE LINK BETWEEN UNEMPLOYMENT AND INFLATION

In the late 1950s, Professor Phillips identified that over the previous 100 years there had been an inverse relationship between the rate of change of money wages and the level of unemployment. In the short term this intuitively makes sense. If unemployment is low, workers can demand higher wages, and vice versa. As wage inflation is a very important component of general inflation, it could thus be argued that there is an inverse relationship between unemployment and inflation – if unemployment rose, inflation would fall, and vice versa. This implied that governments could in principle choose the trade-off between inflation and unemployment that best suited their overall objectives.

Unfortunately, almost as soon as Phillips identified the relationship, it ceased to apply. Throughout the 1970s, both inflation and unemployment rose steeply at the same time, giving rise to a phenomenon known as stagflation. Gradually over the 1980s, inflation was squeezed out of the system through strict control of the money supply, but only at the cost of continuing high levels of unemployment. Since 1992, unemployment has fallen considerably, while inflation has stabilised at the 2–3 per cent level.

Clearly the simple concept of the Phillips curve no longer applies, but it has been replaced by the concept of NAIRU. This is the level of unemployment at which inflation will be stable. NAIRU appears to have been about 7–8 per cent in the 1970s, but to have fallen to around 3–4 per cent (on the ILO measure) by the early 2000s. One prime objective of governments is to continue to improve the trade-off between inflation and unemployment by lowering the level of NAIRU. This can be done through making the labour market more competitive.

However, as the Bank of England says, 'The level of the NAIRU cannot be determined with any precision for the purposes of setting monetary policy …. It is easier to construct plausible estimates after the event – ie once we have observed inflation – rather than in anticipation of it' (Bank of England 2004a). NAIRU appears to be much lower in the United Kingdom and the United States, with largely deregulated labour markets, than in the eurozone, where labour markets are much more heavily regulated. Of course, there is a political and social, as well as an economic trade-off here – which is preferable, a higher risk of unemployment in the eurozone, or the higher level of benefits that accompany unemployment there?

INTEREST RATES

An interest rate is simply the price of money. However, unfortunately the real world is more complicated. As an individual, you are almost certainly paying and receiving several different rates of interest – perhaps on your bank current account, on your building society account, your Internet savings account, your mortgage, your credit card, your hire purchase agreement. Ultimately these come back to one rate, the official rate set by the Bank of England, at which it will lend money to the banks and other financial institutions. This is set monthly by the Bank's Monetary Policy Committee.

If this official rate changes, the banks and building societies will change the rates for their own savers and borrowers. Equally importantly, an increase in interest rates affects expectations. If interest rates start to rise after a period when they have been static or falling, the expectation is that they will continue to rise in the near future. The Bank of England used this to great effect in 2004, when it made a series of quarter-point increases in interest rates, none of which was particularly serious on its own, but which had a big effect on expectations.

Interest rates and demand

When interest rates are changed, demand can be affected in a number of ways.

- Spending and saving. An increase in interest rates makes saving more attractive and spending less attractive. Consumer spending is likely to fall. At the same time industrial investment will fall, as the margin between what an investment costs and the profit it will produce becomes narrower.

- Cashflow. Higher interest rates mean higher mortgage rates – normally paid monthly – and higher rates of interest on savings – normally paid annually. The short-term effect on the cashflow of individuals is likely to be negative, reducing demand.

- Asset prices. A change in interest rates affects the price of stocks and shares. If interest rates go up, the price of stocks and shares tends to fall, as it becomes more attractive to hold cash. There will be a similar effect on house prices. An increase in interest rates thus marginally reduces individuals' wealth, again making them more reluctant to spend.

- Exchange rates. At the same time, the exchange rate is likely to rise marginally, as it becomes more attractive to hold pounds rather than other currencies. This makes export prices higher, which again reduces demand. At the same time, import prices become cheaper, which immediately reduces inflation (Bank of England 2004b).

An increase in interest rates thus clearly reduces demand in the economy, which will lower the rate of inflation. However, as with everything in economics, this is subject to time lags. Some effects are almost immediate, such as the impact on the exchange rate; some take a matter of weeks, such as the impact on mortgage and savings rates; while others are long-term, like the wealth effect of falling share prices. The Bank of England calculates that it takes up to two years for the full impact to work through the economy. In making its interest rate decisions, the Bank of England thus has to make estimates of the level of inflation two years hence. This produces the apparently perverse result that the Bank can sometimes cut interest rates at a time when current inflation is above target, or vice versa.

CENTRAL BANKS AND INTEREST RATES

The Bank of England

The Bank of England has been involved in setting interest rates for many years, and this system was formalised in the mid-1990s by the Ken and Eddie Show, when interest rates were set at a monthly meeting between the chancellor, Kenneth Clarke, and the governor of the Bank, Eddie George. However, in the last resort, the decision was the chancellor's. This was changed in the first act of the incoming Labour government in May 1997. To great surprise, Gordon Brown announced the granting of operational independence to the Bank. In future, interest rate decisions would be taken monthly by the Monetary Policy Committee (MPC), chaired by the governor, which consists of both Bank and government nominees (a total of nine members).

Interest rate decisions were to be taken in line with the government's inflation target, initially set as 2.5 per cent on RPIX, subject to a margin of plus or minus 1 per cent. The target was thus a symmetrical one, unlike the previous Conservative target, which was 2.5 per cent or less.

Under the Bank of England Act 1998, the Bank's remit was to maintain price stability, and subject to that, to support the economic policy of the government, including its objectives for growth and employment. In its remit for the MPC, this was interpreted as:

> The Government's central economic policy objective is to achieve high and stable levels of growth and employment. Price stability is a precondition for these high and stable levels of growth and employment, which will in turn help to create the conditions for price stability on a sustainable basis.

> (Bank of England 2003)

In December 2003, the target inflation rate was changed to 2 per cent on CPI, again plus or minus 1 per cent. This was a slightly looser target, as 2 per cent on CPI roughly equates to 3 per cent on RPIX.

If inflation moved away from target by more than one percentage point in either direction, the governor was required to send an open letter to the chancellor, setting out:

- the reasons inflation had missed the target
- what the Bank was doing about it
- the time span for remedial action
- how the remedial action met the government's monetary policy objectives.

It is a measure of the success of the policy that such a letter had only been required once by the time of writing – in April 2007.

THE MONETARY POLICY COMMITTEE AFTER 10 YEARS

CASE STUDY 4.2

This case study analyses the performance of the MPC over the period 1997–2007, and in particular, looks at two issues:

- How successful was the MPC at managing the UK economy over this period?

- Why was it necessary for the governor to write an open letter to the chancellor in April 2007, when CPI inflation reached 3.1 per cent?

The MPC's track record is excellent. Throughout the whole of its first 10 years of existence, it held inflation within a 2 per cent range (except for one month). The average inflation rate since 1997 has been 2.4 per cent (RPIX) or 1.4 per cent (CPI). This continues the run of successful performance which started with the introduction of inflation targeting in 1992. This is a much better performance than was expected when the MPC was set up, when it was suggested that inflation was likely to be more than 1 per cent off target around 40 per cent of the time (Bank of England 2007a).

Just as inflation has been stable, so has growth. The average annual growth rate of GDP since 1992 has been 2.8 per cent, better than the post-war average, and throughout this period, quarterly growth has always been positive. Using data dating back to 1661, Benati (2006) estimates that this is the most stable period in UK economic history. Some observers refer to this as the Great

Stability, while Mervyn King, the governor of the Bank of England, refers to the decade 1992–2002 as the nice (non-inflationary consistently expansionary) decade. (King did not expect the next decade to be quite as benign – he called it the not-so-bad (not of the same order but also desirable) decade – King 2007.)

How much credit can be given to the MPC for the stability of the UK economy? It is not enough to say that because the MPC and the stable economy coincided in time, the MPC caused the stable economy. Correlation is not the same thing as causation. Indeed, low and stable inflation occurred throughout the Western world, not just in the United Kingdom.

To investigate the impact of the MPC we need to look at some of the theory surrounding its creation. If interest rates are under the control of the government, there is always a temptation to keep them low, in order to stimulate growth and appease mortgage borrowers, even though this risks higher inflation. Similarly, political considerations tend to lead governments to favour low taxation and higher spending, which again tends to be inflationary. Under such a regime, eventually inflation gets out of hand, leading government to stamp on the brakes, which results in the stop-go economy of the 1960s and 1970s.

When he became chancellor in 1997, Gordon Brown saw independence of the

Bank of England as a way to remove some of the political temptation from government. Given an inflation target set by the government, the Bank of England was given a free hand on how to achieve this.

Brown also insisted that the Bank of England was transparent in its decision-making. Minutes of MPC discussions were published each month, listing how each member voted on the interest rate decision. This increased the Bank of England's credibility.

At the same time, Brown brought in long-term controls on fiscal policy. His 'golden rule' laid down that over an economic cycle the current budget was to be balanced – ie no long-term net borrowing to finance current spending. (The European Central Bank did the same kind of thing, with its maximum inflation target and the Stability and Growth Pact, but both of these were more restrictive than their UK counterparts, leading to lower inflation but lower growth in the eurozone.)

What the Bank of England achieved was not only to lower inflation, but also to lower expectations of inflation. This in itself made it more difficult for firms to put up prices, and for unions to push for higher wages. It locked the United Kingdom into a virtuous inflation cycle. In this sense, it can be said that the MPC was highly successful.

At the same time, other forces on a world level were holding inflation down. One was globalisation, and in particular the rise of China as a manufacturing power. Cheap manufactured imports from China held down price levels in the United Kingdom, and throughout the Western world. At the same time, the threat of outsourcing to China held down wages.

Another factor holding down inflation, particularly since the expansion of the European Union in 2004, has been an increase in immigration. By increasing the supply of labour, this has held down wages, and hence inflation.

A third factor is the strength of the pound.

As inflation has been so low, real interest rates have been relatively high. This has made the pound an attractive currency, and its value has been pushed higher. This makes imports cheaper, and so pushes inflation down further (and real interest rates higher). The cycle becomes reinforcing. At the same time, this also has adverse effects. Exports become more expensive, and this hits manufacturing, leading to a two-speed Britain – a booming finance and services-based south, and a recession-hit manufacturing north (Hall and Henry 2006).

Thus in conclusion we can say that the MPC has been extremely successful, partly as a result of its own efforts, and partly as a result of external forces, but not all of its impacts have been benign.

By the mid-2000s, the world economy was becoming less benign. 9/11 had been followed by the Afghan and Iraqi wars, and the price of oil on world markets had soared, largely as a result of the boom in the Chinese economy, which had also pushed up other commodity prices. Inflation in the United Kingdom was rising, and in April 2007 hit 3.1 per cent on the CPI measure, forcing the governor of the Bank of England to write his first open letter to Gordon Brown. As noted above, the letter had to cover four points, and we shall look at each in turn:

- The reasons inflation had missed the target. Mervyn King put half the blame of world factors – the increase in the price of oil, and a rise in food prices, triggered by world-wide bad weather. He also blamed rapid growth in the economy, making it easier for firms to put up prices – for example the price of furniture and furnishings rose 10 per cent in March 2007, partly so that massive cuts could be made in the Easter sales. King also blamed an increasing volatility in inflation.

- What the Bank was doing about it. As King pointed put, the MPC had already taken action, and interest rates had gone up by 0.75 per cent since August. In future the MPC would do whatever was required to meet the target. However, he stressed that the MPC would not be over-influenced by what he saw as essentially short-term factors.

- The time span for remedial action. King expected inflation to drop very quickly as the worst impact of rising oil prices dropped out of the figures. This indeed happened, and by July, CPI inflation was back just below target, at 1.9 per cent.

- How the remedial action meets the government's monetary policy objectives. This one was easy. The remedial action would bring inflation back in line with target (Bank of England 2007b).

Gordon Brown accepted the governor's analysis in his reply (HM Treasury 2007). Others were not quite so forgiving. Several commentators pointed to the impact of soaring house prices (Warner, 2007, Smith 2007a). King argued that house prices are not directly a cause of inflation (Searjeant 2007). This may technically be true, but it ignores the way in which individuals have taken advantage of higher house prices to release some of the equity in their houses, thus stimulating domestic demand.

The European Central Bank

The ECB was set up in 1998, to manage economic and monetary union, including setting interest rates for the eurozone. Interest rates are fixed on a monthly basis by the Governing Council, which consists of the Executive Board of the ECB, six members appointed by the eurozone countries, headed by the president of the ECB, plus the governors of the 12 central banks of the euro area.

The ECB is totally independent, and sets its own inflation target. The prime objective of the ECB is to maintain price stability, originally defined as 2 per cent or less on CPI. On 2003, this was slightly but significantly modified to 'close to 2 per cent over the medium term' (*Guardian* 2003a). This was slightly less deflationary. The objective was modified again in 2004, when the ECB said that 'without prejudice to the objective of price stability', the eurosystem would also 'support the general economic policies in the Community', including 'a high level of employment' and 'sustainable and non-inflationary growth' (ECB 2004).

The Federal Reserve

The central bank of the United States is the Federal Reserve Board, headed until recently by the octogenarian Alan Greenspan, and currently headed by Ben Bernanke. It has no specific inflation target, but its remit is laid down by the Federal Reserve Act as to 'promote effectively the goals of maximum employment, stable prices and moderate long-term interest rates' (Federal Reserve 2004). Interest rates are set monthly by the Federal Open Market Committee.

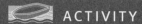

ACTIVITY

4.6 CENTRAL BANKS AND 9/11

In 2001, the terrorist attacks of 11 September hit a world economy which was already sliding into recession. The three major central banks (the Bank of England, the ECB and the Federal Reserve) had already started cutting interest rates before the attacks, as follows:

were made in 2001, while the ECB made most of its cuts in 2002 and 2003.

By 2004, the UK and the US economies had made a robust recovery, while the eurozone still had low growth and high unemployment.

	Previous peak	Rate at August 2001
Bank of England	6.25%	5.00%
ECB	5.75%	5.25%
Federal Reserve	6.50%	3.50%

After the attacks, all three central banks embarked on a medium-term programme of successive interest rate cuts, which troughed at 3.50 per cent (Bank of England), 3.00 per cent (ECB) and 1.00 per cent (Federal Reserve). In the case of the Bank of England and the Federal Reserve, most of the cuts

Question

How far do you think that the relatively more effective recovery of the United Kingdom and the United States from 9/11 was due to:

a) the actions of the three central banks?
b) factors inherent in the terms of reference of the three banks?

PUBLIC OWNERSHIP, PRIVATISATION AND PFI/PPP

PUBLIC OWNERSHIP

When most people think of public ownership, they think of the nationalisations of the Labour government in the late 1940s. But public ownership goes back a lot further than that. The beginnings of a state system of welfare came with the Elizabethan Poor Law in the sixteenth century. The Post Office dates back to the seventeenth century, and developed telegraph services in the nineteenth (the precursor of British Telecom). The Metropolitan Police was founded in 1829, while a primitive system of policing through parish constables goes back hundreds of years before that. A state system of education dates from 1870, and in the 1840s Gladstone gave the state reserve powers to nationalise the railways if necessary. In the late nineteenth century, gas, electricity and water services were developed by local authorities ('municipal socialism').

During the First World War, the state obtained a controlling interest in what later became BP, in 1919 the Forestry Commission was set up to manage Britain's woodlands, and the BBC came into public ownership in the 1920s.

These early examples illustrate some of the driving forces behind public ownership:

- to ensure adequate coverage of services (Post Office, Poor Law, schools)
- to safeguard interests vital to the State (BP, Forestry Commission, BBC)
- to control natural monopolies (police).

The nationalisations of the 1940s added a further motive, a socialist desire to control the 'commanding heights' of the economy in the interests of the state. But even here things were not entirely straightforward. When the Bank of England was nationalised in 1946, it had been effectively under total state control for at least 100 years. The nationalisations of water, gas and electricity involved taking over municipally owned companies rather than private ones. The railways were in private hands, but had been subject to compulsory amalgamations in the 1920s. The NHS took over Poor Law hospitals, by this time under local authority control, as well as charity hospitals. The truly socialist thing about the NHS was the concept of services free at the point of use, rather than ownership. Perhaps the only truly socialist nationalisation was the National Coal Board, which took over from the generally hated coal owners. Generally, the force behind the 1940s nationalisation could be seen equally as a desire to exercise effective centralised planning (Kay 2003).

The nationalised industries had a mixed record of performance, but suffered from a number of systemic flaws:

- John Kay has argued that in order for any type of organisation to operate efficiently and effectively, it must be subject to 'disciplined pluralism'. Because there was no requirement to make a profit, there was little pressure to achieve greater efficiency, ie no discipline. And because the nationalised industries were monopolies, there was also no pluralism (Kay, quoted in Palmås 2005).

- Although day-to-day management was given to the public corporations which controlled the industry, there was a great temptation for governments of all hues to interfere, and government also strictly controlled the level of investment. Nationalised industries thus tended to be used as an instrument of macroeconomic policy, with their investment levels moved up or down depending on the state of unemployment or inflation.

- Nationalised industries were at their height in an era before most businesses, public or private, gave much attention to customer service. As a result, allied with the strength of trade unions, nationalised industries tended to be run in the interests of staff rather than the customer – television in the 1970s loved to expose 'jobsworths' in the nationalised industries and local government. On the other hand, public-sector staff did tend to share a 'public service ethos', which in the case of the railways, for example, led to a high emphasis on safety, and a determination to 'muddle through'. Thus trains kept running during the terrible winter of 1963 in a way which in many cases they failed to do during the floods of 2007.

PRIVATISATION

The Thatcher/Major governments between 1979 and 1997 embarked on an extensive programme of privatisation, starting with British Telecom in 1982 and ending with British Rail in 1996. Most of the big privatisations were public offers of shares to the general public, while others, like the National Freight Corporation and National Bus, were trade sales.

The arguments for privatisation were partly financial and partly political. Privatisation raised very large sums of money for the Treasury, and so permitted tax cuts (memorably criticised by Harold Macmillan as 'selling the family silver'). It also reduced the role of the state (a key element in Thatcherism), which it was hoped would give managers more autonomy to manage efficiently. If the privatised businesses became leaner and meaner, they would be better able to compete effectively in a globalised economy. Privatisation was also intended to stimulate personal share ownership. To ensure that the privatised companies did not exploit their monopoly positions, they were subject to detailed regulatory controls, particularly over pricing, which were intended to force efficiency.

However, just as with nationalisation, flaws in the model gradually become apparent. First, there is no evidence that personal share ownership was significantly expanded. The small investors who bought shares in the privatised companies usually have no other equity investments.

In most cases, prices to the consumer have been reduced, but it is impossible to say whether this is the result of privatisation. In the case of BT, for example, privatisation coincided with a period of rapid technological advance and globalisation in telecommunications. It appears more likely that it is intense competition which has transformed BT rather than privatisation. Privatised industries that are not subject to competition, like water and railways, have been much less successful.

There is also the problem that once an industry is privatised, the state loses effective control over it. One way to try to alleviate this was the system of golden shares – a single share, held by the state, which gave it veto powers over the ownership of the privatised company. For example, the state retained a golden share in the airport operator BAA, which capped a single shareholding at 15 per cent. In other words, the state could veto any takeover of BAA. This was declared illegal by the European Court of Justice in 2003, as it was against EU rules on free movement of capital (Osborn 2003). The hostile takeover of BAA by the Spanish company Ferrovial duly followed in 2006. Other privatised industries that did not have a golden share, such as water and electricity distribution, are now effectively in the hands of French and German companies, including the state-owned Electricité de France. Surely if a key part of the economy is to be in public hands, those hands should be British rather than French!

A fourth problem is what happens when a privatised company fails. By definition, the services provided by a privatised company are vital, and it is important that there is continuity in their supply. Two examples where this happened, Railtrack and Metronet, are discussed below.

Finally, although often regarded with amused contempt, the nationalised industries had a fund of goodwill from the public. When things went wrong, as with train crashes under British Rail, these tended to be regarded as 'acts of God' rather than the fault of the company. The privatised companies have not been successful at building up a similar fund of goodwill. Thus the drought in Yorkshire in 1996 was widely, if unfairly, seen as the fault of the (privatised) Yorkshire Water (Kay 2002).

PUBLIC INTEREST COMPANIES

The advent to power of the New Labour government in 1997 revived interest in a third way of delivering public services, which was neither a nationalised industry or a privatised company. This was the public interest company (PIC). These had three main characteristics:

- They do not normally have shareholders.
- They are independent from the state.
- They deliver a public service.

Legally the PIC is normally a company limited by guarantee. A typical PIC is a housing association, providing and managing social housing.

As Maltby (2003) points out, it has always been an over-simplification to see a simple dichotomy between privatised companies and nationalised industries. In fact there is a continuum of types. Going from pure public sector to pure private sector, we have:

- nationalised industries
- public plcs, where a company operates as though it is in the private sector, but is wholly owned by the state (a good example is the Post Office)
- public interest companies
- public–private partnerships, including PFI contracts (see below)
- regulated private companies – typically privatised companies
- private companies – ordinary plcs.

PICs appealed to New Labour for two main reasons: they represented a Third Way between nationalisation (socialism) and privatisation (capitalism), and they provided an opportunity to give formal influence to stakeholders. As Palmås (2005) argued, PICs combined the management freedom, efficiency and innovativeness of the traditional plc, the public interest ethos of the public sector, and the stakeholder governance of mutuals and the voluntary sector.

Dwr Cymru Welsh Water is a leading example. Originally privatised, it has been owned and managed by Glas Cymru as a PIC since 2001. All financial surpluses are reinvested for the benefit of customers, and since 2001 it has returned £98 million to customers as 'customer dividends'. It has also reduced its level of borrowing from 91 per cent to 75 per cent, so lowering its level of risk (Article 13 and CBI 2007).

An opportunity to experiment with the PIC model on a large scale came with the collapse of Railtrack in 2001. Railtrack had been set up as a result of rail privatisation in 1996, with responsibility for running the rail infrastructure (train services were provided by train operating companies such as Virgin and GNER which rented track use from Railtrack).

At first Railtrack was very successful in financial terms, mainly because it laid off 65 per cent of its staff and outsourced most of its maintenance. It was then hit by a series of accidents, culminating in the Hatfield crash of 2000, caused by a broken rail. In response to public pressure, Railtrack was forced to impose drastic speed restrictions on the network while rails were checked. As a result, Railtrack's profits were shattered, leading to a £534 million loss in 2001. However, Railtrack then paid out a dividend of £137 million.

Railtrack's fortunes continued to decline, and in October 2001 the company was put into administration. By this time its share price had dropped from a peak of £17 to 280p. Eventually, in the spring of 2002, the government effectively bought Railtrack at a price of 250p a share, and handed its management to a new PIC, Network Rail (Palmås 2005).

Network Rail's governance was in the hands of a large group of individuals representing major stakeholders, including 30 drawn from companies already heavily involved in rail, including Amey, Jarvis and London Underground, 34 public members drawn from a range of organisations ranging from Eurotunnel to the National Farmers Union, and 51 individual members selected by a membership panel, who were mostly drawn from 'the great and the good' who frequently appear on the boards of quangos (*Guardian* 2003b).

The government argued that the members of Network Rail represented a fair cross-section of those with an interest in the railways, but it could be argued that too many represented vested interests. It is also unclear exactly what influence the members have on the operation of Network Rail. There is an argument that Network Rail is effectively answerable to no one. In these circumstances, argues Jeremy Warner, 'the engineers are taking over' and 'all [they] want is a shiny new train set' (Warner 2003). However, because Network Rail did not have to distribute profit to shareholders, it was unlikely to be as obsessed with the short term as Railtrack.

NATS: A New Labour privatisation

CASE STUDY 4.3

Until 2002 National Air Traffic Services (NATS), the body responsible for air traffic control in British airspace, was a wholly owned subsidiary of the Civil Aviation Authority, the state body responsible for regulating air transport in the United Kingdom. Its top priority was air safety, it was a natural monopoly, and its prices (paid by airlines) were strictly regulated. All of this would suggest that NATS was the last government service to be seen as a candidate for privatisation. Indeed, at the

1996 Labour Conference, the shadow transport secretary declared 'our air is not for sale' (Grayling 2000).

However, there were some pressures for privatisation. One was the desire to separate out services from the body regulating them. This called for a more rigid separation between the CAA and NATS. The other was the need for heavy investment (£1.4 billion over 10 years) in computer systems to ensure that NATS was able to cope with an expected explosion in air traffic, and Gordon Brown's determination that this investment should come from the private sector rather than the government.

Privatisation was not the only alternative on offer. Another possibility was a state-owned plc, along the lines of the Post Office, which could raise capital from the private sector. Another was a PIC, as adopted by Canadian air traffic control, NavCanada (Grayling 2000).

The decision to go for privatisation was taken in 1998. The model proposed was a part-privatisation. The shareholding of NATS was to be divided into three – 49 per cent retained by the government, 46 per cent sold to a 'strategic partner', which would take responsibility for day-to-day management, and 5 per cent to NATS employees.

However, there was a snag. The CAA, as the responsible regulator, proposed a tough pricing regime for NATS, based on the 'RPI – x%' formula used to regulate other privatisations. CAA's proposal was RPI – 5%, which required NATS to make efficiency savings in real terms of 5 per cent a year. The privatisation met with a lot of political opposition, including claims that the proposed price regime would seriously compromise safety. As a result, in 2001 the CAA eased the pricing regime, and the privatisation finally gained parliamentary approval.

Four bids were received for the 46 per cent privatisation stake – the Airline Group, representing seven British airlines; Serco, the UK facilities management group; the Novares consortium, led by the US company Lockheed Martin; and Airways Corporation, the New Zealand state-owned

air traffic service provider. The Airline Group was selected. This had a certain logic, as British airlines were the major customers of NATS (Done 2001). Each airline paid £50 million for its stake, while new debt raised by the company repaid £450 million debt to the government. Government proceeds from the partial privatisation were thus around £800 million.

However, as soon as it came under its new ownership in July 2001, NATS was savaged by the backlash from the 11 September attacks on the United States, which led to a collapse in transatlantic air travel, and a corresponding collapse in NATS's revenues. The government was criticised for not having contingency plans in place to deal with the crisis. Although no one could have foreseen 11 September, similar effects had been seen to air travel in the past from emergencies including the oil crisis in 1973 and the Gulf War in 1991–2 (Done 2002).

Recovery from 9/11 was slow, and NATS did not break even until the year ending March 2004. Thereafter it moved into steady profit of around £80 million a year, enabling it to pay a dividend for the first time in 2005 (Done 2006).

Was privatisation right for NATS? The use of British airlines as strategic partners, and a staff shareholding, were consistent with a stakeholder approach to corporate governance, but this could have been achieved equally effectively with a PIC. Perhaps the decision to go for privatisation was a devious one. When NATS pays a dividend to its airline shareholders, this could be seen as an indirect subsidy, a partial repayment of their air traffic control charges, which otherwise would be illegal under EU regulations.

THE PRIVATE FINANCE INITIATIVE AND PUBLIC–PRIVATE PARTNERSHIPS

Public–private partnership (PPP) refers to any financial collaboration between the public and private sectors. For example, in the 1980s local authorities were forced to put many of their services out for tender to the private sector under the compulsory competitive tendering system. The result today is that the council dustman has virtually disappeared. Instead, garbage operatives are employed by private waste disposal companies, although their job is still to collect people's rubbish.

Other examples include the use by schools of private security companies, and the way in which the BBC uses private production companies to produce many of its television programmes. Some PPPs are really public–voluntary partnerships – the transfer of local authority social housing to housing corporations, for example, since 1989 (Ward 2000).

The Private Finance Initiative (PFI) is a specialised type of PPP. Set up by Norman Lamont in 1992 after the United Kingdom was forced out of the EU Exchange Rate Mechanism, it was seen as a way simultaneously to stimulate the economy and to hold down public spending. Say the NHS wants to build a new hospital. Under the old system, the capital cost of the hospital was financed by the state, and so increased public borrowing. Under PFI, the private sector provides the cash, which is repaid with interest once the new hospital opens. The NHS (and the government) avoids a high capital payment up front, but it is committed to monthly payments for the next 25–30 years, which will amount to much more than the hospital would have cost in the first place. Deals include penalty clauses if the terms of the contract are not met – if the heating system fails, for example. The private sector company gains a guaranteed flow of income for 25–30 years, but takes the risk if there are cost over-runs.

Many PFI deals went much further. Not only would the contractor in effect lease the hospital to the NHS, but the contract also included the provision of ancillary hospital services, typically catering, cleaning and security. This included the transfer of NHS jobs to the private sector, where they were subject to the EU Transfer of Undertakings (TUPE) regulations.

When New Labour came to power in 1997, it was at first thought that the days of PFI were numbered. Instead the system was expanded. The opportunity for Gordon Brown to keep public-sector capital spending off the public sector borrowing requirement was too good to miss. However, Labour did bring in some safeguards. The system of compulsory competitive tendering for local authorities was changed to Best Value, where the local authority could continue to provide services in-house if it could establish that it provided as good value as outsourcing. PFI was also stopped for small projects, where the cost of the tendering process outweighed any financial savings, and for IT projects, where many contracts had proved expensive failures. It was also stressed that PFI could only be used where it did not come at the expense of employees' terms and conditions.

Several possible models for PFI/PPP were identified by the Institute for Public Policy Research in 2001. These were:

- Public sector default – the public sector provides all services, which is broadly the position for police and fire services.

- Private sector rescue – the private sector acts as provider of last resort only if the public sector is seen to be under-performing, for example some failing local education authorities have been taken over by the private sector.

- Level playing field – equal treatment between different organisations seeking to deliver public services, broadly the position with local authority Best Value.

- Public sector rescue – the public sector acts as provider of last resort only if the private sector is seen to be under-performing, as in the replacement of Railtrack by Network Rail.

- Private sector default – the private sector provides all services, as with the building and operation of new prisons.

The Treasury stressed that one of the main benefits of PFI was that it transferred risk to the private sector. The public authority received the certainty that specified services would be delivered at the cost at which they were contracted. In 2006 the Treasury estimated that PFI would total 10–15 per cent of total investment in public services, and in the five-year pipeline were 200 projects worth £26 billion.

In 2003, Tony Blair seemed to herald a big expansion of PPP into clinical services in the NHS. He said, 'We are anxious to ensure that this is the start of opening up the whole of the NHS supply system so that we end up with a situation where the state is the enabler, it is the regulator, but it is not always the provider' (Carvel 2003).

Treasury research in 2006 also established that on the whole the public sector was satisfied with the results of PFI:

- 79 per cent said service standards are delivered always or almost always

- overall performance of 96 per cent of projects was at least satisfactory

- 70 per cent of public sector managers believe relationships with private sector partners are good or very good.

Only 20 per cent of PFI projects are late, compared with 70 per cent of non-PFI contracts, while 20 per cent are over budget, compared with 73 per cent of non-PFI projects (HM Treasury 2006). However, there are many criticisms of PFI:

- They lock the public sector into contracts that are too long. It is very difficult to forecast demand for facilities as far ahead as 30 years. Schools, for example, are frequently surplus to requirements long before 30 years because of changes in local population. Government NHS policy is to shift significant portions of the work of hospitals into the community. This again puts in doubt 30-year contracts (Batty and Weaver 2006).

- A PFI contract may deliver on time, but this does not take into account the length of time required to finalise contracts – frequently a matter of years. The contracting process itself is also extremely expensive, and the contracts frequently too restrictive. The process also creates a 'contract culture', with endless arguments over exactly what the contract does and does not require.

- PFI threatens the public sector ethos. For example, when cleaners in hospitals were employed by the NHS, they were driven by a desire to produce the best possible service for the patients. When the same people are employed by the private sector under PFI, they are ultimately contract and profit-driven – they are not permitted to go beyond the terms of the contract, because this will cost their employer money.

- Many PFI companies are moving into areas well away from their core expertise. The leading firms involved in educational administration are Jarvis and Atkins, both primarily civil engineering specialists, and VT Education, the service arm of defence and shipbuilding firm Vosper Thorneycroft. In a Fabian report, Colin Crouch argued that the main expertise of these companies lies in their experience in lobbying and negotiating large contracts with the government (Woodward 2003).

- PFI drains public services of current spending power. At the end of 2006, £8 billion worth of NHS hospital PFI schemes were operational or under construction in England. On these, the NHS would have to pay £37 billion in debt payments over the next 30 years. It is estimated that 50 per cent of NHS trusts with major PFI schemes are in financial difficulties, a much higher than the average proportion across the NHS. Some, like South Tees and Queen Elizabeth Woolwich, both in substantial deficit, are paying 20 per cent of their turnover to PFI partners (Hellowell 2006). In the case of Queen Elizabeth, the PFI deal cost £9 million a year more than an equivalent hospital built with money borrowed directly from the government (Batty and Weaver 2006).

- In practice, risk is not completely transferred to the PFI partner. In 2004, the PFI contractor Jarvis was in severe financial difficulty following its involvement in the Potters Bar train crash, where it was responsible for track maintenance. At the time Jarvis was responsible for 14 PFI projects, all of which ground to a halt as the City sorted out a rescue package for Jarvis. Part of the problem appeared to be that Jarvis had been 'lowballing' – bidding too low in order to secure bargain-basement PFI contracts, and then running into trouble when unexpected problems appeared. At the very least, Jarvis's failure led to delays and waste for its public sector partners; at worst, contracts would have to be renegotiated with another partner, leading to higher costs than originally budgeted (Hirst 2005).

The next Activity examines in detail the biggest PPP of them all, the London Underground.

 ACTIVITY

4.7 THE COLLAPSE OF METRONET

In 1997 New Labour came to power and one of its first acts was to set up a Greater London Authority, headed by a mayor. Among other things, the mayor was to be responsible for transport in London, including the tube system, London Underground. Much to the government's embarrassment, the London mayoral election was won by the socialist maverick Ken Livingstone, who defeated an official Labour candidate, and as a result was expelled from the Labour Party.

The government then faced the issue of what to do with the London Underground. Both it and Livingstone were agreed that London Underground, under the control of the mayor and his transport authority, Transport for London, would operate the trains, but there was a bitter dispute over who would be responsible for maintenance of the track and signalling, and refurbishment of the system. Livingstone, and his transport supremo, the American Bob Kiley, who had rescued the New York subway system from collapse, argued for control by London Underground, financed by a bond issue. The government, led by the chancellor, Gordon Brown, insisted on a PPP solution, with the underground system divided into three, and each sector becoming the responsibility of a private-sector consortium.

Expert and public opinion both backed Livingstone. Rail experts argued that the proposal fell into the same mistake as rail privatisation, of dividing train operation from the infrastructure. The principal rail safety inspector warned of 'growing concern' about the impact of the government's plans on safety, while a MORI poll in 2000 found Londoners two to one against the PPP, convinced that the Tube would be less safe, less reliable and worse value for money (Milne 2000).

The fight was long and bitter, including an unsuccessful High Court action by Livingstone and Kiley, but in the end the government got its way and the PPP came into force in 2003. After a tendering process costing nearly half a billion pounds, of the three 30-year contracts, worth a total of £30 billion, two were won by Metronet, a consortium formed by WS Atkins, Balfour Beatty, Bombardier, EDF Energy and Thames Water, and the third by Tube Lines, formed by Bechtel, Ferrovial and Jarvis (Jarvis later sold its share to Ferrovial).

Fast forward four years to 2007, and Metronet was in severe financial difficulties. Its costs were way above those that had been budgeted. Station refurbishments averaged £7.5 million per station, while the budgeted figure was £2 million. Refurbishment of deep-level track and tunnels cost £5.7 million per kilometer, against a budget of £3 million (Wright 2007a). Losses on the deep-level

contract were £550 million, and it was thought that losses on the surface contract were similar.

Metronet claimed £551 million from London Underground (LU), alleging that the cost over-run on the deep level contract was solely caused by additional demands from LU. The case went to the PPP arbiter, Chris Bolt, who decided that Metronet should receive only £121 million (Hencke 2007). Metronet then went into administration.

Its five shareholders lost the £70 million each which they had invested in Metronet, but Metronet also had £2 billion of debt. Under the terms of the PPP, 95 per cent of this was guaranteed by Transport for London (TfL). However, this debt was frozen for one year, while TfL sought a refinancing. Meanwhile, the administrators continued to fulfil Metronet's contracts, and London Underground continued its monthly payments as before (Milmo 2007).

Why did Metronet fail? The most likely reason seems to be the way in which Metronet handed out contracts to its shareholders – known as a tied supply chain. Bombardier, for example, had £3.3 billion of contracts from Metronet (Wright 2007b). Tube Lines, the consortium responsible for the third PPP contract, put all its contracts out to open tender, and so was able to negotiate much better terms. As a result, Tube Lines is operating on time and on budget.

Question

Is the failure of Metronet an example of the success or the failure of PPP?

COMPETITIVENESS

In the 1970s, the United Kingdom was widely seen as a failed economy. It was subject to wide fluctuations in economic performance, and suffered from high inflation and unemployment. Taxation was high, the economy was heavily regulated, and trade unions were widely seen as too powerful. Some of these shortcomings were tackled by the Thatcher governments between 1979 and 1991, which lowered taxation, cut back on regulation and attacked the power of the trade unions. The result was an increase in the efficiency of the economy, although this was largely a function of the contraction of manufacturing. The manufacturers that survived were inevitably more efficient than those that failed.

However, the impetus behind the reforms of the Thatcher governments were as much political as economic. Policy changed with the advent of the Major government in 1991. This was much less ideological. Policies were to be followed because they were effective, rather than because they were politically correct.

This approach was continued by New Labour in 1997, with an almost seamless transition from Ken Clarke to Gordon Brown as chancellor of the Exchequer. Competitiveness became the watchword, and pragmatism the policy. The aim was to reform the British economy so that it could compete with the best in the world.

PRODUCTIVITY

Competitiveness has a large number of facets, from a tightening of anti-trust legislation to the promotion of a higher skills base in the United Kingdom, and stabilisation of macroeconomic policy. What ties them all together is the concept of productivity. This is a measure of how much the economy is producing per worker employed. This is dependent on both the efficiency of the worker and on the hours worked, so a better measure is probably output per worker hour.

In 2002, productivity measured by output per worker was 39 per cent below the United States, 15 per cent below France and 7 per cent below Germany. However, France and Germany work fewer hours than the United Kingdom, and the United States works more, so on the better measure, output per worker hour, the United Kingdom is 26 per cent behind the United States, 24 per cent behind France and 11 per cent behind Germany. This is known as the productivity gap (Philpott 2002).

The 2002 figures represented a considerable improvement on the position in 1991, when the United Kingdom was 35 per cent behind France on output per worker hour, and 30 per cent behind Germany (Daneshkhu 2007a). The improvement continued after 2002, and by 2007 the United Kingdom was 18 per cent behind the United States and 20 per cent behind France, although the gap with Germany had widened slightly, to 13 per cent (Daneshkhu 2007b). Between 1995 and 2006, UK labour productivity growth was 2.1 per cent per annum, France's 1.9 per cent, Germany's 1.7 per cent, and Italy's 0.4 per cent (Giles 2007).

Since the 1950s, the underlying rate of growth of productivity in the United Kingdom has been around 2 per cent. Government policy is to try to increase this underlying rate, with a wide range of detailed polices put forward in two White Papers, *Building the knowledge driven economy* in 1998 (www.dti.gov.uk/competitive), and *Opportunity for all in a world of change* in 2001 (www.dti.gov.uk/opportunity for all). Success in doing so would increase the United Kingdom's long-term rate of economic growth, and would also lower

NAIRU, allowing the UK economy to control inflation at a lower level of unemployment (Philpott 2002). A similar programme was launched by the European Union at the Lisbon Summit in 2000 (EU 2004), which set the objective of becoming the most competitive, dynamic, knowledge-based economy in the world by 2010. Its detailed proposals included creating an environment that was conducive to business start-ups, a fully operational internal market, education and training suitable for a knowledge society, and a raising of the EU employment rate from 61 per cent in 2000 to 70 per cent in 2010, thereby creating 20 million new jobs. Of these, 5 million had been created by 2003 (Philpott 2003).

In 2004 a group appointed by the European Union, under the chairmanship of the former Dutch prime minister, Wim Kok, reported on progress (Hutton 2004). They proposed that:

- EU members should spend 3 per cent of GDP on research and development (the United Kingdom at present spends 1.9 per cent)

- there should be a European Research Council supporting centres of scientific excellence

- degrees and qualifications should be mutually recognised, in order that researchers can develop career paths within the European Union rather than joining the brain drain to the United States

- there should be an EU-wide patent law.

However, in 2005 the *Economist* pointed to slow progress towards the Lisbon targets, and blamed this on the failure of Germany, France and Italy to open up their economies to competition, citing their opposition to the EU Services Directive, intended to liberalise cross-border trade in services (*Economist* 2005b).

An increase in productivity depends on changes in a number of factors. These include:

- Capital investment. The more modern the equipment with which people work, the more efficient they will be. Historically, investment in the United Kingdom has been low, and increases in productivity have come more through the shutting-down of the most inefficient plant than the building of new plant. A telling comparison with the United States is that while the United Kingdom produces the same volume of manufacturing output with half the capacity of the 1970s, the US produces twice the output with the same capacity.

- Economic stability. One key factor which deters investment is economic instability. Investors need to be convinced that there will be a consistent demand for what they produce, and that inflation will be stable. Here the United Kingdom has made great advances over the last decade. De Grauwe (2001) has argued that a comprehensive and reliable welfare state is also necessary, although this does not seem to be required in the United States.

- Research and development. The United Kingdom is excellent at scientific research but much less good at the applied R&D needed to convert this into practical products and processes. It is significant that the United Kingdom's only world-class industry, pharmaceuticals, is the heaviest investor in R&D.

- IT and the Internet. During the dot.com boom of the late 1990s, the Internet was seen as the Holy Grail of productivity, and some US economists put forward the concept of a new economic paradigm, where the business cycle was abolished and growth would continue indefinitely. This rosy view was shaken by the dot.com crash in early 2000, and shattered by 11 September 2001. Of the dot.com companies, virtually only Amazon, e-Bay and a few business to business (B2B) companies are profitable.

- Restrictive practices. Restrictive practices by the trade unions were tackled by the Thatcher governments, so the main concern is restrictive practices by industry. The United Kingdom has anti-trust laws (covered in more detail in the chapter on regulation), but they are much less tough than in the United States. One change here has been to make participation in price-fixing activities a criminal offence, subject to imprisonment – a measure in force in the United States since 1890 (Lennan 2001).

- Management. The quality of management in the United Kingdom is widely perceived as being poor, despite the spread of management qualifications such as the MBA. As with the whole of UK industry, there are some very good examples of management practice, but a very long tail of poor performers. The average standard needs to be raised to be nearer the best. Two main failings are a short-termist approach, which discourages long-term investment and development, and a failure to introduce modern management practices such as just-in-time and continuous improvement. Many sectors of industry still experience high levels of stress and alienation, and many managers refuse to consider a partnership approach with their workers.

- Infrastructure. The United Kingdom has the most congested roads in the European Union. This adds to business costs and makes the operation of techniques such as JIT more difficult (see the Road Pricing Activity).

- Flexibility. Industry must become more flexible in order to optimise its use of resources. This involves being:
  - Numerically flexible: working time must adjust to meet customer demand – 'the 24/7 society'. This involves the use of techniques such as annual hours.
  - Functionally flexible: skills levels must be improved, and these skills fully utilised.
  - Occupationally flexible: workers must become multi-skilled.
  - Wage flexible: reward must be used as an incentive to higher productivity.
  - Mindset flexible: diversity must be encouraged in order to tap all available talent, and organisations must be family-friendly in order to encourage diversity (Philpott 2002, Merrick 2001, Briner 2001).

- Education. A key element is the need to develop workforce skills. The United Kingdom has a higher proportion of low-skilled workers than other comparable economies. A whole series of initiatives have been introduced, ranging from NVQs to TECs, ILAs to LSCs. The result has been an alphabet soup, without a great deal of impact on the skills base. As usual, the UK pattern is one of excellence at the top, with very effective degree-level provision, a gap in the middle, where technician-level skills are poorly developed, and a long tail of functional illiteracy and innumeracy. However, it is becoming clear that workforce development is a dual responsibility, with the government responsible for developing the basic skills of numeracy, literacy and IT (as stressed in the Tomlinson Report on the reform of 14–19 education in October 2004), and industry being responsible for the development of workplace-specific skills.

The best that can be said at present about the effectiveness of competitiveness policy is that the United Kingdom is holding its own and not falling further behind its main competitors. Short-term gains are unlikely, and these policies should be seen as essentially long term.

In 2003, Michael Porter and Christian Ketels carried out a study for the DTI on the United Kingdom's competitiveness (Porter and Ketels 2003). Their conclusions were rather more optimistic. They said that successive governments have 'fundamentally changed the macroeconomic, and, more importantly, the microeconomic context for competition'. They identified what they saw as the strengths of the UK business environment: its openness to international trade and investment, its very low regulatory barriers to national level competition, and its sophisticated capital markets; but also identified weaknesses, particularly a deteriorating physical infrastructure, skills deficits, and low levels of R&D and innovation despite a strong science base. The challenge for the future was to manage the transition from an economy based on low cost to one based on unique value and innovation.

However, the Porter report has been criticised for its emphasis on economic issues at the expense of behavioural ones. For example, US-owned firms in the United Kingdom have higher productivity than UK-owned ones. Andrew Pettigrew of the University of Warwick points out that the most obvious explanation for this lies in the 'varying abilities of managers to perceive, incorporate or even change [environmental] conditions' (Caulkin 2003).

It is also important to remember that productivity per head is not the only driver of economic growth. As William Keegan pointed out in October 2004 (Keegan 2004b), superior economic growth in the United States is largely caused by factors such as:

- A growing labour force, driven by high rates of immigration. This tends to lower the average age of the workforce, and also forces a high rate of investment to keep pace with the demand created by a growing population.

- Long hours and short holidays.

- Generally expansionary macroeconomic policies.

ACTIVITY

4.8 ROAD PRICING AND THE LONDON CONGESTION CHARGE

Britain has the worst traffic congestion in Europe. This causes a number of costs – damage to the road surface, damage to the climate, damage to other people's health (through both air pollution and accidents), and time wasted while sitting in traffic jams (*Economist* 2005b). It also holds back productivity. Firms cannot rely on deliveries being made just in time, and late arrival of office staff because of commuting delays also costs firms money (*Economist* 2006a). No one really knows what all this congestion costs the economy, although the CBI has suggested an annual cost of £20 billion (*Economist* 2006b).

Congestion costs are an example of what economists call an external cost. Here, costs are not borne by the person who causes them, but by someone else. As congestion costs have been rising, the real cost of motoring has been falling, and in 2006 it was lower than in 1981 (*Economist* 2006b).

Motoring is of course taxed, but the taxes on motoring are not closely related to congestion costs. Vehicle excise duty (VED) is linked to pollution, as less polluting cars pay a lower rate of duty, but other congestion costs are not related to VED. Fuel duty is more closely related to congestion, as the more miles someone drives, the more fuel they use, and thus the higher the fuel tax paid, but the duty is not related to where they drive. The same fuel duty is paid for driving on an empty country road as on a congested city one. Although the fuel is taxed, in effect the use of the road is free.

Two methods can be used to control congestion. One is regulation. This goes back to the Romans – wheeled traffic was banned in Rome during the hours of daylight. Modern versions are traffic-free pedestrian precincts, and systems such as that used in Athens, where cars with particular number plates are only allowed into the city on certain days of the week.

The alternative is to charge the driver for driving in the congested area. This internalises the external cost, and is preferred by most economists. The person causing the congestion is charged for it, and in principle the revenue raised can be used to compensate those who suffer from the congestion.

In this case study we look in detail at one local example of road pricing, the London Congestion Charge, and in less detail at proposals for national road pricing.

The London Congestion Charge was introduced by the mayor of London, Ken Livingstone, on I February 2003. Motorists were charged £5 (later raised to £8) to enter an 8 square mile zone of central London (the City and parts of the West End), between 7 am and 6.30 pm, Monday to Friday. The revenue raised from the scheme was to be used to invest in public transport.

The scheme was a great success. it reduced traffic in the Congestion Charge area by 15 per cent, and increased traffic speeds by 22 per cent. Congestion was reduced by 30 per cent (*Economist* 2005b). The Congestion Charge raised gross revenue of £160–180 million a year, with net revenues of £80–90 million. The mayor's Transport Strategy Revision document in 2004 claimed that time savings, reliability improvements and accident reductions produced a benefit to society of £150–210 million a year. The Congestion Charge supported three of the major objectives in the London Plan:

- making London a better city to live in

- making London a more prosperous city with strong and diverse economic growth

- improving London's transport (Mayor of London 2004).

Other cities are interested in the congestion charge concept, and in 2007 it was announced that New York would introduce a very similar scheme (Glaister 2007).

However, not everyone was so happy. The Association of British Drivers, a pro-motoring pressure group, ridiculed the Congestion Charge as the Con Charge, and drew attention to Ken Livingstone's well-known dislike of cars. In 1999 he had said, 'I hate cars. If I ever get any powers again I'd ban the lot!' (ABD nd). The London Chamber of Commerce said in 2004 that 79 per cent of retailers within the Zone claimed that takings were down, with 42 per cent blaming the Congestion Charge (*Grocer* 2004).

In February 2007 the Congestion Charge was extended westwards to cover most of the London Boroughs of Westminster and Kensington and Chelsea (the Western Extension Zone – WEZ). The WEZ was controversial. Westminster Council opposed it, and so did the John Lewis Partnership, whose flagship department stores in Oxford Street and Chelsea were now both affected by the charge (John Lewis 2007).

The WEZ also changed the whole character of the Congestion Charge. The original charge area was ideal – a travel to work business area, with very few residents. The WEZ was different – largely residential with little employment except for retailing. Residents were given a 90 per cent discount, which ironically reduced their cost of driving into central London. As a result, traffic in the original charge area was forecast to increase (Wolmar 2007).

To economists the Congestion Charge, though better than nothing, was still technically flawed. The charge is flat rate (£5, later £8), the same at 8.30 am, when traffic is very heavy, as at 1.30 pm, when it is relatively light, and also the same whether the driver spends five minutes in the charging zone, or five hours. More

sophisticated and sensitive methods of charging are available, based on a variation of the Global Positioning Satellite (GPS) navigation system, which can charge a variable rate, collected through a direct debit charge, based on traffic density, and time spent in the zone. Such a system is already used in Singapore, and to charge lorries for use of the German autobahn (Wolmar 2007).

In May 2007, Manchester announced a very similar scheme. A tag would monitor journeys on 15 of the most congested routes into the city centre, but would only charge during rush hours, with the charge varying on how far into the city centre the motorist went (McVeigh 2007).

This leads us into the concept of national road pricing, based on some variation of the GPS system. In 2005 Alistair Darling, then Transport minister, proposed a scale of charges ranging from 2p to £1.34 per mile, depending on the level of congestion. Other car taxes (VED and fuel duty) would be lowered to ensure that the change was revenue-neutral (*New Statesman* 2005). The government will carry out road pricing trials in nine areas by 2009, with the aim of introducing a national pricing system in 2014.

Questions

1. How is it possible to estimate the costs to society of traffic jams and road accidents?

2. In the spring of 2007, the government invited pressure groups to launch online e-petitions, as part of its e-government programme. The petition against road pricing attracted 1.8 million signatures, more than all the other petitions put together. Why do you think so many people oppose road pricing?

INVESTORS IN PEOPLE

CASE STUDY 4.4

Investors in People (IiP) was introduced in October 1991. It is one of the key competitiveness-promoting initiatives which has been truly non-political, enthusiastically backed by both the Major and the Blair governments. By 2001, 25,000 organisations had qualified for the standard, employing 24 per cent of the UK workforce.

Research carried out for IiP suggests that 73 per cent of organisations awarded the standard more than 12 months ago feel that it has increased their productivity. However, there is a counter view, put forward by Scott Taylor of the Open University, that IiP frequently has little impact on performance (Brown 2001), and this is supported by research from the Institute of Directors, where only 15 per cent of 275 company directors felt that IiP had increased profitability, and a quarter thought it had increased productivity (Nelson 2001).

Arguments in support of Taylor's contention could include:

- Some organisations see IiP as a marketing exercise. The standard is treated as 'just another badge on the wall' rather than a development tool.

- Achievement and maintenance of the standard involves considerable amounts of management and worker time. These have to be offset before there can be any overall improvement in productivity.

- There is considerable emphasis on measurement of outputs. There is a risk that too much emphasis may be put on the targets rather than the processes. To many people, the present government seems obsessed with targets, which can cause distortions. In a recent case, patients waiting for accident and emergency assessment were held in ambulances outside an A&E department, because there is a target for maximum waiting times in A&E, but the clock does not start ticking until the patient actually enters the building! (Boycott, 2004).

- More generally, IiP can only succeed where it is seen not as a box-ticking exercise, but as a fundamental change in values and attitudes. As with similar initiatives such as Total Quality Management, a belief in the virtues of development must be internalised in the organisation and become an integral part of its culture. Many organisations of course do this, and it is clear that in many cases IiP has been a total success.

CONCLUSIONS

This chapter has analysed the legislative process and influences on policy formation in the United Kingdom and the European Union. The key components of the economy were analysed, as were the objectives of government policy and the tools which the government can use to achiever them. Detailed case studies of inflation and interest rates of competitiveness and productivity and of third world development were also analysed.

KEY LEARNING POINTS

- Legislation in the United Kingdom is normally initiated by the government, whereas in the European Union it is initiated by the Commission. The role of parliament is much greater in the United Kingdom than in the European Union.

- Political parties and their members have some influence on policy formation, but this influence is tending to decrease.

- Pressure groups are of two main types, interest or sectional groups and attitude or cause groups. They have considerable influence both on the evolution of government policy and on its implementation.

- There are crucial differences between gross domestic product and standard of living or quality of life.

- All governments, of whatever political colour, are striving to achieve economic growth, full employment, stable prices, and equilibrium on the balance of payments.

- Policy instruments available to governments include fiscal policy, monetary policy, competitiveness policy and exchange rate policy.

- Interest rates in the United Kingdom are set by the Bank of England, subject to an inflation target set by the government.

- The inflation target in the United Kingdom is symmetrical, and therefore less restrictive than that of the European Central Bank.

- A drive to increase productivity and competitiveness is a key aim of both UK and EU economic policy, but does not lead to quick results.

- Despite their very different political systems, both India and China have been very effective at stimulating economic growth.

QUESTIONS

1. What is the difference between a Green Paper and a White Paper?

2. Through what stages does a bill pass in the United Kingdom before it becomes an Act?

3. What are the differences between RPI, RPI-X and CPI? Which do you think is the best measure of inflation?

4. What is the Stability and Growth Pact? What do you think are its major weaknesses?

5. What are the five tests on whether the United Kingdom should join the euro?

6. What is a public interest company?

7. What is the difference between PFI and PPP?

8. What major competitiveness weaknesses of the UK economy were identified by Michael Porter?

TRENDS TO WATCH

- Trends on inflation. Does it accelerate, or is there a tendency towards deflation, as appeared to be the case in the early 2000s? What action does the Monetary Policy Committee take?

- Is there any reform of the European Union's Stability and Growth Pact?

- Does the United Kingdom decide to join the euro?

- Does the Private Finance Initiative survive the next General Election?

- Does China continue to be the main locomotive of world economic growth?

EXPLORE FURTHER

For the underlying economic theory, see Lipsey and Chrystal (1999, recommended in Chapter 2). For the evolution and application of policy, the Bank of England (www.bankofengland.co.uk) and the Department of Trade and Industry

(www.dti.gov.uk) websites are useful. John Philpott, the CIPD's chief economist, produces an occasional series for the CIPD entitled *Perspectives*, which is invaluable.

 SEMINAR ACTIVITY

ECONOMIC DEVELOPMENT IN INDIA AND CHINA

Between 1985 and 1995, GNP growth in the developing world averaged 6 per cent a year, more than twice that of the developed world (World Bank 2000). This suggests that the developing world will soon catch up with the developed world. Unfortunately, this hopeful forecast ignores two key factors. One is the rapid rate of population growth in the developing world. When this is stripped out, and growth converted to GNP per head, the growth rate per head in the developing world falls to 3.8 per cent, while that of the developed world falls to 2.1 per cent.

Second, the developing country figures are distorted by the outstanding success of the two most populous countries, India and

China. In the period 1985–95, India's GNP per head rose by 3.2 per cent a year, and China's by an impressive (although possibly unreliable) 8.3 per cent a year. Stripping out India and China from the figures, the rest of the developing world actually had a GNP per head which fell by nearly 1 per cent a year. Since the 1990s growth in both countries has accelerated, to 10 per cent or more in China, and 8 per cent in India.

China's success has been particularly remarkable. It took England 58 years to double its GDP after 1780, the United States 47 years from 1839, Japan 34 years from 1885, and South Korea 11 years from 1966 (Meredith 2007). It took China nine years from 1978. It then doubled again by 1996, and doubled yet again by 2006 (Hutton 2007).

Why have India and China done so well? To some extent both countries are returning to their historic position in the world economy. At the time of the Roman Empire, China had 26 per cent of the world's economy, and India had 33 per cent. Even by 1820, China had 33 per cent, India 16 per cent (compared with western Europe at 24 per cent, and the United States at 2 per cent (Smith 2007b). It was only in the nineteenth century that the Indian and Chinese economies collapsed. China's GDP per head in 1950 was only three-quarters of its 1820 value. By the early 1970s, China's share of world output was only 5 per cent, and India's 3 per cent, compared with western Europe's 26 per cent and the United States and Canada's 25 per cent.

India and China have some distinct similarities in their economies. Both had their year zero in the 1940s, when their political and economic status was transformed – India's by independence in 1947, China's by the victory of Mao and the Communists in 1949. Both have huge populations, and a dominant agricultural sector, employing more than half of the population. Both went through the same sequence of economic development, of emphasis on heavy industry and a planned economy, followed by agricultural reform, followed by export-led growth, with greater emphasis on the market (Goyal and Jha 2004).

The main difference comes in their political systems. China has been a unitary state since the time of the first emperor (he of the terracotta warriors) in the second century BC. Throughout most of its history, India has been a cultural rather than a political entity, and has only been a single state under foreign conquerors, from the Mughals in the fifteenth and sixteenth centuries to the British in the eighteenth to twentieth centuries. China is a one-party state with power centralised in the Communist party, India is a multi-party democracy. China is relatively homogeneous racially, with few major religious or racial minorities, while India is a heterogeneous state both racially and religiously, with a very large Muslim minority population (India has a bigger Muslim population than Pakistan), and significant numbers of Sikhs, Buddhists and Christians.

Both initially made economic mistakes, but both laid the foundations for their future success immediately after their respective year zeros. Mao took over a state where illiteracy was rife, with a male illiteracy rate of 70 per cent, and female illiteracy up to 99 per cent in rural areas (Hutton 2007, p76). Mao immediately instituted a crash programme of primary education, and by the mid-1990s adult literacy was up to 80 per cent. It is forecast that by 2025 there will be more English speakers in China than there are native English speakers in the rest of the world (Smith 2007b, p100). China's economic policy was eccentric and destructive until the 1970s. The Great Leap Forward between 1958 and 1961 tried to industrialise China through village communes, which predictably proved to be a failure, while the whole Chinese economy was torn apart by the Cultural Revolution between 1966 and 1976.

India after independence went for a moderate socialist economy similar to that constructed in the United Kingdom in the 1940s, with extensive nationalisation of key industries, and also, following the ideas of Gandhi, opted for economic self-sufficiency (autarky). Small industries were encouraged, and tariff barriers were high. The economy was also highly bureaucratic (known as the Permit Raj), and this discouraged entrepreneurialism. However, many small to medium-sized firms prospered under this benign and protectionist regime, and India developed skills in small-scale manufacture.

The first prime minister of India, Pandit Nehru, was also, like Mao, committed to education. His legacy was the foundation of a group of seven Indian Institutes of Technology, founded in 1947. Although small, these were excellent, rated in 2005 as the third best institutions of technology in the world, behind only MIT and the California Institute of Technology. Graduates from the IITs were later to develop the Indian software industry, as well as much of Silicon Valley.

China's switch to a high-growth economy began in 1978, when the veteran communist Deng Xiaoping came to power. Deng realised that results were more important than ideology. One of his sayings was, 'It doesn't matter whether a cat is black or white as long as it catches mice.' Deng dismantled the rural communes, giving land back to the peasants, which immediately led to a rise in agricultural output. He ensured that state enterprises were run by managers rather than party bureaucrats, and he set up special economic zones, tax-free enclaves which welcomed foreign investment, initially from the Chinese diaspora in Hong King, Singapore and Taiwan, but later from the West, particularly the United States. He cut tariffs on imports, and launched a huge programme of infrastructure investment, with tens of thousands of miles of motorway and dozens of new international airports being built. The combination of good infrastructure and plentiful, cheap but well-educated labour proved irresistible to foreign investors. China's manufactured exports have boomed, although there has been some criticism that the result is that goods are 'made in China', but not 'made by China' (Hutton 2007, p114). There are very few major Chinese-owned companies, and none which are truly world-class.

For over 40 years, India bumbled along, with some economic growth, but not sufficient to cut rural poverty significantly (what J K Galbraith described as 'functioning anarchy' (Smith 2007b, p172). Despite the success of the IITs, illiteracy remained high, especially in rural areas, and India was also held back by its caste structure. Since independence, discrimination against *dalits* (untouchables) has been illegal, but in practice it persisted. Only 20 per cent of rural residents are *dalits*, but they make up 38 per cent of the very poor. A further 11 per cent are *adavasis* (members of tribal groups), but they are even

poorer, making up 48 per cent of the very poor (Meredith 2007, p119).

India's point of change came in 1991, when the country faced a financial crisis. This led to reforms introduced by Manmohan Singh, the finance minister, and now prime minister of India. He liberalised external trade and deregulated the domestic economy, copying Deng's concept of special economic zones. The growth rate accelerated, reaching 8 per cent by 2000. India built on its strength in small and medium-sized manufacturing, backed by highly skilled craftspeople.

Whereas China was the country of choice for mass production, India concentrated on short, highly specialised production runs. More important, India latched on to the boom in new technology in the 1990s. Not only did it scoop the market in call centres and business process outsourcing, by the 2000s taking a 48 per cent share of the world market (Smith 2007b, p132), but it also developed a software industry, centred on the southern city of Bangalore, where Infosys and Wipro are world-class and rapidly growing companies. The software for Apple's highly successful iPod was developed in India (and the product assembled in China) (Meredith 2007, p102) Older industry also started to flourish, led by the long-established conglomerate Tata, which now owns Corus (the ex British Steel) as well as a range of Western companies including Tetley Tea. In 2007 it was rumoured to be preparing a bid for Jaguar and Land Rover. India also had great institutional strengths – the English language, a vibrant democracy, a free press, and universal acceptance of the rule of law. Hutton sees these soft attributes as key. However, like China, India has weaknesses. Its literacy rate lags well behind China, and its physical infrastructure is very weak. Its roads, with a few exceptions, are appalling, and anyone who has experienced Agra airport will know that the same can be said for most of its airports. Each of the 28 Indian states has its own border controls and regulations. Smith describes a lorry journey from Kolkata (Calcutta) to Mumbai (Bombay), a distance of 2,150 kilometres, which took eight days, including 32 hours waiting at border toll booths (Smith2007b, p164).

Like China, India also suffers from endemic corruption. In 2007, Andrew Wileman described an attempt to transport a bull elephant from Kerala to Bangalore in order to take part in a Hindu ceremony at one of the IT companies, Aditi. The 300-mile journey involved the payment of £250 in bribes at every state border to and from Bangalore, because 'elephant transportation papers were not in order'. He also tells the story of the auto-rickshaws in Delhi. Apparently there are 500,000 of these, but only 100,000 official licences. The other 400,000 stay in business by paying regular 'fines' to the traffic police (Wileman 2007).

As a democracy, India is relatively slow to take decisions, and to make major shifts in policy. On the other hand, decisions in India have democratic legitimacy. China can take quick decisions, and tends to be better at taking long-term decisions, as its government is not answerable to an electorate, while decisions in India are shorter-term, and geared to the electoral cycle. As a result, China was better placed to make long-term investments in its education and health programmes, and to steamroller through its infrastructure improvements. Despite its centralised political system, China has been very effective at decentralising economic decision-making. It has given a great deal of economic autonomy to the growth areas of Shanghai, Quangdong and Hong Kong.

China has also been more effective at opening its economy to the West and at encouraging foreign direct investment through a stable exchange rate and low real interest rates. India has gained through the widespread use of English in its higher education system, which has led to the outsourcing of large numbers of service jobs from the West. China has tended to gain from the outsourcing of manufacturing rather than service jobs. This has led to a big increase in Chinese exports, particularly to the United States and Japan.

Both countries clearly have economic systems which are highly effective at generating economic growth. As an authoritarian stare, China has been able to be more single-minded in its pursuit of growth, and as a result has achieved a higher rate of growth. However, there are costs in the Chinese system. As the development economist Amartya Sen has pointed out, no democratic country has experienced a devastating famine, whereas authoritarian states like China have (Steele 2001).

It appears that a combination of authoritarian political control and a decentralised market-run economic system are highly effective at producing economic growth, but with accompanying costs like loss of freedom, economic inequality and social disruption.

However, it is possible to over-hype the success of China (Hilton 2004). It took until 1993 before China's exports were back at the level they reached in 1928, before the Japanese invasion, and despite its vast population, China's GDP in 2000 was only a quarter that of Japan. The dash for growth has also caused enormous environmental degradation. China has 16 of the world's 20 most polluted cities.

Question

Which do you think is more likely to sustain its economic growth in the long term, India or China?

There are three excellent books, all published in 2007, which provide background material for this Seminar Activity. Two are journalistic accounts of the economic rise of India and China. David Smith's *The dragon and the elephant: China, India and the new world order* (2007b) examines the issues from a UK perspective. Robyn Meredith's *The elephant and the dragon: the rise of India and China and what it means for all of us* (2007) covers much the same ground from a US perspective. Will Hutton's *The writing on the wall* (2007) takes a more analytical approach, concentrating on China, and is as much a critique of the West as it is of China.

CHAPTER 5

Regulation

LEARNING OUTCOMES

By the end of this chapter, readers should be able to:

- understand the essential features of the UK legal system, including the sources and types of law and the courts system, including tribunals

- analyse the significance of existing and new regulation for particular sectors and organisations, and discuss the type and nature of responses to regulations

- identify the nature of regulation in respect of contract, consumer and competition law and the implications for stakeholders to whom the law applies

- discuss the effect regulation has on health and safety and employment law, advising on its current strengths and weaknesses.

INTRODUCTION

In March 1984, Arthur Scargill led the National Union of Miners into a national strike to try to improve working conditions in the mines and to prevent a massive programme of pit closures. He dismissed the legislation passed two years earlier requiring a ballot before a strike action could be taken, taking the view that 'bad laws should be ignored', just as the trade union movement had successfully done in 1972 against earlier Tory trade union legislation. In a defining moment of the Thatcher administration, the government brought the full force of the establishment – police, army, public opinion – to restore the 'rule of law', supporting the concept that laws passed in a proper democratic process must be obeyed by individuals and organisations. The view was widely promulgated that 'Societies where the rule of law can be flouted with impunity cannot survive', and it was the almost unanimous support of this view across the United Kingdom that ultimately sealed the miners' fate.

The legal system, then, is at the heart of a democratic society. It sets out the rules within which people and organisations live and do business with each other; it reflects the current views on morality held by the majority of its citizens; it defines the punishments for breaking these rules; it establishes the nature of the contracts between the individual, the organisation and the state whereby the state is paid (through taxation) to protect the interests of all parties in a fair and impartial way. It allows everybody to plan their lives with the fair certainty of foreseeing what actions and behaviour are allowed and what is forbidden.

This chapter provides a general introduction to the structure of UK law, details some of the specific legislation that sets out a level playing field for business and the consumer, indicates the main protection for employees in the workplace, examines how law regulates particular sectors and labour markets, and suggests ways that employers can respond to new legislation. Law is a complex subject, and organisations and individuals regularly call on experts to advise them, so the outline provided in this chapter is primarily to raise awareness of the legal contours.

LEGAL CONTOURS

LEGAL CONCEPTS

There is a clear *division of authority* between the judiciary and the executive, a factor that distinguishes true democracy from a dictatorship. Judges are independent, and once appointed cannot be dismissed, except in extreme cases such as when they are convicted of corruption or another serious offence. If they take decisions the government does not like (and this is increasingly happening with the increased use of judicial review), the government simply has to accept their decisions.

Precedent requires courts to follow decisions laid down in earlier cases where the facts are broadly similar. To give an example, in decisions made on unfair dismissal claims soon after the Industrial Relations Act was passed in 1972, higher courts confirmed the circumstances under which an employee could claim constructive dismissal, including the need for the individual to resign immediately and leave the employment once the incident had occurred. If a claim reaches a tribunal today and the claimant delayed by a few weeks in leaving the employment after the incident occurred, then the tribunal would be required to follow the precedent and throw out the claim.

When lawyers are advising on a case, then, they need to be well read not just in the law itself, but in the way it has been interpreted by the courts as shown in the precedents involved. They need to read the *obiter dicta*, which are the judges' recorded comments justifying their decisions. Faced by precedents which indicate that a case would be unsuccessful, lawyers either advise their clients to withdrawal or try their best to argue that the facts of the case are significantly different so the precedent does not apply.

That is not to say that precedents cannot be changed. One of the duties of the Court of Appeal is to examine precedents argued before them and judge whether such precedents are out of date for changing social times or preserve a system that is clearly unfair. In such cases, they may decide they need to be altered at the margins or completely reversed. A well-known example of reversal was the Walker *v* Northumberland County Council case (see Case Study 5.1).

CASE STUDY 5.1

CHANGING A PRECEDENT

John Walker was a social work manager who returned to work after having had a mental breakdown brought on through an excessive workload. He requested a reduction in his duties and additional resources to allow him to cope with his responsibilities and serve the community. His employer did very little to help him and he subsequently suffered a further extended breakdown which ended his career. Prior to this case, the precedent had been that the employer had a clear duty of care in respect of preventing foreseeable physical illness but not mental illness brought on by stress. The Court of Appeal confirmed that this duty of care should be extended to foreseeable mental illness because there was no logical reason that it should be excluded from the scope of the Health and Safety at Work Act. Walker was awarded £175,000 in damages and this decision established a change in precedent. Consequently, employers have had to give much more careful consideration to issue of foreseeable stress and subsequent mental illness amongst their staff.

Source: Walker v Northumberland County Council 1995 IRLR 35/95.

In serious criminal cases (and surprisingly, civil cases for libel or slander), the final decision is made by a jury – people are judged by their peers. In jury trials, even the judge's advice can be overturned under the belief that it is a matter of whose word can be trusted and a jury of 12 people is the best way to test this.

TYPES OF LAW

The law is divided into two main divisions, civil and criminal law.

Civil law

The ground rules dealing with relationships between individuals and between an individual and an organisation are laid down under civil law. Where one side believes that the law has been broken, it will take the case up in the civil courts and aim to have the wrong righted and/or obtain compensation. The main areas under which civil cases are brought are breach of contract (where it is claimed that one party has broken the terms of a legally enforceable contract) and torts, which are civil wrongs independent of contract, such as negligence, nuisance or defamation (see example).

Example of a tort

Your next door neighbour has allowed a tree to grow so large that parts are overhanging your small garden and take away most of your light. You have asked him civilly to take some action but nothing happens. You therefore bring a case claiming *nuisance.* Before the case comes to court, a gale brings down a large branch which smashes your fence and greenhouse. You therefore add a further claim for *negligence* to the case.

The remedies you can obtain are:

- compensation (damages) – but only to the extent of your proven loses, plus costs you have expended
- specific performance – where the court instructs the plaintiff to carry out an action (see the example)
- injunction – where the court instructs the plaintiff to *not* carry out an action, such as demolishing a listed building.

Example of specific performance

You have successfully bid for a painting at an auction but you learn subsequently that the owner decided to withdraw the painting from sale. You believe you have a valid contract and ask the court to instruct the owner to complete the contract and deliver the painting to you. You have set your heart on obtaining that unique painting and no alternative or compensation would satisfy you.

Criminal law

Here offences (crimes) are defined which society believes need to be punished. The court case is a result of a police investigation and a case brought by the Crown Prosecution Service. Very occasionally, a private prosecution takes place, such as by the parents of the murdered teenager Stephen Lawrence in the 1990s. In general, however, these have a very low success rate and can be stopped by the Attorney General if they are not regarded as in the public interest.

Cases are divided into *indictable offences*, generally serious crimes – such as murder, rape, serious fraud – where conviction can result in imprisonment, and *summary offences* – such as parking offences and petty theft – which are less serious and where conviction brings a fine.

 ACTIVITY

5.1 ORGANISATIONAL CRIMES

In 1994, a small outdoor pursuits company in Dorset was convicted of manslaughter after the death of four teenagers on a canoe trip. Its owner, who was identified as being ultimately responsible for decisions relating to the trip that resulted in the deaths, was subsequently sent to prison. Under what other circumstances can an organisation commit a criminal offence?

FROM WHERE DOES THE LAW ORIGINATE?

We are so used, these days, to a flood of new legislation (statute law as explained in Chapter 4) emerging from Parliament each year that it is a common fallacy to believe that this process is the only source of law. However, there are two other main sources.

Common law

Up until the nineteenth century, most law was 'common', which meant that it had come into effect through judges recognising custom and practice (and common sense), and this was spread around the country by judges on their circuits. These decisions made up the precedents. In most areas today, common law decisions have been incorporated into statute, but there are a number of fundamental common law concepts which remain, such as those relating to the law of contract and employee rights (see later in the chapter). There also remain some more isolated specific rights under common law, such as the grazing rights held by New Forest Commoners.

Codes of practice

Although codes of practice are not technically law, formal codes have a strong influence on decisions taken by the courts. For example, an organisation facing a tribunal claim for unfair dismissal which has not followed closely the ACAS Code on Disciplinary and Grievance Procedures is less likely to make a successful defence. Similarly, an employer facing an equal pay claim should ensure that the Commission for Racial Equality's Code on Equal Pay has been incorporated into its procedures.

It should also be noted that much of the statute law originates from the European Union, whose legislative processes were also set out in Chapter 4.

THE COURTS SYSTEM

In Figure 5.1, the courts system for England and Wales is set out (Scotland has had its own somewhat different system for more than 500 years). Courts are distinguished through their regulation of civil or criminal law, and whether they are courts of first instance or hear appeals, or both.

Civil cases

Claims start in the county court or, if the amount at issue is less than £5,000, the Small Claims division. Speed, accessibility and informality are the keynotes here, with representation frowned upon, and costs normally limited to the value of the summons. The judge acts alone as the arbitrator. The Small Claims Division provides an opportunity for businesses and individuals to claim small debts, and for torts to be examined and resolved. One day it may be resolving the overhanging tree dispute; the next, dealing with a claim from an ex-employee for unpaid overtime. There are around 300 county courts situated in cities and market towns, with judges still going on 'circuits' to try to ensure a degree of consistency, although small claims courts are overseen by a registrar.

Figure 5.1 The court system in England and Wales

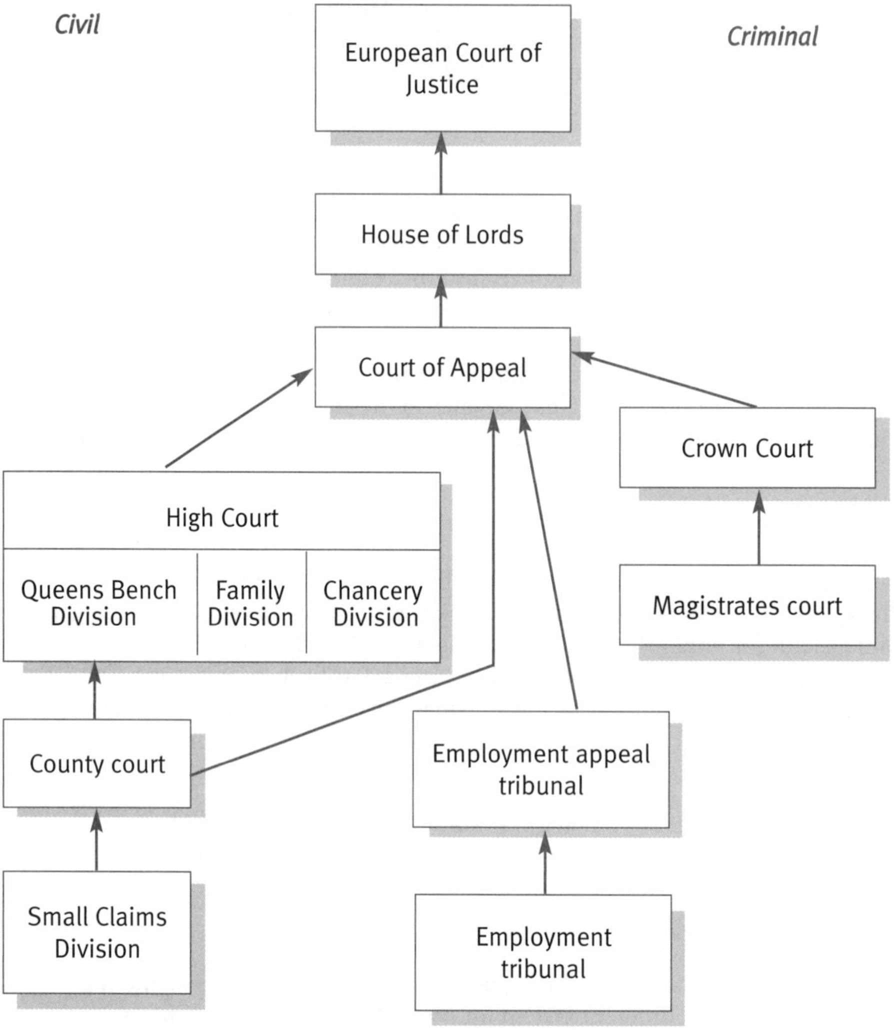

Civil   *Criminal*

```
                    ┌─────────────────────┐
                    │ European Court of   │
                    │      Justice        │
                    └─────────────────────┘
                              ↑
                    ┌─────────────────────┐
                    │   House of Lords    │
                    └─────────────────────┘
                              ↑
                    ┌─────────────────────┐
                    │  Court of Appeal    │
                    └─────────────────────┘
           ↗              ↑    ↑        ↖
  ┌──────────────────────────┐      ┌──────────────┐
  │       High Court         │      │ Crown Court  │
  ├──────────┬───────┬───────┤      └──────────────┘
  │ Queens   │Family │Chancery│            ↑
  │ Bench    │Divis. │Division│     ┌──────────────────┐
  │ Division │       │        │     │ Magistrates court│
  └──────────┴───────┴───────┘      └──────────────────┘
       ↑
  ┌──────────────┐   ┌──────────────────┐
  │ County court │   │ Employment appeal│
  └──────────────┘   │    tribunal      │
       ↑             └──────────────────┘
  ┌──────────────┐            ↑
  │ Small Claims │   ┌──────────────────┐
  │   Division   │   │   Employment     │
  └──────────────┘   │    tribunal      │
                     └──────────────────┘
```

Note: the tribunal route indicates the process for employment law only.

In the county courts, actions for less than £15,000 are heard together with some others up to £50,000 by agreement with the parties, depending on their complexity (although this can vary depending on the nature of the claim). Additional subject areas at the county courts, apart from contract and tort cases, include probate disputes, bankruptcy, undefended divorce, consumer credit issues and some land questions. Around 2.5 million summonses a year are taken out at county courts, but only around 5 to 10 per cent arrive in court and an even smaller percentage are actually defended.

Summonses valued at over £50,000 go directly to the High Court. This has three divisions which deal with cases of first instance and appeals from lesser courts.

The Queens Bench division is the busiest, with jurisdiction over high-value contract and tort cases, and a special commercial court dealing with banking, insurance and other financial services cases. It has an admiralty court to hear cases involving ships and aircraft, while it also hears some appeals from county courts and a comparatively small number of criminal appeals from crown courts. The Family division handles matrimonial cases, including wardship, adoption and custody claims. Finally, the Chancery division, the oldest court of all, has jurisdiction over high-value tax cases, trusts, partnership disputes, patent and copyright actions and land disputes.

Criminal cases

The magistrates courts manage most criminal cases, determining around 98 per cent of all crime. Around half of their caseload of 2 million or so consists of motoring offences. They handle all forms of petty crime, with the maximum penalty they can apply being six months prison sentence, although few prison sentences are awarded. There are special arrangements to handle juvenile cases, and magistrates courts act as a preliminary hearing in serious crime cases, deciding on 'committing' to a Crown Court and agreeing bail/custody arrangements. There are 550 magistrates courts, with 27,000 magistrates on the bench. They are a mixture of stipendiary (paid) officials and unpaid appointees. Stipendiary magistrates can sit alone. It is possible for those accused at a magistrates court to decide to be heard in front of a jury at a Crown Court, usually in the hope that juries convict less often than hardened magistrates. Appeals (there are few) go generally to the Crown Court.

There are close to 100 Crown Courts, the most famous being the Central Criminal Court (Old Bailey). Cases are heard by juries, although the judge has a strong influence through control of the proceedings, interventions to clarify issues and the summing up.

Higher courts

The Court of Appeal hears both criminal and civil court appeals, with three to five judges in attendance and a majority decision prevailing, with each judge's reasons published. Their judgements are extremely influential, much used to clarify the law and to set the ultimate precedent. Cases are sometimes referred to this court when new evidence has come to light that casts doubt on the validity of criminal convictions, cases that may have been heard as long as 20 years or more ago. An appeal to the House of Lords can only be on a legal issue, and the decision is final, except where the case comes under European law, where much of employment law resides. If so, the case is heard by the European Court of Justice which gives a ruling and then refers the case back to the UK court for implementation.

Tribunals

The most well-known tribunals are those in employment areas, such as unfair dismissal and sex, race and disability discrimination. However, there are numerous tribunals set up by statute in other areas. There are rent tribunals, set up to help protect tenants from unscrupulous landlords, social security appeal tribunals, to provide an opportunity for citizens to question decisions made about their right to benefits, such as unemployment and sickness, and various tribunals related to appeals over taxation. They all have the same intention, which is to provide a formal yet accessible process for aggrieved citizens to have their cases heard fairly, impartially and thoroughly by persons not involved in the original decision. The accessibility comes about through, first, some discouragement of legal representation, as with the Small Claims court, by generally not awarding costs; and second, by ensuring that help in the initial stages is provided by the tribunals themselves and by volunteer bodies such as the Citizens' Advice Bureau.

In the employment area, the tribunals are bound by rules of evidence and precedent, but the three-member tribunals are allowed to operate a much more informal and inquisitive approach than the higher courts. Appeals to the employment appeal tribunal and subsequent appeals to higher courts can only be on the basis of law.

Ombudsmen

A final grouping of quasi-legal intent is the sets of Ombudsmen, set up by legislation to investigate complaints of maladministration, mostly in the public arena. There are a number of commissioners (Ombudsmen) in areas such as local government, the National Health Service and Parliament, whose reports have no precise legal standing but put pressure on the bodies concerned to rectify mistakes and improve their services. An example of the cases they deal with is set out in Case Study 5.2.

PARLIAMENTARY OMBUDSMAN REPORT ON PENSION LOSSES

CASE STUDY 5.2

Between 1997 and 2005, 400 private sector pension schemes were closed with outstanding deficits. The main reason for the closures was the demise of the company or its financial inability to continue to contribute to the scheme. The outcome was that 85,000 employees, ex-employees and pensioners did not receive the pensions they had been promised under the scheme. Some, indeed, lost all of their pension entitlement.

In 2005, the Parliamentary Ombudsman was asked to investigate the Department for Work and Pensions (DWP) role in encouraging employees in this debacle. In March 2006, Commissioner Ann Abraham reported that the DWP had been guilty of maladministration. Its official guidance to employees was 'inaccurate, incomplete, unclear and inconsistent'. Much of the criticism was directed at government information leaflets which gave a misleading impression of the security of the schemes. They had not given sufficient warnings of the possibility of scheme closures and loss of pension rights.

The government responded by dismissing the report, pointing out that employees did not rely exclusively on these leaflets as a basis for their financial decisions. They declared that the government could not take on the heavy financial responsibility for the failure of private pension schemes. They were not obliged under legislation to take any further action and would not do so.

Pension campaigners then took the matter to the High Court, and in 2007 they obtained a decision that the government had wrongly rejected the Ombudsman's findings. The court confirmed that the DWP had committed maladministration in its advice on the schemes.

This put additional pressure on the government, which was forced, in April 2007, to make concessions in the form of compensation to many of those who lost out. The government agreed to cover 80 per cent of the losses at a cost of around £2 billion.

LAW OF CONTRACT

Contracts are at the heart of all business and employment activity, and the common law governing their operation goes back further in time than most other law. For centuries, the judges interpreted the law in a way that reflected the 'laissez faire' approach to all business, with the state interfering very little and people in business and employment being left alone to run their affairs. This was partly to preserve the inequality of the 'master and servant' relationship and partly because most business contracts were on a relatively equal basis. To buy a pair of shoes, a customer went to the local cobbler and negotiated a price, a process in which both parties were fairly equally balanced. However, this was to change by the mid-nineteenth century, as the Industrial Revolution and the development of capitalism created large enterprises in commerce and industry which produced many unequal bargaining situations. In the next section, we shall see how the state intervened over the last 100 years by introducing legislation to provide a more balanced situation.

The essence of a contract is to provide a legally binding format to a set of mutual promises. In general, the contract involves one party providing goods or a service and the other paying for them, and a typical organisation will have scores of contracts with suppliers, customers, service providers, intermediaries, staff and contractors. These contracts do not have to be in writing to be legally binding (apart from those related to land), although for clarity and certainty, most of them are confirmed in this way. However, any informal changes that both parties agree to, even if not confirmed in writing, will supersede those written into the contract, as long as one side can produce compelling evidence that such an informal arrangement took place.

Interestingly, there are some very important contracts where the parties have agree that they are not legally binding. These are agreements between employers and trade unions where, by tradition, both sides reserve the right to go back on the deals they make should they choose to do so. This is an interesting reflection on the trust between the parties under British employment relations.

There are six main elements in any contract:

- Offer and unconditional acceptance. For each contract, the offer must state all the terms, be communicated effectively, and must be clear and unambiguous. It is different from what is known as an 'invitation to treat'. When shops first started putting prices in their shop windows, the courts were asked to intervene to distinguish between what appeared to be a legal 'offer' and what was merely an invitation to people to come into the shop and start negotiating. They decided that the prices marked on goods in the shop window or in advertisements are not 'offers' (or even 'special offers'), and a potential customer cannot go into the shop and demand the legal right to buy the goods at the prices shown. It needs the shopkeeper's acceptance to make this a contract.

Acceptance must be unconditional, and within the stipulated (or reasonable) time. An offer can be withdrawn at any time prior to acceptance. If the acceptance stipulates conditions, then this becomes a counter offer. If both parties act as if they are working under an agreement, then a contract is deemed to have been agreed.

An area that still provides some difficulties with the courts is that of standard terms and conditions. One business will ask for tenders for providing goods (an invitation to treat). Another company will respond, making an offer on documentation which has its standard terms and conditions of trading printed on the back. The first company then accepts the offer on documentation with its own standard terms and conditions on the back. If the terms differ, it could be held to be a counter offer, of course. If there is a dispute over some small detail which differs between the companies, the courts have tended to decide that the last set of documentation applies, but will be influenced by the actions of the parties and any evidence that can be offered to support the view that a particular term applied. It still does lead to problems, however, which are regularly resolved by an arbitration service.

- Genuine agreement. Each party must have the same understanding of what makes up the contract, and there must be no misrepresentation. For example, if the car seller knowingly indicates a mileage that is not genuine, then the contract will be void and the buyer can claim damages. What often needs to be clarified under this heading is the distinction between 'representations' ('I think this is a most reliable motor') and the actual terms of the contract (the tyres are three months old). A buyer acting on representations has no redress. Contracts must not be entered into under duress or undue influence, including drink or drugs. If this is the case, the contract can be voided.

- Capacity to contract. The parties must have the ability to make a contract, so minors are excluded, except for necessities (such as sweets and bus journeys!) but not including larger items. The same applies to those of an unsound mind. An interesting area is that it can be assumed that employees of an organisation who appear to have the authority to contract do in fact have this authority. This is to avoid the situation where an organisation can go back on a contract it subsequently decides is not in its favour.

- An intention to create legal relations. In general, legal relations between close relatives are rarely upheld by the courts, unless there is clear evidence to the contrary. The opposite applies to all business relationships, where the presumption is that there is an intention present.

- Legal purposes. The contract must be for purposes that are in conformity with the law. A contract is void if, for example, payment is made as 'cash in hand' where national insurance should be paid or the contract is set up purely to evade taxation.

- Consideration. There must be some consideration, which is normally money, although it can be any right or benefit which can be held to be of monetary value either currently or in the future, and contracts of barter are legal (ie international contracts of grain in exchange for oil). Without consideration, as in an agreement to paint the house of a friend for nothing, there can be no enforceable contract. In the voluntary world, this still provides some problems of course. The payment must refer to the future and not to some past payments or obligations. Finally, the payment does not have to be adequate, fair or reasonable – that is up to the parties concerned.

A contract of employment arises directly out of contract law. A job must be offered and unconditionally accepted; there must be genuine agreement with no misunderstanding of the essential terms and conditions, such as the need to work night shifts or the type of company car provided; the contract must be legal, with no illegal activities such as ' cash-in-hand'; there must be consideration, a wage or salary, as voluntary work is not enforceable. Only those over 13 can have an employment contract, with strict regulations relating to the employment of those under 18. Interestingly, the courts recognise the employment of wives and husbands as long as there is clear evidence of a contract existing.

There are more details on employment law on pages 159 to 167.

REGULATING BUSINESS AND PROTECTING THE CONSUMER

On a hot summer's day in 1930, a young man bought a bottle of ginger beer for his lady friend at the end of a walk. She gratefully drank up, but as she finished the opaque bottle, the remains of a decomposed snail appeared. Not surprisingly, she became very ill. On recovering, she wanted recompense for her unhappy experience, but she could not sue the shopkeeper because she had no contract with him, nor could she sue her boyfriend because there was no consideration – the bottle was a gift. Nor did she have a contract with the manufacturer. However, a lengthy legal case was commenced which, two years later, appeared at the House of Lords (Donaghue v Stevenson) where the landmark decision was reached that manufacturers can be guilty of the tort of negligence.

Prior to the case, 'caveat emptor' (let the buyer beware) applied in all consumer purchases, but Donaghue v Stevenson established that manufacturers have a duty of care to their customers not to be negligent and to avoid any acts or omissions which can be reasonably foreseen as likely to kill or injure the consumer or a member of the public, or to damage property. Subsequent cases have clarified guidelines, such as drug manufacturers having a greater duty of care than newspaper publishers because the consequences of faulty goods are far more serious.

Donaghue *v* Stevenson was an important case, and the outcome was a distinct improvement in the degree of protection for consumers. By the late 1960s, however, governments started to take a more supportive view for the consumer. There were a number of reasons for this:

- The growth of huge multinational corporations made it much more difficult for the view to be held that a contract was made between equal partners.

- Mergers and acquisitions were growing to the stage that some companies had control of substantial sectors of the marketplace and could dictate terms.

- The growth in practice of large organisations inserting 'small print' into contracts, where special conditions were inserted and liabilities excluded to the detriment even of the observant consumer.

- Pressure had developed from consumer organisations, such as *Which?* magazine, which helped develop consumer awareness of shady practices, and politicians appreciated they needed to take notice of this pressure.

- Britain decided to join the European Union in the early 1970s and some legislation was required to bring the United Kingdom into line with European law.

- Trading practices were changing in line with technological and monetary developments and there were gaps in the law in these areas.

The legislation can be divided into the *macro* area, to control and enhance competition generally, and the *micro* area, where specific unfair business practices are made illegal.

CONTROLLING AND ENHANCING COMPETITION

Fair Trading Act 1973

It was considered essential that a watchdog with wide powers of investigation should exist to champion the consumer interest and provide independent advice to the government. The Office of Fair Trading (OFT) took this role, and its powers have been increased with subsequent legislation, including the Competition Act 1998 and the Enterprise Act 2002. The Director-General of Free Trading has responsibility to investigate commercial activities which may appear to be against the interests of consumers and advise the government if it believes action is necessary. The scope of activities investigated is wide, covering all sectors, businesses large and small, and dealing with contract terms, selling methods, packaging and promotion. Although its powers have limits, the fact that an investigation can take place and that it can seek orders from the government to stop certain activities are, in practice, strong deterrents, and have often changed the way business is carried out. In its early days, it investigated pyramid selling and ensured its abolition.

Restrictive Trade Practices Act 1976/Competition Act 1998

This legislation was passed to prevent the use of monopoly power by either individual companies or groups of companies colluding. A restrictive practice is defined as collusion on prices, terms of supply, manufacturing processes, and any activity that is likely to have the effect of restricting, distorting or preventing competition. The OFT has the right to enter premises and demand documents, and to enforce restrictions on movement or destruction of evidence. If an organisation refuses to co-operate, then it can be penalised to the extent of 10 per cent of turnover.

When a practice is found to exist, it can only be successfully justified by the argument that it:

- protects the public from injury
- is a counterweight to another monopoly (such as in negotiations with the Royal Mail)
- provides extensive benefits to exports.

Examples of investigations in recent years include extended warranties (see Case Study 5.3), operation of small pharmacies and the major chains, private dentistry, consumer IT services and estate agencies. The OFT has also investigated some business methods, including doorstop selling and public sector procurement. A number of investigations were carried out in the 1980s and 1990s regarding price-fixing by colluding cement companies (see Chapter 2 for a discussion of the economic aspects of collusion), which eventually resulted in the cartel being broken up and cement prices being substantially reduced.

 OFT REPORT ON EXTENDED WARRANTIES

CASE STUDY 5.3

In 2002, the OFT carries out an investigation into the £500 million market in extended warranties, chiefly for electrical goods, and referred the matter to the Competition Commission to decide on action. It found that the bulk of warranties were purchased at the point of sale of the goods. They could add 50 per cent to the price of the product and were generally poor value. Bad practice reported included:

- sales staff emphasising the risk of product failure

- customers being told that independent repairs were difficult to obtain and were expensive

- consumers not being encouraged to shop around.

It was also reported that self-regulation had not worked and that the large electrical retailers were exploiting their monopoly situation to the detriment of consumers.

Source: OFT website 2002.

The OFT reports to the government, which can decide to refer the matter to the Competition Commission for either a decision or, in the case of an impending merger where the organisation will have 25 per cent or more of the market, a fuller enquiry to decide whether the merger is in the public interest and under what terms the merger would be allowed to progress. Full-scale investigations by the Commission in recent years have included one into the position of Nestlé (which found that it did not have excessive monopolistic power on coffee prices), video games (which recommended the abolition of licence controls) and UK car prices (which found that the exclusive dealership system operated against the public interest).

Investigations of potential wrongdoing, or the threat of referral to the OFT or the Competition Commission, have a huge impact on organisations and their future planning of possible mergers. A raid by the OFT on premises can cause the company's share price to drop 10 per cent, and many mergers have been decided by the policy of the Competition Commission.

 ACTIVITY

5.2 DOORSTEP SELLING

The OFT carried out a survey of doorstep selling in response to complaints from the Citizens Advice Bureau. Its report in 2004 recommended that legislation needed to be updated to combat the psychological tactics employed by many salespeople.

The study into the practice of selling goods and services on the doorstep and in the home, worth at least £2.4 billion a year, found that a range of sales tactics and influencing techniques can lead consumers to make inappropriate purchases which they later regret. This highlights a gap in consumer protection. The current legislation gives consumers who are cold-called a seven-day period in which to cancel a contract. This protection does not apply to consumers who asked for the visit.

Buying in the home provides a unique setting for a business transaction – salespeople effectively have a captive audience. Nearly 40 per cent of consumers have bought goods or services in the home. While 70 per cent of

those were satisfied, a significant minority of 30 per cent experienced problems: at least 15,000 complaints a year are made to trading standards departments regarding doorstep sales. Most respondents to the OFT's consumer survey said they felt buying in the home was more pressurised than other settings.

The OFT recommended that the government should extend the legislation to give cancellation rights to solicited visits as well as unsolicited. The OFT also proposed to run a consumer education campaign in conjunction with interested groups to raise awareness of consumers' rights and alert them to the psychological techniques used and how to combat them.

Look up the Office of Fair Trading's website and examine two more of its recent investigations, including the remit to the OFT, the decisions it has made and the justification for those decisions.

CONSUMER PROTECTION

Economic theory would argue that rational behaviour by consumers makes their protection unnecessary. Poor-performing products should not survive and consumers should simply walk away from poor service. To a large extent that it is true, but consumers are not always in a position to behave rationally. They may not have sufficient information about the product (hence the need for a product description on the label), they may not have a choice of products if an uncontrolled monopoly exists, and they may not be able to challenge a large and unscrupulous supplier. So a whole raft of legislation has been passed in recent years covering all business–consumer relationships and attempting to tighten up legal loopholes. Much of the legislation encoded the common law in place and then extended it. Here is a brief summary of the key features.

Trade Descriptions Act 1968/Consumer Protection Act 1987

These two Acts protect against traders who deliberately give false descriptions about the price, quality and nature of service. These are criminal offences and can result in fines and even imprisonment for repeated offences. The act is policed by local government trading standard officials, who, incidentally, also assist the OFT in gathering information. Examples of cases include:

- advertisements showing massive price reductions when the prices had only been increased the day before (regulations now state that goods must have been at the pre-reduction price for 28 continuous days during the previous six months)

- cars being advertised with 'one owner' which was a leasing company that had leased the car out for long periods to five different drivers

- prices being advertised net, with no indication that VAT is to be added.

 MISLEADING REDUCTIONS

CASE STUDY 5.4

MFI was fined £18,000 in 1993 by magistrates in Enfield, North London, for giving out false information on nine counts. It advertised 'massive reductions' and '30% off' furniture suites when in fact the prices had been the same for the previous six months, with a number of suites actually having gone up in price at the time of advertising.

The Consumer Protection Act also places strict (but not absolute) liability on suppliers for damage and death/injury caused by defects in their products. There is no need to prove negligence or a contractual relationship, but there is a defence that the state of scientific and technical knowledge at the time the product was supplied was not sufficiently advanced for the defect to be recognised (the 'state of the act' defence).

Unfair Contract Terms Act 1977

Introduced to prevent 'small print' removing consumers' rights, generally without their knowledge, this Act has two parts. First, the seller cannot remove the liability for death or injury through negligence under any circumstances. Second, a trader cannot enforce a contract term that the courts hold to be unfair. For example, a coach company advertised a tour by luxury coach with videos, toilet, etc but added in the small print that it reserved the right to substitute a coach of inferior quality. The courts held this to be unfair as it gave too much leeway to the coach company, and most customers would not have picked up this particular item among the small print. The claimant was awarded compensation. Most decisions in this area are now dealt with by the OFT through an 'informal undertaking' agreed with the company, and an 2007 example of this is set out in Case Study 5.5.

CASE STUDY 5.5

UNFAIR CONTRACT TERMS – CARPETRIGHT PLC

Carpetright had a series of clauses in its contracts which the OFT considered unfair. These included provisions that:

- all delivery dates were not legally binding

- time was not an essence of the contract

- the fitter, not the company, was responsible for any liability arising from the work carried out

- liability was excluded if the consumer did not inform the company of nature of the existing floor surface

- gave the right to charge for cancellation of an order without limit.

After consultations between the two parties, these were removed or altered by the company.

Source: OFT website 2007.

A number of well-publicised cases and the constant vigilance of consumer societies and other pressure groups have resulted in much greater honesty in communicating the real (and generally reasonable) contract terms by suppliers since this Act was passed.

Sale of Goods Act 1979/ Supply of Goods and Services Act 1982

These Acts enable dissatisfied customers to take civil action against suppliers. The Acts require that:

- goods and services must match the description given
- they must be of merchantable quality – in appearance, finish and durability
- they must be fit for the purpose

- services provided must be carried out with reasonable skill and within a reasonable time.

As the Acts have been interpreted, the issue of reasonableness is key. A very cheap pair of canvas shoes is fit for the purpose if it lasts six months, while a pair of expensive, hand-made leathers would not be fit if it wore out after four years' light wear. In essence, it has been for the court to decide what are the bounds of reasonableness, and we shall see this again in the field of employment law.

If the product fails to meet the tests under the Acts, consumers have the remedy of the right to their money back, or to receive a credit note, or for the goods to be replaced free of charge. Alternatively the consumer can take the goods at a reduced price.

Consumer Credit Act 1974

This was introduced following the boom in hire purchase and credit agreements in the 1960s and 1970s which led to high-pressure selling, especially in people's homes, and high rates of interest. The Act took two main directions. First, it aimed to clean up the industry by enforcing licensing of lenders for all credit activities, including credit cards. The licensing involves an inspection regime and a requirement for effective staff training and proper funding of the business.

The second direction was to ensure that contracts were not oppressive. All credit contracts and all contracts signed outside business premises have a seven-day 'cooling-off' period where the consumer can cancel without loss to either party. The terms of the credit can be altered by the courts if they regard the rate of interest as excessive. The consumer has the right to full details of the agreement before signing, including the annual rate of charge (calculated by means of the OFT current formula), the full cost of the loan, the debtors' right to pay the loan off early and the terms under which they can do so. The Act does not apply to loans over an upper limit, currently £25,000, and only applies to consumer credit, not corporate credit.

Additional EU-wide consumer protection has been introduced for ordering on the web (Electronic Commerce Regulations 2002) and mail order (Consumer Protection (Distance Selling) Regulations 2000). On pages 177 to 182 we look in more detail at the effects these laws and additional regulations have in specific sectors and industries.

EMPLOYMENT LAW

The regulation of employment relationships has changed out of all recognition over the last 40 years. Originating from the individual 'master–servant' contract, the fundamental inequality of the parties to the employment relationship became clear by the mid-nineteenth century, and a political party (the Labour Party) was set up essentially with the aim of rectifying these inequalities through legislation by establishing employee rights and removing legal restraints on collective bargaining. It was clear that there was a major difference between a conflict over an employment contract, which can lead to unemployment and abject poverty, and one over buying a pair of shoes. Moreover, the evidence of unscrupulous use of dominant employer power was widespread.

Although much progress was made in these areas in the early twentieth century, especially in the collective bargaining field, the stimulus to enacting more radical and extensive employee protection has come from the European Union. At the same time, the political consensus in recent times has been that the rights granted to trade unions in the collective bargaining field went too far, and they were reined in by Conservative governments in the period between 1980 and 1992.

SOURCES OF THE EMPLOYMENT CONTRACT

The terms of an employment contract come from a surprising number of sources. It does not comprise just the *express terms*, which are those specifically included in the contract (usually set out in the offer letter) such as salary, notice and holiday entitlement. Terms from other sources are of equal importance:

- There are a number of *implied terms*, originating from common law. These include the duty of the employee to co-operate with the employer in such areas as reasonable changes to the job, exercise due care in looking after the employer's goods and property, and show loyalty demonstrated by not disclosing confidential information. The employer also has duties, such as to exercise due care over the employee's health, safety and well-being (see pages 168–169ff), to provide work, indemnify the employee if he or she incurs loss, expense or liability in carrying out the employer's instruction, and to pay wages on time and correctly.

- Many contracts incorporate *collective terms*, negotiated between the employer(s) and union(s) at either a local or national level. These may deal with issues such as overtime payment, holidays and disciplinary procedures.

- Contract terms are also incorporated through the *employee handbook* which sets out rules and policies determined by the employer to which the employee must sign up.

- Many more unwritten contract terms reflect *employment laws* covering employee rights and benefits (see below).

An additional complication is that the *contract terms do not need to be written down*. Rules relating to, say, employees swapping shifts, which have operated informally for some years (ie through custom and practice) with the full knowledge of management, become part of the contract. In claims for unfair dismissal, the tribunal is very keen to establish whether terms written into contracts are those that actually operate in practice. For example, if an employee is dismissed for fighting (as clearly laid out in the employee handbook) but it comes to light that the last two occasions when a similar incident occurred, the employees were merely warned, then the tribunal can take the view that custom and practice is that dismissal is not the normal punishment under the contract.

That is not to say contractual terms cannot be changed by either party. An individual employee can request changes to his or her holiday arrangements which are different to the standard contractual terms. Alternatively changes can be negotiated on a collective basis, usually through unions but sometimes through a works council. An employer can change shift arrangements and introduce different work practices and systems. In doing so, it should consult with the workforce, be able to justify the changes for business reasons and ensure they are published widely. It does not need to get every individual's signed agreement to the changes. An employee who continues to work under the changed conditions is deemed to have accepted the changed contract.

A further complication is differentiating between the normal employee contract, called a *contract of service*, and the contract for the self-employed, who work under a *contract for services*. The legal implications are great, in that a different tax regime applies (hence considerable interest by HM Revenue & Customs in this area), and the self-employed have none of the rights and benefits detailed below. Legal tussles have occurred in areas such as commission-only salespeople and those providing occasional but regular services, such as consultants. Although a complex area, the courts examine the degree of control and the nature of exclusivity of contract, which can sometimes overcome the apparent clarity of the payment and tax arrangements.

Under the Employment Rights Act 1996, employers are required to give to each employee within two months a long statement of certain contract terms under 16 headings, which includes details such as the date that continuous employment started, hours of work and holiday entitlement. This is called the 'principal statement' but, to repeat, it is not the actual contract of employment.

EMPLOYEE RIGHTS

The bulk of employment law since the 1970s has been enacted to improve the minimum level of benefits for employees and to protect them from potential employer abuse. There was some earlier legislation in this area, such as the prohibition of child labour and the nine-hour working day in the coal mines from the nineteenth century, but the recent legislation has taken the process much further and allowed employees to benefit extensively from the changes.

Employee protection has been enhanced in the following areas.

Protection from discrimination

Since the 1970s, groups seen as vulnerable in the employment field because of well-evidenced discrimination, harassment and bullying have been given legal protection. The various Acts make it unlawful to discriminate on the grounds of sex, ethnic origin, disability, age or religion. Discrimination has taken three forms:

- Direct discrimination. Examples here are an advertisement for a 'Girl Friday' and the use of different criteria for men and women for selection for promotion. In the case of race discrimination, an example is an employer indicating to a recruitment agency that it does not want black casual workers.

An employer might turn down a deaf or partially sighted applicant specifically because of this disability. In each case, an individual or group is treated less favourably than another on the grounds of sex, race or disability. The employer has no defence even if it genuinely believes what it is doing is right. The motives are irrelevant.

- Indirect discrimination. This occurs where the employer treats all applicants or employees the same but a practice, condition or policy adversely affects one sex or race more than another, or it affects the disabled more than the able-bodied, or the elderly more than the young. The way it normally adversely affects that group is because the proportion of people from a particular group able to meet the condition or policy is considerably smaller. Moreover, the employer cannot objectively justify the practice, policy or condition. If the employer cannot convince the tribunal that the defence is genuine and substantial, then the employer will lose the case. Tribunal cases have included:

  - a requirement restricting applicants geographically by residence to a specific area, which discriminated against ethnic minorities, whose representation in that area was slight
  - recruiting only through word of mouth on an employment site dominated by white males
  - promoting internally when the work force was unbalanced.

  The Equal Pay Act (1970) prohibits discrimination in pay and benefits between men and women, where work is 'like' or rated as similar under a job evaluation scheme. In addition, an employee can claim that his or her work is of 'equal value' to that of another employee of the opposite sex.

- Harassment and bullying. Described as 'unwanted behaviour which a person finds intimidating, upsetting, embarrassing, humiliating or offensive', the courts have increasingly punished harassment and bullying, using both the concept of an employer's duty of care and discrimination legislation, supported by the EU Equal Treatment Directive (amended in 2000). This reflects the changing social attitudes in society where a predominately male, white culture in workplaces, where power may be exercised over staff in a vulnerable position, is no longer acceptable in a modern state. It has been accepted by the courts that the judgement whether behaviour is acceptable or not comes from the subject(s) of the harassment. There can be additional compensation awarded for 'loss of feelings'.

No service requirement is necessary in any area of discrimination. Protection applies from day one of employment.

Protection from unfair dismissal

Since 1972, employees with at least one year's service have been protected from arbitrary and unfair dismissal. To successfully defend a claim, the employer has to show that it had justifiable reason for dismissing the employee (usually based on poor performance, conduct or redundancy), and that it carried out the dismissal using the correct procedures. If it fails, the tribunal awards compensation up to a maximum of £63,000 (2008), and occasionally can order the employer to reinstate the employee.

ACAS has provided codes of practices in dealing with dismissal and redundancies which organisations need to observe to defend claims successfully. For example, where the offences are deemed to be misdemeanours (such as timekeeping, attendance, poor performance), warnings are required, whereas with gross misconduct (for example theft or violence), instant dismissal is permitted. Employees' rights must be observed, including a fair hearing, a colleague to help support their case and a fair appeal procedure.

The same protection is also afforded against dismissal as a result of pregnancy or for being a union activist (see Case Study 5.6).

CASE STUDY 5.6

DISMISSAL BECAUSE OF PREGNANCY

Hildreth, a finance manager, endured a campaign of harassment, intimidation, embarrassment and verbal abuse by the company owners after she told them she was pregnant. They indicated strongly that they would not want to continue to employ her in a pregnant state. Her position became so difficult that she resigned and successfully claimed constructive dismissal, receiving £8,000 in compensation.

Case: Hildreth v Perdu Bars EAT 2007.

Protection from working excessive hours

Arising from a EU directive and essentially a health and safety measure, the Working Time Regulations 1998 have had a controversial history. They have established that employees cannot be forced to work in excess of 48 hours a week, averaged over 17 weeks. Employees should have 11 consecutive hours of rest in any 24-hour period and a 24-hour rest in every seven-day period, plus a 20-minute break if the shift exceeds six hours. The regulations also insist on the provision of 24 days holiday.

The controversial aspect is that employers and employees can agree to 'opt out' of the regulations so that they often apply as a voluntary measure. How 'voluntary' they are and whether the opt-out should remain is discussed later.

Protection when being transferred

The Transfer of Undertakings (Protection of Employment) Regulations 1981 (known as TUPE) were introduced as a result of the EU Acquired Rights Directive. The philosophy here is that employees need to be protected when their organisation is sold to or merged with another organisation, or they are outsourced with their work. Prior to these regulations, employees' terms could be altered fundamentally and unilaterally, with the employees having only the choice of accepting the altered terms or leaving the job.

Under the regulations, all employment terms and conditions are protected (except pensions) and prior service is recognised. This does not stop the new employer having the right to change terms at a later date, but the right is limited by statute. Full consultation must take place with the employees being transferred.

Protection of deductions from pay

Under the Employment Rights Act 1996, employees have the right of an itemised pay statement and deductions can only be made with prior authorisation from the employee in writing.

BENEFITS

Table 5.1 provides a summary of the minimum benefits introduced through legislation.

CASE STUDY 5.7

THE RIGHT TO RETURN TO THE SAME JOB

Blundell, a primary school teacher, was allocated a different class on her return from maternity leave. She claimed she should have returned to teach the same class in the same room. The employment appeals tribunal held her job was to teach at the school, not to teach the same class. The terms and conditions of the job gave the school head discretion in allocating staff, and although staff could indicate a preference, they could not insist on a particular class. The school also pointed out that staff were rotated to different classes and the change in Blundell's class was because of this rotation. But the school lost on its procedure. It did not consult her because she was away on maternity leave (all other staff were consulted) and this was held to be sex discrimination.

Case: Blundell v St Andrew's Catholic Primary School UKEAT/0329/06.

REGULATION OF CONTRACTS THROUGH COLLECTIVE BARGAINING

In the nineteenth century, legislation was put in place to stamp out the infant trade unions which were attempting to interfere with the employment contract. Over the last 200 years the pendulum has swung, firstly to provide a legal framework for union immunity so union activities are protected in tort, and then back the other way under Thatcherite reforms, where tight restrictions on this immunity were introduced to protect employers from arbitrary union power.

Under a variety of Acts in the period 1980–95, legal immunity is only available for unions in leading their members to break their contracts through strikes or other industrial actions when they:

- hold a secret ballot before action is taken (with strict requirements for notifying the employer, how the ballot should be carried out and who is entitled to vote)

- only take action against their own employer (so-called secondary action against suppliers or customers is not protected)

Table 5.1 Employee benefits introduced through legislation

Minimum benefit	Legislation	Summary of key details
Minimum wage	National Minimum Wage Act 1998	Provides low minimum (£5.52 for employees age 22 and over in 2007), includes bonuses and tips with lower rates for employees under 22. Aims to eradicate exploitative pay in vulnerable sectors, such as home workers and hospitality.
Holidays	Working Time (Amendment) Regulations 2007	Minimum entitlement, including public holidays, is 24 days, rising to 28 days from 1 April 2009.
Maternity pay	Employment Rights Act, 1996 amended by Employment act 2002	Payable by employers for 39 weeks. Six months qualifying period paid at 90 per cent of average earnings for six weeks then £113 per week (January 2008) for remaining 20 weeks.
Ante-natal care	As above	Right to paid time off during working hours for all ante-natal care and treatment.
Maternity leave	As above	On top of paid maternity leave, an additional 26 weeks unpaid maternity leave can be taken, with the right to the same job back upon return (see Case Study 5.7).
Paternity leave and pay	Employment Act 2002	Six months qualifying period. Applicable to father of child, mother's husband or partner who is expected to have some responsibility for the upbringing of a child. Paid for two weeks at £113 per week (January 2008).
Adoption leave	Employment Act 2002	One of the parents can take up to 26 weeks unpaid leave when an adoption takes place. Six months qualifying service.
Parental leave	Maternity and parental leave Regulations 1999	Parents with children under 5 (or disabled children under 18) can take up to 13 weeks unpaid leave with the right to return to the same job. One year qualifying service.
Time off for dependants	Employment Rights Act 1996	Reasonable unpaid time can be taken off to provide assistance when a dependant dies, falls ill, gives birth or is injured/assaulted, or any school problems or results from disruption to existing care arrangements. It is not applicable simply to provide normal care on a regular basis and only applies for an immediate crisis. In Qua v John Ford Morrison Solicitors, EAT confirmed a fair dismissal when Qua took 17 different days to look after her child who had medical problems.

continued overleaf

Table 5.1 continued

Minimum benefit	Legislation	Summary of key details
Flexible working	Employment Act 2002/Employment Rights Act 1996 Work and Families Act 2006	Provides the right of a parent of a child under 6 (18 if disabled) to apply for change in working arrangements, including to work flexibly in order to care for the child. Employer can refuse on the basis of burden of additional costs, detrimental effect on ability to meet customer demand or quality of service, disruption of staff/department. Six months qualifying period. These rights were extended in 2007 to employees responsible for caring for adults.
Time off for public duties	Employment Rights Act 1996	Reasonable unpaid time can be taken off relating to work as a member of a local authority, health authority or similar.
Time off for trade union duties	TULRCA 1992	Officials of independent trade unions have right to time off with pay during working hours to carry out reasonable and relevant trade union duties and to undertake training, as specified by ACAS Code of Practice.
Statutory Sick Pay (SSP)	Social Security Contributions and Benefits Act 1992/Statutory Sick Pay Act 1994	Employers are responsible for payment of SSP for up to 28 weeks of sickness/injury in any single period of entitlement.
Redundancy consultation, time off and pay	TULRCA 1992	Consultation with employees/ representatives must take place 90 days before redundancies take effect if 100 or more employees are redundant (30 days if between 20 and 99 employees) and adequate information must be provided by employer. Redundancy pay entitlement at one week's pay (1.5 weeks at age 41 and over, 0.5 from 18 to 21) for each year of service, up to 20 years. The maximum weeks' pay is £310 at Jan 2008. Reasonable time off with pay must be given to look for alternative work.

Notes
These benefits are correct at the time of writing but are subject to amendment both in terms of the pay arrangements and in other details.
These are minimum benefits and employers can (and do) improve them by granting pay where there is no entitlement under the legislation, increasing the rates or enhancing the terms and conditions.

- carry out picketing only at their own place of work and in very small numbers (to prevent the dangerous and oppressive mass picketing which took place during the 1984 miners strike)

- do not insist on a 'closed shop' – employees can join or not join a union as they wish

- ensure they elect their full-time officials on a regular basis under strict governance and follow their own rules on disciplining and expelling members.

The social aspects of this highly influential legislation are discussed in Chapter 7.

Since the 1997 election of a Labour government, the pendulum has swung back somewhat towards improving the regulation of relationships with the workforce, chiefly through organised labour. First, the statutory recognition procedures in the 1999 Employment Relations Act have served to support union members who wish to negotiate formally in the workplace (see Activity 5.4). Second, the European-initiated Information and Consultation Regulations 2004 gave rights to employees to be informed and consulted about the business for whom they work. Third, the requirement for proper grievance and disciplinary procedures to be in place and operating fairly in all organisations was set out in the Employment Act 2002 (Dispute Resolution) Regulations 2004.

However, not all attempts at legislation in this field obtain the desired result. The main intention behind the Dispute Resolution Regulations of 2004 was to cut down on tribunal claims by encouraging employers to set up and follow appropriate procedures and insisting that employees exercised their rights to hearing and appeals under such procedures. Either side would be penalised when it did not follow the procedures. However, after three years of operations, the number of unfair dismissal claims has actually increased, chiefly as a result of the number of disputes over the nature and operation of such internal procedures and the legal wrangles associated with such disputes. Cases have taken longer to settle, and the whole process was reviewed in 2007, a process that led to the regulations being abandoned.

 ACTIVITY

5.4 UNION RECOGNITION

An application was made to the Central Arbitration Committee (CAC) in 2004 by the Amicus union for the right to carry out a recognition ballot for manual staff at Japan Airlines. The employer had provided a number of reasons that this should not take place, concerned mostly with the nature of the bargaining unit requested. The union claimed that 110 out of the 210 manual employees were already union members. CAC carried out an investigation. It found only 96 members out of 229 total staff, but it approved the bargaining unit in 2005 and gave the right for the union to carry out a recognition ballot.

Look up the website for the CAC and examine a further two of the decisions it has taken recently, including the parties involved, the background to the dispute over recognition and the justification for the decision.

REGULATING HEALTH AND SAFETY

INTRODUCTION

Regulation of health and safety in the United Kingdom is very extensive, with over 100 current pieces of legislation. Although there has been a steady decline in the number of deaths and serious accidents over the past decades, over 200 people are killed in accidents at work each year, including nearly 100 members of the public. Not only is this a huge waste of human resources, it is very costly for the economy. The main aim of the regulation, therefore, is to reduce the number of accidents and resultant ill-health and to ensure that a safety-conscious culture becomes widespread so that businesses can operate more efficiently.

This section begins with an introduction to the main legislation, examines how it is enforced and considers the important role of human resources in ensuring initiatives are taken and the law is followed so that all employees work in a safe environment.

HEALTH AND SAFETY AT WORK ACT 1974 (HASAWA)

This influential legislation, born of general consensus between the political parties, is essentially an 'enabling' Act, with wide-ranging, if imprecise, provisions which require interpretation by the courts or putting into effect through Regulations sanctioned by Parliament.

The main aim of the legislation was to provide a comprehensive cover for all employees, protect all personnel on site and impose criminal liability to ensure compliance. At the same time it was important to encourage self-regulation through developing codes of conduct and emphasising personal responsibility from everybody involved – managers, employees, subcontractors and designers.

Duties on employers

The Act lays down a fundamental *duty of care* towards the health, safety and welfare of all employees which is the starting point of all considerations, as illustrated by Case Study 5.8.

Section 2 sets out the general duties on employers, which cover:

- the provision of systems of work, equipment and a workplace that are all safe
- arrangements for the use, handling, storage and transport of articles and substances that are all safe
- adequate and necessary information, supervision training and instruction to ensure effective employee safety
- ensuring there are safe means of getting into and out of premises
- adequate welfare provision.

The duties also extend to subcontractors working on the premises and to members of the public. Throughout this section of the Act, the words 'as far as is reasonably practicable' are mentioned for each clause. This limits the absolute

HICKSON AND WELSH

In 1992, five workers were killed at the chemical company Hickson and Welsh, in Castleford, West Yorkshire. The accident followed the first cleaning in 30 years of the sludge from a tank of volatile mononitroluene (MNT). The job had not been properly assessed for risk and was left to a junior team leader who had only recently returned to the MNT section. Incorrect cleaning tools were used, a monitoring thermometer was inadequate, the sludge content had not been analysed and the whole approach had been 'casual'. During the cleaning operation, a fireball suddenly burst from the tank, torching a frail control cabin next door and leaving the factory's main office block with shattered windows and burnt-out rooms.

The company was fined £250,000 with £150,000 costs in the High Court for breaches of its safety duties and for not providing a safe system of work. The managing director of the plant, the operations director and manager all left the company shortly after the accident.

Source: Wainwright (1994).

responsibility of employers and allows them to achieve a balance between the assessed risk of an unsafe practice and the cost of avoiding that risk. Employers each day need to consider issues such as replacement of older, potentially dangerous machines, reducing noise levels and improving ventilation, balancing the cost and practicality against the safety requirements. These may be finely judged decisions and ultimately, should an accident or incident arise before the employer has acted, it is down to the courts to decide whether the action was 'reasonably practical' or not. If the court decides the employer should have taken action as part of its 'duty of care', the employer could be punished for its failure to carry out its statutory duty.

There is a requirement to use 'best practical means' to solve safety problems. This is an ever-tightening noose trying to prevent employers from carrying out botched jobs or taking short cuts. In industries where safety is an absolute paramount, such as nuclear power and defence, 'state of the art' safety systems are the expectation.

The duty of care extends to a degree of monitoring sickness, absence and health in the organisation. Each establishment has its own specific areas of danger, and certain places are prone to a higher level of sickness if nothing is done.

Duties on employees

The Act recognised that responsibility for safety was not just one way. Confirming the common law implied term of the employment contract, that the employee is obliged to follow the safety instructions, sections 7 and 8 go further by stating that employees must co-operate with safety initiatives and the training that accompanies them, to take reasonable care of their own health and safety and not recklessly interfere with machines, plant or processes so as to make them unsafe. The clear implications are that employees have to wear the required safety gear and follow all authorised safety rules. They also risk dismissal if they refuse to follow other important health and safety instructions, including restrictions on smoking in the workplace, which was banned by UK legislation in 2007.

Duties on designers, manufacturers, suppliers and installers

Duties here under section 6 include incorporating safety features at the design stage, testing for risks to health and providing full safety instruction and hazard details. Again, this aspect clarified the rather unspecific common law obligations and has made a large difference in the way products are designed and marketed. Since the Act, for example, all commercial guillotines require the operator to have both hands on separate buttons for them to operate. Furthermore, one manufacturer of numerically controlled tools was successfully prosecuted because the design allowed the override of a guard while the machine was still working.

THE HEALTH AND SAFETY COMMISSION AND HEALTH AND SAFETY EXECUTIVE

Both the Health and Safety Commission and the Health and Safety Executive were set up under HASAWA. The Commission has between six and nine lay members drawn from bodies representing employers, trade unions and local authorities. It is primarily an advisory body and its main responsibility is for carrying out the policy of the Act and providing advice to local authorities and others to enable them to discharge the responsibilities imposed on them by the Act. The Commission arranges for research to be carried out, submits proposals for new regulations, produces codes of practice and generally works to reassure the public that risks are being properly controlled through information and responsiveness to public concerns. The Health and Safety Executive are responsible for the policing and enforcement of HASAWA and other Acts involving safety.

CONTROL OF SUBSTANCES HAZARDOUS TO HEALTH REGULATIONS (COSHH) 1988

These Regulations and associated codes of practice are designed to protect employees who work with any substances which could be hazardous to their health unless they are handled and utilised in a properly controlled way. They apply to all workplaces, large and small, and include all substances except those for which regulations were already in force, such as lead and asbestos.

The principal requirements in these regulations are fivefold:

- A risk assessment must be made to identify all potentially hazardous substances and to set out the precautions required. Employers are required to carry out the risk assessment every five years.

- A system must be put in place to prevent or control these risks. Consideration must be given to replace hazardous substances or to provide better controlled working arrangements where they are used.

- The employer must make sure these controls are effectively put to use and keep records of the monitoring process.

- Employers must regularly conduct health surveillance of staff engaged in work associated with these substances where there is a known identifiable risk.

- Employees must be informed of the hazards and trained in the control processes, including the precautions that they need to take.

REGULATIONS ARISING FROM EUROPEAN UNION DIRECTIVES

It has been an objective from the early days of the European movement that laws relating to health and safety should be applied consistently across Europe. This ensures that the free market between states can operate efficiently without manufacturers and traders having to deal with different regulations in each country. The Framework Directive, implemented by Member States in 1992, contained general safety principles and objectives, such as the prevention of occupational risks and providing balanced participation between the parties affected. Regulations arising from this Directive include the Manual Handling Operations Regulations 1992, covering requirements on systems and training for lifting, and the Health and Safety (Display Screen Equipment) Regulations 1992, covering the requirements on regular eye testing, design of work stations and the need for regular breaks.

Regulations have also come into effect relating to the provision and use of protective equipment, the control of asbestos at work, measures to set minimum standards for the safe use of machines and equipment, and the protection of young people and pregnant women in the workplace.

REPORTING OF DISEASES AND DANGEROUS OCCURRENCES REGULATIONS (RIDDOR) 1995

All statistics on safety arise from a system of reporting by employers, and this revised system was introduced to produce more accurate information and extend it to dangerous situations where nobody was hurt. All deaths and serious injuries must be reported immediately and a written report sent within 10 days. Lesser accidents or work-related ill-health which cause an employee to be off work for more than three days must lead to a completed form being sent to the enforcing authorities. There were 35 million days lost in 2006–7 through work-related injury and ill-health, with the average absence being 16 days (HSE 2008).

ENFORCING THE LAW

External authorities

Local authority enforcement officers mostly deal with service industries such as hotels, restaurants, offices and warehouses, while inspectors, working for the Health and Safety Executive, deal with factories, mines, railways, schools and hospitals. Their enforcement authority consists of rights to:

- enter premises, with or without notice, at any reasonable time (accompanied by the police, if obstructed)

- take samples, measurements and photographs or recordings
- carry out tests
- direct that work be left undisturbed
- examine books and documents
- take statements from any employee concerned.

Their main enforcement activities, if persuasion has not achieved the desired results, are to issue improvement notices and prohibition notices. Improvement notices are issued where the inspector is satisfied there has been a contravention of a statutory provision. The improvement notice will give the employer a certain time within which that contravention must be remedied. Work can continue in the meantime. A prohibition notice, which means the work must cease immediately, is issued when the inspector considers that the activity involves a risk of serious personal safety or of a severe safety hazard to the employees or the public. Around 15,000 notices are issued each year, and the records of such notices are on public view for up to three years, providing a deterrent to safety transgressors.

Internal authorities

The main authorities within an organisation are safety officers and safety representatives. There is no specific requirement for an organisation to have a safety officer, but most industrial sites employing over 200 have a full-time appointment. Smaller organisations may have a part-time employee or make use of consultants. The role of safety officers is to ensure that the safety requirements imposed by legislation are met by the organisation. They will set up safe systems of work, carry out risk assessments, investigate accidents and dangerous occurrences, and generally try to ensure that a 'safety culture' operates in the workplace.

Safety representatives are appointed or elected by the employees, either directly or through their trade unions. Their rights were set down in the Health and Safety (Consultation with Employees) Regulations 1996. They must be recognised by employers, involved in the consultation process through a safety committee, and given reasonable paid time off to carry out their duties, together with basic facilities such as the use of a telephone and a filing cabinet. Their duties are, to a large extent, in tandem with the safety officer with whom they will work closely in practice, in that they investigate accidents, make regular safety inspections, assess risks and bring forward employee complaints and suggestions regarding safety. If two or more safety representatives request the formation of a safety committee, the employer must set one up.

RISK ASSESSMENT

Risk assessment does not apply only to materials and substances under the COSHH Regulations, although these Regulations stimulated interest and experience in this process. Under the 1992 Code of Practice for the Management of Health and Safety at Work, it became a legal duty for employers to assess and record health and safety risks. It requires the appointment of 'competent persons' to assist in this and other safety tasks.

There are three main stages in the process of assessing and controlling risks:

- identifying hazards (the potential causes of harm)
- assessing risks (the likelihood of harm occurring and its severity) and prioritising action.
- designing, implementing and monitoring measures to eliminate or minimise risk.

Risk assessment continues to be a matter of balance. The test of 'reasonably practical' is still used in the context of cost and difficulty balanced against likely danger. It is important, therefore, that organisations have set out policies and procedures which help them to achieve a fair balance and which will highlight actions that they have to take speedily.

 ACTIVITY

5.5 RISK ASSESSMENT

Suggest how a system can be set up which identifies and assesses the seriousness of risks and the action that should be taken, which can apply to any working situation.

OCCUPATIONAL STRESS

Stress has become one of the most serious health issues of recent years. A survey by the HSE (2006) estimated that stress cost nearly £10 billion per year in the United Kingdom, over 2 per cent of gross domestic product, close to £400 per employee per year. The number of work-related stress cases reaching the courts has increased from 516 in 2002 to 6,428 in 2003 (Palmer and Quinn 2004), and 12.8 million working days were lost to stress, anxiety and depression in 2004/5 (Yarker and Lewis 2007). Employees aged between 34 and 44 suffer the most, while the problems worsen the longer they stay in the same job.

The causes of occupational stress are numerous. They are associated with perceptions of job insecurity, increase in work intensity, aggressive management styles, lack of effective workplace communication, overt or insidious bullying and harassment, faulty selection for promotion or transfer, and lack of guidance and training (Cartwright and Cooper 1997). Employees may be exposed to situations which they find uncomfortable, such as continually dealing with customers, excessive computer work, repetitive or fragmented work or having to make regular public presentations. Probably the most common cause, however, is the constant fear of organisational change through restructuring, takeovers, mergers or business process re-engineering. A lack of control over their work, their environment or their career progression can also be stressful (Rick et al 1997).

When a work environment containing these cultural aspects is added to personal problems, such as divorce or separation, ill or dying relatives, difficult housing conditions and financial problems, then it is not surprising that the employer will be faced with a good proportion of employees with stress-related problems.

Stress is not only manifested in high absence levels; fatigue, increases in infections, backache and digestive illnesses are commonly found. Irritation, hostility, anxiety and a state of panic can arise in the workplace, with knock-on effects on working practices and relationships between employees. The end result may be that the employee is 'burnt out', unable to cope with pressures that previously had been regarded as challenging and stimulating. Employees may also turn to palliatives, such as alcohol or drugs.

The employer that neglects the problem of occupational stress may face legal action. The first legal breakthrough for an employee was John Walker, a social work manager with Northumberland County Council who, having had a mental breakdown arising from his occupation, returned to his job but received no positive assistance from his employer to help him to cope successfully. (For details of this case see page 145.)

Subsequent cases have included a primary school head who won £100,000 after suffering two nervous breakdowns allegedly caused by stress brought on from bullying and harassment. An out-of-court settlement was reached in 1998 between an NHS trust and the bereaved spouse of an employee who committed suicide. In a later case, Birmingham City Council admitted liability for personal injury caused by stress when it moved a 39-year-old senior draughtsman to the post of a neighbourhood housing officer without sufficient training. The nature of the work was so different and the interpersonal demands were so great that she had long periods of ill-health leading to early retirement on medical grounds. She was awarded £67,000 (Miller 1999).

Greater clarification on the employer's responsibility in the case of psychiatric injury based on exposure to unacceptable levels of stress was given by the Court of Appeal in 2002 (Sutherland v Hatton). The court held that an employer was entitled to assume an employee was able to withstand the normal pressures of the job, and to take what the employee said about her own health at face value. It was only if there were indications which would lead a reasonable employer to realise there was a problem that a duty to take action would arise. In terms of whether the injury to health was foreseeable, factors that should be taken into account include whether:

- the workload was abnormally heavy
- the work was particularly intellectually or emotionally demanding
- the demands were greater than those placed on similar employees.

If the only way of making the employee safe was to dismiss him or her, then there would be no breach of duty by letting the employee continue if he or she was willing to do so (IRS 2002).

All of these cases show that employers need to consider carefully the way that work demands affect their employees, and ensure that they investigate each case, taking appropriate action to ameliorate potentially health-damaging situations (Earnshaw and Cooper 1996). A further consideration is the level of employees' expectations on welfare provision. Special provision for the personal and individual needs of employees is a sure sign of a sympathetic and caring employer. Finally, a CIPD study (Tehrani 2002) showed that employers that had some form of 'wellness' programme incurred annual employment costs of between £1,335 and £2,910 less per employee than employers that did not.

ACTIVITY

5.6 STRESS REVIEW

You have been brought in as a consultant to carry out a review of the level of stress in an organisation. Having investigated safety and welfare statistics, and carried out an employee attitude survey, you report on the following indicators of stress:

- the absenteeism levels had risen from 6 per cent to 9 per cent over the last three years, of which 3 per cent was reported as being caused by stress-related illnesses

- the number of staff off work with long-term sickness had increased from eight to 14, with six incidents of stress or other mental problems

- the level of reported accidents had doubled from 12 to 24 over the same period

- there had been three incidences of violence inside the site, two of which

were alcohol induced, five employees had been dismissed arising from these incidents, and two had resulted in claims to employment tribunals

- the staff attitude survey showed that over 70 per cent considered that they worked excess hours which caused stress 'occasionally' or 'regularly'

- 20 per cent of staff found that their relationships with their managers were 'poor' or 'very poor'

- 30 per cent believed that urgent improvements in their physical environment were required.

Question

What advice would you give to the employer to alleviate the causes of stress in this organisation?

ROLE OF HUMAN RESOURCES

In the majority of organisations where separate Human Resource departments exist, they either have responsibility for health, safety and welfare issues in that organisation or they play a major part in those activities. The main activities consist of:

- Formulating policies and procedures. This activity is more than a formality required by law. It is essential that new employees understand how safety works within an organisation, and the policies and procedures will set out how the safety responsibilities are structured, and the requirements from each employee. Specific references to areas (such as responsibility for checking lifting gear, or guards) should be spelled out clearly. The document should give a statement of management intent over how safety issues will be treated in the workplace. Detailed procedures should be set out for dealing with emergencies, safety training, information arising from the investigations under COSHH, and procedures should be set out for all departments where hazards have been identified. Human Resources should ensure that such documents are logical, readable and have been circulated correctly.

- Monitoring policies and procedures. At regular intervals, all procedures need to be examined to see whether they need updating to take account of new processes, materials and layouts. By attending management and safety meetings, Human Resources can ensure such necessary revisions are identified and put into place.

- Advising management and employees on safety legislation. New regulations continue to emerge, especially from Europe, with different levels of importance and different implementation dates. In 2007, for example, the Corporate Manslaughter and Corporate Homicide Act was passed where an organisation will be guilty of corporate manslaughter if a fatality was caused by a 'gross breach' of a duty of care, and the handling of the organisation's activities by senior management contributed substantially to the breach. Although the Act does not apply to individuals and there are no prison sentences, the maximum penalty is an unlimited fine and courts will be able to make a 'publicity order' forcing guilty employers to publicise their offence and the penalty.

- Designing, providing and recording health and safety training. Systematic training is essential if procedures are to operate properly. It should start with induction training to ensure that employees who are involved in any hazardous operation have instruction in key areas before they set foot on the work site. Safety instruction should be incorporated into any new processes or where new materials are introduced onto site. New safety representatives have the right for time off for training, and this should be encouraged by the organisation so they can operate efficiently.

- Liaising with the safety inspectorate. Building a relationship with the enforcing authorities is essential. Making use of their advice and extensive knowledge can be valuable, especially where new processes or production lines are being planned. A list of necessary actions arising from a late visit by the factory inspector could cause an expensive delay to a new production facility.

- Helping create a healthy working environment. All the research indicates that a healthy workforce will be a successful one and a higher performing one, so being proactive in introducing and encouraging initiatives to support health programmes can make a substantial difference to organisational performance, as shown in Case Study 5.9.

A test of overall success is whether a safety-conscious culture pervades the organisation. This is shown through management operating systems and procedures not just because of the legal requirements but because they see that it makes good business sense, in terms of both reducing costs arising from accidents and establishing a caring relationship with the labour force.

CASE STUDY 5.9

IMPROVING EMPLOYEE HEALTH AT KIMBERLY-CLARK

Kimberly-Clark, which makes products such as Kleenex and Huggies nappies, made cost savings of £500,000 per annum and reduced long-term staff absence from 6.8 per cent to 0.5 per cent after launching schemes in 2002 aimed at improving the health of its 174 UK staff. Under the programme, the company introduced work–life balance coaching sessions, massages for desk workers and sleep management workshops to improve employees' sleep quality. It also provided free fruit twice a week to promote healthy eating. Evidence that the scheme was getting immediate results was that, after six months, only 19 per cent admitted they suffered sleep problems, which was down from 68 per cent before the scheme started.

Source: Watkins (2003).

IMPLICATIONS OF REGULATION

Earlier in this chapter the roles of the Office of Fair Trading and Competition Commission in disseminating, regulating and enforcing commercial and consumer legislation were set out. Additional industry-specific regulation has been put in place over the last 20 years, and this section examines the operation of a selection of these regulators and the implications in the fields of privatised utilities, financial services, communications and areas of the public sector.

INDUSTRY REGULATORS – PRIVATISED UTILITIES

During the period 1980 to 1995, public utilities in the United Kingdom were privatised in what is now seen as a momentous and generally successful business revolution. The Labour Party ideology of nationalisation of key industries, which led to coal, steel, gas, electricity, railways and many others coming under state control in the post-war period until 1976, was replaced by the free trade and competition philosophy, promulgated by Milton Friedman (1970). It had become clear that the philosophy of veering towards a centrally controlled interventionist state operation, which had operated for the previous 20 years in the Western economies, had failed to produce the economic success that had been promised. Managers in state-controlled industries complained of constant ministerial interference, starvation of investment and regular changes in strategic direction. At its peak, almost 10 per cent of GDP came under government control. By 2002, after privatisation, this had been reduced to only 1 per cent.

Detailed studies (Martin and Parker 1997, Electricity Association 1998) have shown that labour productivity has risen at an average of 15 per cent, service provision has improved substantially and prices have generally fallen, especially in telecommunications and electricity.

Chapter 3 discussed the issues associated with the privatisation of state monopolies. The model for privatisation was essentially one of attempting to break up state monopolies, introducing a variety of methods to stimulate competition and to keep a measure of control through regulation in the interests of the consumer. *Unbundling* has involved separating out the potentially competitive areas (eg electricity generation, telecommunication value-added services) from the monopoly part (eg transmission and distribution grids, telephone lines to homes). This picture has been repeated across Europe, with only a handful of mostly Scandinavian governments owning the state telecommunications company, reinforced by EU Directives requiring Member States to establish independent regulatory agencies to provide a 'level playing field' for potential competitors (Pollack 1997, Curwen 1997).

In each sector privatised, a *regulator* has been appointed to oversee the operation of the business for the benefit of consumers (business and private) and to try to ensure that the form of privatisation actually works in practice. The main responsibilities of the regulator are to:

- set out the pricing model (with or without agreement from the participants)
- establish and monitor service standards
- encourage the working of a competitive market
- for products such as gas and electricity, ensure stable sources of supply
- prevent the exercise of any remnant of monopolistic power
- ensure the industry meets social and environmental responsibilities.

The regulator is appointed by the government but is independent of government control. Each industry has been faced by a specific business context, and the model of regulation has constantly been changed as the nature of the competitive challenges within each sector has altered. For example, one of the major issues in the telecommunications industry has been the role of the dominant provider, BT, which originally controlled landlines into most UK homes. The challenge was to encourage competition to this control, achieved mainly through encouraging the development of cable and mobile phone systems, complex agreements allowing other companies access to the landlines to provide alternative services, and acting as a mediator in resolving disputes between the parties, such as the dispute in 2004 over NTS discounts. The telecommunication industry has, in fact, moved from one monopoly provider in 1984 (BT) to over 75 providers in 2007, while the degree of competition in the power industry has extended so far that 2,600,000 British customers switched their electricity supplier in the first six months of 2007. In 2004, Ofgem fined Powergen £700,000 after the company stopped more than 20,000 domestic customers from switching to new gas/electricity contracts.

In another regulatory area, companies in the water industry were allowed by the regulator, Ofwat, to make a substantial increase in prices in the early 1990s to fund the substantial investment required to transform sewage treatment, reduce effluent discharge and thereby improve water quality around the UK coastline. In 2007, Ofwat fined United Utilities Water £8.5 million for breaching rules governing trading arrangements with associated companies and threatened to revoke its licence.

The abilities to set pricing models (unsuccessful challenged in the courts in the mid-1990s by the gas industry) and to discipline players in the industry have given the regulator substantial power over operating companies. However, the need for establishing a fair pricing model has been reduced in recent years as more sophisticated markets have been introduced into gas and electricity, as mentioned earlier, allowing more providers to enter the market and create more competition, while natural competition has developed in the telecommunication industry.

INDUSTRY REGULATION – FINANCIAL SERVICES (FSA) AND COMMUNICATIONS (Ofcom)

A second strand of regulation covers two industries that the state regards as needing special forms of regulation, namely financial services and communication. These are industries which generally, have not been government owned (apart from the BBC and BT), but where there is a strong public interest. This interest is not just to preserve or encourage competition but to inspire confidence in the financial or communication systems, regulate ethical behaviour and act as a watchdog over technical developments.

Ofcom, set up in 2003, covers activities previously controlled by, among others, the Broadcasting Standards Commission, Radio Authority, Oftel and the Independent Television Authority. It has a duty to 'balance the promotion of choice and competition with the duty to foster plurality, informed citizenship, protect viewers, listeners and customers and promote cultural diversity'. Its activities include:

- competition policy
  - reform of public service broadcasting, the effects of digital television on the BBC's channel provision and the regular licence review
  - policy on awarding of radio and ITV licences
  - policy on television advertising under a single terrestrial commercial provider (ITV)
  - advising the government on foreign takeover of major communication players, such as national newspapers

- protecting small players – producing codes on the ability of independent programme producers to retain their programming rights

- technology reviews – advising on the digital switchover between 2007 and 2012

- protecting public morals – advising on television programme content in terms of sex and violence.

Regulating financial markets has in recent years been a key part of government economic activity. Understanding that confidence is at the heart of a country's financial system and fearful of the 'melt-down' that could occur should this confidence suddenly evaporate, governments have established systems of financial supervision to try to avoid rogue activities. Much of this authority has been delegated to the Bank of England but a good part of the detailed supervision, investigation and enforcement has gradually been taken up by the Financial Services Authority (FSA), whose main aims are set out in Table 5.2.

The FSA certainly has teeth. Examples of disciplinary action in 2007 included:

- fining BNPP £350,000 for having weak anti-fraud controls which allowed a senior employee to fraudulently transfer £1.4 million of clients' accounts
- fining David Whitstance, a former finance director, £30,000 for failing to exercise due skill, care and diligence in respect of regulatory requirements over a three-year period
- fining Charterhouse Consulting Wealth Management £122,500 for switching clients' funds without their permission
- fining GE Capital Bank £610,000 for failure to have adequate systems and controls in place when selling payment protection insurance, inadequately training their staff and not providing information to customers at point of sale.

The responsibilities of the FSA can overlap with those of the Bank of England. In the Northern Rock crisis of 2007–8, much of the problem has been attributed to the confusion between the three regulatory bodies (see Case Study 10.8 on page 333).

REGULATION AND THE PUBLIC SECTOR

The Audit Commission carries out a different form of regulation in the public sector. It is a true 'watchdog', carrying out investigations into the operations of local authorities, health services and government departments. It principally

Table 5.2 Aims of the FSA

Aim	Activities
Securing the right degree of protection for consumers	Vetting firms and individuals trading in specific areas, such as financial advisers and credit providers, for honesty, competence and financial soundness. Monitoring how these standards are met in practice. When problems arise, investigation takes place and, if appropriate, disciplinary action or prosecution results.
Promoting public understanding of the financial system	Communications and publicity to try to ensure that consumers are more knowledgeable and can manage their financial affairs more effectively
Maintaining confidence in the UK financial system	Supervising exchanges, settlement houses and market infrastructure providers (IT, etc), conducting market surveillance and monitoring transactions
Helping to reduce financial crime	Investigating cases that may involve money laundering, fraud and dishonesty and criminal market misconduct such as insider trading

examines issues of efficiency and ethical behaviour, endeavouring to establish realisable targets, examples of best practice and to shame poor performers into change by publicising their faults. Although it has no executive power to change an organisation's policies or practices, the government takes note of its findings when it takes decisions over funding, especially with local authorities. It has had a degree of success in leading public organisations to examine carefully their methods of operation and benchmark their performance against similar bodies.

REGULATION AND OTHER SECTORS

Although most sectors operate without a specific regulator, they are touched by regulation in a number of ways:

- Their practices may be investigated by the OFT and Competition Commission, such as the doorstep selling example described earlier.

- A planned merger or takeover can be referred to the Competition Commission to decide whether it breaches the monopolies guidelines, such as was threatened in the 2003 battle over Safeway plc. (See Case Study 10.11 on page 346.)

- Their detailed operations can be constrained by UK or European law in areas such as labelling and packaging, information to consumers or environmental regulations.

- Planning laws have become increasingly intrusive, such as the government policy in 2000 to reject any further out of town shopping developments, including supermarkets, because of their effect on traffic growth and decline of the local high street.

CODES OF PRACTICE

Each of the regulators is authorised to produce codes of practices. Ofgem, for example, have produced a code of practice for the action that should be taken when a provider proposes to cut off a consumer's gas or electricity supply, and Ofcom has a Code of Advertising Practice. They do not in themselves have a force of law but they have strong influence on business behaviour. They help to raise standards throughout the industry, stopping organisations from indulging in dubious practices which, although not illegal, give the industry a bad name. Many organisations are happy to accept and influence the production of a code rather than having legal restrictions imposed on them.

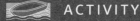

ACTIVITY

5.7 REGULATORY BENEFITS

What are the benefits of a regulatory system as opposed to a state controlled system?

KEY LEARNING POINTS

- UK law can be divided into criminal and civil law and originates chiefly from legislation emanating from the European Union, the UK Parliament and common law. Courts are bound by precedent.

- The last 30 years have seen a substantial increase in the volume and intensity of legislation to protect employees and consumers with increased regulation of business activity.

- The burden of this legislation has been borne by businesses, which need to adapt their operations to ensure compliance.

- A larger emphasis has been put on organisations carrying out safety audits and risk assessment to ensure accident prevention and a healthier workplace.

- Few sectors now manage to avoid some form of regulation, with a substantial presence in the privatised utilities and the financial and communications sectors, where regulators have considerable legal powers.

- Consumers are also protected through the regulation of markets to prevent the use of monopolistic powers by large organisations.

QUESTIONS

1. What are the main roles of the Office of Fair Trading?

2. What duties have been imposed on employees under Health and Safety Legislation?

3. Set out the main influences on governments which have led to the enhancement of consumer rights through legislation from the 1960s onwards.

4. What are the main sources of the employment contract?

5. Describe the main roles of a regulator in the utilities sector.

6. Give six examples of legislation introduced in the United Kingdom to give protection to employees.

7. Trace the path of a tribunal application through the UK/European courts.

8. What are the main roles of an HR practitioner in the field of health and safety?

10. What are the responsibilities of an employer concerning stress in the workplace?

TRENDS TO WATCH

Governments of all shape, EU and UNK, find it difficult to restrain themselves from introducing legislation, so watch out for developments in the following areas:

- In the employment law area, the extension of flexible working rights in the United Kingdom beyond working parents and carers, and a resolution of the long-standing debate on the rights of what the European Union call 'atypical workers', such as agency workers.

- In the consumer protection area, greater clarification and consistency on the roles of regulators, the OFT and the Competition Commissions, with a more consistent approach across Europe.

Demography

INTRODUCTION

Demography looks at populations – their sizes, characteristics and the way they change. It sounds like a dry and academic subject but that is far from the truth. Population changes throughout the ages have been one of the major determining factors in economic development, political activity and social change. A growth in population can have a number of consequences. It can lead to wars, such as when the Roman Empire constantly fought with the barbarians in the search to extend its boundaries to secure more extensive food supplies for its growing population, and the sweeping hordes out of Mongolia and the Far East a few centuries later. It can also lead to extensive economic growth. It was only possible for the Industrial Revolution to get under way in UK factories in the late eighteenth century with the growing supply of surplus labour from the countryside, following the enclosure movement and technological agricultural developments. Nor would the vast choice of international food and restaurants we enjoy today have happened without the post-war migratory patterns, firstly from the new Commonwealth countries, followed by young entrepreneurs from all around the world.

Rapid movements in demography have occurred in recent years. Throughout history, the human race has been young, but now that is changing. In the next 50 years, both birth rates and death rates will continue to decline so fast that populations will age dramatically. For the first time in history, there will be more older people than young people, with the average age rising from 22 in 1978 to 38 in 2050. In a growing number of countries, the population will actually start to decline. It is, indeed, likely that the world population itself will peak around the middle of the century (Wallace 1999).

These changes will change economies and working habits, revolutionise pensions and healthcare provision and even alter some of the markets for goods and services.

DEMOGRAPHY: THE FACTS

POPULATION GROWTH

In the year 1000, the world population has been estimated to have been around 300 million. It grew slowly over the next 750 years to 728 million in 1750. Over the next 250 years there was a spectacular growth, with a doubling of population to 1,500 million by 1900 and a further doubling to 3 billion by 1960. It has taken only 40 years for the population to double again to 6 billion.

The breakdown by continent of the growth from 1800 to 2005 is shown in Table 6.1.

It can be seen that the growth has not been consistent across the world. Up until 1900, population increased rapidly in the developing world, but stayed relatively subdued in the poorer developing world. Since 1900 the bulk of the world population growth has been in the developing world, with an astonishing tripling of population in Africa and Latin America since 1950. This has been accompanied by a rapid slowing in growth in the developed world, especially in Europe, with some countries, such as Germany, showing an absolute decline in recent years.

In the ex-communist countries, the population is already falling sharply in the Ukraine and Bulgaria and is expected to drop by over 10 per cent by 2025 in Russia, Georgia, Belarus and Rumania (Lucas 2006).

In the United Kingdom, as shown in Table 6.2, the spurt in population took place in the nineteenth century and has slowed considerably since 1900, with

Table 6.1 World population 1800 to 2005 (in millions)

	1800	1850	1900	1950	1975	2000	2005
Asia	635	809	947	1,402	2,395	3,683	3,905
Africa	107	111	133	224	416	784	906
Europe	203	276	408	547	676	729	741
Latin America and Caribbean	24	38	74	166	322	519	561
North America	7	26	82	172	243	310	331
Oceania	2	2	6	13	21	30	33
World total	972	1,262	1,650	2,524	4,073	6,055	6,477

Source: United Nations (2006).

Table 6.2 UK population (thousands)

	1801	1851	1901	1951	2001	2005
England	8,305	16,764	30,515	41,159	50,035	50,432
Wales	587	1,163	2,013	2,599	2,988	2,959
Scotland	1,608	2,889	4,472	5,096	5,258	5,095
Northern Ireland		1,443	1,237	1,371	1,701	1,724

Source: National Statistical Office 2007.

growth in Scotland going into reverse in the early twenty-first century. The effects of the potato famine and lack of industrial development in Ireland can be seen, with an actual decline in population from 1851 to 1901 when vast numbers of young people left Ireland to go to mainland England, America and the colonies. In fact, Ireland has also reversed the UK trend with a considerable growth in population since 1951, reflecting a more buoyant agricultural and industrial economy arising principally from joining Europe in 1973; greater economic opportunities have also halted mass migration abroad. The increase in population since 1991, however, has slowed to 0.3 per cent per year.

DRIVERS OF POPULATION CHANGE

Taking the world as a whole, the only two factors controlling population change are the level of the birth rate and the level of the death rate. Within any particular country or region, another factor is important, namely the migration into and out of that country or region.

Birth rate

The birth rate is usually expressed in terms of the number of live births per 1,000 population. The fertility rate is the average number of births for each woman of

Table 6.3 Birth statistics, United Kingdom

	Actual births – average for decade (thousands)	Fertility rate
1900	1,091	3.5
1931	824	1.8
1951	839	2.2
1961	962	2.6
1971	736	2.0
1981	757	1.8
1991	744	1.7
2001	701	1.65
2006 (actual year)	748	1.87

Sources: Office of Population Censuses/Office for National Statistics (2007).

child-bearing age. A rate of 2.1 is required to maintain the population over an extended period of time, excluding migration.

During the twentieth century, the fertility rate peaked at 2.95 in 1964, while the lowest year for births was 1977 (657,000).

It is clear from Table 6.3 that there has been a steady drop in the birth rate since 1900, with the exception of a baby boom in the 1960s (plus a similar shorter boom in the period 1946–9). The birth rate has mirrored the fertility rate, although the latter has had greater variations. It is currently well below 2.1, and this has been the main cause of the slowing-up in the rate of population growth.

However there has been a reverse in the decline of births in the United Kingdom during the early 2000s and a slowly rising fertility rate. This has been due to the continuing economic affluence providing the sense of economic security, the influence of government policies to encourage working women through a raft of measures including enhanced maternity pay and new rights to apply to work flexibly, and the influence of an increased migrant population, especially from the Indian subcontinent, where larger families are the norm. Women are having children much later in life. The mean age of women having their first baby was 23.7 in 1970 but this had increased to 27.3 in 2005. An increasing number of women are childless. One in five women in their 40s has no children compared with one in 10 in the 1940s.

Table 6.4 compares the UK fertility rate with other countries, showing that it is generally higher than the rest of Europe but lower than most developing countries.

The suggested causes of the reduced fertility rate in the developed countries are as follows:

Table 6.4 World fertility rates

	2005	Estimate 2030
UK	1.87	1.85
USA	2.04	1.85
Japan	1.33	1.72
Germany	1.32	1.69
Greece	1.25	1.57
China	1.85	1.85
Hong Kong	0.94	1.31
India	3.07	1.85
Pakistan	4.27	2.43
Brazil	2.35	1.86
Nigeria	5.85	2.95
Algeria	2.53	1.93
World	2.65	2.17

Source: United Nations (2006).

- Women are taking charge of their fertility. The widespread use of the contraceptive pill and other modern devices from the 1970s onwards allowed decisions to be taken on family planning unheard of previously. Many women (and couples) have decided not to have families or to have just one child, often so that two careers can be pursued. This is connected with postponing starting a family until later. Having children usually brings a savage reduction in household income as one member, usually the mother, may stop working or go part-time.

- It is no longer necessary to have a large family as an insurance against obtaining care in older age. The extended family has generally declined in importance as the state has stepped in to provide or support services that have traditionally been carried out by family members.

- The cost of bringing up families has risen, especially if university costs are expected, so the average expenditure on children has not fallen with the birth rate – it is simply a case of each child representing a larger financial investment, despite government financial incentives.

- In the wider world, children are no longer as useful as they once were. Fewer people live on farms where children can help out, and child labour, although still an area of international concern, is far less prevalent. Strong attempts have been made to eradicate this practice in recent years.

About three-quarters of the African countries are presently participating in various family planning programmes. Most governments encourage private planned parenthood associations to carry out various phases of the programmes. In some countries as many as eight or 10 agencies and organisations may be co-ordinated in this effort. Governments often integrate family planning in their maternal and child health services by emphasising birth spacing for health reasons.

In addition to active family planning programmes, many African governments have taken legal measures to reduce fertility. For example, some countries have raised the legal age for marriage. Others have outlawed polygamy. Some countries also now limit child allowances for government officials to no more than three or four children, and some limit the number of maternity leaves (Tarver 1996).

Death rate

As measured by deaths per 1,000 population, the UK rate has fallen from 23 in 1851 to 11 in 2000. The advances of medicine, reduced infant mortality and generally improved health, clean water supply and sanitation facilities have allowed life expectancy to increase as shown in Table 6.5.

The UK life expectancy is around the European average, but some developed countries such as Japan and Singapore have longer rates. As people live longer, the death rate falls. The actual number of deaths, however, has not fallen by the same proportion because the population has increased substantially. In 1900 the number of UK deaths was 624,000, and the figure for 2006 was 577,000.

JAPAN FACES CONTRACTION PAINS

Japan is getting old at an astonishing pace, a far cry from the position just after 1945.Then, the over-65s were around 5 per cent of the population, well below the figure for the other major economies. In 2007, the elderly account for 20 per cent of the population and average life spans have increased from 50 in 1947 to 82. By 2015, the proportion of the elderly will have risen to 25 per cent, thanks mainly to an unusually large post-war baby-boom generation who are now starting to retire at 60, the normal corporate retirement age.

The fertility rate fell below the 2.1 replacement level in 1970 and reached a low of 1.26 in 2005 before stabilising at 1.32 in 2007. In 2005, the actual population began to fall in absolute terms, with very little migration allowed to balance the picture. From 127 million in 2007, it is estimated that the population will drop to 95 million by 2050, with the elderly accounting for 40 per cent of the total.

As the proportion of elderly citizens increases, so the number of young people declines. Around 16 million are currently in their 20s but in the next 10 years alone this will drop to 13 million. Recent graduates are already reaping the benefit, with more job offers than labour available, pushing up the price of graduate jobs. However, the flip side is that today's young graduate must support an ever-larger proportion of retirees. By 2030 there will be two employees for each retiree; by 2050 the ratio will fall to 1.5 employees per retiree. Most commentators regard this as unworkable, as do most graduates, the majority of whom are not paying the fixed portion of their state pension scheme, which indicates that they expect the scheme to be closed before they retire.

The biggest falls in population are taking place in the countryside, where younger villagers have been migrating to the towns since the 1970s. The hugely inefficient agricultural sector has been subsidised

equally hugely for 50 years, backed by massive tariffs to keep out foreign rice and other products. While the economy grew strongly, Japanese society went along with supporting traditional agricultural cultures and values, but the young voted with their feet and joined emerging, innovative industries and services. Now the over-65s make up 40 per cent of rural communities and 60 per cent of all farmers, so many communities have become unviable.

In response, one small isolated hamlet, down to nine villagers all aged over 60, has contracted with an industrial waste company to sell its valley and all its farms so it will disappear under 150 feet of industrial ash. On a larger scale, Yubari, a former mining town on Hokkaido island, has had a population fall from 100,000 to 13,000 since 1950 and has gone bankrupt through spending too much money trying to (unsuccessfully) promote the town's profile. Another town decided to actively shrink its physical environment, moving public institutions from the suburbs back into the centre of town and refusing permission for all additional dwellings outside a prescribed (and smaller) town boundary.

On the macroeconomic front, the government has taken radical decisions over state pensions. Eligibility for the fixed part of the pension will rise from 60 to 65 in stages by 2014, and eligibility for the flexible (and larger) part will rise to 65 by 2026. Most commentators regard this as not fast enough. Businesses have a cultural problem with a higher retirement age. Pay is based very much on seniority, so employees staying longer in the work place would cost the organisation much more money. However, because older employees are respected, it would be extremely difficult to impose pay cuts when employees stay on to a later retirement age.

If the retirement age is delayed until 65 or

70, it would go some way to solving the decline of the supply of labour. Japan already has one of the highest proportion of the elderly still in the workforce. This is not because Japanese simply like to work or do not feel a useful part of society otherwise. For many it is that they have to work to survive. Most of these jobs are 'downshifting' into menial work such as repairs and nightwatchmen, with wages that are mediocre.

However, a bigger influence would be to increase the participation rate of women, which was at 63 per cent in 2007, compared with 68 per cent in United Kingdom and the United States. Cultural problems are even greater here, with male chauvinism dominating offices, a work culture of long hours and a shortage of childcare facilities. Japan still, apparently, does not have an expression for 'work–life balance'. Large numbers of women permanently drop out of the labour market when they have children. As the average Japanese father does not help in the home (partly because of the long-hours culture), this engenders anxiety from the wife about extending the family. By the time their children have grown up, couples then have caring responsibilities for their ageing parents, who often live with them.

In 2002, the Japanese government

announced that every Japanese woman who gives birth is to receive the equivalent of £1,700 plus up to £15,000 worth of help with childcare. The fact that this initiative is likely to cost around £5 billion indicates the degree of anxiety over the continuing decline in Japan's birth rate. So far the effect seems to be marginal, even in the cities, as the attraction is limited of bringing up families in tiny Japanese apartments, where beds are folded up during the day and the father is not seen until late at night.

A rapidly ageing population, supported by fewer and fewer working people, could keep Japan in a state of semi-permanent recession. It is estimated that if current trends continue, young people in 2025 will have to pay around 25 per cent of their salary as a tax to simply keep pensions at their current level. It remains to be seen whether the financial inducements, the availability of 'baby shops' to help women with childcare and 'grandmother networks' to support young families, will make any difference, or whether women will continue to wait until their aspirations in the workplace have been better satisfied.

Sources: Norton (2002), *Economist* (2007b), Woronoff (1996).

Table 6.5 UK life expectancy

	Male	Female
1901	48	52
1950	66	72
1990	72	78
2006	77	81

Source: ONS (2006a).

The picture is not rosy throughout the world. Although life expectancy in Europe averages 74 and in Asia it is 67, 28 per cent of all countries have a life expectancy of less than 60. The average for Africa is 50 and there are still sub-Sahara African countries where societies live with the appalling situation of life expectancy being less than 50. The worst example is Sierra Leone, where expectancy is currently only 39 for women and as low as 36 for men. On top of poor health, there are numerous outbreaks of war and disease (especially HIV/AIDS and SARS), while poor living conditions are very common.

In developed countries, the main feature of a dropping death rate is the rapid ageing of the population, with a rapid growth in the numbers over retirement age.

Migration

The third factor determining population levels is the number of people migrating into or out of a country. Clearly, if more people enter a country than leave it, the population will rise. International migration has always been substantial. Human beings' original ancestors migrated out of Africa to populate the world, and most of North and South America, Oceania and parts of Southern Africa have been colonised by migrants who have replaced the small indigenous populations.

It has been estimated that about 125 million people live outside their country of birth or citizenship (Martin and Widgren 1996). Political, social, economic and environmental upheavals have been the spur to large-scale movements. Religious dissent encouraged puritan migration to America in the seventeenth and eighteenth centuries, and persecution has forced Jewish populations to leave their homelands, such as Russia in the nineteenth century and Germany under the Nazis. Because of very poor economic and social prospects, the Irish migrated all over the world for 150 years. Chinese labour was used to build the American railroads and much of Dubai's current building boom is being built using Nepalese and Indian skilled craftsmen. Britain eagerly recruited in the West Indies and the Indian subcontinent in the early post-war years to staff the health service and public transport when local labour was in short supply. At the same time, there was a substantial outflow of skilled labour to take up new lives in Australia, Canada, New Zealand and South Africa, often under 'assisted passage' incentives.

On a world scale, certain migration paths are especially important, as Dicken explains:

> [T]here are massive movements across the Mexico-United States border and from parts of Asia to the United States. Australia has become an important focus of migration from South East Asia ... and from countries around the Mediterranean to Germany.
>
> (Dicken 2003, p521)

In general terms, the twentieth century has seen far more restrictions placed upon migrants by governments fearful of the economic and social consequences of mass immigration. Although immigration was never easy (both the United States and Australia veered towards operating a 'whites only' policy for decades), the latter half of the twentieth century has seen severe restrictions imposed by countries all over the world, exacerbated by fears of terrorism in the twenty-first century.

In the case of the United Kingdom, the Commonwealth Immigration Act in the mid-1950s imposed severe limitations on free entry for most would-be migrants, and subsequent legislation tightened the regulations further. Commonwealth immigration dropped sharply from 150,000 per annum to a third of this within a few years, and has continued at around this rate since that time. However, since the mid-1990s the net inflow of migrants has escalated substantially, as shown by Table 6.6.

Table 6.6 Average annual migration into and out of the United Kingdom, 1989 to 2005 (thousands)

	1989–1993			1999–2000			2005		
	Inflow	Out	Net	Inflow	Out	Net	Inflow	Out	Net
New commonwealth	50	26	24	71	23	48	125	75	50
Old Commonwealth	53	58	-5	84	68	16	70	80	20
European Union	66	61	5	83	80	3	250	130	120
USA	25	35	-10	23	27	-4	15	30	−15
Middle East	9	11	-2	12	11	1	5	10	−5
Rest of Europe	12	9	3	17	10	7	15	30	−15
South America	2	3	-1	5	3	2	−5	10	−5
Africa and others	24	19	5	86	56	30	−50	30	20
All countries	242	222	19	381	278	103	565	395	170

Source: ONS (2006b).

Where the figure is negative, it means a net outflow of population. These figures show the substantial rise in migration in recent years. From a net balance of only 19,000 per annum in the four years up to 1993, it has risen to 103,000 by 2000, and the figure continued to rise sharply to 170,000 in 2005 (ONS 2006b). The increases have been from all areas of the world including, surprisingly, the Old Commonwealth countries such as Australia. However, the largest recent increase has been from the 10 countries that joined the European Union between 2004 and 2006. The effect of those movements is analysed in Case Study 6.2.

On another front, there was a significant rise in the number of asylum seekers to the United Kingdom in the early 2000s, which peaked at 103,000 in 2002 but fell to 23,000 in 2006 (ONS 2007). Government actions to speed up the system of dealing with applications caused some reduction in applications but did not eliminate the problem. Only around 20 per cent of asylum seekers have their application accepted but many are able to stay in the United Kingdom while their appeal is heard, which can take many months.

The reasons for the increasing numbers of migrants include:

- The UK's economic performance in since the mid-1990s has been very positive, better than most of Europe.
- There is a strong culture of entrepreneurship, with open opportunities for small businesses to flourish, perhaps more so than other parts of Europe, although not so strong as in the United States.
- There are established ethnic communities from all parts of the world, allowing greater ease of transition and community support.

MIGRATION FROM EASTERN EUROPE AND ITS EFFECT ON THE LABOUR MARKET

Research has examined the effects of the migration from the countries that acceded in 2004 and on whom no restrictions on movement and work were placed by the UK government. These were Poland, the Czech Republic, Estonia, Hungary, Latvia, Lithuania, Slovakia and Slovenia, the so-called A8 countries.

Level of migration

Nearly 580,000 migrants from the A8 countries registered for work between 2004 and 2006 (Home Office 2007), and a further 100,000 have been estimated to be working on a self-employed basis. Poland is the main source, totalling over 300,000 migrants, and the effect on the internal Polish labour market has been so great that Poland has had to ease its own restrictions on entry of labour from Ukraine, Belarus and Russia to fill skilled vacancies and gaps in the seasonal agricultural market (Polska 2006).

This is way in excess of the official UK government forecast in 2003 of around 10,000 per year. Expectations have been massively exceeded because:

- a large number of migrants were already working unofficially in the United Kingdom and their registration allowed their work to be 'legal'

- most of the A8 countries have high unemployment figures (20 per cent in Poland, for example)

- earnings in A8 countries are typically six times lower than in the United Kingdom

- working conditions, including health and safety provision, are often at a lower standard than in the United Kingdom

- the arrival of cheap flights and coach travel has made the regular journeys cheaper and easier

- the degree to which agency intervention would apply was greatly underestimated, especially in the building, agriculture and hospitality sectors.

On top of that, the freedom of entry from these countries has meant that an unspecified number have been able to settle permanently, without restriction in most cases. Of that number, it is estimated that 380,000 have stayed on a permanent basis. However, this is only an estimate as there is no register of A8 migrants leaving the United Kingdom.

Nature of migrants, chosen work and pay levels

Most were young, with 80 per cent under 35, while 80 per cent had some form of qualification (mostly technical) although only 5 per cent had degrees. Only 6 per cent had dependants arriving with them. Around 70 per cent worked in low-paid, unqualified work, such as process operation/packing and in warehousing (40 per cent), hospitality (18 per cent) and farming (4 per cent), while 6 per cent worked as care assistants and sales assistants. The average pay was between £4.50 and £5.99 an hour.

Good for the economy?

The government has spelled out the apparent benefits of this unprecedented migration. It identified fewer jobs unfilled, less inflationary pressures (which could fuel higher pay increases) and faster economic growth. The Ernst & Young ITEM club estimated that the activities of the migrants reduced interest rates by 0.5 per cent and GDP was around 0.2 per cent higher (ITEM Club 2006). The Bank of England concluded that the level of unemployment that could be sustained without raising inflation was lowered as migrants took the low-paid jobs that often remain vacant (Blanchflower, Salaheen and

Shadforth 2007). Moreover, responses by employers rated migrants higher than conventional employees in terms of productivity, reliability, attendance and quality of work (CIPD/KPMG 2005).

On the down side, however, there was some increased strain on the social infrastructure, notably housing, transport, hospitals and welfare. Overall, the picture looked very positive.

Sources: Philpott (2007), McSmith (2007).

- The number of low-paid unskilled jobs available is very high, especially in the hospitality, caring and building industries. Some are in the black economy, encouraging asylum seekers and illegal immigrants.

- In the education field, there has been a huge growth in undergraduate and postgraduate courses taken up by international students, who are able to help their financing through part-time work.

Europe has been faced with a similar situation. While the United Kingdom's number of asylum seekers represents 0.5 per cent of the population, Sweden's 330,000 represent nearly 4 per cent, while Austria's proportion is 5 per cent. Asylum seekers to France and Germany are currently running around half the UK rate.

ETHNICITY OF THE POPULATION

An inevitable development of the increase in migration has been a growth in the ethnic variation in most developed countries. In the United Kingdom, around 7 per cent of the population, about 4 million people, are from ethnic minorities, double the figure in the 1970s. The largest group are from the Indian subcontinent – around 55 per cent of the total – while West Indians make up a further 15 per cent (actually a declining proportion as many retire back to their countries of origin), with the remainder from Africa, Asia and the Middle East.

They have generally settled over the years in urban localities, with large congregations in inner East London boroughs and towns in the Midlands and the North. As a whole, they have a lower age profile than the indigenous population, with a much smaller percentage over 65, chiefly because migrants tend to be in lower age categories. Also, many migrants retire to their countries of origin. The effects of the increase in ethnic minority sectors are discussed in Chapter 7 under social effects.

Ethnic variety in the population is far greater in the United States, as shown in Case Study 6.3.

Migration is a very emotive subject, bringing to the mix a number of political, economic, social and psychological issues. Broadly speaking, there are a set of reasons for encouraging migration and another set for discouraging it as follows.

CASE STUDY 6.3

'LATINOS' ARE A MAJOR FORCE IN THE US ECONOMY

People of Hispanic origin (or Latinos, as many prefer to be called), make up 12 per cent of the US workforce today, but this will become at least 25 per cent in 50 years' time, as a result of their much larger families and current age profile. They originate from across Latin America but predominantly Mexico, and their growth rate is 3 per cent per annum, compared with 0.8 per cent for the rest of the US population. As a group, they are a key catalyst for economic growth. In some of the larger cities, such as Los Angeles, they make up the majority of the under-18 age set. Their disposable income jumped 29 per cent from 2001 to 2004, double the pace of the rest of the population, and they have a growing influence on all consumer patterns, especially food, clothes and entertainment.

The Latino boom brings a welcome charge to the economy at a time when other countries' population growth has slowed to a crawl. Without a steady supply of new workers and consumers, a greying United States might see a long-term slowdown along the lines of ageing Japan.

Yet this demographic change produces potential problems. One of the major issues relates to language. With a huge Spanish-speaking minority, there could be pressures for recognition of an official second language, much as French is in Canada today. This could harm assimilation and encourage a form of separatism in states such as California, just as it has been a major cause of conflict in Quebec.

Another issue is the perception that large numbers of poorly educated, non-English speakers undermine the US economy. Although the steady influx of low-skilled workers helps keep America's gardens tended and floors cleaned, those workers also exert downward pressure on wages, causing friction with other groups of workers in this sector.

A case in point is Harris County in Texas, which includes the city of Houston where the population increased by 21 per cent during the 1990s. Forty-two per cent are of Hispanic origin and this ethnic group was responsible for 80 per cent of the growth. There are no zoning laws in the county so developers can build wherever they think there is the demand. At the new 28,000 acre community of Woodlands, a three-bedroom house costs around $130,000 (about £65,000) compared with an equivalent house in San Francisco costing $700,000. The area is surrounded by woodland and crime is very low.

Rapid growth in this form may eventually cause environmental problems but it greatly slows the pace at which America ages.

Sources: *Business Week* (2004), *Economist* (2006).

Encouraging migration

- We live in a global economy and we need to make the best use of all talents from whatever the source.

- Migrants have energy and enthusiasm and a willingness to succeed. They have made a substantial effort to move from their home country, and experience indicates that they are motivated to work hard.

- Most migrants are in the age group 18–40 and, in an ageing population, it is important to have a good source of younger labour.

- Migrants make up such a large proportion of the labour force, estimated at 7 per cent (Salt 2006) that the labour market would tighten dramatically if this source was reduced or eliminated. In fact 15 per cent of firms employ 10 per cent or more migrants in their workforce (Smedley 2008).

- Migrants can fill the low-skill jobs that are currently difficult to fill – they prevent wage rates rising too high.

- It is not unusual for migrant entrepreneurs to offer ethnic goods and services which expand the marketplace to the benefit of the consumer. Thai food and ethnic textiles are obvious examples.

- It is arguable that it is more beneficial for the UK economy for migrants to carry work in the United Kingdom rather than for work to be outsourced to a migrant's home country.

- Why should migrants be prevented from benefiting from the United Kingdom's successful economy? After all, for 200 years, the United Kingdom benefited from running the economies of its colonies so it is time for those benefits to be shared.

Discouraging migration

- The United Kingdom is very densely populated and an inflow of immigrants leads to pressure on housing and jobs.

- Where there is a large source of low-skilled labour, it discourages employers from becoming more productive by automating production or innovating the services provided.

- Too much migration encourages the black economy, which reduces tax revenue and is associated with crime.

- The process of policing and administrating prospective migrants is very expensive and difficult to carry out efficiently and fairly.

- Migrants can be socially marginalised, staying in their own communities, retaining their own cultures and religions and not integrating effectively. This can create social problems and difficulties with the next generation.

- Excessive migration can cause security problems with international conspiracies leading to terrorist activity (Nichiporuk 2000).

OTHER DEMOGRAPHIC CHANGES

Working population

Table 6.7 shows the state of the mid-2004 UK labour market.

Compared with the early 1990s, there has been a growth of around 4 million in the total working population, made up of a natural growth in the population, a reduction in unemployment and an increase in the participation level. The rate of employment for women has risen much more steeply that for men, with the women's total rising by more than 2 million over the last 10 years (see Chapter 7

Table 6.7 The UK labour market 2006 (in thousands)

	Male	Female	Total	
Employed	12,800	12,480	25,280	
Self-employed	2,780	1,020	3,800	
Total labour market	15,580	13,500	29.080	
Part-time	1,600	5,700	7,300	
Temporary	700	800	1,500	
Unemployed			1,400	
Economically active			31,160	(79%)
Economically inactive			8,120	(21%)

Source: ONS (2006b).

for a discussion on the feminisation of work). The steady fall in unemployment, which has halved in the same period, has also led to a more confident labour market, so the number of temporary employees has declined. The number of people self-employed has stayed steady in risen years, having increased substantially in the 1980s under the Thatcher period, when entrepreneurial activity was strongly encouraged.

The decline in the birth rate leading to an ageing population has already affected the size and nature of the potential working population, those within the age range 16 to 60 (female) or 65 (male). Table 6.8 shows this information starkly.

Table 6.8 UK population age distribution, 1901 to 2026 (in percentages)

	Under 16	16–24	25–44	45–64	Over 65
Males					
1901	34	20	28	15	4
1931	26	18	29	21	7
1961	25	14	27	25	9
1991	21	14	30	22	13
2001	21	11	31	23	13
2011*	19	12	27	27	15
2026*	18	10	26	26	19
Females					
1901	31	20	28	15	6
1931	23	17	30	21	8
1961	22	13	25	26	14
1991	19	12	28	12	18
2001	20	10	29	23	18
2011*	18	11	26	26	18
2026*	17	10	25	26	22

* forecast

Source: Office for National Statistics.

Table 6.8 shows that the younger male working population, aged 16–44, has fallen from 48 per cent of the population in 1901 to 39 per cent in 2001, and is expected to decline further to 36 per cent by 2026, with a similar picture for women. The percentage in the age group 16–24 has actually halved. On the other hand, there has been a considerable growth in the older employee groups. In fact, the number of employees aged 50 and over increased by 1.3 million (about 26 per cent) in the 10 years up to 2004. Not all pensioners are an immediate drain on the economy, as many chose to work after retirement age. There are around a million in this category, a figure that has risen by 34 per cent over the last 10 years. However, they do face a degree of discrimination, as shown in Research Focus 6.1.

Given that far more young people go on to further and higher education, with the UK government having a target of 50 per cent attending some form of higher education, this reduces the younger working population even further.

RESEARCH FOCUS

6.1 AGE STEREOTYPES AND DISCRIMINATORY ATTITUDES TOWARDS OLDER WORKERS: AN EAST–WEST COMPARISON

This study compared age stereotypes among 567 respondents sampled in the United Kingdom and Hong Kong, and examined how these stereotypes were related to discriminatory attitudes at work. Compared with the Hong Kong sample, UK respondents saw older workers as more effective at work, but less adaptable to change. As expected, respondents' own age was predictive of positive age stereotypes, although for supervisors this relationship was moderated in the case of perceptions of work effectiveness. Stereotypical beliefs were found to significantly affect respondents' attitudes towards the training, promotion and retention of older workers, their willingness to work with older workers, and their support for positive discrimination. Findings also suggest that anti-age discrimination policies in the respondent's organisation had a positive impact on beliefs about the adaptability of older workers and possibly also on attitudes towards providing them with training. Implications of the findings were discussed in light of the existing sociopolitical environment in the United Kingdom and Hong Kong.

Source: Chiu *et al* (2001).

Participation rates

People used to work until they reached pensionable age. (Many, of course, did not last that long, worn out by heavy industrial work or poor diets.) As late as 1975, 84 per cent of men age 60–64 were 'economically active' in the United Kingdom, but this fell to 65 per cent by 1995. This was chiefly the result of the recession in the early 1990s, when many older men lost their jobs and found it difficult to obtain alternative employment. Many were disabled and obtained disability benefits, which are higher than unemployment benefits. Organisations

ACTIVITY

6.1 ATYPICAL EMPLOYMENT

A development in the working population in recent years has been the growth of what is known as 'atypical employment', which is not full-time 9-to-5 employment. It covers part-time, shift-work, teleworking and a host of variable working arrangements. What are the driving forces for this growth?

also encouraged older employees to take early retirement, sometimes providing generous redundancy payments or enhanced pensions.

By the early 2000s, this position was changing. For example, in the 12 months to December 2004, the number of people aged 50 and over in employment rose by 190,000, including a 73,000 increase in those over retirement age. Participation rates for men 50 to 64 rose from 65 per cent to 79.5 per cent from 1995 to 2005 (ONS 2007), and for those over retirement age it had risen from 7.5 per cent to 9.2 per cent by 2003 (*Economist* 2004). This is partly to do with the prosperous economy where many part-time jobs are available, especially in the service sector, and partly to do with the decline in pension prospects arising from the stock market crash of the early 2000s, where the value of personal pensions declined by as much as 50 per cent, although there has been a substantial recovery since that time.

For women, there has been a substantial increase in the participation rate, rising from 63 per cent in 1979 to 74 per cent in 2004. Women have developed their careers, continued at work while raising a family or returned to work much quickly than in previous decades. They have also taken up new careers and skills through obtaining qualifications, many through some form of government initiative. Other support has come through the strengthening of equal opportunity legislation, where the barriers to women's employment and development have been steadily removed.

The economically inactive can be regarded as a 'reserve army' that can be drawn on during periods of tight labour markets. Smallwood explains that:

> There are huge economic benefits associated with a growing workforce, mirrored by the severe problems that arise when a country's population starts to decline. After all, gross domestic product growth over the longer term is the sum of the growth in the employed workforce and the rise in productivity of that workforce, so the faster the working population goes up, the faster the economy grows. Over the past decade, the growth in the working population has added well in excess of £50 billion to GDP, and swelled the treasury's coffers by nearly half that.
>
> (Smallwood 2006, p6)

The growth in European participation rates mirrors the UK situation, although the average rate was lower at 78 per cent for men and 60 per cent for women in

2000. In France, for example, the male rate was 75 per cent and female 62 per cent, while the Italian rate for women was as low as 46 per cent in the same year.

ACTIVITY

6.2 BUILDING UP THE PARTICIPATION RATE

Two organisations have just set up in an area of high unemployment and low participation, with the support of various government grants and loans. They are as follows:

- Jones Supermarkets have set up a regional distribution centre to employ 450 staff in warehousing and logistics positions on 24/7 operations.

- Williams Toys and Games have established a manufacturing and distributing centre to employ 200 staff. There is a seasonal element to the work

so a number of staff will be working flexibly, including evening shifts and weekends for the busy autumn period. Most of the toys and games are imported finished or semi-finished so the work is essentially unskilled and semi-skilled and involves a high element of packing and distribution.

Given that setting up in the area will help reduce the unemployment rate, are there ways in which the organisations can help further improve the participation rate?

Sectoral employment

The number of people working in manufacturing has been declining since the 1950s, when it stood at over 6 million. The 1990s saw a particularly steep drop both in real terms and as a percentage of total employment, as shown in Table 6.9.

Every part of the service sector has increased, with the sharpest increases (more than 25 per cent) in hotels and catering, real estate, IT-associated business activities, health, education and community/personal needs. This shows two trends. The first is a reflection in the changing pattern of consumer demand, where we spend much more money on property and leisure activities – holidays, eating out, shopping and at the hairdressers. (In fact the highest rate of growth of any individual job from 1990 to 2002 was for hairdressing.) Second, there has been increased expenditure by the Labour government on health and education, as promised in their election manifestos, which has led to an increase in jobs in both sectors.

But the biggest increase of all is the category involving computer-related jobs (although this category is a rather vague one and does include some non-computer activities), which has risen by 40 per cent. This will reinforce what you will read in Chapter 8 on technology, where IT developments (automation, communications) have replaced the need for skilled and unskilled labour in manufacturing. The major improvements in productivity have all taken place in this sector, so output has risen, prices have come down and overall industrial employment has diminished. Also, much of the manufacturing has migrated to parts of the world where labour is cheaper and the products are then imported into the United Kingdom.

Table 6.9 Sectoral employment 1993 to 2006 (thousands)

	1993	2006	Change
Manufacturing	3,952	3.044	- 592
Construction	966	1,269	+296
Service sector	17,419	22,073	+3,575
Sections of the service sector			
Warehousing/retailing	3,906	4,649	+743
Hotels, catering	1,360	1,798	+438
Post, telecommunications	437	491	+54
Real estate	256	446	+190
IT, renting, research, etc	2,546	3,851	+1,305
Public administration	1,467	1,540	+73
Education	1,892	2,369	+477
Health	2,511	3,345	+834
Other community/personal needs	1,069	1,429	+360
Transport	925	1,098	+173
Financial service (banks, etc)	1,014	1,083	+69

Source: ONS (2006c).

ACTIVITY

6.3 CLOSING DOWN

Consider the scenario where the main manufacturing employer in a country town, employing 1,500 staff, announces it is closing down. What are the implications for the local economy? What are the overall implications for the United Kingdom of the decline in manufacturing employment?

Changes in family structure

The move to smaller families and a higher participation rate for women has led to changes in the structure of families and the role of family members. Working women (especially those in full-time work) spend less time in domestic routines, which has led to a considerable growth in industries devoted to convenience foods, eating out and hired-in domestic help. Information from the Family Expenditure Survey shows that the proportion of income spent on eating out increased by 50 per cent over the period 1980 to 2000. The changes in the labour market have led to changes in the nature of society, as shown in Research Focus 6.2.

Other changes have involved the caring responsibilities for children becoming more evenly shared between spouses, while there are many examples of active grandparents taking a substantial responsibility for day-to-day care of younger children.

6.2 CHANGING SOCIETY IN SOUTH WALES

Doreen Massey carried out a survey of the implications of the massive closures of the steel and coal-mining industries in the early 1980s, and identified the difference between the former labour market, which was heavily male-dominated with a high proportion of manual and semi-skilled labour, and a new labour market that had grown up with economic restructuring. This was typified by new jobs in the electronics industries and a high level of female employment. The previous labour market had created a patriarchal society that had remained relatively stable over many generations. The new market offered less stability and less security, and led to changes in social patterns and family organisation.

Source: Massey (1984).

ACTIVITY

6.4 DECLINING MANUFACTURING

What actions can the government take to mitigate the negative consequences of areas of declining manufacturing?

On the other hand, there is the challenge of looking after older relatives, with around half living into their 80s and many into their 90s and beyond. In the past, many have lived with their offspring, making an extended family, but, in Europe this practice is declining, although it is still the norm in Japan. The need for a degree of personal privacy, the day-to-day medical and psychological challenges of coping with an elderly relative and the widespread growth in sheltered accommodation have been reasons for this trend.

Another trend has been the decline in marriage, as shown by Figure 6.1. This is not just a UK phenomenon. In Scandinavia, over 50 per cent of children are now born out of wedlock (Kurtz 2004). The issue of declining marriages and rising divorces (157,000 in 2001) is discussed further in Chapter 7 on social trends, but the rising number of single-parent families and the dependence of many such families on the benefit system, which is especially strong in the United Kingdom, presents a further financial challenge to governments as well as implications for housing provision and, in certain areas, an effect on crime (Haskey 1993).

Changes in geographical population location

A final aspect of demography is the internal movement of population within countries. For over 200 years, there has been a steady movement away from the land and into the cities around the world as agriculture has become mechanised and farms consolidated. In the last 100 years or so, this movement has extended in

Figure 6.1 Marriages in the United Kingdom

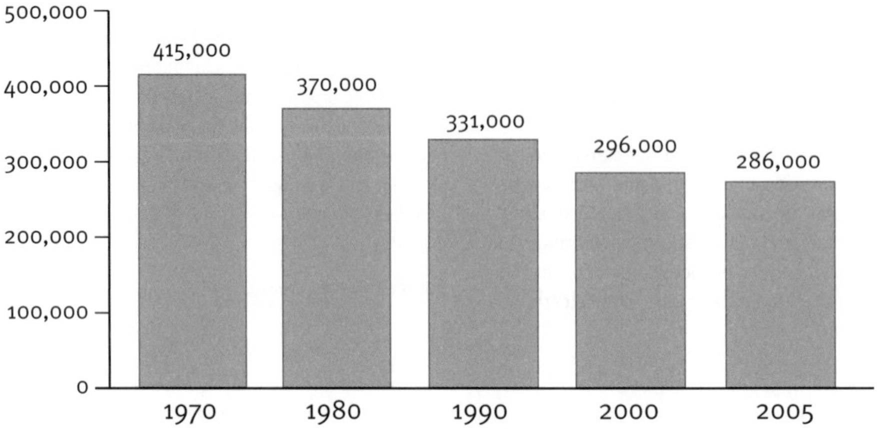

Source: www.statistics.gov.uk.

certain countries to widespread geographical patterns. In Italy, it has been a mass movement from the poor, rural south to the more prosperous urban north. In the United Kingdom the movement has been in the opposite direction, with a general move from the industrial areas, especially in the north, to the more balanced economies of the south and east (Stilwell, Rees and Boden 1992). The population of the north-eastern counties of England actually dropped in the 1990s, and population increases in Yorkshire and Lancashire were quite small. On the other hand, counties in the south-east, such as Cambridgeshire, increased by 10 per cent or more as an estimated 250,000 citizens moved from north to south (Brindle 1999).

TRENDS TO WATCH – AND THE FUTURE?

If the world's population continued to increase at its current rate, all estimates show such a growth to be completely unsustainable. Food and energy would run out, leading to the Malthusian nightmares of war, pestilence and disease, causing a decline in population to sustainable levels. Economists have been divided on the likely scenario at 2050, with some estimates of world population at 10 billion and still growing, and others indicating a more conservative outcome. Happily, those with an optimistic viewpoint are becoming more plentiful. At a 2002 United Nations conference the director of the population division, Joseph Chamie, confidently predicted a peak of 8 billion at 2040, followed by a falling world population at 2050 for the first time since the Black Death.

The conference was called to discuss the implications of unexpectedly fast declines in fertility in dozens of countries, including some very large ones. Mexico, India and Brazil have all forecast a decline in their birth rate below replacement level within 20 years. The assumption that as nations developed their economies, women would settle down to having an average of 2.4 children, now appears erroneous. Women in developing countries appear to be to striving for the freedoms achieved in the developed countries, where the decisions open include choosing not to have a family at all, or to have just one child. Bangladeshi women today have 3.3 children while the Vietnamese have halved their fertility rate in 10 years to 2.3, just above the replacement level (Pearce 2002). So far fewer births will automatically result in eliminating population growth.

There is also a question mark over increasing life expectancy. It is still likely that we can all expect to live a little longer every decade, but AIDS has had a serious effect in sub-Sahara Africa and is spreading its tentacles into other areas, with rapid growth in HIV in Eastern Europe, South America and the Far East. So the increase in life expectancy, although in itself it will have important consequences, will only marginally influence the long-term decline in population.

In the United Kingdom, the stabilisation of the fertility rate at around 1.8 will inevitably bring to an end the natural population growth, probably around 2035 or 2040 where it will peak at around 66 million, according to the latest predictions. However, the Government Actuary's Department has reported that life expectancy is growing faster than previous predictions, and should rise to 81 for men and 85 for women by 2030 (Doward 2003). If this occurs, then the population will continue to grow for a little longer, although the average age will rise.

However, there is no doubt that the population will become older. In 2030 15 million will be over current pensionable age, compared with 11 million now. In 2007 there are more pensioners than children. The average age is set to rise from 38.8 in 2000 to 42.6 in 2025.

The factor that is unknown is the net migration effect, which depends on government policy and the way the policy works out in practice. One government estimate is that net migration will be as high as 135,000 per year for the next 25 years (Baird 2001), adding over 3 million to the population over this period.

To summarise, the world population will continue to grow rapidly for the next 20 years but this growth will then start to taper off and will probably reverse by the mid-century point. Populations in developed countries will become distinctly older and internationally diverse. Populations in developing countries will also age but from a very low base figure, and will become internationally mobile.

IMPLICATIONS OF DEMOGRAPHIC PREDICTIONS

As indicated at the start of this chapter, demographic trends will have substantial implications across the world at local, national and international levels. We shall examine these implications in outline for the following groups:

- organisations, especially in the UK private sector
- governments, especially the UK government
- international society.

IMPLICATIONS FOR ORGANISATIONS

A slowdown in population growth and an ageing population have effects on both the nature of the marketplace and the sources of labour. Adaptations to their current business practices could take the following forms.

Sources of labour

With far fewer school leavers and younger people generally, organisations will have to look elsewhere for labour, particularly if the economy continues to grow steadily under the full employment conditions we have seen in the late 1990s and early 2000s. Alternative sources can involve moving away from the traditional full-time 9-to-5 job design and to a more flexible model where much greater use is made of part-time jobs, job shares, flexible hours and working from home. These flexible modes can meet the working needs of those with caring responsibilities, principally (but not exclusively) women, and older people generally who are retired or semi-retired. Some retailers, such as B&Q and Tesco, have specifically targeted older potential staff, which has led not just to an easing of recruitment difficulties but to considerable customer satisfaction arising from the knowledge such staff bring to the job. As a spokesperson for Nationwide Building Society explained, 'Many customers prefer dealing with more maturity and experience and older workers tend to be more loyal and committed' (*Economist* 2004). An example of a local authority following the same path is shown in Case Study 6.4.

It is also unlikely that the offers of early retirement with enhanced pensions will be so generous in the future. The UK government has already moved away from funding such arrangements centrally, requiring each department or agency to bear the costs involved. This has already led to a substantial reduction in such offers, and employees choosing early retirement now mostly have to fund this out of their own pension schemes.

Given these factors, it is not surprising that a greater proportion of those over retirement age choose to continue to work. However, as in the example of Japanese older workers in Case Study 6.1, there is the danger of 'Balkanisation' of labour markets, where employees at both ends of the demographic market have poor job security, menial work and low pay (Roberts 2006).

In the commercial sphere, many companies are changing their policies towards the employment of older employees. Retailer Asda offers a variety of flexible working practices, including 'Benidorm leave', where employees can take up to three months unpaid leave in the winter to take an extended holiday. It also offers grandparents' leave and carers' leave, together with a seasonal colleagues scheme which attracts older people to work 10 weeks a year at the peak times. Store managers are encouraged to visit older people's clubs, and these policies resulted in the number of 65+ employees rising to 3,500 in 2006 (CIPD 2007).

Change in markets

As the patterns of population change, their consumer needs alter accordingly. With an ageing population, there will be a decline in demand for products for

CASE STUDY 6.4

AGE POSITIVE SUCCESS AT BRIDGEND BOROUGH COUNCIL

In the late 1990s, Bridgend Council began to appreciate the growing demographic effects as its employee average age had risen to 41 and the reduced number of school leavers were being snapped up by major competitors in the area such as Sony and Ford. Action was needed to ensure the continued maintenance of a skilled workforce and to ensure that suitable employment was available, irrespective of age.

Recent initiatives have included:

- the abolition of age limits in advertisements

- eliminating the date of birth on the application form

- employees who work beyond their normal retirement ages can continue to contribute towards their pension scheme up the maximum of 40 years' service

- introducing a mentoring scheme that will involve those who intend to retire coaching younger employees to ensure valuable skills are not lost

- ignoring an employee's age when considering training and development opportunities.

What has been more important is the changing culture where being 'age positive' is built into the way the Council is run, where it is seen as open-minded, flexible and committed to people's development. For example, employees are encouraged to continue working as long as everybody is comfortable. This has worked well in areas such as social care, where maturity can be a positive benefit, and with specialist positions, such as continuing to employ a fitness instructor (well into his 70s) on a part-time basis.

Success in this area has been recognised by a national award from Age Positive – the government body campaigning to tackle workplace ageism.

Source: Persaud (2004).

the young, such as baby foods and prams, and eventually for products for teenagers and the age group 18–25. The brewing industry has seen a substantial decline in the demand for beer as the largest consumers have traditionally been those aged 18–25, a declining age group, although their drinking habits have also changed. Similarly, sales of teenage fashion goods – clothes, compact discs, jewellery – have become sluggish in recent years. Although the per capita spending has increased as the general level of prosperity has risen, it does not make up for the reduced population in those age brackets.

On the other side, there are some sectors of industries that gain from an ageing population. The most dramatic is the travel and tourism industry, as older people spend a higher proportion of their income on holidays than most other groups. For a number of cyclical reasons, they also have become a much wealthier segment of the community. Saga, floated on the stock market for close to £1 billion in 2004, is the clearest winner, providing a vast range of holidays – active and inactive – to a growing market, and broadening its product range to insurance and other financial services.

On the financial front, it has been estimated that worldwide, people over the age of 55 hold around 70 per cent of the planet's wealth, and there is a huge market here for service providers involved in investments, pensions and general financial security, as shown in Case Study 6.5.

CASE STUDY 6.5

WEALTH ADVICE FOR THE ELDERLY IN THE UNITED STATES

Examples of some of the services provided especially for older US citizens are:

- **Reverse mortgages.** In 2006, 76,000 US citizens took out mortgages where they receive a lump sum or a line of credit and do not pay any interest while the mortgage is running. All the fees and accumulated interest are paid off when the house is sold, usually (but not always) when the mortgagee dies. Currently the federal government guarantees such mortgages, so that if a homeowner's debts are greater than the value of his or her home at the time of death, the estate will not have to make up the shortfall. This partly explains why the number of reverse mortgages taken out increased by 77 per cent over the total for 2005. However, fees can be very high for this financial instrument (as much as 10 per cent) and the mortgagee's heirs are not always happy by the way that the inheritance is eroded by high fees and interest payments.

- **Elder Services Group.** A product marketed by Wells Fargo and other providers to the banks' ageing and generally prosperous clientele, the bank will handle investments, pay regular bills, process insurance claims, arrange and monitor healthcare (including the high costs associated with surgery and treatment in the United States) and provide regular reports on the client's financial situation. Some go further and give advice on funeral arrangements, nursing homes, organise taxi contracts when eyesight fails and even deal with regular logistics for pills and other pharmaceutical products.

- **Wealth management.** An increasing number of providers are entering the market to handle investments for the elderly. Citigroup, for example, has built 17 regional 'planning centres' for its wealthy customers – mainly baby-boomers on the edge of retirement with more than US$5 million in assets to invest. They bring together tax and trust lawyers, specialists in insurance, philanthropy and experts in small business sales so all the options are covered. Wachovia has developed a financial programme that allows it to focus on customers with a minimum of US$250,000.

Because of the complexity of this financial area and the declining faculties of some of the clients, the providers are increasingly attempting to avoid the 'hard-selling' approach. A number, including HSBC Bank, are using older or even semi-retired employees to carry out the sales negotiations, so it is hoped that claims for mis-selling will be reduced.

Source: *Economist* (2007).

Housing presents an interesting reflection of demographic changes. Although the population is now growing only slowly, the price of houses has risen substantially, due mostly to a somewhat unexpected higher demand. This has come about

ACTIVITY

6.5 SERVICES FOR THE OLDER CONSUMER

Summarise the effects of an ageing population on the tourism, retailing and banking industries.

because, as the fertility rate drops and the population ages, there is no corresponding drop in the number of households. Whereas young children live with their parents, older people live mostly in their own housing unit. Many stay in their own homes looking after themselves to the end, or nearly the end, of their lives, assisted by a benefits system that encourages such behaviour. Add to this the increase in divorce which often creates additional demand for housing, and the rise in students living away from home, and perhaps the rise in house prices is not so unexpected. Among the winners here have been the construction companies that provide retirement homes, such as McCarthy & Stone.

Other clear winners in the demographic stakes are those who market products specifically for the elderly. There will be growing markets for mobility products and those aimed at improving healthcare, from pharmaceutical products to private hospitals. These include:

- 'Nutraceuticals', including vitamins, nutrients, minerals and herbal extracts, a market estimated to be worth $8billion in the United States alone. Nutritional scientists are working on a new array of food products that are scientifically designed to improve health and longevity, and which will have specific appeal to the middle-aged and elderly.

- There are more than 100 US biotech companies actively researching age-related disorders (Wallace 1999), such as the role of telomeres in cell ageing that may keep skin young and elastic, and tissue engineering, which may offer the prospect of replacement parts for the body.

- Stannah stairlifts has become another household name, while magazines devoted to older readers (such as *Yours*) have substantially increased their circulation.

The same reasoning can be applied to the next age group down, which we can call 'middle aged', where their demands for financial services (savings products, pensions) and some luxury products (Mercedes cars, boats and homes in the sun) have grown very strongly in recent years.

IMPLICATIONS FOR GOVERNMENTS, ESPECIALLY THE UK GOVERNMENT

For governments, the biggest potential difficulty arising from the ageing population is the increase in the **dependency ratio** (see definition).

Dependency ratio

This is the ratio of working-age population to the dependent population.

The dependent population are children under 16 and older people over retirement age.

As the proportion of the population over retirement age increases, it puts a much greater strain on the working population who need to fund the services for older people. As detailed above, there has been much greater reliance on the state for looking after older people. There is no doubt this strain will be with us soon, as shown in Figure 6.2.

Figure 6.2 (which does not take into account the number of dependent children under 16) shows the startling change in dependency that has occurred already and will get worse in the future. Currently just over four employees provide earned income to support one pensioner. This will decline to just over three by 2026. The position is worse for other countries. For Germany and Japan, the ratio will be less than three by the same year, and it is estimated that the German rate will be around two by 2040.

The problem for governments is how to raise the increased revenue required from what could be a dwindling source of working population. It has been estimated that each pensioner costs the government around £10,000 per year, net

Figure 6.2 UK dependency: the ratio of 16–64 year-olds to over-65s

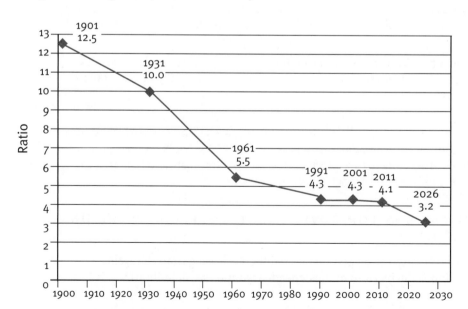

of any tax receipts, through the old age pension, a variety of benefits (housing, disability, etc) and the vast range of medical care (primary care, free prescriptions, hospital stays). Older people are much more prone to illness and therefore impose much greater costs on the health services. It could be argued that some of the additional money required can be raised by savings on services to young people, with reduced expenditure on maternity units and compulsory schooling, although any closure or reduction in services is met by solid resistance from the community. One research estimate is that the additional funding for health is about £1 billion a year, which can be saved by reducing school expenditure, but state pension provision will cost an additional £4 billion a year under existing arrangements (National Institute of Economic and Social Research, quoted in McCrone 1999). Because employees in their 40s and 50s earn more than employees in their 20s, it is expected that increased tax revenue will go some way towards filling this gap.

The pension implications are tough for the United Kingdom and North America, but at least there is reasonable private pension provision that is located in properly funded systems. This, however, is the exception compared with the rest of the world. For most of Europe and other developed countries, the proportion of pensions paid by the state is very much higher, and this is funded as transfer payments under a pay as you go (PAYG) basis, that is directly out of taxation income, rather than from an actual fund of money that has been invested.

Table 6.10 shows the implications for selected countries in terms of the huge government expenditure necessary to pay the pensions as a proportion of their GDP (gross domestic product).

Table 6.10 Public pension expenditure as a percentage of GDP

	1995	2020	2040
United Kingdom	4.5	5.2	7.1
United States	4.1	5.2	7.2
Netherlands	6.0	8.4	12.1
France	10.6	11.6	14.3
Sweden	11.8	13.9	14.9
Spain	10.0	11.3	16.8
Germany	11.1	12.3	18.4
Italy	13.3	15.3	21.4

Source: Eurostat.

There are already substantial problems in France, Germany and Italy over sizeable public sector borrowing. The European Union attempted during 2002–4 to fine these countries as part of the Stability Pact arrangements made at the time of the establishment of the euro to prevent governments incurring excessive expenditure to buy themselves out of financial difficulties. Many commercial organisations are moving production out of these countries to the United Kingdom, Eastern Europe and the developing world to avoid existing high

ACTIVITY

6.6 THE OPTIMISTS

Not all writers regard the pension liabilities as insurmountable or see the necessity of huge increases in taxation or reductions in benefit to solve the pensions problem. What do you consider to be the basis for their optimism?

taxation rates. So how such pension liabilities can be met is sorely testing the economic advisors and central banks in these countries.

A further problem arises from irregular internal migration. Those parts of the country that attract population are faced by considerable pressures on housing, transport and infrastructure services. For example, the housing shortages in London and the south-east have produces continuous shortages in essential public services, especially teachers and nurses who cannot find affordable housing, especially in their early careers. Similar problems occur in the Milan and Turin areas of northern Italy. The governments are faced with planning dilemmas. If they allow housing on green belt land in and around London, it arouses massive opposition. If new roads are built to alleviate congestion, traffic merely increases within a short time to clog up the system (Champion 1993).

In some parts of the world, all these difficulties gel into a bleak prognosis. In California, for example, the State Department of Finance has forecast a 75 per cent increase in population to 60 million by 2050, making it a 'country masquerading as a state' (Kyser 2007). This will lead to a water and power catastrophe, decaying infrastructure, education funding gaps and huge state debt.

Finally, there are problems associated with the skills base. As Jackson explains:

> One reason why the market has been unable to absorb the … unemployed has been the increasing demand for employees with appropriate skills and capabilities. Gaining entry to the labour market has become more difficult as manual occupations have declined and as employers have become more selective about recruits to jobs in the service and quaternary sectors. Britain needs a better trained workforce if it is to meet the challenge from its competitors in Europe and overseas and the current skills gap means that many find themselves excluded from the opportunities of employment.

(Jackson (1998, p125)

Options for governments

Governments will need to either raise taxes or reduce benefits. Some countries have already taken bold steps, such as New Zealand which has abolishing the universal right to an old age pension, and the UK government is raising the age when women can claim the pension to 65 by 2010. However, this can be very damaging politically and is not taken to be lightly. Certainly people can be encouraged to increase their savings for the future by making a larger contribution to their pension schemes, which is done by most governments. In Japan, this has been very successful and the Japanese are the highest savers in the world. (Incidentally, this high saving and reduced consumption has contributed towards a prolonged recession in Japan through most of the 1990s and early 2000s.)

It is also likely that when the full effects of the higher dependency ratio reach the population as a whole, society will be much more affluent and willing to pay the additional costs as part of the understanding that a measure of the decency of a society is how it looks after vulnerable groups, such as the elderly. This will have the effect of placing a greater emphasis on community care for the elderly (Bartlett and Peel 2005).

An alternative approach is to attempt to reverse the demographic trends and to encourage bigger families. This can be done by providing greater financial incentives (tax reliefs and maternity/child benefits) and by encouraging organisations to be more family friendly so that women are able to combine motherhood and a job more easily. The problem is that such actions by governments, such as shown by Japan in Case Study 6.1, appear to have only a marginal effect on the indigenous population. Despite actions in similar forms by many governments in developed countries, it has done little to reverse the flagging fertility rate.

A drastic action could be to open the doors wider to migrants from developing countries. This makes a great deal of long-term economic sense but has a number of political obstacles to overcome in terms of the perceptions of migrants 'taking jobs' and the additional pressures on housing and transport.

One response to the overcrowding in some parts of the country has been to attempt to disperse government departments (as long ago as the early 1970s, the Department of National Savings was moved to Durham, for example) and to provide additional tax and benefit incentives to businesses to move to poorer regions, which is a major pillar in the European Union's economic policy.

The most drastic governmental action seen so far has been in Ulyanovsk, in Russia, where 12 September has been declared 'Conception Day' and couple that conceive under the 'Give birth to a Patriot' scheme can win cars, fridges or cash prizes (*Sunday Times* 2007).

Not everybody, however, insists that an ageing population is so great a problem. Mullan (2002) argues that demographic ageing has no determinate relationship to national economic activity, and that modest levels of economic growth will be more than sufficient to create the wealth required to sustain the costs brought on by greater numbers of elderly dependants.

IMPLICATIONS FOR INTERNATIONAL SOCIETY

The global economy

The most worrying aspect of the current demographic changes is that a mature and ageing population appears to lead directly to reduced economic growth.

Europe and Japan have seen the fastest decline in fertility rates and have also seen the slowest economic growth in the early twenty-first century. The United States, on the other hand, has had a milder strain and has managed to maintain a faster growth rate over the period. In the 'Tiger' economies – China, Korea, Taiwan – and on the Indian subcontinent, where fertility rates, although falling, still remain at or above replacement level, there is a much higher rate of economic growth.

The United Nations has projected that the United States, with its higher fertility rate and greater migration, with catch up Europe's population by 2040 (currently it is 100 million less) and exceed it by 40 million by 2050. The economic implications are far-reaching. The working population of Europe will start to decline in 2010, but for the United States, the current steady growth in its workforce will even start to accelerate in 2025. This will result in the US economy growing twice as fast as that of Europe for the next 50 years. In 2000, the United States accounted for 23 per cent of global GDP compared with Europe's 18 per cent. By 2050, the United Nations estimates the US share will be 26 per cent while Europe's will have shrunk to only 10 per cent. By 2050 the US economy will be two and a half times as big as Europe's, with all the additional political clout that this implies (Smallwood 2003).

In reality, the only way this situation could be reversed would be by radically changing Europe's tight immigration controls, which is a very unlikely event, or if the fertility rate in the US dropped sharply, as it becomes a mature economy.

International migration of work

In the early 2000s, Barclays Bank and other financial institutions announced that they would be cutting their workforces and transferring chunks of their customer service and 'back-office' administration work to other countries, particularly India. The costs of carrying out this work in developing countries are just a fraction of UK costs and the work forces are young, educated, English-speaking and flexible in their approach to working hours and the nature of work. These decisions were made because the demographic changes, and the responses made by governments (India has invested heavily in English-speaking education), have made such countries good substitutes for UK labour.

This situation has been replicated around the globe. In the United States, work migration is an important political issue dividing the parties, while German

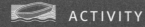

ACTIVITY

6.7 NURSES ON THE MOVE

In 2003, the South African government placed a prohibition on UK companies recruiting qualified nurses to work in the NHS, viewing the exodus of skilled workers such as nurses as a matter of long-term disaster for the country? Do you agree with this viewpoint? Discuss the issue from both viewpoints.

EXAMPLES OF GERMAN JOBS EXODUS 2002–4

Lufthansa: European ticket sales based in Krakau, Poland. Aircraft engines serviced in Hungary, China and the Philippines.

Motorola: 600 engineering jobs moved to China. Repair work moved to Eastern Europe.

Deutsche Bank: Deutsche Software subsidiary moved to India with 4,000 jobs.

SAP, business software and systems: Created 1,500 jobs in Bangalore, India and new 120-strong R&D centre in Shanghai.

Continental Tyres: three German factories closed, work transferred to three new factories in Romania, Czech Republic and Slovakia.

Source: Woodhead (2004).

unions have had to respond to threats to move industrial work in companies such as Volkswagen to Eastern Europe by agreeing to reduce hourly wages (see Case Study 6.6).

THE WORLD'S RESOURCES

In the twentieth century, the inventiveness, organisational powers and application of technology from farmers, merchants, entrepreneurs and companies of all sizes, allowed the tripling world population to be adequately provided for in terms of food, water and power. Not completely of course, with intermittent famines and a growing imbalance between rich and poor countries. However, it had been considered unlikely that such expansion of resources could continue at this breakneck pace for another 100 years.

The forecasts of a levelling out of the population by mid-century must be regarded, therefore, as good news for everybody. The strains on space and exploitation of a limited land mass, especially where global warming appears to be reducing capacity, may now be much lessened, although these pressures are brought about not just by numbers of population but by their overall demands. A richer, more consuming population still has the capacity to wreak enormous damage on our planet's infrastructure.

- The major demographic trends across the world are a major decline in the birth rate, population ageing and increasing migration, both of people and jobs. These trends are strongest in the developed world, especially Europe.

- These trends are likely to continue to produce a reversal of world population expansion around 2050. Developed countries are likely to be faced by declining populations before that time unless they change policies and allow higher rates of migration.

- These demographic changes provide opportunities for organisations to move into new product and service areas. The reduction in the availability of younger labour means that organisations will need to reorganise work patterns to encourage greater participation from women, older people and other groups.

- Governments will increasingly be faced by the need for higher expenditure on pensions, benefits and health services as a result of demographic changes. At the same time, the higher dependency ratio is likely to necessitate higher levels of taxation to finance this expenditure. Initiatives to combat these difficulties can include encouraging larger families through incentives, reducing benefits and stimulating personal savings for pensions and health.

- It is likely that an ageing population will be a less production one, providing challenges for the world economy and wealth creation. There has been a rapid transfer of jobs and services around the world as an outcome of globalisation.

1. What have been the main changes in sectorial employment in the United Kingdom since 1992?

2. Provide five reasons why migration can provide benefits for an economy and set out five problems that migration can bring.

3. What have been the main causes of a reducing fertility rate in Europe since 1970?

4. How can the UK government handle the current crisis in pension provision as a result of the ageing population? What options does it have?

5. What is the 'dependency ratio'?

6. How is the 'participation ratio' measured and what has caused the rate to rise in the United Kingdom since the late 1990s?

7. Why has the number of migrants to the United Kingdom increased since the mid-1990s?

8. What are the implications for organisations in terms of changing markets arising from demographic changes?

9. How can organisations react to the reducing number of younger people coming onto the labour market?

10. How can demographic changes affect HR activities and policies?

CHAPTER 7
Social trends

LEARNING OUTCOMES

By the end of this chapter, readers should be able to understand, explain and critically evaluate:

- major theories of social stratification

- the main socioeconomic classifications used in the United Kingdom

- the nature and extent of social mobility in the United Kingdom

- reasons for the slowing rate of social mobility in the United Kingdom, and its effects

- the extent and nature of inequality and poverty in the United Kingdom

- changes in the industrial and employment structure in the United Kingdom, and the growth of flexible forms of organisation

- the nature and importance of the psychological contract

- work–life balance

- similarities and differences between equal opportunities and diversity

- the changing nature and role of trade unions, particularly New Unionism.

INTRODUCTION

This chapter analyses recent trends in society and social structure in the United Kingdom. We start with an analysis of social stratification, including a discussion of social class. We then analyse social mobility and inequality, and the continuing existence of poverty in the United Kingdom. We then look behind the class structure and analyse the factors that have led to social change, including changes in the industrial structure, the nature of work and attitudes to work. We conclude with an analysis of the current role and position of trade unions.

CLASS

KARL MARX

The concept of class as a social concept goes back to the writings of Karl Marx in the mid-nineteenth century. To Marx class was related to ownership of the means of production. He divided society into two classes, the bourgeoisie, or capitalists, who owned the means of production, and the proletariat, wage workers, who owned only their own labour. The relationship between the two classes was one of exploitation. The capitalists, through their ownership of the means of production – factories, machines, etc – controlled the production process, and used this power to exploit the workers. In particular, the capitalists pocketed the difference between what they paid the workers and the value of the goods produced – what Marx called 'surplus value'.

One thing that will strike you immediately about Marx's analysis is that he recognises only two classes – capitalists and workers. There is no mention of the class that is generally seen as numerically dominant today, the middle class. This is inevitable given Marx's approach. You were either a 'have' (a capitalist) or a 'have not' (a worker). He recognised that there were managers who ran the factories on behalf of the capitalists, and who would not see themselves as workers. These managers later became a key segment of the middle class, but Marx dismissed any aspirations they had to separate themselves from the working class as 'false class consciousness'. In the last resort, he saw them as being as much pawns of the capitalists as the proletariat was.

MAX WEBER

The German sociologist Max Weber, writing at the end of the nineteenth century, argued that Marx's class system was over-simplistic. Class, based on the ownership of property, was important, but it was only one element of social stratification. Unlike Marx, he recognised a significant middle class, including the self-employed, civil servants, clerks and professionals. Weber argued that status and power were also important. Status is a measure of social standing, and refers to the way that society regards individuals and groups. For example, in many societies, doctors or teachers have a high social standing, based on their education and skills. Power is the ability to influence decisions, This is mainly to do with access to political power, which could be used to gain wealth and prestige, as in Italy in the 1980s, or much of Africa in the 1990s.

His concept of class was different from Marx's. Whereas Marx emphasised the ownership of property, Weber saw class as being much more a function of market capacity – the skills and attributes that individuals bring to the labour market, and which determine their success or failure.

Runciman (1990) has combined the Marxist and Weberian approaches by stressing the concept of economic power. He sees this as having three dimensions:

- ownership – legal title to the means of production (nowadays more often through share ownership rather than direct ownership)

- control – a contractual right to direct or manage the means of production (ie managers)

- marketability – skills or capacity with a value in the labour market.

An individual's position in the social hierarchy can derive from any of these dimensions.

Putting the Marxist and Weberian models together, and incorporating Runciman's approach, we can produce a stratification system as shown in Table 7.1.

Table 7.1 A class stratification system

Class	Characteristics
Upper class	Owners of the means of production Very advantageous life chances
Middle class	Non-owners of direct productive wealth, but owners of personal wealth and some indirect productive wealth(houses, pension funds, unit trusts etc) Advantageous life chances due to market capacity from non-manual skills
Manual workers	Non-owners of productive wealth, very little personal wealth Disadvantageous life chances as a result of falling demand for manual skills
Underclass	Non-owners of any sort of wealth Grossly disadvantageous life chances as a result of marginal position in the labour market

Source: adapted from Bilton *et al* (1996).

SOCIOECONOMIC CLASSIFICATIONS

There are several different ways in which social stratification is measured in the United Kingdom. One of these is the National Statistics Socio-economic Classifications Scale (NS-NEC) used by the government for the first time for the 2001 census.

This divides the population into eight categories:

1   Higher managerial and professional occupations. This is subdivided into:
   1.1   Employers and managers in larger organisations (company directors, senior civil servants, senior police and armed forces officers)
   1.2   Higher professionals (doctors, lawyers, clergy)

2   Lower managerial and professional occupations (nurses, journalists, actors, prison officers)

3   Intermediate occupations (clerks, secretaries, driving instructors)

4   Small employers and own-account workers (publicans, farmers, taxi drivers, window cleaners)

5   Lower supervisory, craft and related occupations (printers, television engineers, train drivers)

6   Semi-routine occupations (shop assistants, hairdressers, bus drivers)

7   Routine occupations (labourers, waiters, refuse collectors)

8   Those who have never had paid work and the long term unemployed.

The theoretical underpinning for this classification is to differentiate social position in relation to type of employment relationship. The key criterion is thus how much freedom someone has over their work, rather than the amount of money they earn. The higher the degree to which someone controls the terms and conditions of their working life, the higher their classification (ISER 2002).

A similar classification is the JICNARS market research classification:

A   Upper middle class: higher managerial, administrative or professional (bank manager, bishop, coroner, professor)

B   Middle class: middle to senior management and professionals (police chief inspector, priest, probation officer, senior buyer)

C1 Lower middle class: junior management, supervisory, secretarial and clerical (accounts clerk, bank cashier, staff nurse, receptionist)

C2 Skilled working class: manual trades (bus driver, bricklayer, carpenter, train driver)

D   Working class: semi and unskilled workers (refuse collector, bus conductor, ratcatcher)

E   Pensioners, widows and those on the breadline.

 ACTIVITY

7.1 SOCIAL STRATIFICATION

- How useful do you think the NS-NEC and JICNARS classifications are in explaining social class in the United Kingdom?

- If you were a marketing manager, what further classifications would you find useful for your job?

SOCIAL MOBILITY

Social mobility is the movement of people up or down the social hierarchy, either within one generation (intragenerational mobility) or between generations (intergenerational mobility). Intergenerational mobility is easiest to measure, by taking the occupation of fathers and comparing this with the occupation of their offspring.

CASE STUDY 7.1

THE DEATH OF CLASS

In his book *Sociology* (5th edn, 2006), Anthony Giddens discusses the theories of Jan Pajulski and Malcolm Waters, and their book, *The death of class*.

The core of their argument is that whereas class was fundamentally a function of production, social stratification in the twenty-first century is based primarily on consumption. The more a person is able to engage in 'status consumption' (cars, clothes, houses, holidays etc), the higher his or her status in society.

They also argue that globalisation and its effects have led to an international division of labour, which has lessened the importance of class within a country like the United Kingdom. The First World is post-industrial – there are fewer manual working-class occupations, because these have shifted to countries like China and India. Skilled manual jobs have given way to knowledge and service-sector jobs. As a result, collective class-based communities, and the class solidarity they displayed, such as those associated with coal mining, have vanished.

They claim that society is now 'individualised', and that behaviour and attitudes are now primarily influenced by factors such as race, gender, age and national identity.

There are clear parallels between the 'death of class' thesis and the 'embourgeoisement' thesis, popular in the 1950s, which argued that the working class was becoming more like the middle class. This thesis was examined in detail in the 1960s by John Goldthorpe in the *Affluent worker* study (1968–9). Based on his study of car workers in Luton, Goldthorpe found that affluent workers, although they had incomes comparable with those of the middle class, did not associate with white-collar workers in their leisure time, and they did not take on middle-class norms and values. However,

Goldthorpe did agree with Pajulski and Waters that collective class solidarity had evaporated. The affluent workers were individualistic, with a home-centred outlook, and little interest in collective concepts like class.

There have been no strictly comparable studies since Goldthorpe's work, but anecdotal evidence would suggest that divisions between the working and middle class have lessened considerably since the 1960s. Margaret Thatcher's wholesale sale of council houses to sitting tenants ensured that large numbers of the working class now own their own house (estimated at 50 per cent). Another factor which may well have lessened class differences is the much greater influence of television compared with the 1960s – in particular the way in which 'soaps' like *EastEnders* have become universal viewing.

However, affluence alone is not enough to bourgeoisify the working class. As Ken Roberts says, 'something only has to become normal within the working class for it to lose any middle-class associations' (Roberts 2001, p99). This has happened with package holidays, deserted in droves by the middle class, and with ex-council houses, which are regarded as very much second rate in the housing market.

In addition, whether or not it is strictly class-based, the fact remains that inequality still exists in the United Kingdom, and is increasing, and that social mobility is lessening, as we discuss in greater detail below. The boundaries of class may have changed, and it could be argued that the fundamental class divide is now between the 75 per cent who own their own houses, and the 25 per cent who do not – and, given current levels of house prices, have little prospect of ever doing so.

We return to the classless society concept in a later Activity.

Another distinction is between absolute social mobility (the number or proportion of people who move from one social class to another) and relative social mobility (the probability of a member of a social class moving to another class). Opportunities for social mobility are one dimension of an individual's life chances, the opportunity to better his or her quality of life. Other dimensions are the absence of poverty, and access to decent standards of health and education. Quality of life varies with social class, ethnic group, gender and locality (Aldridge 2004).

Until the Second World War, there was considerable absolute social mobility in the UK, but downward mobility was nearly as common as upward. Since the Second World War, upward absolute social mobility has considerably outweighed downward, with the trend increasing – it is much higher for men born in 1950–9 (the latest available figures) than for men born in 1920–9 (the first group to have reached maturity after the Second World War). The main reason for this upward mobility is that there is 'more room at the top'. In 1900, the middle class made up 18 per cent of the population, while the working class made up 62 per cent. By 2000, the middle class was 42 per cent of the population and the working class 38 per cent.

While the picture on absolute social mobility looks positive, the picture is very different when we look at relative mobility. Because the middle class is bigger, this means that children of middle-class parents have less risk of falling down into the working class, ie downward social mobility has fallen. The result has been that the chances of a working-class child making it to the middle class have changed little – it is estimated that a working-class child is 15 times less likely to make it into the middle class than a middle-class child is to stay in the middle class.

Most worryingly, there is some evidence that social mobility, however it is measured, is slowing down. This is best shown by figures on income. Studies have been made of the correlation between fathers' earnings and offsprings' earnings. A correlation of 0 would imply complete income mobility between generations (ie that a father's income has no influence on his offspring's income) while a correlation of 1 would imply total immobility (ie that an offspring's place in the income scale is exactly the same as his or her father's). For the United Kingdom, correlations have been found of between 0.4 and 0.6 for sons' earnings, and between 0.45 and 0.7 for daughters. The higher the correlation the less income mobility, and, by implication, the lower the level of social mobility.

Closer examination of the correlations shows two disturbing trends:

- Correlations are much higher in the United Kingdom than in countries such as Canada, Sweden and Finland.
- A comparison of those born in 1958 with those born in 1970 shows the correlations increasing – ie social mobility in the United Kingdom is falling.

One study compared two sons, both born in 1958, who left school in the 1970s. The parents of one earned twice as much as the parents of the other. By their early 30s, the son of the richer parents earned 17.5 per cent more than the poorer son. For two comparable boys born in 1970 who left school in the 1980s, the income gap had widened to 25 per cent (Blanden, Gregg and Machin 2005).

In 2007 the educational charity the Sutton Trust researched the educational backgrounds of 500 leading figures in the law, politics, medicine, journalism and business. They found that over half had been educated at an independent school, although these only educate 7 per cent of the population, and that this figure had barely changed over the past 20 years. In addition 47 per cent of the top 500 were Oxbridge educated (Sutton Trust 2007).

CASE STUDY 7.2

SOCIAL MOBILITY: MANAGERS AND PROFESSIONALS

Both managers and professionals are clearly members of the middle class. However, as Fielding (1995) has showed, the two groups have different experiences of social mobility. Using the OPCS longitudinal study (a 1 per cent sample of the population), he tracked mobility over the period 1981–91.

He found that managers were much less socially secure than professionals. Of those who were in professional positions in 1981, and were still in the labour market in 1991, 69 per cent remained in a professional position, but only 51 per cent of managers were still managers. One in three managers experienced downward social mobility over the decade, compared with one in six of professionals. The difference was even more marked for women. Of women managers in 1981, nearly half had experienced downward mobility by 1991, while this was true of only 30 per cent of male managers.

Why should there be this difference between managers and professionals? The most likely explanation is that most managers in the United Kingdom have received no specific management education. Their status depends on their position within a particular organisation, and is not easily transferable to another organisation. A professional, on the other hand, has a highly transferable educational qualification.

INEQUALITY

Inequality in society can be measured in a number of ways, but the easiest are distribution of wealth or income. Wealth is extremely unevenly distributed in the United Kingdom, although rather less unevenly than in the 1950s, and much less unevenly than in the 1920s, when the top 1 per cent owned over 60 per cent of marketable wealth (Abercrombie and Warde 2000). (See Table 7.2.)

Several points can be drawn from these figures:

- Inequality in wealth fell over the period from 1954 to 1981. The main reason for this seems to have been the spread of home ownership, from perhaps 20 per cent just after the war to around 75 per cent by 1994. For the first time this gave most of the middle class, and some sections of the working class, access to wealth.

Table 7.2 Distribution of wealth in the United Kingdom (%)

	1954	1975	1981	1994	2002
Top 1 per cent	43.0	23.2	18.0	19.0	23.0
Top 10 per cent	79.0	62.4	50.0	51.0	56.0
Top 50 per cent		92.0	93.0	93.0	94.0

Source: ONS (2004).

- Wealth inequality has widened since 1981 (in reality from the election of the Thatcher government in 1979). Drastic cuts in the higher rates of tax, privatisation and the long-term rise in the stock market have all contributed to this trend, which has not been reversed under New Labour. The top 1 per cent hold 75 per cent of privately held shares, the top 5 per cent own 90 per cent.

- The bottom half of the population has never owned significant wealth, and this has not changed in recent years.

If we exclude the value of dwellings, wealth is even more unevenly held. In 2002, the top 1 per cent held 35 per cent of all marketable wealth less value of dwellings, the top 5 per cent 62 per cent, and the top 50 per cent 98 per cent (ONS 2004).

A slightly less pessimistic picture comes if we include the right to a state old age pension as part of wealth. If we do this, the share of the top 50 per cent for 1994 falls from 93 to 83 per cent.

The same pattern emerges if we examine distribution of income, as shown in Table 7.3.

Key points from this table are:

- Income inequality narrowed marginally between 1961 and 1979, but has widened again since 1979.

- Income distribution in 1997 was more uneven than it had been in 1961.

- Margaret Thatcher's 'trickle-down' theory, that increasing the wealth and income of the rich would produce a trickle down of greater income and wealth lower down the scale, appears to be a myth.

Table 7.3 Distribution of income (United Kingdom) (before housing costs)

	1961	1979	1994	1997
Top 10 per cent	22.0	21.0	26.0	26.0
Top 20 per cent	37.0	35.0	41.0	41.0
Top 50 per cent	70.6	68.0	72.0	72.0
Bottom 10 per cent	4.2	4.2	3.1	3.1

Source: adapted from George and Wilding (1999).

- Even when inequality was lessening, this did not benefit the bottom 10 per cent.

Since 1997, the share of the bottom 10 per cent has improved slightly, largely as a result of Gordon Brown's use of tax credits targeted at the poorest, but inequality generally seems to have continued to increase. An increased emphasis on indirect rather than direct taxes, which started well before 1997, has tended to hit the bottom end of the distribution harder than the top. Since 1979, the proportion of income paid in tax by the lowest 20 per cent of taxpayers has risen from 31 to 42 per cent, while the proportion paid by the highest fifth has fallen from 37 to 34 per cent. (Clark 2004). Yes, the poor pay a higher proportion of income in tax than the rich!

Inequality is still increasing. The highest 1 per cent of earners have increased their share of national income by 3 per cent since Labour came to power in 1997, the share of the top 0.1 per cent is now the same as it was in 1937, and the share of the top 20 per cent grew in 1996–7, as the share of the bottom 20 per cent fell (Milne 2007).

A method used by statisticians to measure inequality is the Gini coefficient. This expresses income distribution on a scale of 0 to 100, with 0 representing total equality. The higher the figure, the more uneven the distribution. The Gini coefficient figures have changed as shown in Table 7.4.

Table 7.4 Gini coefficient (before housing costs)

1961	1970	1979	1991	1997	2002
26	26	25	34	33	36

Source: George and Wilding (1999) and Clark (2004).

On the Gini figures, inequality was constant over the period 1961–79, widened under the Thatcher governments, narrowed slightly under the Major government, and has widened significantly under New Labour since 1997.

POVERTY

Absolute poverty in the Ethiopian sense does not exist in the United Kingdom. A more useful definition is relative poverty, and this is inescapable in a society in which income is distributed unevenly. However, relative poverty can be defined in many different ways – assistance level, assistance level plus x per cent, half median earnings, 60 per cent of median earnings, before or after housing costs. The definition standardised throughout the European Union is household income below 60 per cent of median income (after housing costs) – approximately £12,000 a year in 2004. On this definition, poverty rose steadily throughout the Thatcher and Major years, reaching a peak of 13.9 million people (nearly a quarter of the population) in 1997, falling since to 12.4 million in 2004 (Clark 2004). Of 16 industrialised countries measured for poverty in 1995, the United Kingdom was twelfth, with twice the level of poverty of Sweden and Finland, and slightly less than Ireland, Greece, Italy and the United States (Aldridge 2004).

Poverty is particularly influenced by three factors:

- Children. The percentage of households with incomes below 60 per cent of the median was around 20 per cent of the whole population in 2000–1, but around 30 per cent for households with children. The proportion for single-parent households was even higher. When New Labour came to power, one of its main objectives was to eliminate child poverty, which had grown from one in seven in 1979 to one in three in 1997. By 2003, the government had reduced it to one in four, but 72 per cent of children of lone parents were still classed as poor in 2007 (Toynbee 2007). One in four of all children (2.7 million) were in a lone-parent family in 2001 (Carvel 2003).

- Gender. Despite 30 years of equal pay legislation, average female hourly earnings are still only around 75 per cent of male earnings, and women on average work fewer hours than men. This particularly hits single-parent households headed by women (the vast majority).

- Ethnicity. Ethic minority groups are likely to have lower incomes than whites – average weekly male pay in 2000 was £297 for whites, £264 for Chinese, £254 for Afro-Caribbeans, £222 for Pakistanis and £142 for Bangladeshis. Only Indians, at £307, have a higher income than whites. However, after we take account of the fact that Indians on average have higher educational qualifications than whites, their 'like for like' earnings are lower. In 1995, more than a third of the ethnic minority population was in the poorest fifth of the population (George and Wilding 1999). In 1991, unemployment rates for all ethnic minority groups were twice those of the white population, and unemployment rates for Bangladeshis were three times as high for men and five times as high for women.

Poverty matters because it affects future life chances. Infant mortality rates are twice as high for unskilled manual groups as they are professionals. Life expectancy for male professionals in 1997/9 was 79, and for female professionals 83, while for unskilled manual groups the corresponding figures were 75 and 77. The lower your income, the more likely you are to be a victim of burglary.

The percentage of children aged between 5 and 15 experiencing mental disorders is between two and three times higher for those living in households with an income of less than £100 a week than it is for those in households earning over £700 a week. Most poor children fail. Their depressed parents are unable to give them aspirations (Toynbee 2004).

Poverty persists across the generations. Of people whose families were poor when they were in their teens in the 1970s, 19 per cent were poor in their early 30s, while where families were not poor in the 1970s, 10 per cent were poor as adults. Dividing 19 per cent by 10 per cent shows that the odds of being poor as an adult were doubled if one's parents were poor. For teenagers in the 1980s, the odds of being poor were quadrupled when their parents were poor (Blanden and Gibbons 2006).

Research in 2007 by the Joseph Rowntree Foundation examined public attitudes to poverty. More than half of the UK population felt that there was quite a lot of poverty in the country, and 46 per cent thought poverty would increase over the next 10 years. Seventy-three per cent of the UK population in 2004 felt that the gap between high and low incomes was too large. While they did not necessarily think that those on low incomes were underpaid, they felt that those on high incomes were very overpaid. However, only half as many people supported redistributive measures to reduce poverty as felt that the income gap was too great (Orton and Rowlingson 2007).

ACTIVITY

7.2 POVERTY AND INEQUALITY

a. In 2001, the average chief executive officer in the United Kingdom earned £509,000, while the average manufacturing worker earned £20,475, a differential of around 25:1. German CEOs averaged £298,000, 11 times a German manufacturing worker. The ratio in the United States was 32:1. Executive pay in the United Kingdom had soared by 29 per cent between 1999 and 2001, and has risen relative to average wages since 2001 (Duncan 2001). What do you think the impact of these differentials is likely to be on the motivation of manufacturing workers in the United Kingdom?

b. Why should social inequality matter to employers? What can they do about it?

c. The Joseph Rowntree Foundation in 2007 identified five types of household:

  ● core poor: income poor, materially deprived and subjectively poor

  ● breadline poor: living below a relative poverty line

  ● asset wealthy: holding assets which reach the inheritance tax threshold

  ● exclusive wealthy: so much wealth that they are outside the norms of society

  ● average: everyone else.

Figures for these groups in 1980 and 2000 were (%):

	1980	2000
Core poor*	10	12
Breadline poor	17	27
Exclusive wealthy*	7	6
Asset wealthy	17	23
Average	66	50

* Core poor is a subset of breadline poor; exclusive wealthy is a subset of asset wealthy. Exclusive wealthy declined sharply during the 1980s, then rose from 1990 to 2000.

The research also found that poor, rich and average households are less likely to live next door to each other in 2000 than in 1970. Both the poor and the wealthy have become more and more clustered in different areas (Dorling et al 2007).

What do you think are the social consequences of the trends identified above?

d. What can the government do to increase social mobility and equality of opportunity, and to reduce poverty?

How easy is it to move out of poverty? The answer seems to be not easy, but not impossible. Evidence from the British Household Panel Survey shows that just over half of the individuals who were in the bottom quintile (lowest 20 per cent) for income in 1991 were still there in 1996. In other words, half had escaped from dire poverty. Over a one-year time span, 65 per cent stayed in the bottom quintile, and of those who escaped, most stayed in the bottom two quintiles (ie the bottom 40 per cent) (Giddens 2006). McKnight (2000) found that the unemployed are most likely to gain employment in the lowest-paid sectors when they do find work, and that the lower paid are more likely to become unemployed than the higher paid.

Even after recent falls in child poverty, the United Kingdom has the fourth worst figures among the EU 25. Only Italy, Portugal and the Slovak Republic have higher rates. Contributory factors include pay inequalities, a high proportion of lone parents, their low chance of working, and less generous welfare benefits. (Barnard and Goulden 2006). Child poverty could be ended, but at a cost. It would involve a massive increase in child tax credits, estimated at £30 billion up to 2020. Barnard and Goulden point out that this only represents one year's economic growth. Money alone will not be enough. Considerable practical and emotional support in increasing the self-esteem of lone-parent families will also be needed, through the expansion of educational programmes such as Sure Start and employment programmes like New Deal.

TRENDS IN EMPLOYMENT

CHANGES IN THE INDUSTRIAL STRUCTURE

In 1951, manufacturing accounted for a third of GDP and nearly 40 per cent of employment. By 2001 employment in manufacturing had fallen to 14 per cent of the workforce, although as the size of the workforce had increased considerably, the number working in manufacturing had only fallen from 8.7 to 3.7 million. Part of the reason for this fall is the shift of manufacturing jobs to Eastern Europe and the Far East, a consequence of globalisation. Another reason was peculiar to the United Kingdom – the chronic over-valuation of the pound since the late 1970s, which made UK manufacturing uncompetitive, and triggered recessions in the early 1980s and early 1990s. The trend continues: the pound is still high, and there is much talk of a two-speed economy, with booming services and recessionary manufacturing. Where manufacturing has survived, the nature of work within it has changed, from skilled and semi-skilled manual work to much more knowledge-based and less manual work.

The fall in mining and quarrying was even more marked, from 880,000 workers in 1951 to 76,000 in 2001 (Philpott 2002). The share of public services in GDP has fallen markedly since the early 1950s, although employment has remained more or less constant at around 5 million. Falls in privatised public corporations and the armed forces have been matched by growths in education and the NHS. Services of all kinds have boomed, and grew from about half of employment in 1966 to around three-quarters in 2001 (Gallie 2000).

There have also been changes in the occupational level of the workforce. The share of manual workers in the workforce fell from 64 per cent in 1952 to 38 per cent in 1991, with the biggest proportionate fall among unskilled manual workers, whose percentage fell by nearly two-thirds. Skilled manual workers fell from 25 per cent of the workforce in 1951 to 12 per cent in 2001, while the managerial, professional and technical workforce rose from 12 per cent in 1951 to nearly 40 per cent in 2001, and relatively poorly paid service sector jobs also increased.

The above trends are typical of most of western Europe, although the proportion of workers in manufacturing is higher in Germany and Italy, and the proportion working in services higher in the Netherlands (Gallie 2000).

THE FEMINISATION OF THE WORKFORCE

Male participation rates (the proportion of the population of working age who are in employment) have fallen steadily since 1951 (and indeed since 1911). They were 88 per cent in 1951 and had fallen to 71 per cent in 1998 (Gallie 2000). The fall is explained by early retirement, and greater levels of sickness incapacity. Female rates over the same period have risen from 33 to 54 per cent. As a result the share of women in the labour force has risen from 30 to 44 per cent. All of the gain in female employment has come about as a result of the increased participation on the labour force of married women. The single participation rate has fallen from 73 per cent in 1991 to 64 per cent in 1991, while the married women participation rate has risen from 22 to 53 per cent. It is difficult to remember that in the early 1950s women in occupations like the civil service were routinely expected to resign when they married!

Women are under-represented in the higher professions, managers and administrators, and manual work, while they are over-represented in lower professionals and technicians (primarily education and the NHS), clerical work and sales. Women are expected to account for two-thirds of all expected job increases over the period to 2010 (Green 2003).

Why has the work force become feminised? Giddens (2006) puts forward three main reasons:

- Demographic trends. The birth rate has declined, and women are having children at a later age. As a result, they work for longer before they have children. As families are smaller, it is easier for them to return to work after having children. Domestic housework has also become much less labour-intensive, and men are at last tending to take a greater share of it. Women spend nearly three hours a day on housework, but men spend one hour 40 minutes (ONS 2003).

- Financial pressures. Single mothers often have little choice but to work, and increasingly this is being encouraged by the working of the welfare support system. Even two-parent families often find they need two incomes to maintain their desired standard of living.

- Personal fulfilment. The women's movement in the 1960s and 1970s increased women's self-esteem, and a desire among women for more independence.

A fourth reason could be that women workers are particularly attractive to employers, because they are much more likely to want to work part-time. In 2004, there were 5.2 million women in the United Kingdom in part-time employment, as against only 1.2 million men. Part-time workers are much more flexible than full-time ones, and this gives a considerable advantage to employers.

CASE STUDY 7.3

THE FEMALE FORFEIT

In the 1990s, Rake (2000) examined the lifetime earning experiences of women. Women suffer two detrimental effects in the labour market: the female forfeit – how much less a woman would earn in a lifetime than a comparable man, even if she has no children – and the mother gap – how much less a woman with children would earn compared with a childless woman. Together these make up the parent gap – the female forfeit and the parent gap combined.

Three case studies were put forward:

- Mrs Low Skill has no qualifications and works as a shop assistant. She has two children, takes nine years out of the labour market (because she cannot afford expensive childcare), and then works part-time. Her female forfeit is £197,000, her mother gap £285,000, and her parent gap £482,000.

- Mrs Mid Skill has GCSEs and works as a secretary. Again she has two children, is out of the labour market for two years and then works part-time. Her female forfeit is £241,000, her mother gap £140,000 and her parent gap £381,000.

- Mrs High Skill is a graduate teacher. She also has two children, works part-time for a year, then works full-time (because she can afford childcare). Her female forfeit is £143,000, her mother gap only £19,000, and her parent gap £162,000.

It appears that inequality in the labour market hits the poor much more than the (relatively) rich. To some extent this is deceptive, because it takes no account of childcare costs. As all three examples above are married and part of an enduring nuclear family, childcare costs presumably fall on the family unit rather than on the woman herself. However, single mothers have to meet childcare costs themselves (albeit with some state support).

ACTIVITY

7.3 SOCIAL CLASS

'There is no such thing as society' (Margaret Thatcher); 'The classless society' (John Major); 'We are all middle class now' (anon).

Explain each of these statements. Do you agree with any of them?

THE FEMINISATION OF MANAGEMENT

CASE STUDY 7.4

The National Management Salary Survey has been carried out by the Chartered Management Institute and Remuneration Economics for 34 years. The last two surveys (2005 and 2006) throw interesting light in the feminisation of management.

The 2005 report found that women made up 35.7 per cent of managers and directors, up from 31 per cent the year before. Women were a majority of managers under the age of 29, although female representation fell rapidly after that age. Between 35 and 39, women made up only a third of managers, and only 11 per cent of those aged 50 or more (CMI 2006). Women received more rapid promotion than men, however. The average female team leader was 37, the average male team leader 42. For department heads, the corresponding ages were 40 and 43 (CMI 2007).

For 10 years up to 2005, the pay gap between male and female managers narrowed. The gap was 13.6 per cent of earnings in 2003, and narrowed to 11.8 per cent in 2005, but in 2006 it rose to 12.2 per cent. The only sectors with anything approaching wage equality were the public sector and charities, where the gap was only 0.7 per cent. In HR the gap was 40 per cent, with female managers earning on average £35,198, and males £47,502 (Carvel 2007).

ACTIVITY

7.4 THE HARLOW ECONOMY

Harlow is a New Town in the county of Essex in south-east England, designated in 1947, and about 25 miles from central London. Harlow's population peaked around 1980, fell to 75,000 in 1991, and rose again to nearly 80,000 in 2001. The original population moved into Harlow between the early 1950s and the late 1960s, attracted by the twin offers of a job and a house. The number of people of pensionable age in the Harlow population is on a steep upward trend, from 5 per cent of the population in 1971 to 16 per cent in 1991 and 21 per cent in 2001.

Harlow attracted the growth industries of the 1960s, including printing, electrical and mechanical engineering, and distilling. Like the rest of the United Kingdom, it has experienced a decline in manufacturing industry, although this was much more rapid than elsewhere. As recently as 1985, the split between manufacturing and service employment was about 50:50, a much higher emphasis on manufacturing than in the United Kingdom in general, but by 1993 manufacturing had fallen to 28 per cent, and by 2000 to 24 per cent (still higher than in the United Kingdom generally). Service employment had risen to 68.5 per cent by 1993, and to 72 per cent by 2000.

The biggest employers in Harlow today are research and development, in the pharmaceutical and electronics/telecoms industries, and the NHS. The Harlow economy is dominated by large employers to a greater extent than the rest of Essex. It has 4.5 per cent of the county's total number of businesses, but 7.1 per cent of the county's employment. There are relatively fewer small businesses than elsewhere in Essex – 373 VAT registrations per 10,000 population, compared with 562 for Essex as a whole. However, there is a mismatch in skills between the resident Harlow population and the growing employment sectors. Nearly half of all those employed in Harlow live outside the town. Conversely, there is considerable commuting from Harlow into London. The average wage of people employed in Harlow was £444 a week, while for those living in Harlow it was only £383. This shows that higher-paid jobs in the town are predominantly taken by people from outside.

In 1989 unemployment in Harlow was roughly half the national average, but by 1993 this had increased to slightly above the national average. Although unemployment in Harlow is now about the national average, large areas of Harlow are defined as socially deprived, and Harlow is the third most deprived community in the East of England.

Sources: Harlow District Council (1993, 2002), Harlow Renaissance (2007).

How would you explain the changing economic and social structure of Harlow? In particular consider:

Questions

a. the delayed collapse in manufacturing (Harlow manufacturing was barely affected by the 1981–2 recession, but was hard hit by that in the early 1990s)

b. the changing patterns in unemployment – from below the national average to above the average, to equal to the average

c. the extent of in-commuting

d. the extent of social deprivation.

WORK ORGANISATION

THE FLEXIBLE ORGANISATION

The typical organisation in the 1950s and 1960s was large, monolithic and rigid, typified by the nationalised industries like the National Coal Board and British Railways – businesses employing tens of thousands, even hundreds of thousands, with many levels of management and a bureaucratic culture. Status was all-important, and the objective of a manager was to climb up the ladder of the hierarchy. The ethos was male, and based on conformity.

This rigid type of organisation was faltering by the 1970s, although in Japan it was to survive until the depression of the 1990s. By the 1970s, the dominant form was the conglomerate, with groups of disparate businesses held together by a small strategic headquarters. The view had developed that a successful manager could manage anything, hence it did not matter that the activities of the conglomerate bore little relation to each other. There was also slightly more flexibility, as a career could develop across the conglomerate. Again the conglomerate structure survived longer in Japan than anywhere else, where it formed the basis of the *keiretsu* system.

By the 1980s, conglomerates were going out of fashion, and the new orthodoxy was that expressed by Peters and Waterman in *In search of excellence* (1982) – 'stick to the knitting'. The spread of computers and IT-based management techniques also lessened the importance of economies of scale, and made smaller businesses economically viable. 'Stick to the knitting' was pushed further and further, as organisations started to outsource their non-core functions, leading in the ultimate to the concept of the 'virtual corporation'. Here advanced IT and communication techniques permit the organisation to become totally fluid, consisting of individuals who come together to perform particular tasks, and then separate again.

Changes in the external environment have increased the pressure on organisations to become more and more responsive. Not only have organisations become smaller, they have also changed their internal organisation. The old 'smokestack' structure of large monolithic vertical departments, each with its own hierarchy, and little contact with each other, has proved too unresponsive, and increasingly has been replaced by a more flexible and fluid matrix type of organisation, based around teams, which can form, dissolve and reform to tackle particular problems. The result has been a delayering within organisations, with many fewer layers of management. Either a manager has to adjust to this new paradigm, and settle for a series of lateral moves, or he or she must change organisations.

The idea of the flexible firm was first identified by Atkinson (1984), and the concept was refined by Handy (1991). Atkinson identified four types of flexibility:

- numerical flexibility, achieved by altering working hours or altering the number of workers employed through part-time working, etc
- functional flexibility, achieved by training workers to perform a wider range of tasks (multiskilling) and breaking down barriers to deploying workers on different tasks (demarcation)
- distancing, replacing employees with subcontractors
- pay flexibility, switching from centralised collective bargaining and rigid pay scales to individually negotiated pay and benefits.

The result is a segmentation of the workforce into core and peripheral workers. Core workers are those key workers who are central to the organisation's core functions. They will be long-term employees, possibly with guaranteed employment, and highly trained. They will be committed to the organisation, and the organisation will be committed to them. Peripheral workers will be those performing non-core services, often as subcontractors. They will be hired and fired as required, and will serve as a buffer protecting the core workforce from fluctuations.

Handy developed the core–periphery concept into his Shamrock model. This type of organisation has three interlocking leaves consisting of three distinct groups of workers who are treated differently and have different expectations – specialist core workers; a contractual fringe, who may or may not work exclusively for the organisation, and who are paid a fee based on results rather than a wage based on time taken; and a flexible workforce, who are likely to be employed on a temporary or casual basis.

Remember, however, that what Atkinson and Handy are discussing is a theoretical model of organisations. Although many organisations have moved towards this kind of structure, many have not. As with other new management techniques, UK management tends to be conservative and reluctant to adopt new ideas (Marchington and Wilkinson 2000).

ACTIVITY

7.5 THE CHALLENGES OF FLEXIBLE WORKING

What problems are posed by the movement towards more flexible ways of working?

THE FUTURE OF THE WORKPLACE

Moynagh and Worsley (2001) put forward three possible scenarios for the future development of the workplace by 2020. They identified two key variables:

- The degree to which organisations must adapt to their workers, and conversely the degree to which workers must adapt to organisations. Tight labour markets will shift power to workers, while more intense competition in the product market will shift power to organisations.

- The stability of networks. Will employers favour stable networks that allow them to retain knowledge in the organisation, or will rapid change lead to virtual teams which change so frequently that long-term relationships between their members become unsustainable?

On the basis of these two variables, they identified three possible scenarios for 2020:

- Fragile communities – workers are forced to adapt, but networks are stable. Individualised contracts are widespread, and workers are contracted to perform specific tasks and paid by results, but skills shortages encourage employers to retain knowledge workers. However, this model is unstable, because competitive pressures are forcing rapid change, which puts pressure on networks.

- Stable communities – organisations adapt, and networks are stable. Competitive pressures are lessened as organisations merge or collaborate, and organisations must adapt to the needs of their workers through measures such as work–life balance. However, this may not be viable because of the pressures of globalisation.

- Disposable communities – workers are forced to adapt, and networks are fragile. Labour is seen as a commodity, and employers tap into a global pool of skilled labour. Knowledge is stored electronically, so there is no pressure to retain workers as the corporate memory of the organisation. Workers are insecure and stressed, and may respond to this by opting out of the labour market, through downshifting or self-employment. In the long run, this may make the model self-defeating.

All three of the models are plausible, but all three contain the seeds of their own destruction. The result may be a labour market that oscillates between them.

THE PSYCHOLOGICAL CONTRACT

All employees have a legal contract of employment, but for the employee this is usually presented as a 'take it or leave it' situation. The employee has to accept it or leave. The psychological contract is different. It is implicit rather than explicit, individual rather than collective, tacit rather than written (although elements of it may be incorporated into a social partnership agreement with a trade union) (CIPD 2003a). There are dangers in making it too explicit, as organisational and environmental changes may make it impossible to deliver on an explicit contract (Briner and Conway 2001). It can be defined as 'the perceptions of the two parties … of their mutual obligations towards each other' (Guest and Conway 2002). By its very nature, the psychological contract is dependent on trust between the employer and the employee.

One view of the psychological contract is that it has changed from an 'employment security' contract to an 'employability' contract. This reflects the shift from the monolithic to the flexible organisation which we discussed above. Under the employment security contract, the employee offered time and loyalty in return for security of employment and the possibility of promotion (Kimberly and Craig 2001). As redundancy and downsizing became more common, employers could no longer guarantee their side of the bargain, and gradually it was replaced by the employability contract – employees would still offer time and loyalty, but in return the employer would ensure that they received the work experience and training that would enable them to get another job elsewhere. This has been described as the 'new deal' at work, and as producing a 'free agent' mentality among workers.

If this model is correct (and there is some doubt about this – the 'old' psychological contract often still exists, and where it has gone, it has not necessarily been replaced by an employability contract), loyalty may not be enough to keep the free agent employee on board. The organisation may have to offer more, including possibly empowerment. If workers are to be trusted, they expect trust back from the organisation.

Rousseau (2004) distinguished between relational contracts, based on give and take and on trust in the employer, and transactional contracts, which are more short-term in approach and concentrate on pay and conditions. The CIPD (2005) points to a suggestion that there has been a shift in recent years from relational to transactional, as trust in employers has declined, but refutes this, saying that employee commitment is broadly stable.

Other implications of the new psychological contract suggested by the CIPD include:

- Process fairness: employers need to put in processes which ensure that employees see the way in which decisions are made as being fair.
- Communications: communication mechanisms have to be set up to ensure that employers are aware of the employee 'voice' (this is reflected in the EU Information and Consultation Directive).
- Management style: employees expect to know what is going on – management style needs to change from 'top down' to 'bottom up'.
- Managing expectations: managers must be seen to be fair, honest and open.
- Measuring employee attitudes: managers need to know what their employees are thinking.

The employability and free agent approaches in many ways put a lot of pressure on employees. They are forced to take responsibility for their own future in a way which, while attractive to many, does not suit everyone. Many people want security rather than opportunity. Those who really crave opportunity may well have shifted to self-employment already (the self-employment rate in the United Kingdom is currently around 12 per cent of the workforce – Philpott 2002). Increasingly employers have to offer something else as part of their side of the psychological contract. This is work–life balance, which we discuss in the next section.

WORK–LIFE BALANCE

Changes in social structure have increased pressure on people in work:

- In the 1950s and even into the 1960s, women routinely gave up work on marriage, and so were at home to care for children. People married young, and had children young, with most families being completed by the age of 30. At the time when children were dependent, many parents also had an extended family to draw on and relatively young grandparents, who probably lived nearby.

- In the 1990s and 2000s, over half of all married women were in work, whether or not they had children, and families had come to expect and need two incomes. The age of marriage had risen, and many women had not had their first child by 30. The extended family had broken down, and by the time the family needed support, grandparents were too old, did not live locally, and increasingly needed care themselves.

- The increase in the rate of marriage breakdown meant that increasing numbers of single parents with children, particularly women, needed to work to support their families, but had no external support networks to draw on. In 1991, 20 per cent of dependent children lived in single-parent families.

- Millions of women in their 50s have to care for an elderly dependent parent.

- There is an increased desire on the part of employers as well as employees for a more flexible workforce.

An Institute of Management survey in 2001 highlighted the extent of the problem (*Professional Manager* 2001):

- 46 per cent of female managers have children

- 26 per cent care for others such as elderly parents

- 27 per cent cite family commitments as a career barrier (up from 17 per cent in 1992).

In 2003, 9 per cent of males and 33 per cent of females had at some time given up work to care for somebody (ONS 2004).

In addition, people without caring responsibilities also feel that they are entitled to a life outside work. One in five people take work home almost every day, and one in 10 work more than 48 hours a week (CIPD 2003b).

There are some legal requirements on employers to meet the needs of their employees for work–life balance. These are mainly concerned with the right to time off to cope with one-off situations or emergencies, and full details are given in the CIPD factsheet *Work–life balance*, cited above (2003b). In addition, from 2003 (under the Employment Act 2002), employees with children under 6 (18 if disabled) can request a change in their hours, time or place of work. The employer must consider such a request, and can refuse it, but only after following a detailed procedure and if the decision can be based on specified business grounds.

Although only parents of young children have the right to request flexible working, any other employee can ask for flexible arrangements, and many employers have granted this. The latest figures (for 2003) are that 18 per cent of men and 27 per cent of women working full-time have some kind of flexible working arrangement. The most common arrangements are listed in Table 7.5.

Table 7.5 The most common flexible working arrangements (percentages)

	Males	Females	All
Flexible working hours	9.7	14.9	11.6
Annualised hours	4.9	5.1	5.0
4½-day week	1.8	1.1	1.5
Term-time work	1.2	5.8	2.9

There are similar patterns for part-time workers, with flexible working hours and term-time working being the most used options. Twenty-six per cent of males and 47 per cent of females had changed their hours or working arrangements to look after someone.

 **ACTIVITY**

7.6 WORK–LIFE BALANCE

a. Our discussion above has been in terms of flexible working hours or time off. What other family-friendly arrangements could employers offer?

b. What business case could you put to your employers to persuade them to adopt family-friendly policies?

c. Among your workforce are two workers, Anne, who is a single parent with a daughter aged four, who has asked to work school hours only, and Peter, who is the sole family carer for his elderly mother, who has Alzheimer's disease. He has asked to work a 30-hour week, instead of the normal 35, and to leave work one hour early, in order to get home before his daytime carer leaves. What response would you make to each worker?

EQUAL OPPORTUNITIES AND DIVERSITY

The United Kingdom is a very diverse society: diverse in terms of race, sex, sexual orientation, religion, age, disability and life experience. Equality of opportunity is based on legislation, and has as its main aim assimilation – that whatever a person's background, all should have the opportunity to achieve the same outcomes. Diversity is much more about difference. The differences between the two are illustrated in Table 7.6.

Table 7.6 Differences between equal opportunities and diversity

Equal opportunities	Diversity
Externally imposed	Internally driven
Groups	Individuals
Assimilation	Diversification
Systems	Total culture
Responsibility of Personnel/ Human Resources	Responsibility of all, permeates the culture

Source: adapted from Ross and Schneider (1992).

In 2005 the CIPD published three related Change Agenda documents on diversity, entitled *Managing diversity: measuring success* (Tatli et al 2005), *Managing diversity: learning by doing* (Taylor, Piasecka and Worman 2005), and *Managing diversity: linking theory and practice to business performance* (Mulholland, Özbilgin and Worman 2005). These are invaluable in an understanding of diversity.

Diversity is traditionally viewed as being concerned with categories of race, gender, ethnicity, age and disability, but true diversity is much wider than this. Anderson and Metcalfe (2003) identify three different types of workforce diversity:

- social category diversity: differences in demographic characteristics such as race and sex (the traditional definition)

- informational diversity: differences of knowledge, experience, functional background, etc

- value diversity: differences in personality and attitudes.

Tatli et al (2005) identify three major benefits from diversity:

- It enhances customer relations and increases market share.

- It enhances employee relations and reduces the cost of recruitment and retention.

- It improves workforce quality and performance in terms of diverse skills, creativity, problem-solving and flexibility.

However, it is important to note that these benefits of diversity do not just happen. Diversity has to be managed effectively. Mulholland et al (2005) liken it to managing change. They quote the example of the turkey producer Bernard Matthews, which was suffering from a shortage of labour in rural Norfolk. This was tackled by bringing in immigrant labour from Portugal, which increased the proportion of Portuguese employees from 3 to 30 per cent of the workforce. However, in order to make it work, Bernard Matthews developed local support networks, promoted local English language training, and created partnerships with the Home Office, Norfolk Police and HSBC to facilitate integration of the new workforce.

Kandola and Fullerton (1994) identify three key elements of diversity:

- Diversity is a source of real value to the organisation.

- Diversity is not only about obvious visible differences, but is about all the ways in which people can differ.

- The aim of diversity is to enrich the organisational culture and working environment.

All of these points are illustrated in the following case studies.

 DIVERSITY

CASE STUDY 7.5

The war against crime

The Metropolitan Police has set up a Cultural and Communities Resource Unit, headed by a (black) detective chief inspector, Keith Fraser. The unit maintains a database of the range of backgrounds, lifestyles and specialisms in the Met and the City of London Police. The unit has 800 people on its books, and has located experts who have helped with 700 criminal enquiries all over the country. Examples of the work of the unit include:

- The murder of an elderly Bengali woman, where white officers were getting no co-operation from the community. Bengali officers immediately got co-operation.

- A Chinese person had been missing in the North of England for two weeks. A Chinese policeman from London found him in a day and a half.

- Tamil officers are investigating violence between rival Tamil gangs.

- A voodoo expert helped interpret seemingly innocuous but actually sinister objects sent to a Bangladeshi man.

As Det Ch Insp Fraser says, 'the unit highlights the true meaning of diversity and the fantastic opportunities and benefits it gives policing' (Cowan 2004).

Sharia mortgages

Islamic finance is regulated by *sharia* law. One of the main principles of *sharia* law is a prohibition on usury, the payment of interest. This makes a conventional Western mortgage impossible under *sharia* law. The solution developed by Islamic banks is a version of sale and lease-back. Customers in effect sell their houses to the bank, pay rent (not interest) on it, and then at a later stage buy the house back from the bank. Unfortunately, under UK law this represented two property sales, each of which is liable to stamp duty. In the 2006 Budget Gordon Brown recognised this, and abolished the requirement for double stamp duty (Parker 2006).

TRADE UNIONS

So far in this section on work organisation we have concentrated on the position of individuals. We conclude by analysing the collective – the role and position of trade unions.

Trade union membership peaked in 1979, at more than 13 million. Since then it has nearly halved, to around 7.5 million in the late 1990s. It has since stabilised, helped by legislation on union recognition in 1999. The nature of trade union membership has also changed. Union density (the proportion of workers who are union members) has fallen from 54 per cent in 1979 to 29 per cent in 2003, but for women it has only fallen from 37 to 29 per cent.

Density is also affected by age. Density among the over-50s is 33 per cent, while for the age group 25–34 it is 25 per cent (ONS 2004b). Density among full-time workers is 32 per cent, among part-time workers only 21 per cent. Density among professional and associate professional workers and personal service workers is higher than among manual workers. Density in the public sector is 60 per cent, while in the private sector it is only 20 per cent.

In 1979 the typical union member was a male manual worker in heavy industry – a miner or a steel worker. By 2003, the typical union member was a female teacher or NHS worker.

Many reasons have been put forward for the decline in union membership. These include:

- the decline of traditional highly unionised sectors of industry
- the anti-trade union legislation of the Conservative governments between 1979 and 1997
- the recessions of the early 1980 and 1990s
- the growth of a flexible workforce, which is more difficult to unionise
- the growth of pay review bodies in the public sector
- the spread of performance-related pay and individualised HRM systems
- the fall in the size of firms
- defeat in highly publicised set-piece disputes like the miners' strike.

The response of the trade unions, led by the Trades Union Congress (TUC), was to change their orientation. The traditional perspective taken by unions was a pluralist one – that management and unions have some common aims, but many more conflicting aims, within the employment relationship. Collective bargaining was seen as managing the balance between the interests of management and workers, and would frequently be adversarial. Many individual union leaders took a more radical Marxist perspective, and saw the management–labour relationship as an exploitative one.

In the early 1990s unions in the United States developed a different approach, known as New Unionism, based much more on a co-operative relationship, recognising that management and unions have basic agreement in wanting the employment relationship to work more smoothly, and that both sides benefit from a high-wage high-productivity environment. New Unionism also recognised that the approach of union members and potential members is an instrumental one – they want a union to protect their individual interests. They buy union membership like they buy a foreign holiday – they want value for their money.

In 1996, the TUC adopted New Unionism. The emphasis in future was to be on developing social partnerships with willing employers, and on stressing casework for individual members (Barber 1998). To further New Unionism, the TUC set up an Academy in 1998 to train union representatives. The typical Academy student was female and from an ethnic minority.

 SOCIAL PARTNERSHIP AT VERTEX

CASE STUDY 7.6

Vertex is an outsourced services company, part of United Utilities, formed in 1996 when North West Water merged with North West Electricity. In five years, it has moved from collective bargaining to union derecognition, to non-union consultation, to collective bargaining based on partnership.

The head of employee relations, Tony Stark, said 'I'd had a bellyful of trade unions after working in the car industry and the docks in Liverpool.' However, he was to lead negotiations with Unison which led to partnership. Even when the union was derecognised, union officials were elected onto the company-wide employee consultation forum, and proved constructive partners.

After the passing of the Employment Relations Act, Unison applied for a ballot on recognition. Rather than fight the request, Vertex set up a working party with the union, which produced agreement on recognition and social partnership. The company and the union put in a successful bid to the DTI's Partnership Fund, which aims to make organisations aware of best practice in partnership. This funded six months of workshops, facilitated by Ruskin College.

The partnership has produced tangible results, including a pay progression agreement, which has helped the company to achieve a retention rate much higher than that prevalent in the call centre industry. The partnership has also helped the company to win contracts with the public sector (Walsh 2001).

New legislation introduced by the Labour government supported the new approach. Under the Employment Relations Act 1999, all workers have the right to be accompanied by a fellow worker or union official to disciplinary proceedings. The Employment Act 2002 set out the statutory rights of union learning representatives, who have a key role in helping to promote learning and development within organisations which recognise unions (CIPD 2004a).

Perhaps most important, the 1999 Act introduced a statutory right to union recognition through ballot, as long as 50 per cent of workers vote in favour of recognition, and at least 40 per cent of those eligible to vote are in favour. This ensures that a small minority of the workforce cannot force through recognition.

Crucial recognition agreements were those with Honda and Sheerness Steel in 2001. Honda is a classic example of the 'good' company which feels that because it is a good company, unions are not needed (Clement 2001), while Sheerness Steel was the scene of a bitter derecognition dispute in 1992 between the ISTC and the then owners, CoSteel (Gall 2001).

 ACTIVITY

7.7 UNION RECOGNITION

What do you think are the advantages and disadvantages to employers of recognising trade unions?

CONCLUSIONS

This chapter has analysed Marxist and Weberian theories of social stratification, and has examined the major socioeconomic classifications used in the United Kingdom. It has examined the nature and extent of social mobility in the United Kingdom, and the social effects of a slowdown in the rate of mobility, including its impact on inequality and poverty. Changes in the industrial and economic structure of the United Kingdom have been analysed, and the flexible firm has been identified as a major developing form of organisation. The psychological contract has been examined, with particular reference to employability and work–life balance. Finally, the changing nature and extent of trade unionism in the United Kingdom has been analysed.

KEY LEARNING POINTS

- Marxist theories of social class are related to ownership of the means of production, whereas Weberian theories are wider, and consider status and power as well as class.

- Throughout most of the twentieth century, social mobility in the United Kingdom was high, as the absolute size of the middle class rose considerably at the expense of the working class, but these trends have slowed in recent years.

- There are considerable inequalities in both income and wealth in the United Kingdom, and these inequalities have been widening in recent years.

- Inequality is closely related to relative poverty, which has persisted in the United Kingdom, and which leads to an impairment of the life chances of the poor.

- Since the 1970s, manufacturing has declined rapidly in the United Kingdom, along with a growth in employment in services. This has helped to lead to an increasing feminisation of the UK workforce. Globalisation and computerisation have also led to the growth of flexible forms of work organisation.

- The labour force in the United Kingdom has increasingly been feminised, although inequality of opportunity between men and women still persists.

- The psychological contract has evolved from an emphasis on job security, to employability, and to work–life balance.

- Equal opportunities is about assimilation, while diversity is about celebrating difference.

- Trade union membership in the United Kingdom has almost halved as a result of changes in social and industrial structure. The response of the unions has been to develop the concept of New Unionism.

QUESTIONS

1. How does Weber's view of class differ from that of Marx?

2. What is the difference between absolute and relative social mobility?

3. What is the Gini coefficient, and what does it tell us about inequality in the United Kingdom?

4. Why do you think that the share of manufacturing in the United Kingdom's GDP has fallen?

5. What three reasons did Giddens put forward to explain the feminisation of the UK labour force?

6. What four types of work flexibility were identified by Atkinson?

7. Identify three main differences between equal opportunities and diversity.

8. What do you understand by the concept of New Unionism?

TRENDS TO WATCH

- What happens to social mobility? Does it continue to slow? If so, what (if anything) does the government do about it?

- Does manufacturing in the United Kingdom continue to decline?

- Do trends towards greater work flexibility continue?

- If net immigration remains high, what impact does this have on diversity at work?

- What changes are there in the role of trade unions?

EXPLORE FURTHER

Social class and social mobility are discussed in any good sociology textbook. Poverty and inequality are covered in Vic George and Paul Wilding, *British society and social welfare: towards a sustainable society* (1999). Excellent overviews of the evidence on social trends are given in two papers by Stephen Aldridge (2001, 2004), an economist in the Prime Minister's Strategy Unit (formerly the Performance and Innovation Unit), and in John

Philpott's CIPD pamphlet *HRH – a work audit*, published for the Queen's Golden Jubilee in 2002. A series of CIPD Change Agendas published in 2005 are valuable for diversity. The CIPD has also published a series of excellent factsheets relevant to this chapter, including *Managing the psychological contract* (2003a) and *Work–life balance* (2003b). On trade unions, the TUC website (www.tuc.org.uk) is invaluable.

SEMINAR ACTIVITY

SOCIAL MOBILITY, EDUCATION AND THE MERITOCRACY

a. After the Education Act of 1944 it was thought that the 11-plus examination, which determined whether children would go to a grammar school (and receive an education leading to middle-class occupations) or to a secondary modern school (leading to working-class occupations) would increase social mobility, by selecting on the basis of intelligence rather than fathers' social class. By the 1970s the theory behind this was discredited, and a switch was made to comprehensive education, whereby all children, whatever their intelligence or social background, would go to the same school. This does not seem to have been effective in increasing social mobility. Why do you think that changes in the education system seem to have failed to increase social mobility?

b. In 1958 the sociologist Michael Young published *The rise of the meritocracy*. In this book he examined the likely consequences of a society in which success was based solely on merit (ie on ability) rather than on social background, and in which there was total social mobility – in other words something very like the aspirations of the 1944 Education Act. However, Young saw considerable downsides to this. What do you think these downsides could have been?

c. The slowdown in social mobility is of increasing concern to Labour politicians. Typical is a speech made by Alan Milburn to the Institute of Public Policy Research in November 2004 (Milburn 2004). Why do you think that New Labour would be concerned about a fall in social mobility?

CHAPTER 8
Technology

LEARNING OUTCOMES

When you have completed this chapter you should be able to:

- identify the key technological developments in information technology and other fields

- understand the direct impact such changes have had on organisations

- reflect on how technology has influenced goods, services and the labour markets

- analyse the concept of knowledge management

- discuss some of the reasons that technology has not always been seen as a beneficial influence.

INTRODUCTION

No one doubts that massive technological advances have changed the world, as set out in the causes of globalisation in Chapter 3. The developments in information and communication technologies (ICT), biotechnology, energy supply and transportation have altered the world beyond recognition over the last 50 years. To put it more accurately, technological change enables massive changes to take place – changes in organisation, communication, products, marketing and distribution, together with associated ways of managing people. The uniqueness of technology is that, once it has been invented, it cannot be 'un-invented'. Other resources can be used up (oil), can suddenly disappear (chief executives), or be replaced (buildings), but technological knowledge will always survive. In fact, once one organisation uses a technology and gains competitive advantage, then it needs to be adopted in some form by all its competitors to ensure their survival.

The speed of technological advance is increasing, prompting even speedier changes in society. In fact, writing about examples is quite difficult because, by the time this is printed, most of the examples will be out of date. The most influential changes of the next 10 years are only known about by small cliques of researchers in multinational research and development labs and their counterparts in leading universities.

WHAT'S HAPPENING IN TECHNOLOGY

PATTERNS OF TECHNOLOGICAL DEVELOPMENT

The common differentiation between humans and other animals is that humans have the ability to design and use tools, so primitive technologies have been utilised for many thousands of years. However, the beginnings of the Industrial Revolution in the mid-seventeenth century saw the early stages of fundamental technological growth, where machines replaced hand operations.

Although technological invention appears to follow a continuous and unrelenting line, a pattern has been identified by, amongst others, Hall and Preston (1988). Named K-waves, after the Russian Kondratiev who first developed the concept in the 1920s, a 50-year cycle for each wave has been identified as outlined in Table 8.1.

There can be much debate about the timing of these waves and the overlapping feature of new technologies, but an economic pattern emerges that shows four stages. First, the invention and diffusion of the technology produces prosperity, especially for the organisations leading the way. However, after a period, demand slackens or competitors catch up, leading to a recession where new investment falls. After such a period, the third stage is that of outright depression arising

 ACTIVITY

8.1 THE DOWN PHASE

There is some evidence that the current technological cycle is swinging towards a down phase. Set out the reasons that this down phase might be occurring, and also explain why the contrary may be true – that the current technological phase is gathering more steam.

from reduced activity, and restructuring with mass unemployment before the final stage, recovery, appears when the economic conditions improve sufficiently for the next wave of technological development.

Table 8.1 The K-waves

Wave no.	Dates	Innovations
K1	1770s to 1830s	Early mechanisation in textiles and water power with the construction of canals which lead to the first large-scale factories and companies
K2	1830s to 1880s	Invention of steam power used in railways and machines which lead to vastly improved communications and location independent of water sources
K3	1880s to 1930s	Inventions of electricity, steel, chemicals and synthetics creating new industries with reliable and powerful energy leading to very large-scale production and control (trusts and cartels) and opening-up of transportation and communication through cars and aircraft. Technologies were integrated to create assembly-line techniques.
K4	1930s to 1980s	Explosion of development of cars and aircraft together with petrochemicals and consumer durables. Controlled through integrated manufacturing processes and by multi-national organisations.
K5	1980s to present day	ICT developments producing ability to source and manufacture flexibly across the world, creating global brands, communicated by television, radio and internet technologies. Robotics allows complex manufacturing and medical processes.

TYPES OF TECHNOLOGICAL CHANGE

Freeman (1987) identified four different types of technological change:

- Incremental innovations – these are small-scale changes made at a local level. For example, a quality circle might come up with a new way to calibrate existing equipment in a factory.
- Radical innovations – these change the way things are done. For example, the development of semiconductors rather than valves in the 1960s changed the ways in which computers could operate.
- Changes of technology systems – these often involve linking together two existing technological systems to form a new system. For example, multimedia entertainment systems bring together computer and television technologies.
- Technology revolutions – these occur about every 50 years or so and

revolutionise our approach to technology. One was the development of the steam engine in the 1770s, another the growth of the railways in the 1830s. The development of the computer in the 1940s and the creation of the World Wide Web/Internet have been the latest two.

INFORMATION TECHNOLOGY

In all technological developments, it is in the field of information technology (IT) that the speed of development has been the greatest, as has the effect upon society. A stream of inventions has followed the arrival of the first commercial computer in the 1950s. In hardware, integrated circuits have become increasingly powerful through the invention of optical chips and biochips, paralleled by the improvements in data storage systems. The price of PCs continues to decline, while ever more powerful laptops allow work to be carried out at any location and on the move. In software, there is the ability to network information so it is available to multiple organisational users; to operate real-time systems so leisure activities, such as flights or theatre tickets, can be booked electronically; in banking, money markets around the world are linked with instant access to information and market changes; programs can control tools to perform any task previously carried out by hand such as cut, weld or burn; controls can be programmed into complex machinery which determine the output and the quality of the process.

All these developments have led to the computer being at the heart of business and, increasingly, private lives. Production, sales, distribution, finance, human resources (HR), are all aided by computer systems which increase the speed of operation, while providing reliable operations, communications and storage. Recent developments, badged as 'business intelligence' (BI), aim to transform large amounts of data, often scattered across the organisation, into the key information that drives informed decision-taking, and deliver it in an easily read form through the computer screen to anybody where and when they need to know. So essential is this intelligence that the estimated worldwide market for BI systems in 2008 is around £20 billion.

COMMUNICATION TECHNOLOGIES

Supporting the development in information technologies have been two major technological developments in communications. First, satellite communication, starting in the mid-1960s, has increased exponentially so that there are now over 100 geostationary satellites in orbit facilitating cheap and instantaneous communication and data transmission.

Second, the invention and development of optical fibre technology has provided a competitor in huge capacity handling at great speed. FLAG Europe-Asia, for example, is a 27,000 km system servicing half the world at lower and lower costs. An example (*Economist* 2000) is that the cost of transmitting the *Encyclopaedia Britannica* electronically from New York to Los Angeles was US$187 in 1970. By 2000, the entire contents of the Library of Congress could be sent the same distance for less than US$40.

Both these developments have led to the creation of mass markets, allowing consumers to be aware of the goods and services on offer. Even if incomes are low, the spread of multinational advertising and brand creation produces images that people can aspire to so that they become future consumers. Television has had the most dramatic effect because it does not demand a good standard of literacy, unlike the printed word. The technological development improvements since its invention in the 1930s, which have consistently reduced the price and increased the quality and reliability, have had two effects on the mass markets. The first effect is direct, in that most television channels are commercial so products and services are directly communicated to the consumer. The second effect is more elliptical in that television programmes show styles of life which create an aspirational effect. This was most pronounced in Eastern Europe under communism, where the nightly broadcasting of Western shows indicated clearly how far behind the communist economic model was compared with the West, and contributed to its eventual collapse.

The swiftness of communication improves the effectiveness of markets. Producers and consumers widely use mobile phones to aid their business choices. Jensen (2007) researched the rapid spread of mobile phones among Kerala fishermen off the Indian coast, and found that they were able to land their catch in the markets which provided the best return. This reduced the overall price for consumers, provided more consistency of supply and prevent the widespread wastage which occurred when fish could not be sold. So a much more efficient market prevailed.

TRANSPORTATION TECHNOLOGIES

The 'shrinking world' is a simplistic but accurate description of the rapid technological change since the 1940s, heralded by the invention of the jet engine and its development into the commercial jet liner. The time difference in travel by air compared with boat and train has been so substantial that it has created two linked mass markets. The first is for the traveller, whether business or pleasure, for whom the swiftness and pleasure of the journey is joined to the associated activities it allows. The second is for the tourist, where the travelling is a means to take holidays in other countries and where a vast supporting infrastructure has been built up – hotels, holiday complexes, leisure activities. The break-up of the nationalised, non-competing flag-carrying airways has allowed the creation of a flood of low-cost carriers, bringing regular travel to the mass market. A weekend flight to Geneva can be cheaper than a taxi journey across London.

Another development, less publicised but of considerable importance, has been containerisation for the movement of freight across land and sea. It is such a simple and obvious development that it tends to be overlooked that it only started in 1956. Before that time, loading and unloading cargo could be a slow, hazardous and wasteful activity. One of the authors had direct experience of the strong union presence in the ports of most developed countries, which threatened strike action against developments that were likely to reduce labour costs or employment. By the 1980s union power had been broken in both America and the United Kingdom, and today the container can be 'stuffed' on the factory site, loaded and unloaded quickly by crane, and its contents enjoy protection against weather and theft throughout its journeys.

THE INTERNET

There has been an astonishingly quick development of Internet technology since its origins in the US Defense Department in the mid-1970s, and its commercial usage since the mid-1990s. It now affects all aspects of work and leisure at a steadily reducing cost, which now puts their utilisation within the grasp of most citizens in the developed world and many in the developing world. Society communicates through e-mails while hard-copy communications (such as letters) are used only in specific situations. Some organisations, such as easyJet, have attempted to become completely paper-free by scanning all incoming post and insisting on all correspondence, internal and external, being carried out through e-mails. The Internet provides a huge range of information that it is relatively simple for anybody to access (although, surprisingly, it has had little effect on book sales). It enables buying and selling transactions to take place at the work station.

 ACTIVITY

8.2 NET COMMERCE

Not all organisations have been enthusiastic about implementing online buying and selling. What holds them back from gaining advantages in this area?

BIOTECHNOLOGY AND MEDICAL TECHNOLOGIES

Biotechnology is the process of altering life forms, essentially through genetic modification. Arising from the fundamental discovery of the structure of DNA in 1953 by Crick and Watson, modification of biological processes allows such interventions as the introduction of new genes into organisms, breeding organisms to form new variants and treating organisms with new compounds.

One example of biotechnology is in the creation of genetically modified organisms (GMOs). Here, plants, animals and micro-organisms (bacteria, viruses) have their genetic characteristics modified artificially in order to give them new properties. This could include a plant's resistance to a disease or an insect, the improvement of a food's quality or nutritional value or a plant's tolerance of a herbicide.

The implications for food production and medical advance are astounding. The biotechnology industry has promised a vast increase in food production which would be sufficient to eradicate all forms of under-nourishment world-wide. In medicine, applications promise the eventual eradication of genetic diseases, such as cystic fibrosis, as well as better understanding and treatment of common diseases and conditions, such as cancer and Alzheimer's disease. Governments around the world have co-operated in the massive genome project to map all human genes, which was successfully completed in 2004.

However, the outcomes in recent years have proved problematical. In food production, there has been considerable opposition to the acceptance of GM foods in many countries, especially the United Kingdom, to the extent that all UK trials of GM cereals were halted in 2004. There have also been very few signs of medical developments. In cystic fibrosis, for example, the discovery of the errant gene in 1984 has not led to any improved treatment because of technical problems of gene therapy processes, and similar problems have occurred in other treatments, as shown in Case Study 8.1.

CASE STUDY 8.1

GENE THERAPY

In 1999 Jesse Gelsinger, a 19-year-old with a rare liver disorder, participated in a voluntary clinical trial using gene therapy at the University of Pennsylvania. He died of complications from an inflammatory response shortly after receiving a dose of experimental adenovirus vector, a new device to direct the new gene to the appropriate location. His death dealt a blow to the confidence of scientists and halted all gene therapy trials in the United States.

Source: Subramanian (2004).

ARTIFICIAL INTELLIGENCE (AI) AND ROBOTICS

Artificial intelligence is the science and engineering of making intelligent machines, especially intelligent computer programs. It is related to the similar task of using computers to understand human intelligence. AI is studied in the overlapping fields of computer science, psychology, philosophy, neuroscience and engineering dealing with intelligent behaviour, learning and adaptation.

Research in AI is concerned with producing machines to automate tasks requiring intelligent behaviour. These are synthesized in what are called 'expert systems'. Examples include control, planning and scheduling, the ability to answer diagnostic and consumer questions, speech and facial recognition. A recent development has been the extension into computer vision, where tests have shown that computers can be trained to 'recognise' complex objects in photographs marginally better than humans can (*Economist* 2007).

As such, the study of AI has also become an engineering discipline, focused on providing solutions to real-life problems, knowledge mining and software applications, together with games. However, the world had to wait until 1977 for IBM's Deep Blue to beat the world chess champion Gary Kasparov. One of the biggest difficulties with AI is comprehension. Many devices have been created that can do amazing things, but critics of AI claim that no actual comprehension by the AI machine has taken place.

From the early days of computers, attempts have been made to create robots that can replicate human activity, with the first industrial robot being used by General Motors in 1961. Robots are utilised in four main ways:

- In place of humans. The most common use has been in manufacturing, where robots have replaced humans in jobs that are dirty, dangerous and difficult. They worker faster, to more reliable degrees of quality, and can operate around the clock. The introduction of paint-spraying in car factories by robots reduced the labour force by 85 per cent and improved quality standards by 90 per cent. They are now seen in all manufacturing environments, as shown in Case Study 8.2. Another example is unmanned surveillance planes both in the military and increasingly in civil surveillance, such as have been used in unauthorised migration watch on the extended borders between the United States and Mexico, and between Russia and its neighbours.

- Doing jobs that humans find difficult. Robots can be miniaturised to work in very confined spaces where access for humans is difficult or impossible, such as drains. They have been designed to work in areas affected by earthquakes or tornados to help to identify the trapped and injured.

- Helping humans perform better. In the military, robots have been utilised for walking through minefields, deactivating unexploded bombs or clearing out hostile buildings. Boston Dynamics has produced a legged robot which can travel at 3 miles per hour, climb steep terrains and carry up to 120 lb in rough terrain impenetrable to wheeled or tracked vehicles. Robots designed to help soldiers on the battlefield have to be carried onto the battlefield by those soldiers. For that reason, robot builders try to design 'man-portable' designs. A man-portable robot can be carried by a single soldier, usually in a special backpack.

  For civilians, robots are developing much more slowly in the field of household gadgets to cook, vacuum and clean buildings. Mitsubishi, for instance, has designed and marketed a 1 m tall humanoid Wakamaru robot, costing around £7,000, to act as a mechanical house-sitter and secretary. It can recognise up to 10 faces and understands 10,000 words, and can be utilised to watch over homes while owners are away, alerting them to possible burglaries, record notes and appointments and remind its owners with well-timed announcements. It can even monitor the condition of a sick person.

- Training for humans – Case Study 8.3 demonstrates the benefits of using robots for simulation purposes.

THE IMPACT ON BUSINESS STRATEGY, GOODS AND SERVICES

The impact of new technology can be seen in two main developments: in business strategies and the method of operation on the one hand, and in new products and services on the other.

INDUSTRIAL ROBOTS ARE RESHAPING MANUFACTURING

It would be tough to find a company seemingly more evocative of twentieth-century, 'old economy' America than Allied-Locke Industries. The family owned and run manufacturing firm has its headquarters about 100 miles due west of Chicago in rural Dixon, Illinois. No one walking onto Allied-Locke's low-light, high-decibel factory floor is going to mistake the place for the clean room at a semiconductor manufacturing plant. Allied's operations appear about as unglamorous and low-tech as you might expect of a maker of chains and sprockets – except, that is, for a smattering of robots.

Although the pervasive grease and grime make these computerised machines with their articulated arms look like they originally came with the place, the robots – all adorned with user-friendly female names like 'Heidi' – are relative newcomers at the 300-employee firm. In 2000 the company picked up four used robots (they formerly resided in a now shuttered Caterpillar plant) for around US$40,000 each to assist in the heated hardening of pins that help form the links in its chains.

Those four robots – along with seven more purchased since then for various tasks

such as welding and loading – have allowed Allied-Locke to get more production out of the same number of workers. And that has helped it avoid new hiring. That sort of situation represents the other face of the well-publicised issue of America's declining manufacturing employment. If American workers aren't losing jobs making Nike sneakers to Vietnamese workers, then they are losing out to machines as companies look to increase productivity.

As the saying goes in manufacturing, 'automate or evaporate'. And robots represent the cutting edge of automation technology in the United States. While Japan is often thought of as most adept at the use of robots, America is now a top market for them. In 2003, North American manufacturing companies shelled out US$877 million for robots and the amount is rising by over 20 per cent per annum.

Materials handling has remained the largest application for robots, followed by spot welding. The automotive industry is still the biggest robot user, ordering nearly two-thirds of robots sold across the United States.

Source: Pethokoukis (2004).

EFFECTS ON BUSINESS STRATEGIES AND OPERATIONS

The biggest effect is that organisations have the ability to be flexible and to be eager to change. New developments put old technologies out of business so quickly. For example, in the 1990s, only luxury cars had air conditioning; in the twenty-first century, few cars, except those at the very cheapest end, will sell without it. Given the extended period of design and development, manufacturers need to build in the ability to alter the standard product quickly and effectively within a very tight budget. In reality, the product must combine the extreme reliability that new technology has brought with design obsolescence to ensure the customer continues to purchase a company's new products.

Associated with this trend is the need to mass-customise products, perhaps

MEDICAL SCHOOLS USE ROBOT BIRTH SIMULATOR FOR TRAINING

The American Institute of Medicine, an arm of the National Academy of Sciences, estimates that as many as 98,000 US patients die annually from preventable medical errors. By using a robot and analysing in detail what went wrong, these errors can be engineered out. Noelle is a lifelike, pregnant robot used in increasing numbers of medical schools and hospital maternity wards.

The full-sized, blond, pale mannequin is in demand because medicine is rapidly abandoning centuries-old training methods that use patients as guinea pigs, turning instead to high-tech simulations. It's better to make a mistake on a US$20,000 robot than a live patient. The robot mannequins range in price from US$3,200–20,000, the most expensive being the closest to approximating a live birth. Noelle can be programmed for a variety of complications, can labour for hours and produce a breach baby or unexpectedly give birth in a matter of minutes.

She ultimately delivers a plastic doll that can change colour, from a healthy pink glow to the deadly blue of oxygen deficiency. The baby mannequin is wired to flash vital signs when hooked up to monitors. The computerised mannequins emit realistic pulse rates and can urinate and breathe.

A training session involves a set of doctors and nurses tending to Noelle, which is hooked up to standard delivery monitoring machines. However, in the corner is an engineer from the manufacturer using his or her laptop to inflict all sorts of complications, through wireless signals to the robot which override any preprogrammed instructions. The medical team learn through their role-plays how to deal with all types of emergencies, and the harm they inflict in making wrong decisions has no consequences.

Source: Elias (2006).

something of a contradiction. Mass production is needed to produce the cost saving, but varieties are required to meet all the customers' varied needs. A good example in services is Compass plc, which delivers thousands of catering contracts across the world, every one different but with some essential common sourcing, marketing and administration systems. The system becomes more complex but IT systems allow control and monitoring of every detail. The customised feature has altered manufacturing approaches to assembly lines, many of which have been abandoned in favour of cell production systems, where groups of multi-skilled employees work in teams to meet the differing production contracts, taking responsibility for quality, waste reduction and innovation.

The vast improvements in efficiencies in production, brought about through robotics and other IT processes, and the ability to manufacture on a global basis have led to a growing *decline in manufacturing in developed countries* as the technology has been transferred to developing countries, which also provide cheap capital and labour.

Technology has offered two additional *marketing opportunities*. Better knowledge of an organisation's customers through manipulation of a vast amount of purchasing data allows much closer targeting of their requirements, a process that retailers such as Homebase and Tesco have developed through loyalty cards. This quantity of information is only available to large organisations, but the second opportunity, the web, can be used by any sized business. In fact, the web has allowed many niche organisations to market, sell and distribute their products and services at low cost, many without the overheads of retail premises. Web-based business activity has expanded exponentially since the mid-1990s, especially business to business where sourcing can be fixed through web-based tendering or even a quasi-auctioning system. Jupiter Research (epaynews.com) has forecast that US online purchases will reach 5 per cent of all retail sales by 2008.

 ACTIVITY

8.3 COMPETITIVE ADVANTAGE

It is evident that some forms of technological development provide organisations with a competitive advantage. One example is the invention by St Helens glassmaker Pilkington of the float glass process in the 1950s. This brought huge competitive advantages in both the quality of the sheet glass and the productivity levels.

Think of a further three examples of this process and explain why such an advantage was gained in this way.

SPECIFIC PRODUCTS

The implications arising from the recent rapid developments in IT and communications for the marketplace are substantial. Here are just a few examples:

- Increasing offering by subscription of movies, music and television/radio programmes by operators such as Disney, Comcast and Rhapsody will mean that programming on demand will take the place of normal television and radio schedules. It is likely that the BBC will eventually set up a subscription service for all its huge archive of programmes. This will allow viewers to choose exactly which episodes of, say, 'Allo, 'Allo! or a set of 1970s *Play for Today* they want to watch, and when they want to watch them.

- Flat-screen, computerised televisions will consistently drop in price and become essential furniture of the networked home, with users demanding ever more bandwidth to fill the high-definition screens.

- Myriad websites compete with television, music and video producers and distributors. Individuals can beam up their own productions onto the web and become their own publishers.

EFFECTS ON LABOUR MARKETS AND HUMAN RESOURCES

Technology both eliminates jobs and creates them. The introduction of railways in the nineteenth century eliminated most jobs in the canal transport industry but created a substantial net increase in jobs in total, in the rail industry itself, in the suppliers to the industry and in the associated expansion of industry and commerce that fast rail transport provided.

The same is true of today's technological changes. The IT software industry has created a huge number of jobs around the world, while the outcomes of their labour have reduced jobs selectively in manufacturing, distribution and administration. Introducing robotics into paint-spraying operations in car production, for example, has reduced the labour requirements in this function by 95 per cent. On the other hand, this technological change, amongst others, has reduced the price of the finished car to the extent that it is affordable to a greater mass market, and employment in car manufacturing around the world continues to show a small overall increase.

It is the nature of the labour force that has changed with technological innovation. A polarisation has occurred, with an increased demand for highly trained professional and technical employees and, at the same time, a reduced demand for low-skilled assembly and production operatives. An even bigger decline has occurred in the demand for semi-skilled employees and those with traditional apprentice-served skills, most of which have been replaced by automation. This is also reflected geographically, with most of the employees in Silicon Valley and other high-tech clusters in the United States and Japan being in the high-skills category, while the actual production of semiconductors, printers and other hardware is carried out in East Asian countries and Mexico with largely low-skilled employees.

The perceived need for a reservoir of highly skilled employees has been the driving force for advanced countries, including the United Kingdom, to lay greater stress on achieving an increased percentage of the population that is qualified through higher education (the current UK target is 50 per cent) or through educational programmes of skills achievement.

INCREASE IN TEMPORARY LABOUR

IT can provide information in a more reliable form and at a much more rapid rate. This allows organisations to respond far quicker to variations in consumer demand which, in turn, requires the labour market to become far more flexible.

Employers have responded in their employment model by making much greater use of non-standard employment, such as part-time and temporary employees. Supermarkets, for example, use their sales data to forecast precisely the number of checkouts required every hour of the year, and use part-time employees to resource the varying needs. The need for temporary staff for Christmas and holiday periods can also be pinpointed precisely through the accurate data provided. This allows them to reach their business target of queues no greater than one or two people.

Case Study 8.4 shows a micro example of this process.

CASE STUDY 8.4

LETTUCE LEAVES AND THE LABOUR MARKET

It has become clear in recent years that consumers are steadily reducing their purchases of whole lettuces and increasingly purchasing packages of prepared salad leaves in a variety of forms. For supermarkets, this has provided an excellent opportunity, with Tesco selling over £150 million worth a year, with a very high mark-up (as applies to most ready-prepared foods). But the packs have a very short shelf life, despite the chemical methods applied during their preparation. In addition, the purchase of such packs (often on impulse) varies very much in line with the weather.

The supermarket response to this scenario is to assemble incredibly accurate information on purchasing trends, adjust for forecast weather conditions and put in orders with a very short delivery time – usually no more than a day in advance, sometimes shorter. The suppliers, who are dealing with large orders they cannot afford to lose, in turn need to adjust their labour requirements flexibly. Most cannot afford to operate a system of on-call labour so they turn to labour service providers. One pack-house, for example, contracted in 2004 for 2.7 million hours of temporary labour for lettuce and other convenience salad packs. The providers, known as 'gangmasters', have large groups of itinerant labour, mostly from overseas, whom they call on a daily basis to meet heavily fluctuating demand in preparing lettuce packs and other highly seasonal goods.

Estimates of the immigrants (legal and otherwise) engaged in such work vary greatly, but it continues to rise with every report. Provista, a major player, recruits regularly from Eastern Europe, which goes some way to explain the vast increase in work permits from that area since the accession of Eastern European countries to the European Union.

Source: *Economist* (2004).

The direct implications for human resource (HR) practitioners of new technologies can be seen in the fields of recruitment and selection, teleworking and call centres, and in the way the human resource operation is structured.

RECRUITMENT/SELECTION PROCESSES

Most organisations use the web to post their current job vacancies, and require applicants to complete their application online, saving considerable costs. Technology also enables telephone screening of applicants to take place, as shown in Case Study 8.5.

A further example of automated shortlisting is the use of equipment to read CVs electronically using OCR (optical character recognition) software. The system uses AI to read the texts and, by using search criteria such as qualifications, job titles and companies where the applicant has worked, will produce a ranking list

TELEPHONE SCREENING AT STANDARD LIFE

Applicants for vacant positions advertised online called a dedicated telephone number and they then went through an automated telephone screening interview. The company sorted through 561 candidates before taking on 15 recruits, and claimed that the screening system saved 143 work days. The phone lines were open 24 hours a day, seven days a week. The system, developed by Gallop, was tested on 100 existing staff and looked for six generic performance attributes: achiever, conscientiousness, responsibility, agreeableness, numeracy and stability.

Source: *People Management* (1998).

of applicants against the mandatory and optional aspects of the person specification.

This system is quicker and more consistent than if the selection were carried out manually, but will only be efficient as the search engine and will certainly miss many potential candidates, let alone the difficulty the technology faces in trying to understand poor handwriting.

ACTIVITY

8.4 APPLYING ONLINE

What are the advantages and disadvantages to employers and employees of online recruitment?

TELEWORKING

The development of the World Wide Web and associated technological innovations have facilitated the process of working at a distance from the employer or main contractor. The process allows a variety of models, ranging from the ability to work for one or two days a week at home with a laptop, to being a fully fledged teleworker hundreds of miles from the employer's office site, where physical contact with the office site is restricted to an annual conference visit. As phones merge with computers, video calls will become far more common, with far-flung teams working on shared documents in virtual meetings.

Advantages of teleworking

- Productivity gains – employees working from home are often more productive. They get away from the frequent interruptions and distractions that pepper the working day. In is also in their interests to show they are more productive so the teleworking arrangement can continue.

- Employees can work out a work–life balance much more easily, with more time spent at home. Caring responsibilities can be balanced with work to be completed, as long as the will and the self-discipline is present.

- Time saving – for mobile teleworkers, the ability to complete tasks at remote locations, rather than return to a central office, saves considerable time and expense. Time is saved on regular commuting to work.

- Reduced accommodation costs – most organisations sell teleworking to their boards through setting out the huge savings in accommodation costs, especially when offices are in central city locations.

Difficulties that could arise

- Teleworking can be difficult to manage without daily face-to-face contact. Managers often want quick answers to questions or a special task performed quickly. This is far more difficult with remote workers. Supervisors and managers need specialised training to manage the remote worker. Contact has to be regular but not too intrusive.

- Performance management systems need to be devised carefully. They must be based much more on outputs and outcomes rather than traditional measures such as attendance. Regular meetings need to be held to discuss the employee's performance.

- Employees may not have work distractions but they may have home ones instead – children, other family members, friends, callers, etc can all disrupt a steady work flow. Relationships with family members can suffer if the borders between work and home are not drawn tightly to everybody's satisfaction.

- Health and safety in the home need to be carefully monitored.

- Dealing with confidential documents in the home setting has to be addressed.

- Some teleworkers feel too remote from the workplace. They miss the comradeship of the office and lose out on the regular gossip and social activities. There is also a general concern that teleworkers lose training and promotion opportunities because of their low visibility.

An example of the benefits of teleworking is shown in Case Study 8.6.

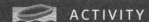 **ACTIVITY**

8.5 HOME ALONE

Research has shown that teleworkers often suffer from social isolation. Can you suggest ways that these effects can be mitigated?

TELEWORKING AT BAXTER INTERNATIONAL

Baxter International is a leading US manufacturer and supplier of technology relating to the blood and circulatory systems, employing over 40,000 worldwide. In the late 1990s, as part of its close technological relationships with Nortel Networks, it implemented Nortel's HomeOffice 2 system, which connects remote workers to the corporate phone system and intranet as if they were still in the office. This system matched the company's need for increased flexibility:

- The global and distributed nature of the business meant staff had to go to the office regularly in the early hours for audio conferences.

- Many of its offices, including the UK base at Compton in Berkshire, were in rural settings so many staff had to drive some distance to get to and from work.

- The life-critical nature of the business means that some staff need to be available all hours to the hospitals and to be able to direct the action required through the organisation's system. This had previously meant 24-hour rotas in the workplace, which was unpopular.

- Similarly, call centre staff at the subsidiary supplying dialysis equipment cover the period from 8 am to 10 pm, with every patient having a named agent. Working early and late was, again, not very popular.

Introduced in 1999, the scheme has become so popular that around 20 per cent of non-manufacturing staff now work from home, working out with their manager how often and when they come into the office. World-wide, over 3,500 employees use the teleworking system.

The set-up cost per employee was around £3,000, including the Nortel system installation, a fax, copier, printer and scanner, a desk and ergonomic chair, fire extinguisher and a smoke detector. There are also ongoing costs as the company paid for ISDN costs and personal calls. Most employees concerned had already been issued with laptops.

The organisation has gradually changed its culture in response to its distributed system of operation. Performance management is now almost totally related to outputs. Managers with homeworkers have needed to be trained in target-setting, measurement and relationships with their staff, for example.

A number of additional benefits have arisen since the scheme began. Retention of existing employees has improved but so has the ability to trawl through a relatively small pool of crucial specialists who no longer necessarily have to relocate to the company's main centres. This ability to avoid family disruption can be crucial in the decision whether to accept a job opportunity, as well as saving a large amount of relocation costs.

In addition, the proportion of staff returning from maternity leave has risen as many have joined the teleworking loop and take part in audio-conferencing to keep themselves up to date.

Overall, the scheme has been seen as very successful indeed, not just for the speed of take-up by staff but by the hard-nosed measures of increases in productivity – estimated at around 30 per cent on average. Alongside this has been the substantial saving in office space.

Source: *Flexible Working* (2000).

CALL CENTRES

The invention and development of the automated call distribution (ACD) system, which both released the need for a switchboard operator and also provided detailed call information, has promoted the introduction of a growing number of call centres. In 2007 it was estimated that over 600,000 UK employees were call centre operatives, a number that was increasing despite the dispersal of many such jobs to the Indian subcontinent where labour rates are cheaper (Peacock 2007).

Operators work with the required database to answer customer queries or process sales and service agreements, and most build in an interactive instruction guide for the employee to follow, which reduces the time and cost for training. The technology also allows management to monitor calls to identify process glitches, training needs and earnings through any incentive scheme. Call centres can take a distributed form, allowing calls to be channelled to teleworkers at distant locations, with the technology allowing access to all necessary data.

The implications for HR practitioners are quite complex here: there has been much debate about the high staff sickness and turnover rates, quality of job design and the ethical nature of the job requirements.

 ACTIVITY

8.6 CALLING OFF

Call centres have some of the highest staff turnover rates (average over 40 per cent) and absenteeism rates (over 6 per cent) in any UK employment sector. Can you suggest why this has happened and what should be done about it?

EFFECT ON THE STRUCTURE OF HR OPERATIONS

Sparrow, Brewster and Harris (2004) and Reddington, Williamson and Withers (2005) have set out some of the opportunities that technology has provided in facilitating new and developing HR systems.

Shared services

The system adopted by many large organisations, such as Standard Chartered Bank (see Case Study 8.7), Whitbread and HSBC, is to extract routine HR processes from operating units and place them with a central service, not necessarily anywhere near a head office. Activities include payroll, record keeping (attendance, starters and leavers, pensions), the operation of recruitment, job advertising and shortlisting together with advice on company HR systems and employment law. Technology allows local managers to have access to the databank of information held at the centre, and video-conferencing arrangements for wider discussion of action on, say, a difficult disciplinary situation. Many shared services have access to a network of experts for areas such as reward and benefits or selection testing.

The savings that are made by using this system involve cutting back on duplication of HR support at each operating unit (averaging 20–40 per cent), moving the work to low-cost locations, savings on purchasing of technology and services at one point rather than many, and a near certainty that consistent decisions will be made, avoiding litigation in discrimination and other legal areas (Reilly 2000).

E-enablement of HR processes

The ability to get HR information to and from, and support onto, line managers' desks without a formal HR intervention allows far more time for the HR department to focus on more strategic areas. The early stages of development here, involving access to policy documents and routine statistical processes, have moved on to empowering line managers to take greater control of their HR responsibilities. They can access external information on pay and benefits, authorise pay increases, select the appropriate standardised terms and conditions to go in an offer letter, process key data on an individual's performance management and manage their staff and training budgets. Norwich Union (Parry *et al* 2007) had four key drivers when it introduced an HRIS self-service functionality in 2006:

- enabling line management – encouraging managers to take more responsibility for managing their people through being able to access and maintain records

- improving and simplifying core processes – providing real-time updates on core data, removing duplication and increasing online processing, increasing standardisation and economies of scale in administration.

- adding value through HR expertise – allowing the HR resource to move from transactional to performance-enhancing activity, facilitating the introduction of new HR activities online, such as competencies and flexible benefits, encouraging individuals to take increased ownership of their own details and career management

- e-enablement of HR – mirroring business practice.

Outsourcing of HR

Service centres and e-empowerment can be organised in-house or the function may be outsourced to firms that have the technological expertise to offer such services at low cost. For example, Arinso Corp has contracted with Shell to produce a shared services system utilised by over 100,000 employees across 45 countries (Glover 2004). HR departments may therefore be reduced in capacity, with interesting implications for career planning. The normal stepped climb up the organisation may instead become leaps between service providers and organisations, not unlike the current career path of senior management.

An example of shared services is given in Case Study 8.7.

An example of an integrated approach to using technology in developing the HR function is given in Case Study 8.8.

SHARED HR SERVICES AT STANDARD CHARTERED BANK

In the early 1990s, Standard Chartered Bank decentralised its decision-making processes to regional centres around the world. However, this led to a patchwork of different approaches, duplication of effort, myopia, constant reinvention of the wheel and a large increase in costs.

In 2001, the company decided to revert to centralising standard transactional processes and delivering them to its 32,000 employees in 56 countries through web technology from Chennai in India. This location was picked because of its technology infrastructure, well-educated workforce and low costs. Here 45 staff handle routine enquiries, supporting the standardised HR systems and processes available on the web. Eighty-five local HR jobs were eliminated in the process, with substantial cost savings.

The local HR teams lost much of their autonomy, with the driving force the concept of 'a single recruitment and reward process so that everybody does it the same way time and time again' (Arkin 2002, p36). The menu on offer includes development planning, scheduling of training courses, talent management tools and e-learning.

Routine calls are handled by staff with a call-centre background. If they cannot solve the query, it is referred to a 'case analyst', who has postgraduate HR qualifications. The remaining HR structure consists of a 12-strong organisational effectiveness team based at head office, responsible for formulating HR strategy and working with the business to improve its performance. The next level down consists of centres of excellence: small, geographically dispersed groups of specialists in resourcing, reward and organisational learning.

Source: Arkin (2002).

KNOWLEDGE MANAGEMENT

So great is the speed of technological innovation and so dominant in the changes that it brings in the form of new products, services or the way with live and work, that commentators have expressed the view that we now live in the 'knowledge economy':

> *A firm's competitive advantage depends more than anything on its knowledge, or, to be slightly more specific, on what it knows, how it uses what it knows and how fast it can know something new.*
>
> (Prusack 1997, pix)

Having knowledge can be regarded as even more important than possessing the other means of production – land, buildings, labour and capital – because all the other sources are readily available in an advanced global society, while the right leading-edge knowledge is distinctly hard to obtain. Linked to this thinking is the concept of 'intellectual capital', which can be bought (and, if appropriate, stored securely) either through purchasing patents or intellectual property rights or through employing the highly skilled/intelligent employees/consultants who possess that capital (Stewart 2001).

IMPACT ON THE CHANGING ROLE OF HR IN NORTEL

The company

Nortel is a recognised leader in delivering communications capabilities that enhance the human experience, ignite and power global commerce, and secure the protect the world's most critical information. The company's next-generation technologies, for both service providers and enterprises, span access and core networks, support multimedia and business-critical applications and help eliminate today's barriers to efficiency, speed and performance by simplifying networks and connecting people with information.

HR structure

Nortel has over 30,000 employees world-wide, servicing customers in over 150 countries, and about 6,500 employees in Europe. The HR structure is based on the Ulrich (1998) model, with HR shared service centres in four global locations, six HR delivery teams, four core HR strategy groups and a number of HR business partners supporting different parts of the business. Because of the volatile nature of the markets for their main products, the businesses have been reorganised on a number of occasions – from centralisation to decentralisation and from a hands-off approach to a more management-controlled style. Underlying Nortel's ability to make these changes has been the significant investment in IT infrastructure and particularly HR information systems.

Changing the system

In 2005, an HR Evolution project was launched which included the deployment of SAP employee and manager self-service modules in 2006. Traditionally, HR had the responsibility for people transactions and processes, but by empowering the managers in HR functions through the self-service tools, HR became able to focus on delivering added value to the business in other areas such as strategy and process design.

Nortel's HR Shared Service Centre (SSC) became responsible for ensuring that the HR transactional services were delivered consistently across the company and for ensuring that any change request approved by the line manager was within company policy and guidelines, a job previously carried out by HR managers wearing their 'policeman' hat.

In effect, the new system empowered line managers to take decisions as if they themselves owned the business. No longer are they involved in a multi-layer, paper-based bureaucratic decision-making process – they are held accountable for the people changes they make that impact on their budget. Much more training has taken place to ensure that line managers are aware of HR policy and practice and the legislative context. It was well understood that previously, there were too many HR staff touching every part of the transactional work. Under the new system, managers are expected to grasp the people action initiative and take responsibility for developing their own people skills, as well of those of their staff. One of the key skills is in clear objective setting and communication of expectations, open discussion of issues that affect performance and honest feedback. No longer can they say 'This is not in my hands, go and see HR.'

When it comes to obtaining advice and information, in the majority of cases line managers can find what they want on the intranet in areas such as recruitment, reward, termination, discipline and benefits. Where they need more help, managers or employees call the SSC and trained team members will guide them on policy interpretation or action required when unusual events have occurred. Where answers are not forthcoming from this source, the question is referred to members of the HR delivery teams, where a specialist in, say, compensation delivery will provide the definitive answer. Their main role, however, is for process design, improvement and delivery, where they work very closely with the SSC. As the processes evolve and new approaches and systems are defined, the delivery team will work out how best to translate the changes into workable end-to-end processes from the line managers, through the systems and on to the SSCs.

The technology is further utilised by constantly reviewing the SSC user metrics to identify regular problems. The skills required to interpret the metrics and then translate them into process improvement activities are a new experience to the more 'traditional' HR professional.

The final part of the HR structure is the Core HR Strategy group, which deals with employee relations, compensation and benefits, talent strategy and diversity. Here the designs for future people strategy are formulated, using data from all other HR groups, together with benchmarking and competitive intelligence exercises.

Technology is at the heart of all these changes. By automating as many processes as possible and devolving others to management through the use of manager self-service, HR has been able to reduce significantly the amount of time spent on routine administration tasks, which thereby facilitates other non-administrative tasks, such as learning, recruitment and strategic analysis. This should allow HR professionals to manage the HR function in a strategic manner and to become real partners in the business.

Source: Parry *et al* (2007).

Activity

a. Consider the operation of HR systems at Nortel and identify where difficulties could arise, for both line managers and HR staff.

b. Identify the likely overall impact of such a structure on:
   - employee engagement
   - communication systems
   - skills of HR staff
   - careers for HR staff.

This capital does not necessarily consist of discoveries and processes that can be patented. Society is developing in such a way that services are becoming the dominant commodity over manufacturing. This means that skilled services in areas such as advertising, design, leisure and even sport can command very high fees – just look at the prices paid for the world's top 100 footballers, film stars or music performers. So wealth created in the economy is increasingly perceived as derived from knowledge and intangible assets (Storey and Quintas 2001).

Because it is such an important asset, organisations are starting to assess their own collection of knowledge bases and ensure they are available for use. This involves

 ACTIVITY

8.7 KNOWLEDGE VALUE

Do you see knowledge as a source of competitive advantage in the marketplace? If so, how?

not just sorting patents but analysing the knowledge gained through the experiences of their skilled staff. In HSBC, for example, a senior manager has been appointed to identify banking expertise among staff and ensure this knowledge is not lost when they retire or leave the organisation, and organise ways that critical knowledge can be shared across the organisation. Part of the role is to develop 'tacit knowledge', such as intuitive approaches to problem-solving in a particular work context, or vague ideas about a new product or service, into 'explicit knowledge' that can be written down and communicated (Stredwick and Ellis 2005).

Consideration must also be given to the development of what Hansen, Nohria and Tierney (1999) refer to as *codification* strategies, where knowledge is codified and stored in databases where it can readily be accessed and used by employees, and *personalisation* strategies, where knowledge is closely tied to the person who developed it and is shared mainly through direct person-to-person contacts. Ensuring a balance between these two approaches is crucial to the success of knowledge management. For example, if greater emphasis is given to personalisation, there needs to be formal encouragement of a highly developed process of social networking to allow informal opportunities to arise for knowledge sharing outside of standard meetings. Many knowledge-based companies organise social events, even organise company holiday weekends for this purpose.

In the HR field, how knowledge workers are recruited, trained and motivated has come under much scrutiny in recent years. As a group, research has shown that they can be distinguished by their demand for greater autonomy in their work, by their intrinsic motivation and greater sense of task satisfaction, and by their emphasis on career-progressing projects rather than immediate financial gratification (Scarborough and Carter 2007). The implication is that recruitment should pay as much attention to skills and potential as to actual knowledge, and that the performance management process is crucial to retention success.

TECHNOLOGY – THE DARKER SIDE

Although technological developments generally lead to improvements in standards of living, not all are seen as universally benign. For every five citizens that welcome new products, job opportunities, improved quality and variety of services, better healthcare and ease of transportation, a sixth will see a darker side with more bleak effects. This can be examined first by looking at three short case studies which have already featured in this chapter.

GENE THERAPY (SEE P251)

In itself this is a dispiriting case of shaken expectations, but there are further difficulties in this area. One of the success stories has been the development of devices to allow accurate screening for genetic disorders. This can be carried out at any age and even for unborn babies. The main benefit is that such disorders can be treated at an early stage so that the prognosis improves. However, this presents a number of problems. First of all, insurance companies (and employers that provide and pay for life insurance for their employees) are very interested in carrying out such tests before accepting insurance risk. For those citizens with no disorders and long life expectancy, life insurance costs would be cheap but pensions expensive. For those with a disorder, the opposite would apply, with life assurance virtually impossible to obtain. There is considerable debate currently on whether such tests should be compulsory, when the outcome would be to leave vulnerable people uninsurable and regarded as second-class. A second problem is the dilemma faced by the parents where pre-natal tests show up genetic disorders. This provides the opportunity for the birth to be aborted and some of the life-long pain averted, but such an irreversible decision is a very hard one to take, and most parents (except those who already have one disabled child) choose to avoid taking such tests.

LETTUCE LEAVES (SEE P257)

There are a number of ethical and regulatory issues surrounding this case. First, it is becoming very difficult to challenge the power of the largest supermarkets in demanding tight schedules from suppliers and, subsequently, their employees. In the United States Wal-Mart, with over 25 per cent of the huge US market, virtually writes the rules, with suppliers being unable to match its negotiating power. The situation in the United Kingdom is somewhat better, with a competing group of supermarkets matched in certain product areas against a similar group of large producers, but the growing dominance of Tesco is creating some worries for regulators. This issue is discussed further in Chapter 5 on regulation. The second issue is whether it is ethical for so much migratory labour, living in poor conditions, to provide fresh food for the community in the twenty-first century. It is hoped that they are protected by the Minimum Wage Act, but many will slip through the net, and the rules concerning deductions for accommodation are very complex, with such situations being rarely investigated. Added to this are some safety issues, as was shown graphically by the death of 20 illegal Chinese immigrants working as cockle-pickers in Morecombe Bay in 2003. Consumers may demand fresh produce at affordable prices but these may come at indefensible cost.

SHARED HR SERVICES (SEE P263)

There are experiences of 'one product fits all' which may not apply in fast-moving, customer-oriented businesses. The quality of the service provided by unqualified staff can be questionable, with a background in call centre work rather than human resources. Many opportunities for seriously effective HR interventions and innovations can occur through regular discussions about routine issues, often in informal settings, which are far less likely to happen under formalised shared-service environments. Moreover, services that are shared across countries run the risk of cultural confusion.

THE DARKER SIDE OF EMPLOYMENT

Alongside the potential problems faced by employees in call centres and teleworkers, there has been much research into the inherent problems that new technology brings to the workplace, demonstrating its dialectical nature, where advances in one direction produce problems in another (Martin 2005). These can take various forms, such as:

- Deskilling of manual work, especially in industries such as house-building where prefabrication, using computer-controlled design and machine tools, has replaced many traditional skills. A major consequence in the United Kingdom has been the near collapse of trade training by large house-builders, which in turn has led to severe shortages of servicing and maintenance trades, such as plumbers and electricians, where the market is dominated by small organisations. Even software work has been substantially automated and routinised.

- The intrusion of surveillance technology has presented dilemmas for employers who have the responsibility and opportunity to monitor employees to ensure no laws are being broken (such as downloading of pornography) but appreciate employees' fears and resentment at such a process taking place. Monitoring attendance (through card-swiping security systems) and performance (such as call centre systems detailed earlier) has become cheap and accurate, but presents challenges to employment cultures where employees' trust and independence of action are highly valued. Surveillance may focus employees' attention on organisational and strategic targets but also has a tendency to discourage innovation (Taylor 2004).

- A special problem of e-business employment is the lack of contact with the customer and a poor level of social interaction. This has led to higher levels of staff turnover than in conventional businesses (PricewaterhouseCoopers 2000). There has also been some sense of alienation related to virtual meetings, where the growth of video-conferencing can be surprising slow, although most evidence would support the view that the correct usage of mobile phones and e-mails has generally enhanced employees' social contact.

- Some commentators picture ICT in a tyrannical frame in the sense that it provides more intensive work through the huge amount of data it provides and the options available, and it also demands longer hours at the workface through its additional ability to provide 24/7 coverage (Green 2002). However, not all research supports this view. In a CIPD-financed project, Nathan, Carpenter and Roberts (2003) provided little evidence that ICT directly impacted on increased working hours. Employees were using more technology and they were working longer hours but the causal relationship was not proven.

- Although many of the accident-riven jobs in traditional industries have been eliminated by automation, new health problems have emerged, both physical (repetitive strain injury, eyesight deterioration) and psychological (stress-related illnesses).

- Many employees have shown considerable reluctance to share knowledge in a formalised system, with doubts expressed over the possible reduction in value of their personal human capital and expertise (Scarborough, Swan and Preston 1999).

In labour market terms, a divide has developed between two major segments of employment: the knowledge-intensive organisations and the knowledge-routinised ones, called the 'hour-glass' model by Coyle and Quah (2004). Knowledge-intensive jobs use advance and complex ICT skills and require high human capital levels. Employees work long and often unsociable hours but their jobs are often (but not always) associated with high pay, extensive training, career development and high personal and job satisfaction. Knowledge-routinised jobs, on the other hand, are low-paid, require much lower levels of human capital, and the routine ICT work provides much less personal satisfaction.

TRENDS TO WATCH – WHAT OF THE FUTURE?

'The horse is here to stay!'

Forecasting the effects of new technology is very tricky, and many serious and well-respected forecasters have got their forecasts very wrong. In an excellent article by Smith (2004), which details some truly awful forecasts, he quotes pioneers in the IT industry from whom we would have expected a clearer vision. For example, IBM forecast in 1952 that its worldwide sales of main frame computers would be 52. Thirty years later it raised the estimate to 200,000, roughly what it now ships each week. Even Bill Gates made gaffes, such as stating in 1981 that '640K should be enough for anybody'. Going further back, the president of Michigan Savings Bank advised people in 1901 against investing in the Ford Motor Company, quoting the statement at the top of this section.

There was a better performance by Kahn in his 1967 book *The year 2000*, where he predicted computers, mobile phones, video recorders and satellite dishes. But he, like many forecasters since, seriously misjudged the effect of technology on working lives. Almost everybody has forecast that we would all be working far fewer hours (30 a week at most, according to Kahn), have much more holiday and retire very early. This was because technology would take away jobs, which it clearly does. What almost all futurologists failed to grasp was that, while some jobs disappear, more arise in their place. Production jobs have disappeared either through automation and robotics or to developing countries with cheaper wages. In their place have arisen industries that provide services – either business services, such as IT, financial services and all the many consultancies, or personal services, such as leisure, health and beauty and personal finance. At the same time, services that used to operate for the few, such as hotels, eating out, travel and tourism, are now used by everybody in increasing numbers.

What is just as significant is that such new and developing industries are generally very labour-intensive (automated hairdressing is still not with us), so technology has released employees from the grind of heavy production but provided instead the more sociable but equally routine (and absolutely vital) activities involved in such activities as 'housekeeping' in hotels and 'care working' in hospitals and old people's homes. This explains why the average working week has decreased only marginally in the last 25 years, and why unemployment in flexible societies, such as the United Kingdom and the United States, remains very low.

- Technological development can occur through incremental innovation, radical innovation, change in technological systems or technological revolution (Freeman 1987).

- 'Business intelligence' is a key concept where the aim is to transform a large amount of data, often scattered across the organisation, into the key information that drives informed decision-taking, and to deliver it in an easily read form through the computer screen to anybody where and when they need to know.

- Technological developments provide the capacity for organisations to be flexible and to be eager to change, in fields such as product design, advertising and marketing (especially on the web), customer relations and quality development.

- Technology has had a profound effect upon labour markets through facilitating novel flexible working practices, such as annualised hours, complex shift systems and multi-skilling, together with the development of sophisticated recruitment and selection processes.

- HR systems have been affected by the technological changes that allow systems of shared services, outsourcing and e-enablement of HR processes.

- It has been recognised in recent years that knowledge management is a vital process to ensure that organisations can collect, store and distribute key areas of knowledge that help create competitive advantage.

- Technological progress produces its own ethical dilemmas in areas such as gene therapy, consumer choice and outsourcing.

1. In what ways does technology offer improved marketing opportunities?

2. Name five difficulties associated with the employment of teleworkers.

3. Provide four examples of how technology helps HR administration and management become more efficient.

4. What is the difference, according to Freeman, between a radical and an incremental innovation?

5. Give three examples of developments in communication technologies and their effect on markets.

6. Provide four examples of how technology can provide difficulties in the employment setting, as well as benefits.

7. What are the four main cycles of K-waves?

8. Give four examples of the use of technology in the recruitment and selection process.

9. What is the connection between technology and flexibility requirements?

10. What are 'shared services' in the HR setting, how are they facilitated by technology and what savings are made?

CHAPTER 9

Ethics, social responsibility and sustainability

LEARNING OUTCOMES

By the end of this chapter, readers should be able to understand, explain and critically evaluate:

- different approaches to ethics and ethical principles
- the problems involved in resolving ethical dilemmas
- whistleblowing
- the nature of professional ethics
- how far business ethics exist as something separate from general ethics
- stakeholder theory
- values and codes of business ethics
- approaches to corporate governance
- the principles and issues underlying corporate social responsibility
- the principles and issues underlying sustainable development
- the role of HR in sustaining corporate social responsibility
- the role of the government in corporate social responsibility
- corporate social responsibility and profit.

INTRODUCTION

This chapter examines the nature of ethics, and different approaches which can be taken to ethical problems. It discusses professional and business ethics, stakeholder theory, values, and codes of ethics. The second half of the chapter analyses corporate governance, corporate social responsibility (CSR) and sustainability, the role of businesses, HR and the government in promoting CSR, and the extent of compatibility between CSR and profit.

ETHICS

The theory of ethics can be extremely complex, and in order to be of use in a day-to-day work situation, it must be made practical. Here we immediately run up against a problem. To philosophers, ethics is about the theory of right and wrong, not about the practical application of those principles. This is the area of morals. Ethics involves the values that a person seeks to express in a certain situation, morals the way he or she sets out to achieve this (Billington 2003).

A wider definition of ethics is given by Connock and Johns (1995). This includes three elements:

- fairness
- deciding what is right and wrong
- the practices and rules that underpin responsible conduct between individuals and groups.

Billington lists five distinctive features of ethics: (2003, pp20–25):

- Nobody can avoid ethical decisions. We all make ethical decisions every day.
- Other people are always involved in ethical decisions. There is no such thing as private morality.
- Ethical decisions matter – they affect the lives of others.
- Although ethics is about right and wrong, there are no definitive answers. The philosopher can put forward principles which should guide decisions, but the ultimate decision is always down to the individual.
- Ethics is always about choice – a decision where the individual has no choice cannot be unethical.

 ACTIVITY

9.1 NO CHOICE

Can you think of any situations where an individual has no choice about what action he or she should take – in a work environment, or any other situation?

ETHICAL PRINCIPLES

Billington identifies three different approaches to ethics:

- **Absolutism.** Ethics are underpinned by absolute values, which apply in all societies and to all situations, such as the Ten Commandments. The problem here is that an absolutist might make decisions which could be seen as morally repugnant. For example, a pacifist who believes literally in the absolutist statement 'Thou shalt not kill' would logically have found him or herself refusing to fight the evil of Nazism.

- Relativism. Ethics depend on the situation, and on the cultural mores prevalent at a particular time or place. Thus for example, racism in Victorian England, or child labour in present-day Pakistan must be seen as reflecting the mores of those societies. This is the 'when in Rome' principle. This approach has been criticised on two grounds – that it freezes the status quo and is therefore inherently conservative, and that in practice every major religion (Buddhism, Christianity, Confucianism, Hinduism, Judaism, Islam and Sikhism) subscribes to the absolutist golden rule (see below) (Snell 1999).

- Utilitarianism. As Jeremy Bentham put it in the early nineteenth century, 'the good of the greatest number is the criterion of right or wrong' (Billington 2003, pp35–40, 119). This begs the question of what 'good' means.

Archie Carroll (1990) widened out these principles into 11 ethical guidelines, which are summarised in Table 9.1.

Table 9.1 Carroll's ethical guidelines

Name of principle	Description
Categorical imperative	You should not adopt principles of action unless they can be adopted by everyone else
Conventionalist ethic	Individuals should act to further their self-interest as long as they do not violate the law
Golden rule	Do unto others as you would have them do to you
Hedonistic ethic	If it feels good, do it
Disclosure rule	You should only take an action or decision if you are comfortable with it after asking yourself whether you would mind if all your associates, friends and family were aware of it
Intuition ethic	You do what your 'gut feeling' tells you is right
Means-end rule	You should act if the end justifies the means
Might-equals-right ethic	You should take whatever advantage you are powerful enough to take
Organisation ethic	Be loyal to your organisation
Professional ethic	Do only that which can be justified to your professional peers
Utilitarian principles	The greatest good of the greatest number

Source: adapted from Carroll (1991).

The three most popular among managers were the golden rule, the disclosure rule and the intuition ethic.

ETHICAL DILEMMAS

Managers face ethical dilemmas at work every day of their working lives. Some typical ones are examined in Activity 9.2. On the basis of interviews with managers in Hong Kong, Snell identified a number of typical sources of dilemmas, summarised in Table 9.2.

Table 9.2 Sources of dilemmas

Source of dilemma	% incidence
Subordinates' perceived deceit, incompetence or disobedience	18
Policy, or request by superior, that is mistaken	25
Policy, or request by superior, that is ethically suspicious, exploitative or unfair	13
Improper, suspicious or unfair request from client, supplier or colleague	6
Conflicting instructions, decisions or directives from above	9
Caught in the middle of a direct conflict between other parties	5
Direct dispute with another party	6
Aware of another's misconduct, neglect or unfairness, but not directly responsible	8
Other	10

Source: Snell (1999, p347).

Snell's interviewees also suggested four possible responses arising from requests by a superior to do something they knew to be wrong (Snell 1999, p348):

- 'little potato' obedience (quiet, fearful, humble, deferential conformity)
- token obedience (following orders half-heartedly and semi-incompetently)
- undercover disobedience (only pretending to obey, and keeping disobedience hidden)
- open disobedience (conscientious objection).

Carroll's ethical guidelines can be used as a template for resolving ethical dilemmas.

Stage 1.   Rank each of Carroll's guidelines from 11 (most important to you) to 1 (least important to you).

Stage 2.   Consider your ethical dilemma against each of the guidelines. If you can justify the action under a criterion, put + in the next column, if you cannot justify action, put –.

Stage 3.   Score each criterion by taking its ranking and putting + or – in front of it.

ACTIVITY

9.2 ETHICAL DILEMMAS 1

a. You are a personnel manager for a medium-sized company, and you are faced with what you see as a series of ethical dilemmas Consider how you would approach each scenario, and what ethical principles you would apply:

Scenario 1. It is the custom in your industry for customers to be entertained lavishly. Your company gives each customer's sales manager a bottle of very good-quality malt whisky on his or her birthday, his or her partner's birthday, and at Christmas. Your purchasing manager expects similar perks from his suppliers.

Scenario 2. Your organisation is undertaking a number of redundancies. You decide who is to be made redundant. The production manager asks you to add a particular worker to the list. This worker does not meet any of your criteria for redundancy, but she is well known for not getting on with the production manager. You point out that if you sack this worker without justification, she will take you to an employment tribunal and will win a claim of unfair dismissal. The production manager's response is, 'Fine, It'll be worth it to get rid of her.'

Scenario 3. You are responsible for training, and you have used an old friend of yours to run a recent training programme. Your friend met all your criteria, and had adequate if not glowing references. However, the feedback from the programme is strongly negative. You are about to repeat the programme, and your friend has asked you if he/she will be given a repeat contract.

b. How far do you think Snell's identified responses to ethical dilemmas are likely to be universally valid, and how far do you think they reflect the culture of Hong Kong?

Stage 4. Add up the scores. If the figure is positive, for you the action is ethically justified; if negative, it is unjustified.

Stage 5. If the overall score comes to 0, change the rank for your most important criterion to 12, and redo the sums.

Remember that this method can only tell you whether or not a particular action is ethically justifiable, not exactly what you should do about it. An example of the scoring is shown in Table 9.3. In this case, the conclusion is quite clear: according to your values, you find this course of action ethically unacceptable, and should not do it.

ACTIVITY

9.3 ETHICAL DILEMMAS 2

You are export sales manager for a large company. You have been approached by an intermediary, who has asked for a large commission to obtain his influence to secure a large overseas deal. Such bribes are a long-established part of doing business with that country. Using the Carroll template, decide whether you should pay the commission.

Table 9.3 Example of scoring a dilemma using Carroll's guidelines

	Rank	+/−	Score
You should not adopt principles of action unless they can be adopted by everyone else	9	−	−9
Individuals should act to further their self-interest as long as they do not violate the law	5	+	+5
Do unto others as you would have them do to you	11	−	−11
If it feels good, do it	2	−	−2
You should only take an action or decision if you are comfortable with it after asking yourself whether you would mind if all your associates, friends and family were aware of it	10	−	−10
You do what your 'gut feeling' tells you is right	6	−	−6
You should act if the end justifies the means	1	+	+1
You should take whatever advantage you are powerful enough to take	3	+	+3
Be loyal to your organisation	4	+	+4
Do only that which can be justified to your professional peers	8	−	−8
The greatest good of the greatest number	7	+	+7
Overall score			26

WHISTLEBLOWING

Whistleblowing describes a situation where an individual is so concerned about the behaviour of an organisation or of individuals within it that he or she feels constrained to raise this with a third party, who may be inside the organisation, but is normally outside.

De George (1999) argued that six conditions must apply before whistleblowing can be morally justified:

- A product or policy of the organisation needs to have the potential to harm members of society.

- The employee should report all the facts to their immediate supervisor.

- If the immediate supervisor does not act effectively, the concerned employee should take the matter higher in the company, exhausting all internal channels.

- The employee should hold documentary evidence to support the charges.
- The employee must believe that whistleblowing will lead to a change in the product or policy (ie don't sacrifice yourself pointlessly).
- The employee must be acting in good faith without malice or vindictiveness.

THE PUBLIC INTEREST DISCLOSURE ACT 1998

The Public Interest Disclosure Act (PIDA) gives some protection to whistleblowers, although it does not give an absolute right to whistleblow, as strict criteria are laid down which must be met. The Act also places the burden of proof on the complainant.

The disclosure must relate to a specified set of malpractices:

- a criminal offence
- failure to comply with a legal obligation
- a miscarriage of justice
- danger to health and safety
- damage to the environment
- deliberate concealment of any of the above.

Internal procedures can only be sidestepped (De George's steps 2 and 3) if:

- the employee reasonably believes he or she would be penalised by the employer for making the disclosure
- the employee is concerned that evidence would be concealed or destroyed
- the employee has previously disclosed essentially the same information to the employer.

If the whistleblowing case falls within the definitions of the PIDA, the employee will be entitled to compensation if he or she has been victimised or dismissed as a result of the whistleblowing act (Fisher and Lovell 2006).

PROFESSIONAL ETHICS

If you think of words to describe a professional, you will probably comes up with words like:

- qualified
- objective
- impartial
- honest
- competent
- accountable.

These words all imply ethical principles, and one main role of a profession is to set and maintain ethical standards for its members. Rosemary Harrison (2002, p139) stresses two aspects: qualified advice, and standing by the integrity of that advice. This implies two ethical responsibilities: to the organisation for which you works (organisational ethics), and to impartial integrity (an absolutist ethic, which lies at the heart of professional ethics).

Most professions lay down ethical standards for their members to follow through a code of ethics, and the Chartered Institute of Personnel and Development (CIPD) is no exception. Its *Code of professional conduct and disciplinary procedures* (2003a) can be downloaded from www.cipd.co.uk.

Lawton (1998, p88) suggests 10 functions for a code of professional ethics:

- to promote ethical, and deter unethical behaviour
- to provide a set of standards against which to judge behaviour
- to act as guidance to decision-making
- to establish rights and responsibilities
- a statement indicating what the profession stands for
- to create a contract between professionals and clients
- to act as a statement of professional development
- to legitimise professional norms and justification for sanctions

THE DISCIPLINARY POWERS OF THE CIPD

CASE STUDY 9.1

In an article in *Personnel Today* in October 2001 (Kearns and Ingate 2001), Paul Kearns argued that the CIPD should be prepared to 'strike off' negligent, incompetent or dishonest members, in the same way that the General Medical Council strikes off doctors, or the Law Society solicitors. He argued that this was essential for the CIPD to have credibility as a profession, particularly given its new chartered status. The implication was that such a striking-off should be public, and that a person who had been struck off should be prevented from practising the profession.

In response, the secretary of the CIPD, Kristina Ingate, made three points. First, a comparison with professions such as medicine or the law is not appropriate. Personnel is not a statutory closed shop, unlike medicine or law, and CIPD membership is not a requirement to work in the personnel field. Second, the CIPD has a disciplinary procedure, and as a last resort, members in breach of its *Code of professional conduct* can be expelled from the Institute, although admittedly this is likely to be for misconduct rather than for incompetence. However, she urges caution. By its very nature personnel work is about human relationships, frequently in stressful situations. As a result, a complaint about a personnel practitioner will frequently be either totally unwarranted, or in reality a complaint against the policies or practices of the employer, rather than the individual practitioner. Third, CIPD members have high standards of both conduct and competence, and members are expected to keep their competence up to date through continuing professional development.

- to enhance the status of the profession
- a statement of professional conduct.

BUSINESS ETHICS

We have now moved some distance from our original concern with individual ethics. As we have seen, professions can impose ethical standards on their members. We now go one step further, and consider whether there is, or should be, a distinct field of study called business ethics. In other words, does a business, organisation or public body have any ethical responsibilities over and above the ethical responsibilities of the individuals who work for it?

Peter Drucker argues that ethics is by its very nature a code of individual behaviour. As a result, a business has no ethical responsibilities separate from those of every individual. An act that is not immoral or illegal if done by an individual cannot be immoral or illegal if done by a business. For example, if an individual pays money to an extortioner under threat of physical or material harm, that individual has in no way acted immorally or illegally. However, he quotes the case of the Lockheed aircraft company, which gave in to a Japanese airline which extorted money as a prerequisite for purchasing its L-1011 airliner, and was heavily criticised for doing so. He says, 'There was very little difference between Lockheed's paying the Japanese and the pedestrian in Central Park handing over his wallet to a mugger' (Drucker 1990, p236).

It seems to us that Drucker's example is a poor one. The mugger can do the pedestrian a great deal of physical harm if he does not hand over his wallet. On the other hand, the airline could not positively harm Lockheed by not buying its plane. We would regard the Lockheed case not as extortion by the airline, but as bribery by Lockheed, and a clear case of breach of business ethics.

 ACTIVITY

9.4 COCO DE MER

Coco de Mer is a sex shop or 'erotic emporium' in London's Covent Garden owned by Sam Roddick, daughter of Anita Roddick of Body Shop fame. Roddick insists that everything she sells is ethically sourced, including fair trade 'spanking paddles' and leather handcuffs, and there is a World Wildlife Fund endorsement for non-toxic sex toys. The business also supports sex-related human rights projects, including Pleasure Project, which educates women in developing countries on how to use contraception while at the same time enjoying sex, and the Belles of Shoreditch, which acts to protect the interests of strippers in East End pubs.

Is Coco de Mer an ethical business? How would your answer differ if we were talking about a manufacturer of cluster bombs rather than a sex shop? (Cluster bombs are bombs that spread large numbers of unexploded bomblets over a wide area, which explode when they are touched, usually by civilians, including children.)

In contrast, Michael Hoffman argues that companies can be held morally responsible (1990, p250). Companies can be morally good or bad according to the consequences of their actions. They espouse values, and individuals coming into the corporation are subject to those values. These values are maintained and reinforced by the culture of the organisation. As a result, it is quite legitimate to talk of business ethics as separate from individual ethics.

STAKEHOLDERS

Stakeholders are 'those individuals or groups who depend on the organisation to fulfil their own goals and on whom, in turn, the organisation depends' (Johnson and Scholes 1997). Stakeholders can be inside the organisation, like shareholders or employees, or outside, like customers or suppliers. In some cases the relationship is legal, as with statutory regulatory bodies or lenders, or moral, as with the local community, or a mixture of the two, as with employees (to meet the requirements of the contract of employment and to respect legal employment rights (legal), and to fulfil the expectations of the psychological contract (moral)). In the case of the public sector, there are no shareholders, but a wide range of client stakeholders.

Note that the CIPD has a narrower definition of a stakeholder. It includes only those parties who have a legal or financial relationship with the organisation. All others are defined as 'other interested parties' – the CIPD specifically mentions the media and the local community (CIPD 2003b, pp6, 30). However, this narrow definition ignores the moral and ethical dimensions of stakeholder theory. For example, a local community may have no legal claim on a company that routinely but legally pollutes its environment, but few would deny its moral claim on the company.

Stakeholder theory states that organisations have responsibilities to a wide range of stakeholders. This can be contrasted with the stockholder theory of corporate governance, which states that the organisation's only responsibility is to its shareholders (who in the United States are known as stockholders). Stockholder theory has been defended from several different angles. One is the agency approach associated with Milton Friedman. He argues that managers are legally the agents of the organisation's owners (its shareholders), and under agency law are thus legally obliged to serve only their interests, as long as they keep within the law. Another is the logical argument put forward by John Argenti, who argues that it is logically impossible for an organisation to pursue multiple objectives – ie it cannot simultaneously serve the interests of a range of stakeholders. In times of prosperity, the organisation might be able to deal out rewards in such a way as to keep all the stakeholders quiet, but in hard times, shareholders will take priority, if only because in the last resort, shareholders can sack the board of directors (Argenti 1993).

Not all stakeholders are equal. Some are much more important to the organisation than others. The relative importance of stakeholders can be analysed using stakeholder mapping (Johnson and Scholes 1997, pp197–203).

OXFORD BUS

CASE STUDY 9.2

The Oxford Bus Company, a subsidiary of the transport group Go-Ahead, has a 'stakeholder board'. This consists of representatives of customers, a local pressure group representative nominated by the National Federation of Bus Users, and the transport strategy officer of a local NHS trust, representing large employers, as well as company employees and managers. The board meets quarterly to discuss company performance and other matters of concern. Although purely advisory, it has been involved in vehicle design, ticketing and customer care issues. In future the company intends that one meeting a year will be held as an open meeting, to which members of the public will be invited (Weldon 2003).

Stakeholder mapping classifies stakeholders by the power they have over the organisation, and the degree of interest they have in it. These can be plotted on a two-by-two matrix as in Figure 9.1.

Figure 9.1 Stakeholder mapping

Level of interest

	Low	High
Low	A Don't bother	B Inform
Power		
High	C Satisfy	D Crucial

Source: Johnson and Scholes (1997).

Stakeholders of type A can effectively be ignored. They are not interested in the organisation, and have little power to affect it anyway. Conversely, type D are critical, and their interests must be taken into account at all times. Type B are interested in the organisation, but do not have the power to affect it significantly. They need to be kept informed, particularly as they may in turn be able to influence other stakeholders. Type C are passive stakeholders. They have great potential to influence the organisation, but at present little interest in doing so. They need to be kept quiet, so that they do not suddenly take an adverse interest in the organisation, and shift into type D.

The implication is that stakeholders have to be actively managed. They can be crucial in mobilising support for the organisation, or if things go badly, they can cripple it.

ACTIVITY

9.5 EDEXCEL

Edexcel is one of three major examination boards in England, Wales and Northern Ireland. It awards 1.5 million qualifications a year, which include GCSEs, A levels, BTEC qualifications, NVQs and GNVQs. Its annual turnover is £112 million. The other major examination boards are AQA (turnover £128 million) and OCR (turnover £77 million).

Edexcel was formed in 1996 as a result of a government-inspired merger between BTEC, a quango (quasi-autonomous non-governmental organisation) which specialised in vocational qualifications, and the University of London Examinations and Assessment Council, owned by London University, which specialised in GCSE and A level qualifications. At this stage Edexcel had charitable status.

Edexcel and the other exam boards are answerable to the Qualifications and Curriculum Authority (QCA), the regulator for the industry, and ultimately to the Department for Innovation, Universities and Skills.

Running an examination board is a high-risk activity. GCSE and A level results are issued in a blaze of publicity each summer, and any mistakes made by the exam boards are picked up by the media in a wave of adverse publicity. Exam boards always seem to get the blame, even for things which are not their own fault.

An extreme example occurred in the summer of 2002. Edexcel had already endured a wave of bad publicity in the winter of 2001–2, which culminated in a threat by the education secretary, Estelle Morris, to strip it of its licence, condemnation by Number 10 as 'sloppy' and 'unacceptable', and a public apology by Edexcel's chief executive John Kerr. Then in the summer of 2002 there was a row over late changing of grade boundaries for A levels, which led to many A level grades having to be changed, and hundreds of university places being put at risk. Ironically, Edexcel was not at fault – the main culprit was OCR – but all the exam boards suffered from the resulting media storm. The chairman of the QCA, Sir William Stubbs, was sacked, and eventually the education secretary herself resigned.

In 2003 Edexcel was taken over by the media giant Pearson, a FTSE 100 company with wide interests, including the *Financial Times*, and the publisher Pearson Education. Pearson already had interests in examination systems overseas, and saw it as its aim to 'globalise the marking process'. It is investing heavily in order to computerise the examination system, including online testing and marking.

Ken Boston, the new chairman of QCA, said at the time of the takeover, 'I see no reason why we should blanch at private sector companies.' However, other commentators were less complacent. Martin Ward, deputy general secretary of the Secondary Heads Association, said, 'the entry of a commercial organisation … has the potential for less accountability', while Ted Wragg, emeritus professor of education at Exeter University, said, 'I feel alarmed about the future …. People want to feel that an examination board is focused on standards, not profit.'

Sources: Lewis (2002) and Curtis (2004).

Questions

a. Identify and map the stakeholders (including 'other interested parties') of Edexcel as at the summer of 2004.

b. Do you think that the public-service role of Edexcel is incompatible with its private ownership?

CASE STUDY 9.3

STAKEHOLDING IN REVERSE: HUNTINGDON LIFE SCIENCES

Huntingdon Life Sciences is an organisation in Cambridgeshire which carries out drug tests on behalf of the pharmaceutical industry. Many of these tests involve experiments on animals. This is legal, but is regarded as immoral by the animal rights pressure groups. Co-ordinated by Stop Huntingdon Animal Cruelty (SHAC), the pressure groups have carried out a long campaign to force Huntingdon to close down.

The animal rights groups have used tactics, including physical violence against employees, which are themselves morally questionable, but this case study is concerned not with the ethics of the situation (do the ends justify the means?) but with the involvement of Huntingdon's stakeholders. Pressure has been put not only on Huntingdon, but also on its stakeholders, including its bankers, its insurers and the market maker that dealt in its shares. In industrial relations this is known as secondary picketing, which was banned by the Conservative government in the 1980s.

The technique has been partly successful. The government has been forced to supply banking and insurance services to Huntingdon itself, and the company has delisted its shares in London, and transferred its legal domicile to Maryland, USA, where company law enables it to operate in much more secrecy than in London.

However, the research facility is still operating, and the company and its stakeholders have found a way to use the law against its opponents. Using the Protection from Harassment Act 1997, which was originally designed to protect individuals against stalkers, both Huntingdon and some of its stakeholders (including in one case the landlord of a stakeholder – tertiary picketing?) have obtained injunctions placing exclusion zones around their premises and the homes of their employees.

Sources: Williams (2001) and Tait (2003).

 ACTIVITY

9.6 THE CHILD LABOUR DILEMMA

You are personnel manager for a UK clothing retailer. In addition to your personnel duties, you are also the company's ethics officer, responsible for implementing the code of ethics. One of your successful clothing lines is T-shirts, which are assembled in Pakistan and imported into the United Kingdom.

Opening your e-mails today, you find a report from one of your buyers of his recent visit to Pakistan. He reports that in a plant in Lahore, he has seen girls who look no older than 10,

sweeping the floor between the rows of sewing machines the other women work on. Your code of ethics does not specifically mention child labour, but it does contain a clause about treating all workers, both directly employed and employed by suppliers, with dignity and respect.

Your first action is to e-mail Mansur Khan, your agent in Lahore, and to ask him to investigate. He reports back that working conditions aren't bad. The girls concerned are aged from 11 upwards, and are the daughters of female production workers. He also says that child labour below the age of 14 is illegal in Pakistan, but there is widespread evasion of the law, which is not generally enforced.

Your first reaction is to tell your Purchasing Department to insist that the supplier stops employing the children, or your contract with it will be cancelled. However, a friend then brings to your attention the view of the International Confederation of Free Trade Unions (ICFTU), which is among the bodies that argues that this is not the best solution. It has called for clauses on labour standards to be incorporated into World Trade Organization (WTO) agreements, despite claims by developing countries that they could be used to prevent Third-World goods competing against Western products.

The ICFTU is concerned about employers that pay low wages, use child labour, ignore health and safety standards and deny staff union representation. Some argue that free trade is exacerbating exploitation by allowing companies to relocate to wherever production costs are lowest, regardless of local employment standards. But non-governmental organisations (NGOs) and developing countries argue that if Third-World countries are to compete in the global economy, they cannot afford to pay the same levels as Western employers, because their productivity levels are much lower. Developing countries should not be denied the competitive advantage they gain from cheaper wages.

You are now thoroughly confused. Do you have the right to impose western moral principles on the factory in Lahore, if there is a risk that as a result the girls and their mothers will lose their jobs?

You decide that the best way forward is use Archie Carroll's ethical principles. Using in turn the golden rule, the disclosure rule, the intuition ethic and the utilitarian principle, think about what your response to this problem would be.

VALUES

Values underpin ethics, and the values of an organisation underpin its business ethics. Organisational values answer the questions 'What do we stand for?' or 'What are the key principles that matter to us?' This is the second of three questions which organisations must ask themselves as they evolve their mission statement (see BITC 2000):

- What are we here to do? (purpose)
- What do we stand for? (values)
- What would we like to see ourselves become? (vision)

Values, as long as they are shared, help to bring together the people in an organisation, and get them working for a common aim (purpose and vision). Successful companies place a high emphasis on values, and share three characteristics (Deal and Kennedy 1990, p108):

- They stand for something.
- Management fine-tune their values to conform to the environment of the organisation.

- The values are known and shared by everyone in the organisation, and are also known, understood and supported by key stakeholders.

A value-driven company is likely to be more consistent in its decision-making, to be single-minded, and not deflected from its long-term vision by short-term expediency. Its staff are also likely to be more committed and motivated, as long as they have ownership of the values. However, values can be counter-productive if top management behaviour is not consistent with the stated values. For example, one of the long-standing values of Marks & Spencer was support of suppliers, and the company lost a great deal of public sympathy when it axed long-standing suppliers in the United Kingdom in order to buy more cheaply abroad.

CODES OF ETHICS

One definition of a code of ethics is 'a written, distinct, formal document, which consists of moral standards which help guide employee or corporate behaviour' (Schwartz 2001, p27). Codes can be of three different types (Brinkmann and Ims 2003, p266):

- educational – aimed at increasing moral awareness and behaviour within the organisation

- regulatory – detailed rules for behaviour, which recognise moral conflicts and help with resolving them

- aspirational – laying down general values, and communicating ideals to individuals within the organisation.

Poor codes of ethics tend to be inward-looking, and to ignore external stakeholders, and they tend to be regulatory and over-detailed. Many companies do not make their codes of ethics available to external stakeholders, and some do not even make them easily available to their own staff (which would seem to make them totally counter-productive).

Good codes of ethics recognise the importance of relationships with all major stakeholders, both internal and external, and involve stakeholders in their preparation. They are also clearly communicated to all stakeholders, and training is provided to stakeholders in order to ensure that they are understood and effective.

Even a good code of ethics is no guarantee of ethical behaviour. The existence of codes of ethics did not prevent the scandalous collapse of Enron and WorldCom in the United States, or the deliberate over-statement of oil reserves by Shell. Just as with values, top management must live the code of ethics at all times. If they do not, all respect for the organisation is likely to collapse.

Finally, a US survey in 1987 measured opinions on codes of ethics among American businesspeople. Respondents were asked to comment on a number of statements, with responses coded from 1 (strongly agree) to 4 (strongly disagree). Table 9.4 shows the outcome.

Table 9.4 Responses to a survey on codes of ethics

	Mean response
Professionals consider codes as a useful aid when they want to refuse an unethical request impersonally	1.8
Codes raise the ethical level of the industry	2.1
A code helps managers in defining clearly the limits of acceptable conduct	1.9
In cases of severe competition, a code reduces the use of sharp practices	2.7
People violate codes whenever they think they can avoid detection	2.5
Codes are easy to enforce	3.3
Codes protect inefficient firms and retard the dynamic growth of the industry	3.3

 ACTIVITY

9.7 MULTIGENOME AND ITS CODE OF ETHICS

Multigenome is a (fictitious) US-based multinational research company. Its code of ethics is reproduced below. Critically evaluate this code of ethics.

'Because we are separated – by many miles, by diversity of cultures and languages – we need a clear understanding of the basic principles by which we will operate our company. These are:

● That the company is made up of individuals – each of whom has different capabilities and potentials – all of which are necessary to the success of the company.

● That we acknowledge that individuality by treating each other with dignity and respect.

● That we will recognise and reward the contributions and accomplishments of each individual.

● That we will continually plan for the future so that we can control our destiny instead of letting events overtake us.

● That we maintain our policy of providing work for all individuals, no matter what the prevailing business conditions may be.

● That we make all decisions in the light of what is right for the good of the whole company, rather than what is expedient.

● That our customers are the only reason for the existence of the company

● That we must use the highest ethics to guide our business dealings to ensure that we are always proud to be a part of Multigenome.

● That we will discharge the responsibilities of corporate and individual citizenship to earn and maintain the respect of the community.

● As individuals and as a corporate body we must endeavour to uphold these standards so that we may be respected as persons and as an organisation.'

CORPORATE GOVERNANCE

Corporate governance is concerned with two questions. In whose interests should an organisation be run? And how should these purposes be determined? The two key issues in corporate governance are conflict of interest and accountability. Conflict of interest comes back to the agency issue discussed above (see p280). Managers are the agents of shareholders, but because of their control over key resources, particularly information, their power is greater than that of shareholders. How should this power be managed, and how should managers be held accountable to shareholders (and other stakeholders)?

CASE STUDY 9.4

CORPORATE GOVERNANCE IN THE VENETIAN REPUBLIC

The Venetian Republic dominated the Mediterranean for a thousand years, from its founding in the ninth century as a group of poor fishing villages, to its abolition by Napoleon in the early 1800s. Much of its success was due to its elaborate system of corporate governance.

The head of the Venetian Republic was the Doge, who was elected for life. However, his power was strictly limited. Each Doge on election signed a contract (*promissione*), which set out and limited his powers, and against which his performance was monitored each year. Over the centuries, these *promissioni* were progressively tightened. Weak or ineffective Doges were retired, and really

bad ones ran the risk of assassination. Even after his death, the Doge was still subject to independent review. If he was found to have been a bad or ineffective ruler, his family could be fined.

Each Doge was assisted by four ducal counsellors, who were independently appointed by the state, not by the Doge himself. Their term of office was short (two or three years), which meant that they could not become too powerful. There were also a whole series of other state committees, which ensured that leadership experience was widely diffused, providing a wide pool of potential Doges and ducal counsellors.

Source: McKee (2003).

Company law in the United Kingdom and the United States (the Anglo-Saxon model) supports the shareholder approach – companies must be run in the interests of their shareholders – although UK corporations do have legal responsibilities to other stakeholders. Other countries take a different approach to corporate governance. In Germany, companies have two-tier boards, a supervisory board and a management board (the Rhine model). The management board runs the company on a day-to-day basis, but is answerable to the supervisory board, which has shareholder, employee and third-party representatives on it, and which represents the interests of stakeholders (Farnham 1999, pp300–301).

Big business in Japan is organised through large integrated corporations called *keiretsu* (Mitsui, Mitsubishi etc). These can be either vertical, where manufacturers, suppliers and subcontractors are members of the same *keiretsu*, or horizontal, where the *keiretsu* companies operate in different markets. Mitsubishi, for example, is involved in gas, chemicals, plastics, steel, aluminium, cement, butter, brewing and paper (Charkham 1994, p77). Customers and suppliers are thus frequently within the same *keiretsu*, and relationships with them are much closer than in the West. (As a corollary, customers and suppliers outside the *keiretsu* might find themselves much more harshly treated, leaving the system open to charges of cronyism.) Japanese society is also heavily based on the concepts of family, consensus and *wa* (harmony). This leads naturally to a heavy reliance on the stakeholder approach. The hierarchy of interests tends to be customers first, employees second, managers third and shareholders last. The controversy over excessive 'fat cat' rewards to top management which is so prevalent in the United Kingdom would be impossible in Japan. However, because the stakeholder approach is supported by culture rather than law, it is vulnerable to changes in that culture, and has been shaken by the long recession in Japan over the last two decades.

Each system has its strengths and weaknesses, as summarised in Table 9.5.

Table 9.5 Strengths and weaknesses of different corporate governance models

	Strengths	Weaknesses
Anglo-Saxon model	Dynamic and innovative Fluid capital investment	Volatile and unstable Short-termism Weak governance
Rhine model	Long -term strategy Stable capital investment	Lack of flexibility Conservatism
Japanese model	Very long-term strategy Stable capital investment	Financial speculation Crony governance Weak accountability

Source: adapted from Johnson, Scholes and Whittington (2006, p174).

The conflict of interest and accountability questions are also tackled in different ways. In the United States, the approach is one of compliance, where corporate governance regulations are laid down by law, and must be followed. Typical is the Sarbanes–Oxley Act of 2002, which followed the scandals in Enron and WorldCom. This states that all companies listed in the United States must introduce codes of conduct, ethics policies and whistleblower hotlines. This also applies to foreign companies seeking a listing on the New York Stock Exchange. However, the key weakness of the compliance approach is that it does not internalise corporate governance in the culture of the corporation. As with other law, determined managers will find ways to obey its letter, but thwart its spirit.

Enron had a code of ethics, and on paper abided by all legal requirements (Crane and Madden 2007).

The UK approach is to use voluntary codes of practice, but to force firms to issue explanations if they choose not to abide by them. The key to the UK approach is separation of powers. In 1992 the Cadbury Report called for separation of the roles of chairman and CEO in listed companies. The CEO represents the executive managers, while the chairman acts in the interests of shareholders. The supermarket chain Morrisons had a combined chairman and CEO (Sir Ken Morrison, the founder), until it took over Safeway in 2003, but its explanation, that in effect it was a family business, was accepted by the stock exchange. Cadbury also called for the increased use of non-executive directors (NEDs) on boards, who again would represent the interests of shareholders. This was strengthened by the Higgs Report in 2003, which called for NEDs to be a majority on boards, and for them to be independently appointed, to avoid charges of cronyism if they were selected through the 'old boy network' from among friends of the chairman or CEO (Fisher and Lovell 2006). Again the example of Enron illustrates the risk of cronyism. The vast majority of its directors were non-executive.

CASE STUDY 9.5

PRIVATE EQUITY – A LICENCE TO PRINT MONEY?

2007 was the year of private equity. In the space of two months, private equity consortiums took over Alliance Boots, failed to take over Sainsbury and bought Chrysler from Daimler. In 2006, private equity groups spent US$725 billion – a figure greater than the GDP of the Netherlands – and companies owned by them are said to employ one in five of all private sector workers in the United Kingdom.

What is private equity? Basically, it describes a situation where a group of investors put money into business. There are three main types:

- venture capital, normally involving start-ups or small businesses

- management buy-outs (MBOs), where private equity funds are used to back an incumbent management team

- management buy-ins (MBIs), where external investors impose a new management team.

This case study is concerned with the last two types, particularly management buy-ins.

There are two key features of private equity:

- It is short-term – the private equity investors aim to get out within two or three years, by which time they hope to have doubled their investment.

- If the company taken over is a public company, it becomes private, ie it is no longer quoted on a stock exchange.

Both of these features have corporate governance implications. As the horizon of the private equity company is at best medium-term, its buyers will look for quick cost savings. The result is that jobs are likely to be shed. The Work Foundation reports that in a survey of MBIs, the average job loss was 18 per cent, and the average worker was £231 a year worse off. Typical is the AA. This was bought from Centrica in 2004 by Permira and CVC

Capital Partners for £1.75 billion. At the time of the takeover it employed 10,600 people, but by 2006 this was down to 7,000, with redundancies including 500 patrol staff. Each patrol worker now attends 6.8 breakdowns a day, compared with 5.2 before the takeover, and the AA has slipped from first to third in *Which?* magazine's ratings of breakdown services. In addition, the GMB union has been derecognised. However, Alistair Maclean of the house union AA Democratic Union disputed that the private equity management was anti-worker – 'the only difference with private equity firms is the speed with which they do it' (Mahony 2007).

In 2007 the AA merged with the travel and insurance group Saga, which had itself been taken over by the private equity group Charterhouse in 2004 for £1.35 billion. The value of the merged group was £6.15 billion, roughly double the value of the two component organisations in 2004. Saga's approach to its workforce had been rather more conciliatory than the AA's. Its workers had been offered employee shares in 2004, and the 80 per cent who had taken this up received an average windfall of £10,500 on the merger (Mahony 2007).

When a company becomes private, it virtually vanishes from the public eye. It no longer has to comply with stock exchange listing requirements, but only with the less rigorous requirements of the Companies Acts. It has nine months after the end of its financial year before it has to publish its accounts, it does not have to publish interim figures, and it does not have to put its annual report on its website.

Other stakeholders also lose out. The way in which MBIs are financed is through debt. A typical example is Debenhams, which was bought by a private equity consortium in 2003 for £2 billion. Of this, £600 million was equity, and £1.4 billion debt. This took Debenhams' debt from £100 million to £1.5 billion. Interest had to be paid on this, effectively wiping out Debenhams' profits, and also its tax bill. A sale and lease-back of Debenhams' property raised £500 million, but again increased the company's costs, as

rent now had to be paid. Further borrowing took Debenhams' debt to £1.9 billion, enabling the owners to draw a dividend of £1.2 billion from the company (twice what they paid for it). In 2006, Debenhams was taken public again, enabling the private equity owners to withdraw.

The result of these financial manoeuvrings is that the company becomes much more risky. The heavy level of debt makes the company much more vulnerable to a trading shock or to a steep rise in interest rates. This puts pensioners at risk, as well as present employees. It also means that the government loses out, as it no longer receives corporation tax on profits which no longer exist. Attacks from the trade union movement are increasing. Brendan Barber, the general secretary of the Trades Union Congress, says that the rise of private equity is fundamentally changing the nature of UK and European capitalism, while the Financial Services Authority warns that the failure of a private equity deal is inevitable.

The biggest private equity deal to date is the takeover of Alliance Boots, the first FTSE100 company to fall to private equity, in May 2007. This is a complex example, a mixture of MBO and MBI, with a Trojan horse already within the company. In 2006, Boots and Alliance Unichem merged to form Alliance Boots. The chairman of Alliance, Stefano Pessina, became executive vice-chairman of Alliance Boots, with a 15 per cent shareholding. In early 2007, Pessina began talks with the US private equity company KKR about a buy-out. This raised serious corporate governance issues – was Pessina acting in his own interests or in those of shareholders as a whole?

Eventually a deal was reached in May 2007. KKR and Pessina would buy out Alliance Boots for £11.1 billion. £3.4 billion of this would be equity, with £1 billion from each of KKR and Pessina, and £1.4 billion non-voting equity from a consortium of banks, who would also lend the balance of the buy-out price. KKR and Pessina thus each had 50 per cent effective control, although each had put up less than 10 per cent of the purchase price. Pessina's 15 per cent stake in Alliance Boots was thus worth £1.5 billion, so even after putting up his £1 billion stake, he was left with an immediate £500 million profit! Like the other directors, he also received a cash payout from the exercise of share options he held.

Not surprisingly, the GMB national officer Paul Maloney described the deal and the payouts as 'obscene and unacceptable'. Alliance Boot's £600 million profits would be swallowed up in interest charges, costing the government £130 million in corporation tax.

The private equity boom may now (January 2008) be over. The 'credit crunch' which spread from the United States in late summer 2007, and the associated collapse of Northern Rock, have made banks much less ready to finance private equity deals. Whether it also leads to the failure of existing private equity deals is still to be seen.

Sources: Thornton (2007), Plender (2007), Mathiason (2007), Finch (2007), Mathiason and Stewart (2007), Hencke and Inman (2007), Treanor (2007), Mahony (2007), Milner (2007).

CORPORATE SOCIAL RESPONSIBILITY

Corporate social responsibility (CSR) is the way in which an organisation expresses its values in behaviour towards stakeholders. The European Commission defines it as 'a concept whereby companies decide voluntarily to contribute to a better society and a cleaner environment' (2001), while the DTI defines it as an organisation which recognises that its activities have a wider impact on society; takes account of the economic, social, environmental and human rights impacts of its activities, and works in partnership with other groups and organisations (2002).

Archie Carroll (1991) put forward a four-part model of CSR:

Economic responsibilities:	required by society
Legal responsibilities:	required by society
Ethical responsibilities:	expected by society
Philanthropic responsibilities:	desired by society.

Several key points come out of these definitions:

- CSR is voluntary. Mere compliance with legal requirements is not CSR. An organisation's CSR behaviour must go beyond the law.
- CSR is active. It involves behaviour, not just good intentions.
- CSR involves environmental as well as social responsibilities.
- CSR is often carried out in partnership with others.
- Although the European Commission only mentions companies, CSR extends to all organisations, public and private, profit-making and not-for-profit.

CSR can take a number of forms. These include:

- Community involvement, frequently in partnership with other organisations.

This can include sponsorship of worthy bodies, or direct involvement of the organisation's employees in community activities.

- Socially responsible investment, which can include ethical banking, and refusal by pension funds to invest in companies making, for example, armaments or cigarettes.

- Corporate governance, concerned with the behaviour of a company towards its shareholders, and including elements like the appointment and responsibilities of non-executive directors.

- Fair trade, buying goods produced by suppliers which are, for example, organic, or non-employers of children, or not based in human-rights abusing countries like Burma.

- Sustainability, acting in such a way as to assist the long-term survival of the planet.

Several of these are illustrated in case studies below, derived from winners of Business in the Community's Awards for Excellence 2004 (www.bitc.org.uk/resources/case_studies).

 THE CO-OPERATIVE BANK

CASE STUDY 9.6

The Co-op Bank launched its Ethical Policy in 1992, after consultation with customers. It launched its Partnership Approach in 1997, identifying seven groups of stakeholders, or Partners, and pledging to deliver value to them in a socially responsible and ecologically sustainable manner. It published its first triple bottom line (profit, society, environment) independently-verified *Partnership report* in 1998. The 2002 *Partnership report* sets out 77 targets, in each case with the name of the individual in the organisation who is charged with its achievement.

It is the United Kingdom's biggest provider of financial services to the credit union movement, which tackles financial exclusion. Its community investment, at 2.7 per cent of pre-tax profits, is amongst the best in the United Kingdom. Its campaigns mobilise its customers to protest on international human rights issues, for example, against the illicit trade in conflict diamonds – a source of finance which has fuelled civil wars and human rights abuses in Africa – and against the use of cluster bombs.

CSR has been criticised as often being little more than a PR stunt, designed to boost sales rather than to benefit society. This is particularly true of community involvement activities. This has been called 'cause-related marketing'. For example, Vodafone sponsors the England cricket team, but in return gets endless exposure of its logo on players' shirts during Test Matches. Tesco runs a Computers for Schools project, which supplies computers to schools, but only after customers have collected vouchers to verify their spend in Tesco stores (for a spirited condemnation of cause-related marketing, see Monbiot 2001).

Early in 1999, Industrial Relations Services carried out a survey of ethics in the

CASE STUDY 9.7

MARKS & SPENCER

Marks & Spencer has pulled together its wide range of community involvement programmes into a more focused approach called Marks & Start. This runs the biggest work experience programme in the United Kingdom, designed to help people who face the biggest barriers to obtain sustained employment.

It also takes responsibility for the total footprint of its business through the manufacture, use and disposal of its products. It is rated number one by Greenpeace on avoiding GM food, and by Friends of the Earth on pesticide reduction. It is supporting an innovative approach to fisheries management called Invest in Fish, which brings together stakeholders (fishers, fishing communities, NGOs and the fish trade), to develop a fishing industry which is successful economically, and socially and environmentally responsible. In 2007 it introduced its Plan A, designed to make the company carbon-neutral.

workplace (IRS 1999). The survey asked why organisations were involved in community activities. Respondents could choose as many of six responses as they wished. The results are given in Table 9.6.

Table 9.6 Why organisations are involved in community activities

		Per cent
1	Enhancement of corporate image	82
2	Moral obligation	62
3	Employee satisfaction	59
4	Develop staff potential	51
5	Promote the business	46
6	Improve profitability	15

Source: IRS (1999).

 ACTIVITY

9.8 IS YOUR OWN ORGANISATION INVOLVED IN THE COMMUNITY?

Find out what community activities (if any) your own organisation is involved in. If possible, also try to find out why the organisation chose these particular activities.

Was the primary motive short-term profits, long-term profits, employee benefit or moral obligation (or a mixture of several of these)?

Short-term profits (no 6) were mentioned by only a small minority of respondents, while long-term profitability (nos 1 and 5), employees (nos 3 and 4) and moral obligation (no 2) were seen as much more important. Perhaps community involvement is a rare example of a true win-win situation. (see also Kelly 1999).

SABMILLER – DEVELOPING A GLOBAL CORPORATE SOCIAL RESPONSIBILITY POLICY

CASE STUDY 9.8

SABMiller (formerly South African Breweries) is the second-largest brewer in the world, with large operations in South Africa, Europe, China, the United States and Latin America. When it was a local South African company, it developed CSR programmes based on the local issues of HIV/AIDS and community development. In Europe, global warming and energy conservation were seen as more crucial issues.

Once SABMiller became a world company, it decided that it needed a global CSR strategy. It developed a sustainable development framework through extensive world-wide consultation, which concentrated on 10 priorities. These included responsible drinking, energy and carbon management, HIV/AIDS, human rights and community development.

All SABMiller operations throughout the world must strive to meet objectives in all 10 areas, but they can decide how far they go on each one. All operations must reach at least what the SABMiller board defines as level 1, the minimum acceptable standard, while the levels currently go up to level 4, which represents admired status in relation to current good practice.

The strategy helps managers to understand that they are part of a global operation with global responsibilities, but at the same time it enables them to prioritise local issues.

Sources: Article 13 and CBI (2007), Kollewe (2007).

FAIRTRADE

CASE STUDY 9.9

Fairtrade is one of the retail successes of the 2000s. Sales of Fairtrade coffee grew from £15.5 million in 2000, to £65.8 million in 2006, when it commanded 18 per cent of the UK roast and ground coffee market. Similar rates of growth have been seen for tea, chocolate and cocoa, and bananas.

Fairtrade is a product labelling scheme, which acts as an independent guarantee that disadvantaged producers in the Third World are getting a better deal. Its standards are set by an international

certification body, Fair Trading Labelling Organisations International, and administered at a country level by national Fairtrade organisations. In the United Kingdom the administering body is the Fairtrade Foundation, a charity set up by Cafod, Oxfam, Christian Aid, Traidcraft Exchange and the World Development Movement.

The majority of coffee and cocoa is grown by small farmers, organised into co-operatives, while bananas and tea are usually produced on plantations. In the former case it is the co-operative that is given Fairtrade certification; in the latter it is the plantation, which guarantees minimum health and safety and environmental standards, and that no child or forced labour will be used.

In return, producers are guaranteed a price which is sufficient to cover sustainable production, plus a premium which is invested in community development. For example, the minimum price paid for Fairtrade cocoa is US$1,600 a ton, plus US$150 per ton premium, as long as the world (New York) price is below US$1,600. If the New York price rises above US$1,600 a ton, the Fairtrade price will be the New York price plus US$150 premium. This means that producers are guaranteed a stable price, and they are insulated from market fluctuations, which is the case of primary products can be violent.

An example quoted on the Fairtrade website is the Juliana-Jaramillo group of banana farmers in the Dominican Republic. Until 1962, the Granada Food Company ran vast plantation estates in the area, providing housing, water supply and schools. In 1962, it pulled out and the infrastructure collapsed. Granada even took the zinc roofs off the estate houses. The government divided 15 per cent of the estates among local farmers, giving each worker about 15 hectares. In 2000, Fairtrade introduced the local farmers to a UK-based company, Mack Multiples, and they worked together to improve the quality of their fruit and to develop sales to Sainsbury. A local farmer, Alfredo Martinez, says that he is now guaranteed a minimum price, receives money weekly, and is making twice what he was before Fairtrade. Environmental standards have been improved, and education and health standards have been restored.

However, not everyone is so impressed with the Fairtrade achievement. First, Fairtrade is

not necessarily the same as ethical sourcing. For example, Marks & Spencer sells Fairtrade cotton clothing. This guarantees that the raw cotton was produced ethically, but not necessarily that the whole of the supply chain was ethical. In any case, Fairtrade cotton only makes up about 1 per cent of that purchased by M&S each year.

Second, there is a feeling that Fairtrade is being exploited by large retailers. They see the Fairtrade label as a way to segment socially aware consumers, who are willing to pay a premium price for Fairtrade products. The result is that the main beneficiaries are the supermarket groups, rather than the Fairtrade producers.

Third, major producers are also jumping on the Fairtrade bandwagon. The best known is Nestlé, whose Partner's Blend coffee has Fairtrade certification. This is seen as unacceptable by some ethical campaigners, who point to the long-standing claims that Nestlé unethically promotes its powdered milk compounds in Third World countries.

Fourth, Fairtrade has been criticised by some economists, particularly Americans, because it is seen as biased towards co-operatives.

Finally, some economists claim that Fairtrade, by guaranteeing a price above the world price, is in effect encouraging over-production. Fairtrade counters by saying that for all commodities, Fairtrade is only a small percentage of world output, and that the Fairtrade price gives farmers surplus income which encourages them to diversify.

On balance, like us, you may well think that Fairtrade benefits the Third World and should be encouraged, but as with most things, the situation is not as simple as it appears at first sight.

Sources: Fairtrade website, Crane and Matten (2007), Murray (2006), *Economist* (2006), Prosser (2007).

SUSTAINABILITY

Sustainability is about our responsibility to the ultimate stakeholder: our own future, and the future of the planet. We are using up the resources of the earth and degrading the planet at an increasing rate, and this can only be at the expense of future generations. Sustainable development is 'development that meets the needs of the present without compromising the ability of future generations to meet their own needs' (Fisher and Lovell 2006, p21). 'To operate sustainably, an organisation must … [be] supportive of the survival of the physical environment and also the communities and economies in which it operates' (Accountability nd).

At the macro level, we have the problem of global warming and the associated climate change, the result of the excess of greenhouse gases, particularly carbon dioxide, in the atmosphere, caused at least in part by our excessive burning of fossil fuel. This can only be tackled at global level (global social responsibility). The Kyoto Treaty in 1999 committed industrialised countries to large reductions in carbon emissions, but this effort has been frustrated by the refusal of the Bush Administration to ratify the treaty. The United Kingdom is fully committed to the Kyoto principles, and has introduced a climate change levy on polluting industries.

At a micro level, sustainability concerns us all, organisations and individuals alike. At an individual level, it is as basic as composting our garden waste, rather than sending it to landfill sites, and turning off our television sets at night, rather than leaving them on standby. At an organisational level, it can be about energy conservation, and also about the kind of activities highlighted in the following case study and activity.

CASE STUDY 9.10

CARILLION PLC

Carillion is one of the United Kingdom's leading construction companies. Its sustainability activities include:

- **Self-sufficient materials strategy** – when building the M6 toll road, much of the required building materials were sourced from within the construction site, saving on vehicle movements. Pulverised fuel ash was used to replace cement in concrete mixture, saving on extraction activities.

- **Waste management** – Carillion is responsible for hospital waste disposal, and better training on the nature of clinical waste has led to a considerable fall in the volume of material going into clinical waste bins.

- **Energy management** – consumption of energy in head office buildings was reduced by 19 per cent.

- **Sustainable construction** – working with its supply chain, Carillion has developed new construction methods which save energy, produce less waste and have lower long-term running costs.

Source: adapted from a Business in the Community case study (www.bitc.org.uk).

PLASTIC BAGS – AN UNSUSTAINABLE OPTION?

CASE STUDY 9.11

Seventeen billion plastic carrier bags are used in the United Kingdom every year, 14 billion of which are given away by supermarkets. Only one in 200 of these is recycled. The rest go into landfill, weighing 100,000 tonnes, where they take up to 1,000 years to decompose. The vast majority of bags are made from oil derivatives. Most are non-degradable, a few are degradable – they break down when exposed to sunlight (but not in landfill) – and a very few are biodegradable, made of corn starch, and do break down in landfill.

Several countries have taken action to control their use of plastic bags. In 2002, Bangladesh banned them outright, as they were causing flooding by blocking storm drainage channels during the monsoon. They are also banned in South Africa, and San Francisco is the first US city to impose a ban. Taiwan has banned plastic plates, cups and cutlery as well as plastic bags, leading to a 25 per cent cut in its landfill.

Ireland took a different route, introducing a tax of 15 cents (about 10p) a bag in 2002. This cut plastic bag usage by at least 90 per cent, although some small bags are exempt. Usage has slowly crept up again since 2002, leading to an increase in tax to 22 cents in July 2007.

In the United Kingdom there are no official restrictions on the use of plastic bags, although the Scottish Parliament considered and rejected a tax of 10p a bag in 2006, and a MORI poll suggested that throughout the United Kingdom 63 per cent would support a 10p tax. London is considering a ban, while the prime minister, Gordon Brown, has said that he would like to see a total ban on single-use plastic bags.

The small town of Modbury in Devon became the first town in Europe to ban plastic bags in April 2007. None of the town's 43 traders, including the Co-op supermarket, issues plastic bags.

Individual stores have taken unilateral action. IKEA charges 10p a bag, and has seen plastic bag use fall by 97 per cent. The discount stores Aldi and Lidl have always charged for bags.

Tesco, the heaviest bag user of all, with 4 billion bags issued each year, costing it £40 million at 1p per bag, introduced a scheme in 2006 whereby customers received one 'green' Clubcard point, worth 1p, for each bag they reused, whether or not the reused bag originally came from Tesco. This is intended to cut Tesco's usage by 25 per cent, or 1 billion bags a year. Each bag saved saves Tesco 1p, so the only net cost to Tesco is when it pays out for other stores' bags. Tesco has also made all its bags degradable (but not biodegradable).

Tesco's move has been welcomed by the government, but criticised by Friends of the Earth as 'a very small step' and a 'greenwash', as it does nothing to cut the excessive amounts of food packaging used by Tesco and all other supermarkets, and because Tesco has chosen not to go biodegradable.

However, the plastic bag industry is fighting back. Barry Turner, the chairman of the UK Carrier Bag Consortium, claims that although plastic bags are made from oil, they use by-products such as naptha, ethylene and propylene, which would otherwise have to be flared off. He also criticises the use of paper bags rather than plastic. Paper bags weigh more than plastic, are four times as expensive to produce, and most seriously, whereas plastic bags in landfill remain inert, paper bags decompose to release the greenhouse gases methane and carbon dioxide.

Although the obvious response to Turner's claims is 'He would say that, wouldn't he?' the situation is clearly more complex than at first sight. Perhaps the ideal solution is that advocated by Sainsbury – the more extensive use of 'bags for life', more heavy-duty bags which sell for 10p, can be reused many times, and which the store guarantees to replace free when they wear out, whereupon Sainsbury sends the worn-out bag for recycling.

Stop press: In March 2008 the government announced its intention to legislate on plastic bags in 2009.

Sources: Turner (2006), Finch and Allen (2006), Butler (2006), *Economist* (2007), Barkham (2007), Aldred (2007), Wintour (2007).

CASE STUDY 9.12

FOOD MILES

The seafood producer Youngs catches langoustine (scampi) off the Scottish coast. It is then shipped to Thailand for processing, and then returned to Grimsby, England, for breading and packaging, a round trip of 17,000 miles!

Surely this is a case of 'food miles' gone mad? Not so, says Youngs. British consumers prefer their scampi to be hand-shelled, rather than machine-shelled. It used to be machine-shelled in Scotland, but the only feasible hand-shelling plant is in Thailand. Independent research by the Carbon Trust found that shipping scampi to and from Thailand is no more

environmentally damaging than machine-shelling it in the United Kingdom, as carbon dioxide emissions from machine-shelling are high, while emissions from shipping the scampi are relatively low.

Clearly the situation is more complicated than it appears at first sight. On the other hand, what the company does not evaluate is the impact of hand-shelling the scampi in the United Kingdom. This would be environmentally the best solution, but would undoubtedly be more expensive for Youngs, and so ultimately for the consumer.

Source: Cooke (2007).

CORPORATE SOCIAL RESPONSIBILITY AND HR

Carroll (1979) identifies four philosophies of organisational responsiveness to CSR:

- Reaction: the company denies all responsibility for social issues, claiming that they are the responsibility of government (the Friedman approach).
- Defence: the company accepts responsibility but fights it, doing the least that seems to be required (the tobacco industry?).
- Accommodation: the company accepts responsibility and does what is expected of it (most major companies in the United Kingdom).
- Proaction: the company does more than is expected (Body Shop, the Co-op Bank).

Who should be responsible for directing an organisation's policy on ethics and CSR? There are three leading contenders, each reflecting a particular perception of ethics and CSR.

- Marketing/PR, if CSR is primarily seen as a marketing tool, and the key relationship is that with customers (defence).

- The company secretary, if CSR is primarily seen as a matter of regulation, and the key relationship is the corporate governance one with shareholders (accommodation).

- HR, if CSR is primarily seen as a cultural issue and about human behaviour, and the key relationship is that with all stakeholders (proaction).

The theory on ethics and CSR would strongly suggest that the policy can only be meaningful if it permeates all the activities of the organisation, and if everyone in the organisation truly internalises the policy, rather than merely paying lip-service to it. This would suggest that HR should be the lead department. However, of even greater importance is that, whichever department is in day-to-day charge, top management, in the form of the CEO, should at all times behave ethically. Just as quality has Total Quality Management, ethics/CSR requires Total Ethical Management.

So what in detail should be the role of HR in ethics/CSR?

- Helping to identify the values of the organisation. HR should have experience with values, and is well placed to canvass opinions on values across a wide range of stakeholders. Here HR has a clear strategic contribution to make.

- Drawing up a code of ethics. HR should be used to drafting policies, many of which themselves have a clear ethical content.

- Behaving ethically in its own relationships with a key stakeholder, the organisation's own staff. Here the concept of the 'psychological contract' is important (CIPD 2003b, pp18–19). This defines the implicit deal between employer and employees, as distinct from the formal deal contained in the contract of employment. It is an understanding about what each side can expect from the other. This has two implications for HR in the context of ethics/CSR: the psychological contract should itself be an ethical one, and the concept of the psychological contract can be extended to relationships with other stakeholders.

- Managing the culture of the organisation. A culture that fully supports ethics does not just happen, it has to be nurtured, maintained and communicated.

- Development. If staff in an organisation are presented with a CSR policy and a code of ethics, it will mean nothing to them until they are thoroughly trained in what they mean and how they should be implemented. This presents HR with a crucial development role, at all levels of the organisation. Some help here is likely to come from the launch of the DTI's online CSR Academy in July 2004 (see *Personnel Today* 2004).

- Maintaining the 'employer brand'. Increasingly companies want brand values to be reflected in everything that the organisation does. An ethical brand value has clear marketing advantages and recruitment/retention advantages (see CIPD 2003b, p23).

ACTIVITY

9.9 INSTITUTIONAL RACISM

In 1999 the Macpherson Report on the murder of Stephen Lawrence identified the principle of institutional racism. The report defined this as:

> The collective failure of an organisation to provide an appropriate and professional service to people because of their colour, culture or ethnic origin. It can be seen or detected in processes, attitudes and behaviour which amount to discrimination through unwitting prejudice, ignorance, thoughtlessness and racial stereotyping which disadvantages minority ethnic people.

(Home Office 1999)

Macpherson argued that because to its ingrained culture (the so-called 'canteen culture'), the Metropolitan Police was institutionally racist. This does not mean that every Met officer is racist, or that there is a deliberate policy of racism in the organisation, but it does mean that the organisation is unthinkingly racist in its attitudes and behaviour.

After the publication of the report, the Met pledged itself to eliminating institutional racism, as did other police forces.

What actions could the police take to eliminate institutional racism?

CORPORATE SOCIAL RESPONSIBILITY AND THE GOVERNMENT

The government has two main roles in CSR. First, the government is itself a major employer and a major purchaser and supplier of services. In this role, it can and should behave ethically just like any other organisation.

However, the government also has a role in the promotion of CSR (Cowe 2004). In March 2000, the first minister for corporate social responsibility was appointed, within the Department for Trade and Industry. The minister, Stephen Timms, made it clear that the government takes its role seriously: 'what we are talking about here is beyond philanthropy. CSR is not an add-on. It must be about the very way we do business, both at home and overseas.'

The main interest of the government has been in securing greater transparency. The Pensions Act of 2000 requires pension fund trustees to make a statement of investment principles, disclosing their policy on social, environmental and ethical issues. Its Company Law Review led to the introduction in 2005 of a requirement on all public companies to include an operating and financial review in their annual report to shareholders. In addition, the government set up a new CSR Academy in 2004.

However, locating the responsibility for CSR within the DTI has inevitably led to an emphasis on the corporate governance aspects of CSR. Other departments clearly also have an involvement in CSR – the Department of Work and Pensions in pensions, the Department for International Development in trade and aid aspects of CSR, and the Environment Department in issues of pollution,

CASE STUDY 9.13

CORPORATE MANSLAUGHTER

The ultimate social responsibility of an organisation is not to kill people. However, it is extremely difficult to convict a company on a criminal charge of corporate manslaughter. In law, corporations do not commit acts, individuals do. To convict a company of corporate manslaughter, it is necessary to prove that an individual who should have acted in ways that could have prevented the death from occurring, was negligent in his or her duties (the identification principle). In addition, the individual must sit at the nerve centre of corporate decision-making, and must be recognised as guiding a relevant aspect of corporate activity (the guiding mind principle).

Not surprisingly, given these constraints, it is very difficult to make a charge of corporate manslaughter stick. In the notorious case of the *Herald of Free Enterprise*, which sank in Zeebrugge harbour in 1987 when it sailed with its bow doors open, it was not thought worthwhile even to attempt a prosecution. This was although crew members had reported five times on the lack of warning lights on the bridge to indicate that the bow doors were open, and although at the subsequent Department of Trade enquiry the company was described as 'from top to bottom ... infected with the disease of sloppiness'.

In practice, only a small business with an identifiable owner-manager is likely to be convicted of corporate manslaughter. One such case was the Lyme Bay canoeing tragedy, where children were drowned in a canoeing accident at an outdoor training company. Another was the Hodgson case in 1996, where James Hodgson, who was responsible for cleaning chemical residue from road tankers, was sprayed in the face with a toxic chemical and consequently died. In this case the company was found guilty of corporate manslaughter and fined £15,000, while the owner was sent to prison for 12 months.

In the case of public companies, such as the rail companies involved in the Paddington rail crash, prosecutions under the Health and Safety at Work Act were used rather than corporate manslaughter charges.

A proposal to tighten up the law on corporate manslaughter was in the Labour manifesto in 1997. In 2000, the Home Office published proposals for reform, *Reforming the law on involuntary manslaughter*. This made six proposals:

● There should be a special offence of corporate killing.

● A corporation could be prosecuted for corporate killing where its conduct fell far below what could be reasonably expected.

● The corporate offence should not require that the risk be obvious.

● The death should be regarded as having been caused by the conduct of the corporation if it is caused by a 'management failure'.

● Such a failure will be regarded as a cause of the death even if the immediate cause is the act or an omission of an individual.

● Individuals could still be liable for reckless killing or killing by gross carelessness.

A corporate killing bill was in the Queen's Speech in 2004, just before the election in 2005. However, to date nothing has happened.

The European Union has proposed a wider reform, covering other offences in addition to corporate manslaughter. A corporation would be responsible for all offences committed by its employees, but would be allowed a due diligence defence if it could show that every precaution had been taken to avoid or minimise such an act occurring.

Source: Fisher and Lovell (2006).

sustainability and climate change. The involvement of the government is likely to increase.

THE BOTTOM LINE

Do CSR and ethical behaviour increase a company's profits? A series of studies suggests that they do.

First, CSR seems to benefit an organisation's reputation. In 2002, Business in the Community carried out a survey on what the public thought of corporate responsibility (BITC 2002). Business leaders in general are not trusted. Only 25 per cent of respondents trusted them to tell the truth – only ahead of politicians and journalists, and well below doctors and teachers. This suggests that business has a lot of ground to make up. The public wants business to be responsible. Only 2 per cent think that companies should maximise their profits, regardless of society or the environment. Eight times as many thought companies should make a major contribution to society, regardless of cost.

Responsible behaviour also affects people's purchases. Eighty-six per cent in 2002 thought it very or fairly important that an organisation show a high degree of social responsibility, up from 68 per cent in 1997. One in six people have actively boycotted a product on ethical grounds in pervious years.

Is this evidence conclusive? No. It is suggestive, but little more. If you were interviewed by Business in the Community, you might have a shrewd idea of the kind of answers the interviewer would like! It is also unfortunately true that there is often a gap between what people say they do, and what they actually do.

The second piece of evidence is *The business case for corporate responsibility,* a report written by the management consultants Arthur D Little in 2003, again for Business in the Community (BITC 2003). This identifies a number of benefits from CSR:

- It offers a means by which companies can build the trust of their stakeholders. This is supported by the US strategy guru Michael Porter, who is reported as saying that how a company is perceived by its stakeholders is becoming a source of competitive advantage (Golzen 2001).
- CSR offers more effective management of risk. CSR encourages firms to understand and empathise with society and the environment, and this makes it more likely that they will be proactive about social and environmental risk.
- CSR helps to attract and retain a talented and diverse workforce.
- CSR stimulates learning and innovation within organisations.
- CSR facilitates access to capital. Over half of analysts and two-thirds of investors believe that a company that emphasises CSR is attractive to investors.
- CSR improves competitiveness, market positioning and profitability. The report quotes from Collins and Porras's *Built to last* (2000), a report on a

pioneering study in the 1990s, which compared successful companies that had been in business for at least 50 years, with a control group that had been less successful. They found that a key characteristic of the successful 'visionary' companies was that they had a core purpose beyond making money.

CASE STUDY 9.14

ETHICAL COMPANIES

Friends Provident

The 200-year-old insurance company is convinced that its Quaker origins and ethical reputation have served to differentiate it from its competitors.

Centrica

After Centrica developed an employee community involvement programme at its Cardiff call centre in 2000, it found higher retention rates among volunteering employees, increased levels of job satisfaction, and lower absenteeism.

The Beacon Press

The Beacon Press has demonstrated that higher standards of quality in printing can be achieved through environmental best practice. This has led them to push the boundaries of technology.

Is the Arthur D Little evidence conclusive? It is certainly very strong. Although some of the findings are based on opinion, others are based on hard evidence of changes in behaviour (see the case study on Centrica).

The third study was carried out by the Institute of Business Ethics in 2003. This examined a sample of FTSE350 companies which were perceived as being ethical (they had had code of ethics in operation for at least five years, they scored highly on *Management Today*'s annual league table of 'most admired companies', and they were rated highly by the specialist ratings agency SERM on their 'socio-ethical risk management'). These ethical companies were compared with a control sample.

The ethical companies were found to score more highly on three measures of financial performance – market value added, economic value added and price/earnings ratio. On a fourth measure, return on capital employed, they did less well until the stock market collapse of 2000, but have performed better since then, suggesting that their profits are more stable (Caulkin 2003, Maitland 2003).

Is this evidence conclusive? Again, it is very strong, but unfortunately it is not conclusive. There is clearly a strong correlation between ethical behaviour and profits, but this does not prove that the ethical behaviour causes the profits. The link may be the other way round – profitable companies may be more likely to be ethical – or both may be the result of some unknown third factor.

A more theoretical approach was taken by Reitz, Wall and Love (1998). They concentrated on the relatively narrow area of business negotiation, and argued that taking an unethical stance in negotiation has four major costs:

- Rigidity. Unethical negotiators will tend to stick to the patterns of negotiation that have paid off in the past. They will thus trap themselves in a rigid bargaining position which can be matched and exploited by their opponents.

- Damaged relationships. If a bargaining partner feels that it has been manipulated through underhand tactics, it is likely to feel embittered and to seek revenge.

- Sullied reputation. Success in business frequently depends on reputation. If you get a reputation for cheating or other unethical behaviour, this will harm your future business prospects.

- Lost opportunities. Negotiation is about finding a win-win situation, whereby both sides gain. A reputation for sharp dealing may lead potential partners to avoid making concessions to you, for fear that you will not make concessions back.

Their conclusion is that ethical negotiation is not only morally desirable, it is also good business.

 ACTIVITY

9.10 CSR AND PROFITS – THE CONTRARY VIEW

A strong case against CSR has been made by David Henderson (2001). He makes the following points:

- CSR involves organisations in higher costs, and, in so far as it means that they may forgo some activities seen as non-responsible, lower revenue. The result will be lower profits (although he admits that in some cases, this could be offset by gains as a result of enhanced reputation). This argument is supported by evidence that in 2003, the Dutch insurance company Aetna spent €20 million in order to comply with the US Sarbanes–Oxley regulations, introduced

after the Enron scandal (Targett 2004).

- Some of the leading CSR companies have gone through spectacular collapses in profits. He cites the US jeans manufacturer Levi Strauss, but the same point could be made about Body Shop and Ben and Jerry's ice cream.

- The CSR agenda is frequently set not by 'society', but non-governmental organisations (NGOs) like Greenpeace, which he sees as anti-capitalist pressure groups, and as unrepresentative of society as a whole.

Critically evaluate these arguments.

CONCLUSIONS

This chapter has analysed the nature of personal and professional ethics, whether or not it is possible to see business ethics as a distinct ethical area, the principles and application of stakeholder theory, the use of values and codes of ethics, and the nature and importance of corporate social responsibility.

KEY LEARNING POINTS

- Three main approaches can be taken to ethics, and these lead to a larger number of ethical guidelines. The most commonly used of these are the golden rule, the disclosure rule and the intuition ethic.

- All managers face ethical dilemmas on a daily basis in their work.

- Professionals have an ethical responsibility both to their organisation and to impartial professional integrity.

- There is a considerable argument over whether a separate business ethic exists.

- Stakeholder theory holds that organisations have responsibilities to a wide range of stakeholders.

- Values underpin ethics, and an organisation's values underpin its business ethics.

- Codes of ethics, unless they are internalised in the organisation's culture, do not guarantee ethical behaviour.

- Corporate governance is concerned with issues of conflict of interest and accountability.

- Corporate social responsibility is the way in which an organisation expresses its values through its behaviour towards stakeholders.

- Sustainability or sustainable development is concerned with safeguarding the environment for future generations.

- HR has a key role top play in promoting CSR.

- The government has an important role in promoting CSR.

- Although the evidence is not totally conclusive, it appears extremely likely that there is a positive correlation between CSR and profit.

QUESTIONS

1. Distinguish between the absolutist, relativist and utilitarian approaches to ethics.

2. Describe the golden rule, the disclosure rule and the intuition ethic.

3. According to De George, what conditions must apply before whistleblowing is morally justified?

4. Does an organisation have any ethical responsibilities over and above those of the individuals within it?

5. How would you define a stakeholder?

6. Define purpose, values and vision.

7. How useful are codes of ethics?

8. Define corporate governance.

9. What are the key features of corporate social responsibility?

10. Define sustainable development.

TRENDS TO WATCH

1. Watch the debate over private equity, and tensions between the private equity and the corporate social responsibility approaches.

2. As a replacement for the Kyoto Treaty on control of global warming is negotiated, what impact does this have on the sustainable development movement?

3. What is the attitude of the US president elected in November 2008 to climate change?

4. What role does the environment play in the next UK General Election?

EXPLORE FURTHER

Stephen Connock and Ted Johns' *Ethical leadership* (1995) is a useful summary of ethical issues from an HR standpoint. The CIPD also published a useful factsheet on Corporate responsibility and HR's role in 2003 (available on the CIPD website www.cipd.co.uk). Another useful website is Business in the Community (www.bitc.org.uk), which contains a number of useful reports on ethics and CSR. Excellent books on ethics are Colin Fisher and Alan Lovell's *Business ethics and values* (2nd edn, 2006), although this is rather heavy going, and Andrew Crane and Dirk Matten's *Business ethics* (2nd edn, 2007).

SEMINAR ACTIVITY

RESPONSIBLE TOURISM

1. In 1999, Richards and Gladwin put forward their definition of a socially sustainable enterprise:

The characteristics of a socially sustainable enterprise are that it would:

1. return to communities where it operates – selling as much as it gains from them

2. meaningfully include stakeholders impacted by its activities in associated planning and decision-making processes

3. ensure no reduction in, and actively promote, the observance of political and civil rights in the domains where it operates

4. widely spread economic opportunities and help to reduce or eliminate unjustified inequalities

5. directly or indirectly ensure no net loss of human capital within its workforces and operating communities

6. cause no net loss of direct and indirect productive employment

7. adequately satisfy the vital needs of its employees and operating communities

8. work to ensure the fulfilment of the basic needs of humanity prior to serving luxury wants.'

Explore Worldwide is a UK tour company, specialising in small-group exploratory holidays. Its brochure stresses its commitment to sustainability.

'Respecting our planet

Our commitment to Responsible Tourism

Explore's dedication to Responsible Tourism is the driving force behind our Environmental Policy. Far from being an abstract ideal for us, Responsible Tourism shapes all our major decisions – from the concept that 'Small Groups Leave Fewer Footprints' to the choice of local agents and suppliers.

Here are our guidelines in a nutshell:

- By operating in small groups, we minimise the impact on the local culture and resources, whilst blending in more easily.

- We issue our travellers with clear guidelines on responsible tourism. These cover a variety of issues from litter and waste disposal in remote areas, to begging and artefacts. We encourage customers to buy local crafts and support local skills, but never to buy products that exploit wildlife or harm the habitat.

- We use locally owned suppliers wherever viable to provide and run services. This ensures that the local economy benefits directly. We also expect local suppliers to meet our standards, with particular consideration for the environment.

- When recruiting Tour Leaders, we assess their environmental credentials and then train them to our own standards. They are also required to complete a Responsible Tourism Audit on each tour.

- Throughout a tour, the Leader will encourage the education of our customers on the social workings of a region. And part of their role is to make sure that the local communities benefit from our visit, ensuring that we will always be welcome.

Explore's passion for travel goes beyond the yearning for discovery. Ours is a reasoned, tried and tested approach to the enjoyment of a truly amazing planet.'

(Explore Worldwide 2004–2005 brochure)

Critically evaluate Explore's Responsible Tourism policy against Richards and Gladwin's principles.

2. Mark Ellingham, the founder of the *Rough Guide* series, has recently declared that 'binge flying' constitutes a threat to the global environment. 'If the travel industry [ignores] the effect that carbon emissions from flying are having on climate change, we are putting ourselves in a very similar position to the tobacco industry' (Hastings 2007).

Is overseas tourism unsustainable?

CHAPTER 10

Strategic management

LEARNING OUTCOMES

By the end of this chapter, readers should be able to understand, explain and critically evaluate:

- the nature of strategic management
- characteristics of strategic decisions
- models of strategy – corporate planning and strategic management
- the elements of strategic management – analysis, choice and implementation
- vision, mission, values and objectives
- the nature and uses of mission statements
- the concept of core competence
- generic strategies and the strategy clock
- evaluation of strategic options – suitability, acceptability and feasibility.
- strategic implementation – transformational and incremental change
- models of change management
- the role of HR in change management
- change leadership.

INTRODUCTION

This chapter analyses the nature of strategic management, and identifies different models of strategy. It analyses the stages of strategic decision-making – analysis, choice and implementation. The last part of the chapter concentrates on the nature and practice of change management.

WHAT IS STRATEGIC MANAGEMENT?

The origins of strategy are military, and concern the art of war. A *strategos* was a general in commend of a Greek army. Quinn (1980) identifies three elements of strategy:

- Goals or objectives. What is to be achieved, and when it is to be achieved? Major goals which affect an organisation's overall direction are strategic goals.

- Policies are guidelines which set out the limits within which action should occur. Major policies are strategic policies.

- Programmes lay down the sequence of actions necessary to achieve objectives. They set out how objectives will be achieved within the limits set by policies.

In other words:

- Where do we want to get?

- What actions should we take to get there?

- How can we carry out these actions?

The essence of a strategy is to build a position so strong that the organisation will achieve its objectives no matter what unforeseeable forces attack it (ie how can we win whatever the enemy does?). Effective strategies should:

- contain clear and decisive objectives – sub-goals may change in the heat of battle but the overriding objective provides continuity over time

- maintain the initiative

- concentrate power at the right time and place

- have built-in flexibility so that one can use minimum resources to keep opponents at a disadvantage

- have committed and co-ordinated leadership

- involve correct timing and surprise

- make resources secure and prevent surprises from opponents.

Strategic decisions have a number of characteristics:

- They are concerned with the scope of an organisation's activities – the boundaries which an organisation sets to its activities.

- They are concerned with matching the activities of an organisation to its environment.

- They are concerned with matching the activities of an organisation to its resource capability.

- They often have resource implications for an organisation – if current resources do not permit a particular strategy, can the necessary resources be acquired?

- They affect operational decisions – a whole series of implementing sub-decisions must flow from the making of a strategic decision.

- They are affected by the values and expectations of those who have power in an around the organisation – its stakeholders.
- They affect the long-term direction of an organisation (Johnson, Scholes and Whittington 2004).

Strategy can be seen at several levels:

- Corporate level, concerned with the overall scope of the operation, its financial performance, and the allocation of resources to different operations.
- Competitive or business unit level – how to compete within a particular market at the level of a strategic business unit (SBU).
- Operational level – how the different functions of the organisation contribute to the overall strategy. This level is often seen as tactical rather than in any real sense strategic, but it can equally be seen as the implementation stage of strategy.

Strategic management is about doing the right things. It is:

- ambiguous
- complex
- non-routine
- organisation-wide
- fundamental
- involving significant change
- environment or expectations driven.

Operational or tactical management is about doing things right. It is:

- routinised
- operationally specific
- involving small-scale change
- resource-driven.

MODELS OF STRATEGY

CORPORATE PLANNING

This was a product of the 1950s and 1960s, a period with a largely placid environment. Detailed corporate plans covering the whole organisation were drawn up by a central planning team and then agreed by top management. The details of the plan were extremely complex, as were the models used, but the planning process itself was relatively simple because the corporate future was seen as programmable since the future was expected to be a continuation of the past. The role of line management was to implement the plan. The main exponent of corporate planning was Igor Ansoff, although Ansoff has since modified his views on strategy. There are clear parallels with the system of central planning as used to run the Soviet Union.

The strength of the corporate planning approach is its rigour, and the vital information which is collected in the course of drawing up the plan. However, it has a number of weaknesses. It is inflexible – the plan is too vast and complex to cope with rapid change in the environment. However, some of the best corporate planners – such as those at Shell – coped with this by developing a range of scenarios about the future environment. One of these forecast exactly the huge rise in oil prices which happened in 1973, with the result that Shell could react very quickly to the new situation.

Centralised corporate planning is also demotivating. Nobody owns the plan except for the planners – the line managers who have to implement it have no commitment to it. At worst, corporate planning was an academic exercise, and the plan was put away in a drawer and quietly forgotten.

STRATEGIC MANAGEMENT

This model emphasises adaptability in the face of a turbulent environment. There is no rigid long-term plan, although there are long-term visions and values. Strategy becomes bottom-up, as line managers react to or anticipate changes in the environment. The organisation has to be very responsive to changes in the environment, which requires managers at all levels constantly to monitor the environment. The organisation becomes a learning organisation in the fullest sense of the term, as it is constantly scanning and learning from its environment.

Leading exponents of the strategic management concept are:

Tom Peters

In search of excellence in 1982 (Peters and Waterman 1982) stressed the importance of a number of attributes for excellence, which emphasised values, simplicity, quick reactions and understanding the customer:

- stick to the knitting
- close to the customer
- productivity through people
- autonomy and entrepreneurship
- hands on, value driven
- bias for action
- simple form, lean staff
- simultaneous loose-tight properties.

Peters followed this up with *Thriving on chaos* (1985), where he argued that the organisation should cope with chaos by becoming chaotic itself – being in a continual state of flux. He also stressed that chaos provides marvellous opportunities for the fleet of foot.

Michael Porter

Porter approached strategic management as an economist. He stressed the importance of the competitive position of an industry (the five forces) (1980), the nature of generic strategies, and the importance of the organisation's value chain in identifying its competitive advantage (1985).

Ralph Stacey

In *The chaos frontier* (1991) and *Strategic management and organisational dynamics* (1993), he developed the application of chaos theory to strategic management. The environment facing organisations is one of chaos. Multiple and ultimately unpredictable reactions follow from a single event – the classic example is the fluttering of a butterfly's wing ultimately leading to a hurricane. The environment facing an organisation is like that facing a weather forecaster – the patterns of weather are forecastable several days ahead, but the further the forecaster looks into the future, the more outcomes become possible. As a result the organisation must be highly responsive and reactive. The role of top management is to develop and support creativity and innovation.

Gary Hamel and C K Prahalad

In *Competing for the future* (1994), they stressed that the key role of management is to manage the organisation in such a way that it is flexible and able to respond to a changed environment. This means identifying and developing the core competencies of the organisation. We shall return to this later. Hamel later developed the 10 principles of revolutionary strategy (1996):

- Strategic planning isn't strategic – it assumed that the future will be more or less the same as the present.
- Strategy making must be subversive – strategy is about breaking rules and assumptions.
- The bottleneck is at the top of the bottle – top managers are most resistant to change.
- Revolutionaries exist in every company.
- Change is not the problem, engagement is – senior managers fail to give people responsibility for managing change.
- Strategy making must be democratic – senior managers must recognise that creativity is spread throughout an organisation.
- Anyone can be a strategy activist – senior managers must see activists as positive, not as anarchists.
- Perspective is worth 50 IQ points – organisations have to use all their knowledge to identify unconventional ideas.
- Top down and bottom up are not the alternatives – both are necessary.
- You can't see the end from the beginning – strategy can often throw up surprises.

James Quinn

In *Strategies for change: logical incrementalism* (1980), Quinn developed the concept of logical incrementalism, that strategy does not consist of a big bang, but rather of a series of small steps (incrementalism).

Say an organisation wants to get from A to E. It does not set out to go straight from A to E, but instead identifies intermediate steps on the road, B, C and D. It then concentrates first on getting from A to B, and experiments with ways of getting there. This may involve several false starts and blind allies, but eventually the firm gets to B. Then it follows the same process to get to C, and so on.

Henry Mintzberg and strategic management

One of the most trenchant critics of corporate planning has been the Canadian guru Henry Mintzberg. His writings include *The rise and fall of strategic planning* (1994). He argues that old-style corporate planning was all about left-brain activity – numbers, linearity, analysis. Strategic management is right-brain – ideas, patterns, relationships, intuition. He talks of crafting strategy, rather than planning strategy. Strategy emerges as a result of a whole series of decisions throughout an organisation.

Mintzberg is famous for his five Ps of strategy:

- Strategy as a plan for action. Here the strategy is made in advance of the actions to which they apply, and it is applied consciously and purposefully. However, as we shall see later, outcomes may not be as expected.

- Strategy as a ploy, a manoeuvre to outwit opponents.

- Strategy as a pattern. A pattern of behaviour becomes a strategy. If a particular course of action tends to lead to favourable results, a strategy emerges. The strategy is the result of events, rather than the cause of them. A variation on this he calls the umbrella strategy, where top management lays down broad principles, and line managers have autonomy to act within these principles. Here strategy is both planned and emergent.

- Strategy as position. Strategy here is about finding a niche in the market, a position which balances the pressures of the environment and the competition.

- Strategy as perspective. Here the strategy reflects how the organisation views the world and its place in it. A classic example is Hewlett-Packard's 'H-P way', where the whole approach of the organisation is based on engineering excellence and innovation. The important thing here is consistency in behaviour.

Planned strategies often require modification as they are implemented, as environmental or organisational factors change. It is very rare that a long-term strategic plan can be implemented over a period of years without modification. The intended strategy may not be realised in practice, and even if it is, it may not achieve the desired results.

There are six possible combinations of intended strategy, realised strategy and results:

CASE STUDY 10.1

THE EGG MCMUFFIN

One innovation introduced by McDonald's was the Egg McMuffin, basically an egg in a bun, the classic American breakfast. Mintzberg posed the question whether this was a strategic change for McDonald's. Some students argued that it was – McDonald's was moving into a new market, the breakfast market. Others argued that nothing had changed – all that had happened was that an egg had replaced a burger.

Mintzberg argued that both were right, and both wrong. McDonald's position had changed by moving into breakfasts, but the perspective was exactly the same – the product was classic McDonald's. The position could be changed easily because it was consistent with the perspective. Mintzberg suggested that a change in perspective would involve McDonald's entering the sophisticated evening dining market with a product like a 'McDuckling a l'Orange'.

Source: Mintzberg (1998).

- What is intended as a strategy is realised with desirable results.

- What is intended as a strategy is realised, but with less than desirable results.

- What is intended as a strategy is realised in some modified version because of an unanticipated environmental and/or internal requirement or change. The results are desirable.

- What is intended as a strategy is realised in some modified version because of an unanticipated environmental and/or internal requirement of change. The results are less than desirable.

- What is intended as a strategy is not realised. Instead, an unanticipated environmental and/or internal change requires an entirely different strategy. The different strategy is realised with desirable results.

- What is intended as a strategy is not realised. Instead, an unanticipated environmental and/or internal change requires an entirely different strategy. The different strategy is realised with less than desirable results.

THE ELEMENTS OF STRATEGIC MANAGEMENT

The analysis so far may seem extremely complex, but the important thing to remember is that the essence of strategic management is very simple. It consists of getting answers to four questions:

- Where are we?

- Where do we want to get?

- How can we get there?

- What do we have to do to get there?

From this we can derive the three elements of strategic management:

ACTIVITY

10.1 HONDA AND THE US MOTORCYCLE MARKET

When Honda established an American subsidiary in Los Angeles in 1959, its intended strategy was to push the sales of motorcycles with 250cc and 350cc engines, despite the fact that the much smaller 50cc model was a top seller in Japan. Honda's top managers believed that the American environment and the US consumer would prefer bigger models. However, Honda's 250cc and 350cc bikes did not sell well.

At this time, Honda's executives were using their own 50cc motorbikes to commute in traffic-congested Los Angeles. The convenience and appearance of the bikes began to be noticed. Orders for the 50cc model began to come in from motorbike retailers, but Honda was reluctant because it did not want its image in the United States to be associated with a small, no-frills motorbike. When the major US retailer Sears Roebuck expressed an interest, Honda management changed its mind. The move was overwhelmingly successful.

Honda's success in selling its 50cc bikes gradually convinced the firm to try again at developing a market for its bigger bikes. This was successful from the late 1960s to the

mid-1980s. Honda's success was partially based on its reliable and sturdy products, but it was also successful because of weak competition. With the exception of a lethargic Harley-Davidson, Honda did not face any serious threat from American companies, and European and Japanese competitors had not matched Honda's investment in the US market.

This scenario began to change during the mid-1980s. Foreign competitors became more aggressive in the US market, particularly for small and medium-sized bikes, while following a management-led leveraged buyout in 1981, Harley-Davidson began to reassert its dominance in the large-bike market. Harley-Davidson increased its market share for the largest bikes from 23 per cent in 1983 to 60 per cent in 1990. Honda's overall share of the US market plunged from 58 to 28 per cent between 1985 and 1990. Hence, as the competitive situation changed rapidly, Honda's results deteriorated.

Identify episodes in the Honda experience which fit the intended and realised strategies outlined above.

- Strategic analysis – tackles the first two questions – what is our current position and where to do we want to go?
- Strategic choice – the third question – how can we get there, ie what strategy should we choose?
- Strategic implementation – what do we have to do to implement our chosen strategy?

STRATEGIC ANALYSIS

Strategic analysis is concerned with the strategic position of the organisation. What are the key characteristics of the organisation, what changes are going on in the environment, and how will these affect the organisation and its activities?

The aim is to form a view of the key influences on the present and future well-being of the organisation:

- Expectations of stakeholders, the culture of the organisation, and most important, the organisation's vision and values.

- The environment, as identified through a STEEPLE analysis and other techniques. Many of these variables will give rise to opportunities, and many will pose threats. The main problem is to distil out of the complexity the key environmental impacts for the purposes of strategic choice. I'm sure you will be delighted to hear that we have already covered the necessary techniques for this part of the analysis – the principles of STEEPLE and SWOT in Chapter 1, Porter's five forces and portfolio analysis in Chapter 2, and the detailed impact of the various elements of the environment throughout the book.

- Resources. Strategic capability is about identifying strengths and weaknesses by considering the key resource areas of the business such as physical plant, management, finance and products.

Classical corporate planning saw environmental analysis as the key element in strategic analysis, while strategic management sees culture and values as most crucial.

CASE STUDY 10.2

WHAT BUSINESS ARE WE IN?

In 2001, Hornby, the model railway company, was in trouble. Shareholders wanted to sell the company, but nobody wanted to buy it. The company was seen as staid and old-fashioned. Seventy per cent of its sales were to adult hobbyists, and 30 per cent to children, and marketing was heavily based on nostalgia for a vanished world of stream railways.

After the failure of the attempt to sell the company, new management was brought in, and Frank Martin became chief executive. He was horrified to find that the old management had just turned down the licence to make a Hogwarts Express set to tie in with *Harry Potter,* and he quickly reversed the decision.

What business is Hornby in? The old management felt that it was a hobby business, and should not be interested in products, like Hogwarts, aimed at children. Martin took the view that this was short-sighted. The hobbyist market was ageing, and unless a new segment of customers was attracted, the business would eventually die. Under his leadership, licensing of media tie-in properties has become an integral part of the business. This seems to have been the right strategic decision, as the share price is now eight times higher than when he first joined the business.

Source: Teather (2007).

GAP ANALYSIS

The extent to which there is a mismatch (a gap) between current strategy and the future environment is a measure of the strategic problem facing the organisation. As Figure 10.1 shows, over time the current strategy is likely to get more out of line with the environment, and a planning gap will grow.

Figure 10.1 Gap analysis

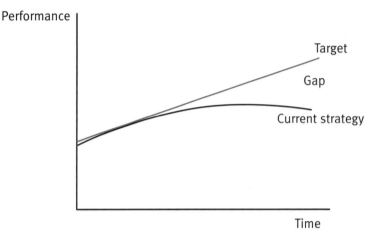

The organisation needs to choose a new strategy which will ensure that this gap is filled.

STRATEGIC CHOICE

Strategic choice involves three steps:

- Generation of strategic options. Three levels of analysis are involved here – what fundamental or generic strategy should be followed; within this generic strategy, what strategic directions are needed; and then what methods of strategic direction are most appropriate.

- Evaluation of strategic options. This involves testing options for suitability (do they fit the generic strategy, and will they provide the desired results?); feasibility (are resources available or obtainable?); and acceptability (do they fit the values of the stakeholders?).

- Selection of strategy – either logically, using some kind of weighting criteria, or politically.

STRATEGIC IMPLEMENTATION

Strategic implementation involves resource planning, organisational structure, systems, change management techniques, etc.

STRATEGIC ANALYSIS

VISION, MISSION, VALUES AND OBJECTIVES

Vision, mission, values and objectives are closely linked, and often confused. However, they are clearly distinguished by Peter Senge in *The fifth discipline* (1990).

- Vision is the what – the picture of the future we want to create, or the desired future state of the organisation (where do we want to get?).

- Mission is the why – the over-riding purpose of the organisation, its scope and boundaries (what business are we in, why do we exist?).

- Values are the how – the underlying beliefs and ethical stance which drives how the business behaves (how are we going to behave while we are getting there?).

Objectives operationalise all the other three – a precise statement of where we want to be and when, which turns the vision, mission and values into concrete quantifiable terms. It is frequently said that objectives should be SMART:

- Stretching

- Measurable

- Achievable

- Relevant

- Time limited.

CADBURY AND A FAILURE OF VALUES

CASE STUDY 10.3

The chocolate manufacturer Cadbury was founded in Birmingham in 1824 by John Cadbury, a local Quaker. Like other nineteenth-century Quakers, Cadbury was a committed social reformer. He campaigned against the use of climbing boys to clean chimneys, and he founded the Animals' Friend Society, which later became the RSPCA. The company remained true to its Quaker principles, and was a shining example of corporate social responsibility long before the term was invented. It took a leading role in promoting education in Birmingham, built the Bournville model village for its workers, was the first company in the country to introduce a half day on Saturday, and launched a pension fund as early as 1906 (Cadbury 2007).

The emphasis on Quaker values continued well into the twentieth century, as long as the company was directly controlled by the Cadbury family. It was a member of the family, Adrian Cadbury, who produced one of the first reports on corporate governance in the early 1990s.

It is clear from the Cadbury website that the company is still very proud of its Quaker heritage, and so it came as a great shock when the company was fined £1 million for a breach of safety regulations which led to a salmonella outbreak. What was worse was that the outbreak was a direct result of the company's own policy. In 2003, it had changed its policy on salmonella contamination from a 'zero tolerance' policy, where product was destroyed automatically if any trace of salmonella was detected on test, to a policy allowing a 'tolerable level' of salmonella. This was despite scientific opinion that no level of salmonella could be regarded as safe.

In January and February 2006 there were 36 positive tests for salmonella, but the company did nothing until it was linked to an outbreak of salmonella poisoning in June 2006, in which at least 42 people were infected (Williams 2007). It then recalled all the products concerned. It is estimated that the recall and the resultant bad publicity cost the company £40 million (Tait and Wiggins 2007).

In the company's trial under food hygiene regulations, it was claimed by the prosecution that the change in policy was a deliberate and cynical act of cost-cutting. The judge said the company had fallen 'seriously short' of its obligations, but accepted the company's defence that although it was negligent, it was not deliberately aiming to cut costs. Simon Baldry, the former managing director of Cadbury Trebor Bassett, was one of the casualties of a management shake-up which followed the product withdrawal (Elliott 2007).

What this case shows is that the higher an organisation's standards and values, the more serious are any shortcomings in failing to meet those standards.

The mission and objectives of the organisation are constrained by four main factors (Johnson, Scholes and Whittington 2004):

Corporate governance

External constraints on the organisation, set by company law; reports of investigations such as the Cadbury Report on non-executive directors or the Greenbury Report on directors' pay; regulatory bodies such as the Financial Services Authority, and targets and controls imposed by the government on public bodies (ie Best Value for local authorities).

Stakeholders

The rights and power of various stakeholder groups were discussed at length in Chapter 9, but basically stakeholders can influence the organisation's strategic direction through their power and/or their interest.

Business ethics

Again this was discussed at length in Chapter 9, but ethics can impact on an organisation at three levels: general ethical policy; how the organisation interprets its corporate social responsibility when it formulates its strategy; and the ethical behaviour of individuals within the organisation. Clearly ethics is all about values, particularly the values of top management.

Culture

Culture in organisations operates at three levels:

- Values, often written down as part of the mission statement, but often vague, like 'service to the community'.
- More specific beliefs, often expressed as policies.
- Taken for granted assumptions – the organisational paradigm – the 'way things are done here'. At grassroots level, these may often be in conflict with the values and beliefs officially expressed at a higher level. For example, the police force in the United Kingdom is totally committed to eradicating 'institutional racism', but at the level of 'canteen culture' there are still racist PCs.

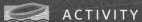 **ACTIVITY**

10.2 LONDON ZOO

In 1993 *Management Today* published an article on the strategy of London Zoo (Sebag-Montefiore 1993). Although the case is an old one, it still deals with some fundamental issues in strategic management.

The zoo, owned by the learned society, the Zoological Society of London (ZSL), had been going through hard times. By 1992, it had lost money for a decade, and had only survived through drastic cost-cutting, including redundancies among keepers which many felt had reduced staffing to dangerous levels. The turnaround led to a small profit in the year ending March 1993.

However, the turnaround plan was only the start of a bitter battle for the soul of the zoo, between the zoo's commercial staff and their supporters – the 'suits', who wanted the zoo to become much more commercial, using high-tech computer displays and interactive technology, and a militant group on the Council of ZSL, the 'beards', who thought that the zoo should stick to its original aims of breeding and conserving endangered species. The suits were led by a property developer, David Laing, and the beards by a left-wing journalist, Colin Tudge. The centrepiece of the suits' plan was a giant interactive aquarium to be built at the zoo.

Each side was vitriolic about the other. The beards referred to the suits' plan as 'animal prostitution', and said that the animals would be reduced to 'bit part actors on a stage', while the suits described Tudge as 'that breeding fanatic' and his supporters as 'Leninists with their heads in the clouds'. However, both sides genuinely thought that their plan would make the zoo more attractive to visitors.

The job of resolving the quarrel fell to Jo Gipps, the director of the London Zoo. His business plan, revealed in 1993, was a compromise, but leaning more towards the beards.

Crucial to the argument was the mission statement of ZSL, which read:

> To achieve and promote the worldwide conservation of animals and their habitats.

Both sides could argue that this supported their argument. The beards pointed to the word 'conservation', while the suits pointed to the word 'worldwide' – in their view the zoo should be fully commercial, and raise money which could be used to support conservation elsewhere in the world, rather than specifically at London Zoo.

Question

What does this case tell you about the importance of vision, values and mission?

THE MISSION STATEMENT

This is the most generalised statement of organisational purpose. It sets the direction of the organisation, and provides a benchmark against which policies can be evaluated.

An effective mission statement should achieve the following:

- It should be visionary and long-term. It is meant to inspire and drive the organisation.

- It should clarify the main intentions and aspirations of the organisation and the reasons the organisation exists.

- It should describe the organisation's main activities and the position it wishes to attain in its industry.

- It should contain a statement of the key values of the organisation in relation to its stakeholders.

- It should be taken seriously within the organisation.

- It should be a focus for activity, which can serve as a continual guide, rather than a closed aim which can be fully achieved.

However, there are two great dangers with mission statements. The first is a risk that they can appear grandiose, or even ridiculous. Too many overblown mission statements have tended in the past to lead to the whole concept being treated with ridicule. Typical is the *Dilbert* website (www.dilbert.com), which contains a mission statement generator, which will produce randomly generated mission statements.

The other danger is that the mission statement may become set in concrete. The external environment may change in a way that renders the mission statement obsolete, and a hindrance rather than a help to strategy formulation (see the case study on Komatsu).

 ## KOMATSU

CASE STUDY 10.4

Komatsu produces earth-moving equipment, an industry where the market leader is the American company Caterpillar. In the 1950s, it was a small company serving only its Japanese home market. In 1964, Yashinari Kawai became president of Komatsu, and announced the company's new mission statement – 'Maru C' or 'encircle Caterpillar'. This was to be the driving force of the company's strategy for the next 20 years.

The statement served Komatsu well – by the 1980s, it was the world's second largest producer of earth-moving equipment, although it had failed to overtake Caterpillar. Unfortunately, while Komatsu had been focusing all its attention and energy on Caterpillar, it had ignored changes in the environment. Demand for basic earth-moving equipment was falling, and new competitors in different but related industries were becoming an (unseen) threat.

Fortunately the new company president, Tetsuya Katada, spotted the danger in time. He decided that the company's new emphasis should be as a 'total technology enterprise', with the new mission statement 'Growth, Global, Groupwide'. Komatsu's sales decline was reversed, thanks entirely to an explosive growth in its non-construction equipment business.

RESOURCE ANALYSIS

Resource analysis is internal to the organisation. It is concerned with the strengths and weaknesses parts of SWOT analysis, and measures the efficiency and effectiveness of an organisation's resources, and their degree of fit with the external opportunities and threats also identified through SWOT. Ideally

ACTIVITY

10.3 THE WEA (NORTHERN IRELAND)

The Workers' Educational Association (WEA) in Northern Ireland publishes its mission statement and WEA values on its website (www.wea-ni.com), as follows:

The WEA Mission Statement

We will make learning accessible to all men and women, especially those removed from the educational experience. As well as offering opportunities to individuals we will assist those who wish to work collectively for the benefit of their communities and for the good of society as a whole.

The Value Base of the WEA

The WEA has been a catalyst for social change since it began in Belfast in 1910. The following values underpin our commitment to social change:

Social inclusion – we make special efforts to reach those most removed from the learning experience.

Voluntarism – we provide opportunities for people to volunteer to work both individually and collectively for the betterment of our society.

Active citizenship – we equip people to play a full role in the social, economic, cultural and political life of our society.

Building alliances – we work closely with others to improve opportunities for learning.

Sharing experience – we share good practice to promote mutual learning

Equality – we promote equality of opportunity through learning.

Evaluate the WEA mission statement against the six characteristics of an effective mission statement listed above.

strengths should support opportunities, and be able to counteract threats. Resources should be seen in the widest sense, to include the organisation's competitive position, as identified through techniques such as five forces and portfolio analysis. However, SWOT analysis has severe limitations. The most important of these is that it is subjective – different analysts will identify totally different strengths and weaknesses. Stevenson (1989) found no consensus among the managers in the companies he studied on the strengths and weaknesses of their companies. Higher-level managers tended to be more optimistic about the balance of strengths and weaknesses than lower-level managers.

Prahalad and Hamel in *The core competence of the corporation* (1990) identified the concept of the core competences of the organisation – those factors that give the organisation its key competitive advantages. Unlike resources, which are tangible, tradeable and easily replicable, competences are based on the accumulated knowledge and skills of the organisation, are unique to it, and difficult to copy. They are based on people rather than things. Examples are the way in which Dell Computer builds all computers individually to order, and the reputation of Body Shop as an ethical crusader. Other analysts have suggested that the crucial competence needed by all organisations is the ability to be nimble, flexible and responsive to rapid and unpredictable changes in the external environment.

Core competences can be based on:

- Cost efficiency. Many advantages based on cost efficiency are not really core competences, as they can relatively easily be copied by other organisations. One which may lead to a core competence is cost efficiency based on experience – the more experience an organisation has, the lower its costs tend to be.

- Value added. Is the organisation more effective than the competition? In the early stages of the quality movement in the 1970s and 1980s, quality could be a core competence. Now it is a given – it is expected of all organisations and does not in itself give a competitive advantage. Value added is more likely to be experienced by the customer through service than through the product itself – Dell does not necessarily sell a better computer, but it gives the customer a flexible computer configured to his or her requirements.

- Managing linkages, between different stages of production, or through alliances with other organisations. For example the low-cost airlines like easyJet and Ryanair pioneered the use of Internet-based ticket booking systems and paperless tickets, giving them both a cost and an effectiveness advantage, as well as allowing a very flexible pricing system. They also offer weblinks to suppliers of hotels and car hire.

- Robustness. How easy is it to ensure that the competences are difficult to copy?

If it can develop a number of core competences, an organisation can greatly strengthen its strategic position. However, there is the danger that over time the core competences may no longer match the external environment. If computing becomes based on mobile phones rather than PCs and laptops, Dell's core competence may prove to be a weakness rather than a strength.

ACTIVITY

10.4 HARRY POTTER AND THE PORTENTS OF DOOM

Bloomsbury Publishing was founded in 1986 by Nigel Newton, still the company's chairman. His mission was to publish books of the highest quality, and to bring quality to the mass market (Bloomsbury 2007a). The company initially grew slowly, and by the early 1990s its turnover was barely £10 million. It then went public in 1994, raising £5.5 million, followed by a rights issue in 1998 which raised another £6.1 million.

By then Bloomsbury's fortunes had been transformed when it accepted a children's book from an unknown author, J K Rowling. This was published as *Harry Potter and the Philosopher's Stone* in 1997, and the rest is history. Bloomsbury owns the English-language rights to *Harry Potter* throughout the world except the United States (where the rights are owned by Scholastic). World-wide sales of the first six *Harry Potter* books totalled 325 million (Jordan 2007).

As the sales of *Harry Potter* soared, so did Bloomsbury's fortunes. Turnover rose from £20 million in 1999 to £109 million in 2005, while profit rose from £2.6 million in 1999 to £20.1 million in 2005 (Bloomsbury 2007b). However, events were then to show how dependent the company was on *Harry Potter*. The sixth book, *Harry Potter and the Half-Blood Prince*, was published in July 2005, and no *Potter* title appeared in 2006.

The result was that both sales and profits collapsed in 2006. 2006 turnover was £74 million, lower than 2003, while profits slumped to £5.2 million, the lowest figure since 2000. All the fall was due to a fall in turnover in the children's division (basically *Harry Potter*) (Shelley 2007).

Fortunately for Bloomsbury, the last book in the series was still in the pipeline, *Harry Potter and the Deathly Hallows*, published in July 2007. In the first 24 hours 2.6 million copies were sold in the United Kingdom, plus another 400,000 English language copies in Germany (Bloomsbury 2007c).

Clearly the success of the seventh and final title will generate healthy profits for Bloomsbury in 2007, but this boost is likely to be short-lived, because of the peculiar nature of the *Potter* market. The major supermarkets all see *Harry Potter* as an ideal vehicle for a short-term price war. The recommended retail price of *The Deathly Hallows* is £17.99, with a wholesale price of £9.89, but the supermarkets are selling the book for prices ranging from £5 to £8.99. It is cheaper for an independent bookseller to buy its stock from Tesco than from a wholesaler (Alberge 2007).

In a sense the fact that retailers make no money out of the book does not matter to Bloomsbury, because they get their £9.89 a copy anyway. But in another sense it does matter. The typical pattern with a best-selling book is that it is initially published in hardback at a high price, with only moderate but very profitable sales. Then a year later, a paperback edition appears, at a lower price, but with greater volume. The publisher has two bites at the apple.

This does not happen with *Harry Potter*. Because of the discounting and hype, people who might have waited for the paperback buy the hardback instead. As a result sales of *Harry Potter* are minimal after the year in which the title is published.

Bloomsbury is a classic example of an organisation whose success is resource-driven. Its key asset is the intellectual property embedded in the *Harry Potter* titles. Like a pharmaceutical company with a blockbuster drug, it must ensure that a stream of new products is developed to replace the blockbuster. If this is not done, as the blockbuster drug loses its patent protection, or the *Harry Potter* series comes to an end, profits collapse.

Question

How can Bloomsbury escape from *The Portents of Doom* and ensure its long-term future?

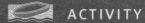

ACTIVITY

10.5 THE WATERSTONE'S TAKEOVER OF OTTAKAR'S

The bookselling industry comprises four broad types of outlet:

- **Specialist booksellers**, including retail chains such as Waterstone's, Ottakar's and Borders as well as independent booksellers.

  Waterstone's. Founded by Tim Waterstone in 1982, and owned by W H Smith until 1998, when it was acquired by HMV. On 31 December 2005 it had 190 bookshops in the UK, including 31 on university campuses. The range of book titles stocked varied between 30,000 and 40,000 per store. Its sales in the year ended 30 April 2005 were £446 million, but like-for-like sales fell in the year 2005–6 its market share in 2005 was 17 per cent.

  Ottakar's. Founded in 1987 by James Heneage and Philip Dunne. On 31 December 2005 it had 141 stores, with a typical store range of 20,000 to 30,000 titles. Its sales in the year ended 28 January 2006 were £176 million, a like-for-like fall of 3 per cent compared with the previous year. Ottakar's market share in 2005 was 7 per cent. The geographical overlap between Waterstone's and Ottakar's is fairly small, as Ottakar's has followed a deliberate strategy of entering small towns without significant competition.

  Borders. The US-based Borders is the second biggest book retailer in the world. It entered the United Kingdom in 1997 when it acquired Books Etc. It specialises in book superstores in out-of-town locations, carrying 50,000 to 80,000 titles. It thus does not directly compete with Waterstone's and Ottakar's, both of which are high-street based. Borders, Waterstone's and Ottakar's all generally provide a coffee shop in their stores.

- **Blackwell's.** A specialist university bookseller, with 56 stores in university towns, many on campus. Borders and Blackwell together have a 15 per cent market share.

- **Retail chains for which books are an important category.** The dominant company in this sector is WH Smith. WH Smith sells a wide range of newspapers, magazines, stationery and entertainment products as well as books. It has 545 high-street stores, of which 365 have a typical range of 5,000 to 10,000 book titles, and the remainder 10,000 to 20,000 titles. WH Smith is estimated to have around 10 per cent of the book market.

- **Retailers which sell books as part of a much wider range of goods (**the major supermarkets, plus Woolworths). Supermarkets specialise in best sellers and lifestyle books, particularly cookery and celebrity titles, and they discount heavily. Tesco increased its book sales by 52 per cent in the year to 25 February 2006. Supermarkets have a market share of 8 per cent, which is increasing rapidly, up from 4 per cent in 2001. Tesco alone has a target of 10 per cent of the market.

- **Distance sellers.** Amazon dominates the Internet market for books. It discounts, although not as extensively as the supermarkets (although unlike the supermarkets it offers discounts on non-best-selling books, making it more competitive against the high-street chains). It also has access to a much bigger backlist than any of the bricks and mortar retailers. The Internet had a 12 per cent of the market in 2005, up from 5 per cent in 2001. Other distance sellers are mainly book clubs, dominated by Book Club Associates, whose market share is 15 per cent, but falling rapidly, from 21 per cent in 2001 (Competition Commission 2006, Table 3, pC3).

Overall, market trends are that high-street retailers are slowly losing market share, book clubs are rapidly losing share, while Amazon and the supermarkets are rapidly increasing market share. Overall demand has risen over the past five years. Total sales in 2006 were £4.24 billion, an increase of 3.4 per cent (Keynote 2007), and are expected to grow by a total of 20 per cent over the period 2006–11.

The Waterstone's takeover

Ottakar's went public in 1998. In the spring of 2005, a management buy-out team headed by the founders of Ottakar's, James Heneage, then CEO, and Philip Dunne (then chairman), launched a bid to take the company private. They offered a price of £3.50 a share, increased to £4 on 6 September 2005. HMV then launched a rival bid at £4.50, and this was accepted by the Ottakar's directors on 13 September. The bid was notified to the Office of Fair Trading as, even though the combined market share was just below the referral threshold of 25 per cent, the size of the bid was sufficient to justify a referral.

On 6 December 2005, the OFT referred the bid to the Competition Commission. On 6 May 2006, the Competition Commission concluded that the merger should be allowed, as it would not be 'expected to result in a substantial lessening of competition ... at a local, regional or national level in the UK (Competition Commission 2006, p41).

The major source for this Activity is the Competition Commission report, *HMV Group plc and Ottakar's plc: proposed acquisition of Ottakar's plc by HMV Group plc through Waterstone's Booksellers Ltd* (12 May 2006), but also used was the Keynote report, *Book selling* (March 2007).

Question

1. Why do you think the Competition Commission allowed the merger?

As part of its research, the Competition Commission carried out a consumer survey to establish reasons why customers choose a bookshop. This came up with the following reasons (respondents could pick more than one answer):

Range of books	91%
Convenience	76%
Value for money	26%
Customer service	17%
Nice environment	12%

Converting these percentages to numbers, and scoring 'range of books' as 10, this gives the following reworked maximum scores

Range of books	10
Convenience	8
Value for money	3
Customer service	2
Nice environment	2
Total	25

The nearer a bookshop scored to 25, the more attractive it would be to customers.

We would give a (purely subjective) score to W H Smith as follows:

Range of books	4
Convenience	7
Value for money	1
Customer service	1
Nice environment	0
Total	13

Question

2. How would you (from your own experience) score Waterstone's/Ottakar's, Amazon and the supermarkets?

STRATEGIC CHOICE

GENERIC STRATEGIES

The concept of generic strategy was introduced by Michael Porter (1985). He identified possible strategies as being:

- Cost leadership. An organisation will succeed if it can achieve lower costs than its competitors, but sell its products at or near the industry average price.

- Differentiation. An organisation will succeed if it can produce a differentiated product which commands a premium price, but at the same time keep its costs to the industry average.

- Focus. An organisation will succeed if it concentrates on a niche market, in which it can achieve either cost focus or differentiation focus.

CASE STUDY 10.5

RYANAIR – A SUCCESSFUL FOCUSED COST LEADER

In 1991, Ryanair was a small, unsuccessful Irish airline, when its newly appointed CEO, Michael O'Leary, went to America to meet Herbert Kelleher, Southwest Airlines' founder. The low-cost carrier had transformed the economics of air travel in the United States. From Kelleher, O'Leary learned the importance of cost control, through the use of one type of plane, point-to-point flights only, and elimination of all frills (*Business Week* 2006).

Since then, Ryanair has pushed the Southwest business model even further, and has become the biggest and most profitable low-cost airline in Europe. Its success is based on three pillars – cut costs to the minimum ('nail down costs'), 'give nothing, sell everything', and efficiency.

Cost cutting

- Ryanair flies only one type of plane – the Boeing 737-800. This enables economies of scale in pilot training and maintenance.

- Ryanair's seat density on the 737 is 189, 15 per cent more than other airlines.

- Ryanair places its orders for aircraft in a counter-cyclical fashion, taking advantage of weak demand to wring better prices out of Boeing. For example, it placed a very big order in the immediate aftermath of 9/11. In 2007, it was rumoured by the *Financial Times* to be selling some of its planes secondhand for more than it had paid for them (Done 2007).

- The company's planes are stripped of all non-essentials – seats do not recline, there are no window blinds, and no seat-back pockets. This shaves several hundred thousand dollars off the cost of each plane.

- Like other low-cost airlines, Ryanair does not use travel agents, thus saving up to 15 per cent commission, but it has gone further than its rivals in promoting booking over the Internet, which minimises handling costs. By 2007, 98 per cent of bookings were made over the Internet.

- Ryanair does not use air bridges at airports – passengers must walk to the plane. This saves on airport charges.

- Ryanair is notorious for using secondary, but very cheap, airports. These are often some way from the city that they nominally serve. Brussels-Charleroi is 40 km from Brussels, Copenhagen-Malmo is actually in Sweden, not Denmark, and Frankfurt-Hahn is 140 km from Frankfurt. As easyJet repeatedly points out, this means that Ryanair's low fares are deceptive, as further transport costs are needed to reach the final destination. The secondary airports used are desperate for Ryanair's business, and are prepared to offer extremely good terms. In the case of Charleroi, allegedly illegal subsides were paid. In 2004, the European Commission ordered Ryanair to repay €4 million of subsidies.

- Advertising on planes is widespread (as well as liveries which attack other airlines).

- Extensive use is made of Eastern European (particularly Polish) cabin crew).

As a result of its rigorous cost-cutting programme, Ryanair's costs are two-thirds of those of easyJet, 60 per cent of UK holiday charter airlines, and half that of full-service carriers (Thompson 2005).

Charges

- Ryanair is notorious for charging its staff for perks normally seen as free: crew must pay for their own uniforms, they must pay for water drunk on flights, and they are banned from recharging their mobiles on company power sockets.

- Like other low-cost airlines, it charges passengers for refreshments on flights.

- Ryanair was the first airline to introduce a charge for baggage. This has the effect of raising revenue, and also of cutting the number of bags carried, so lowering baggage handling costs by an estimated £20 million a year (*Air Transport World* 2006a).

- In September 2007 it introduced a charge for checking in at the airport,

which could only be avoided by checking in online (Milmo 2007b).

- In 2002 Ryanair was heavily criticised when it refused to provide wheelchairs for disabled passengers at Stansted. A court ruling in 2004 judged that the responsibility for disabled passengers was shared between the airport and the airline. Ryanair's response was to place a 33p surcharge on all its ticket prices (attacked by other airlines as a 'wheelchair levy'), which raised far more revenue for Ryanair than the costs it was claimed to cover (Starmer-Smith 2006).

Ryanair has made few friends. On the other hand, millions of travellers like its low fares. The airline is also unquestionably good at what it does.

Efficiency

As Ryanair gleefully points out on its website, the airline is extremely efficient. It claims:

- the best on-time record in Europe (91 per cent on time arrivals in 2003, compared with 83 per cent for British Airways and 82 per cent for easyJet)

- the lowest level of cancellations

- fewest lost bags – 0.6 bags per 1,000 passengers in 2003, compared with BA's 14.2) (Ryanair 2003).

Results

Ryanair's model seems to be successful. In 2005, it had the fourth-highest operating profit in Europe (behind BA, Air France-KLM and Lufthansa), and the 12th highest in the world, the 11th highest net profit in the world, and the 15th highest number of passengers carried (*Air Transport World* 2006b). In August 2005, for the first time it carried more passengers than the entire world-wide BA network (Ryanair 2007).

Conclusion

Ryanair seems to have the focused cost leadership business model cracked. However, there are three potential clouds on the horizon:

- In 2007, Ryanair operated 136 planes. However, it also had orders which would take its fleet size to 262 (Done 2007). Given Ryanair's flight pattern, it requires 250,000 passengers a year to operate a plane profitably. To fill all the planes on order, Ryanair would have to nearly double its present number of about 45 million passengers a year. Can the company's growth rate be maintained indefinitely?

- The full-service carriers are fighting back. They have cut their fares, increased their online bookings, and heavily marketed their own selling features – meals, free drinks, seat allocations, more convenient airports.

- There are ominous signs that O'Leary is being distracted from the business model. In 2006, he tried to take over the Irish state carrier Aer Lingus when it was privatised, with the intention of operating it as a going concern, including its long-haul flights, while in 2007, he announced plans to develop a new long-haul airline, to be called RyanAtlantic. Although this would be separate from Ryanair, it would sell tickets through the Ryanair website.

KwikSave: a failed cost leader

CASE STUDY 10.6

KwikSave was founded in Rhyl, North Wales in 1959, and floated on the stock exchange in 1970. At its peak in 1993 it had over 1,000 stores, made a profit of £135 million, was a member of the FTSE100, and in volume terms was the third-biggest food retailer in the United Kingdom, with a market share of over 10 per cent, more than Asda, and behind only Tesco and Sainsbury.

Its success was due to its aggressive pursuit of a strategy of cost leadership. It aimed directly at the bottom of the market. Its stores were in secondary high-street sites, which were cheap to acquire. It sold only branded tinned and packaged goods, which were sold direct from cardboard boxes, so cutting costs to the bone. It stocked only 1,000 lines, exploiting the 80:20 rule. As it pointed out in 1993, 80 per cent of typical supermarket sales came from only 20 per cent of its lines. KwikSave stocked only these fast-moving lines, ignoring the rest (Tempus 1993). As a result, its prices were more than 10 per cent lower than those of the major supermarkets (Gilchrist 1993a). In value added terms, KwikSave was the most

successful retailer in the United Kingdom, with a value added return of 25 per cent, compared with Sainsbury's 10 per cent (Lord 1990).

However, even at the peak of KwikSave's success, small clouds were appearing on the horizon. Between 1990 and 1994 food sales in the United Kingdom grew much less quickly than floor space (Sivell and Dolan 1995). In the early 1990s the Danish discount retailer Netto entered the UK market, followed by the German companies Aldi and Lidl. All three had long experience in cut-throat European markets, and had deeper pockets than KwikSave. By 1993, Netto had a 2.5 per cent price advantage over KwikSave (Gilchrist 1993b), and KwikSave was warning that a price war would hit its profits (Gilchrist 1993b).

The response of KwikSave was twofold. It cut its prices further, and introduced a No Frills own brand, selling at or below cost. Simultaneously, it tried to move up-market by stocking fresh and chilled food, which had a higher profit margin. However, both proved to be mistakes. The low-price message was diluted, the price cuts provoked Tesco into retaliation, while KwikSave found that although fresh and chilled food could be more profitable, they also required specialised retailing skills which KwikSave did not possess (Sivell and Dolan 1995).

In 1994–5 profits were down from their peak, and like-for-like sales were down 2.5 per cent (Bagnall 1995). KwikSave shoppers were voting with their wallets, and deserting the high street for the out-of-town superstore.

KwikSave called in Andersen Consulting, whose solution was that KwikSave should become more like Tesco – widen its range, and widen its margins. The advice was disastrous – KwikSave shoppers had shopped at the chain because it was different from Tesco. If it became the same as Tesco, why not shop at Tesco? KwikSave also accelerated its store opening programme, spending money and lowering its return on capital. By 1996, KwikSave's profits were still falling, Tesco had matched its 3p price for a tin of baked beans, and the continental retailers were taking 1.5 per cent of the market, soon expected to rise to 5 per cent (Stevenson 1996, Cope 1996).

In February 1998 KwikSave merged with Somerfield in the hope that their greater combined size would enable them to overcome their trading problems. However, Somerfield was nearly as weak as KwikSave. The merger was described with ironic understatement as 'not quite the deal of the century', while an analyst said, 'Both of them would have hit a brick wall at some stage. Now they will just hit a bigger one' (Hollinger 1998).

Although it was nominally a merger, it soon became clear that Somerfield held the whip hand. The KwikSave head office in North Wales was scheduled for closure, and plans were announced to rebrand all the KwikSave stores as Somerfield. This proved a disaster, and within 18 months some ex-KwikSave stores were announcing falls in sales of up to 50 per cent (Cope 1999). At the end of 1999, 350 ex-KwikSave stores were put up for sale, only for the sale to be abandoned four months later when no realistic offers were received. The merger was described as 'one of the most disastrous in corporate history' (Finch 2000). Another U-turn saw the KwikSave brand resurrected. A further blow came late in 1999, when Asda was taken over by Wal-mart. Asda was even more aggressive on price than Tesco, and now had the bottomless pockets of Wal-mart behind it.

KwikSave-Somerfield sales continued to decline, and eventually in October 2005, the company was taken over by a private equity consortium headed by billionaire Robert Tchenguiz (Finch 2005). The new owners quickly off-loaded KwikSave to another company, Back to the Future, in February 2006 (Rigby 2006). By the end of 2006, KwikSave sales had collapsed to a market share of 0.2 per cent. By May 2007 the group was boycotted by its suppliers, by June it could not pay its staff, and in July it went into administration (Finch 2007).

What this case shows us is the very high risk associated with a cost leadership strategy. Caught in a vice between the continental discounters and Tesco and Asda, KwikSave was slowly squeezed to death.

MARKS & SPENCER SIMPLY FOOD: A SUCCESSFUL FOCUSED DIFFERENTIATOR

In the late 1990s, Marks & Spencer's inexorable growth seemed to hit the buffers. Its clothes ranges were tired, and the company seemed to have run out of steam. However, this did not apply to its food ranges, which seemed to be exactly what the consumer wanted. Research showed that M&S was highly rated for the quality of its food, for offering more unusual items, for its high reputation, and its ready meals. It scored low on value for money and on convenience (Hamson 2004).

M&S decided to capitalise on its food reputation, and in July 2001 opened the first Simply Food outlet in Surbiton, Surrey. The store was aimed at commuters, with a high footfall but a low spend per customer, selling 4,000 food lines, plus newspapers and magazines. At 2,500 square feet, it qualified legally as a convenience store, and so is entitled to open extended hours on a Sunday (8 am to 6 pm). (Bruce 2001).

The format proved successful, and expansion was rapid. By the summer of 2003, 30 stores had opened, and there were plans to develop a further 40 stores on railway stations in partnership with Compass (Bruce 2003). The first Simply Food store on a motorway service station followed in August 2003. The stores were also made more flexible. Some went above the 3,000 square feet convenience store limit, while stores would now carry between 800 and 15,000 lines, depending on local demand, rather than the 4,000 lines per store originally planned (*Grocer* 2003).

The stores that proved most successful were those which generated annual turnover in excess of £3 million, and were situated well away from other M&S stores (Watson 2004).

It also became clear that the railway station and motorway service station stores served different types of customer. On the railway stations, customers were in a hurry, and their spend was lower. The priority here was to have an adequate number of tills to cope with the high footfall. Motorway service station customers were prepared to spend longer in store, and also almost by definition had cars, so their average shop was higher (Hamson 2005).

Expansion accelerated in 2006, when M&S acquired 28 ex-Iceland stores. The stores were cherry-picked with great care, using a number of key success criteria:

- strong footfall from high-street shoppers
- high penetration of affluent shoppers
- strong comparable premium retailer offering
- proximity to public transport
- large local resident population
- large work-based grocery expenditure.

Stores that scored highly on these criteria included Torquay and Hertford (*Grocer* 2006a). A trial with BP on BP petrol station forecourts in late 2005 also proved successful (*Grocer* 2006b).

Partly because of Simply Food, M&S has increased its share of UK food grocery sales to 4 per cent, with like for like sales in 2006 growing by up to 6 per cent (Durston 2006). By November 2006 M&S was operating more than 200 Simply Food stores, with a further 100 planned for 2007, of which 60 would be on BP forecourts (*Grocer* 2007).

Why has Simply Food been so successful? Because it:

- builds on the M&S high reputation for food quality
- successfully extends the M&S brand
- avoids cannibalisation by developing new types of site – railway stations, motorway service stations, smaller towns, petrol station forecourts

- had very careful site selection

- works with franchise partners (Compass and BP) which lowers risk and level of investment, and also brings in outside expertise

- has an offer that is carefully tailored to the type of outlet.

The result is that 50 per cent of Simply Food shoppers are in the 16–34 age band – a much younger demographic than for traditional M&S stores (Durston 2006).

CASE STUDY 10.8

NORTHERN ROCK: A FAILED FOCUSED DIFFERENTIATOR

Over a weekend in the middle of September 2007, the United Kingdom experienced the first serious run on a bank for a century. Hundreds of people queued for hours outside the branches of Northern Rock, desperate to withdraw their savings before the bank collapsed. How had a previously well-respected bank come to such a pass?

Northern Rock dates back to 1850, when the Northern Counties Permanent Building Society was formed, followed by Rock Building Society in 1865. The two merged to form the Northern Rock Building Society, based in Newcastle, in 1965. It was a typical building society – taking in deposits from its members, and lending them out as mortgages. It was safe, solid and respectable. Its share of the national mortgage market was 2 per cent. It was also very popular in the north-east because it had been very sympathetic to miners in mortgage arrears during the mining strike of the early 1980s.

In 1997 it demutualised, forming Northern Rock plc, and its status changed from a building society to a bank. As a public company its priorities changed. Rather than providing a service for its members, its priority was now to make profits for its shareholders. Within months, it showed a new face when it was criticised by the Office of Fair Trading of being 'cavalier' for unilaterally changing the terms offered to its depositors (Hughes and Tighe 2007).

Unlike some of the other demutualised ex-building societies, Northern Rock did not attempt to develop general banking services, but continued to specialise in mortgages. However, it was faced with problems in expanding in this area. First, it only had 79 branches, mainly concentrated in the relatively impoverished north-east. This limited its ability to raise funds from depositors (known as retail funds). By comparison, the leading building society, Nationwide, had over 700 branches, and the big high-street banks had thousands.

Northern Rock tackled this problem by raising funds through the interbank market, from other financial institutions (known as wholesale funds). As a building society, it would have been limited by law from raising more than 50 per cent of its funds from the wholesale market, but no such restrictions applied to banks (BBC2 2007). At its peak in the early autumn of 2007, Northern Rock raised more than three-quarters of its funds from the wholesale market, on terms ranging from overnight to three months.

Wholesale borrowing is generally regarded as more risky and volatile than retail borrowing. Although retail depositors can in theory withdraw many of their funds on demand, in practice they are highly unlikely to do so. On the other hand, other banks will move their money elsewhere if they think they can get a better return. Northern Rock's reliance on wholesale funds was described by one experienced banker as akin to overtaking a queue of traffic on the outside of a bend – 'everyone knows it works (for a time), but only fools or the inexperienced would attempt it' (Croggon 2007).

Even when Northern Rock obtained more funds, it still had to persuade people to take out more of its mortgages. It did this through aggressive lending policies. It became known as the bank which would lend even if you had a patchy credit record. It was also prepared to lend more than other banks or building societies. In 2002 it introduced its Together loan, which allowed a borrower to borrow up to 125 per cent of a property's valuation, or six times annual income. As other lenders were not prepared to lend more than four times income, borrowers flocked to Northern Rock. By the end of 2006, its share of the mortgage market was up to 7 per cent.

Massive expansion continued throughout the first half of 2007, at a time when increasing warnings were being issued of the frothy state of the UK housing market, and of a worrying level of consumer debt. In the first half of 2007 Northern Rock took a 25 per cent share of the new mortgage market, making it the biggest mortgage provider, shooting past traditional lenders such as the Halifax and the Nationwide (Collinson and Seager 2007).

With hindsight, it was clear that Northern Rock was over-trading, and taking unacceptable risks. In June 2007 it was forced to issue a profits warning, and its shares started to fall. Its strategy was described by Professor Willem Buiter, one of the founder members of the Bank of England's Monetary Policy Committee, as 'an extremely aggressive and high-risk strategy' (Duncan and Webster 2007).

Northern Rock might still have got away with it had it not been caught up in the backlash from a separate but related financial crisis, the sub-prime crisis in the United States. Here, US financial institutions had pursued a Northern Rock-style strategy of aggressive lending to poor credit risks (the sub-prime market), eventually leading to a collapse of the US housing market in the summer of 2007. One consequence of this was a freezing-up of the interbank lending market in the United Kingdom, as well as the United States. This meant that Northern Rock, which continually needed to roll over its wholesale borrowing, faced a liquidity crisis.

The crisis for Northern Rock came to a head on Thursday 13 September, when the bank applied to the Bank of England for emergency assistance (known as 'lender of last resort'). On Friday 14 September the Bank of England agreed to lend virtually unlimited funds to Northern Rock, but at a penal rate of interest, believed to be 7 per cent.

This should have been the end of the crisis, but Northern Rock retail depositors interpreted this as a sign that the bank was about to fail, and a run on the Bank's cash started and quickly accelerated. Bank deposits are guaranteed, but only up to a maximum of £35,000, and only up to 90 per cent. On Friday and Saturday, a sum estimated to be between £2 billion and £3 billion was withdrawn from Northern Rock branches. Eventually, to stop the run, the Chancellor, Alistair Darling, announced on Monday 16 September that the government would guarantee all deposits in Northern Rock, without limit. The immediate crisis was over.

This case illustrates several important points. One is that Northern Rock's strategy differentiated it from the rest of the mortgage industry, but only at the price of unacceptably high risk. Second, the case demonstrates the nature of moral hazard. The Bank of England was reluctant to intervene at an earlier stage in the crisis because of the risk of moral hazard – that in effect a rescue would reward Northern Rock for its reckless behaviour, and might encourage other institutions to be reckless in the future. Eventually, the Bank of England had no choice, and was forced to intervene to safeguard the stability of the whole banking system, as there was a risk that the panic might spread to other institutions. The bail-out safeguarded not only Northern Rock's depositors, who were innocent victims, but also the bank's management and shareholders, who should have known better (Davies 2007). Third, an ethical issue is involved. Northern Rock's depositors have a 100 per cent government guarantee for their funds, yet when the life assurance company Equitable Life failed in 2000, no such protection was extended to its policy-holders. Was this fair?

Porter's generic strategy concept has been further developed by Bowman (Bowman and Faulkner 1996), who proposes the strategy clock, based on a combination of price and perceived added value. He identified eight possible strategies:

- low price/low added value – not likely to be feasible in the long term unless the organisation operates in a protected niche

- low price/standard added value – equates to Porter's cost leadership

- low price/high added value (hybrid) – the strategy pursued by Japanese companies in the 1970s and 1980s, when they were gaining a foothold in European markets

- standard price/high added value (differentiation) – this would be a sensible strategy as a progression from the hybrid strategy

- high price/high added value (focused differentiation) – likely to be a niche strategy, similar to Porter's differentiation focus

- high price/standard added value – not a long-term viable strategy; why should customers pay more if they are not gaining added value?

- high price/low added value – only feasible for a monopoly in a market which is not contestable

- standard price/low added value – not viable in the long term; what is in it for the customer?

SELECTION OF STRATEGIES

This is concerned not with what strategies should be chosen, but how they should be chosen. Johnson and Scholes propose four models:

- Formal evaluation. Here the choice is based solely on analytical techniques. The decision process is impersonal and rational, and appears to be objective. This avoids the risk of taking decisions solely on gut feeling, but it should be remembered that a lot of the analytical techniques are themselves in practice subjective.

- Enforced choice. Here choice is imposed on the organisation from outside. This may be because of the dominant influence of an external stakeholder – for example, a supplier to Marks & Spencer has very little control over its own strategy. However, in the long term, even a firm in this situation does have some strategic choice – to widen its customer base, for example.

- Learning from experience. The emphasis here is on incremental change on a pilot basis with operating units, and then the application of the experience learned from this throughout the organisation. This method is increasingly used by government, which trials new policy initiatives through a pilot study before going for a national launch, and by many manufacturers, which test market new products before attempting a national launch. It is similar to Quinn's concept of logical incrementalism, which we discussed earlier. The advantage is that it pushes responsibility for strategic development down the organisation, but there is the possible disadvantage that there is never a fundamental strategic rethink – the organisation can suffer from strategic drift.

- Command. Here the dominant stakeholder (who may be the CEO, the biggest shareholder or a government department) selects the strategic direction, and imposes it on the organisation. This has been the experience of the NHS, which has had fundamental strategic change imposed on it by successive governments at regular intervals.

EVALUATION OF STRATEGIES

Possible strategies should be evaluated on three levels, suitability, acceptability and feasibility.

SUITABILITY

Is this a strategy which will produce a sound fit between the organisation and its environment? Will it exploit opportunities in the environment and avoid or neutralise threats? Will it capitalise on the organisation's strengths and core competences and avoid or neutralise weaknesses? Various analytical techniques can be used to help answer these questions:

Life cycle analysis

The consultants Arthur D Little have identified the life cycle/portfolio matrix (see Johnson, Scholes and Whittington 2004). Here the strategies that should be adopted depend on the stage of the product/industry life cycle (embryonic, growing, mature or ageing), and the competitive position of the organisation (dominant, strong, favourable, tenable or weak). For example, the prescribed strategies for a strong firm in a growing industry are fast grow, catch-up, attain cost leadership or differentiation, while for a weak firm in an embryonic industry they are find niche, catch-up or grow with industry. The model is open to criticism, as the definition used are subjective (what is a favourable position in one environment may be a weak one in another), and because, like all models, it ignores all variables except those actually built into the model (stage of maturity and competitive position). For example, it ignores speed of technological development.

Portfolio analysis

We discussed the Boston matrix in Chapter 2. Briefly, this categorised product lines on a matrix of market share and market growth rate, as:

- cash cows: low market growth, high market share
- stars: high market growth, high market share
- question marks: high market growth, low market share
- dogs: low market growth, low market share.

Here the preferred strategic option is to attempt a balance to portfolio between stars and cash cows. Stars are profitable, but they do not generate much cash, while cash cows may be less profitable but are highly cash-generative. Hence use cash cows to finance stars. As with the life cycle model, this is superficially attractive, but again it ignores other variables.

Value chain analysis

Value chain analysis is yet another model developed by Michael Porter. He says that the activities of an organisation should be seen as a sequence of primary events:

- inbound logistics, deliveries, storage, etc
- operations
- outbound logistics (warehousing, wholesalers, deliveries, etc)
- marketing and sales
- service

while underpinning all of these are support activities:

- the firm's infrastructure
- human resource management
- technology
- procurement (purchasing, raising capital, recruitment).

All of these serve to add value for the organisation and form the value chain. The greater the synergies between the various elements, the greater the added value. Conversely, the whole value chain is only as strong as its weakest link. The aim of strategy should therefore be to strengthen the value chain as a whole, by building on existing strengths, or correcting weaknesses.

For example, the primary part of the chain might be strong, but the organisation might have problems caused by high turnover of staff. The strategic choice here would be to concentrate on improving staff turnover using HR techniques. Alternatively, the product might be strong, but its reputation is let down by poor after-sales service. After digging deeper, it might be discovered that the IT systems supporting service are inadequate.

The strength of the value chain technique is that it forces an analysis of how the organisation actually functions, and it avoids over-concentration on some of the more obvious strategic possibilities like merger or takeover. The weakness is that it is exclusively inward-looking. It should be combined with a rigorous analysis of fit with the environment.

ACCEPTABILITY

Strategies have to be acceptable to internal and external stakeholders. This can be assessed in three ways: return, risk and stakeholder reaction.

Return can be assessed using a range of standard accounting techniques, including profitability analysis (discounted cashflow etc), shareholder value analysis (looking at the overall increase in value for the shareholder), using techniques such as economic value added, or cost–benefit analysis (looking at non-financial as well as financial factors).

Risk can be assessed using techniques including:

- break-even analysis – if the break-even point for the new strategy is a very high percentage of capacity, the project is highly risky
- ratio analysis – if the new strategy will result in very low levels of liquidity, as measured by standard ratios, it is high risk
- sensitivity analysis – how sensitive is the profit of the project to a shortfall in any of the key financial variables?

Stakeholder reactions can be assessed using techniques such as stakeholder modelling (discussed in the Chapter 9). Stakeholders may well have strong views on risk, and these should be taken into account.

FEASIBILITY

Strategies have to be feasible in terms of resource availability. Techniques to measure this include:

- Funds flow analysis – what is the implication for future cashflows? If sufficient cash is not currently available, can it be acquired on reasonable terms?
- Break-even analysis – what is the break-even point given the present cost structure? If the break-even point is too high, can the cost structure be improved?
- Resource deployment analysis – what are the key resources and competences required for each strategy? Does the organisation already possess them? If not, can it reasonably acquire them?

STRATEGIC OPTION SCREENING

Several methods can be used to screen options to see whether they meet criteria on suitability, acceptability and feasibility. These include ranking, decision trees and scenario planning.

Ranking

Here options are assessed against key factors in the environment, resources and stakeholder expectations, and a score (or ranking) established for each option. To take a very simple example, assume that a company has two strategic options, A and B, and two success criteria, profitability and stakeholder acceptability. It has established that it regards profitability as more important, and has given this a weighting of 70. Stakeholder acceptability has a weighting of 30 (producing a total weighting of 100).

CASE STUDY 10.9

STAKEHOLDER ACCEPTABILITY

An acceptable strategy – Ben & Jerry's and Unilever

Ben & Jerry's ice cream was one of the leading lights of the ethical business movement. It was not only concerned to trade ethically, it also wanted to change the world. It donated heavily to radical causes, and was deeply involved in the anti-globalisation movement. These values were fully supported by its staff and customers, both key stakeholders.

In April 2000, Ben & Jerry's was taken over by the strait-laced Anglo-Dutch conglomerate Unilever, a classic representative of the globalisation that Ben & Jerry's had opposed. Although it had a good ethical reputation, Unilever was in no sense radical. Ben Cohen, the joint founder of Ben & Jerry's, forecast that the takeover would lead to the destruction of the company.

However, when Unilever appointed a 25-year Unilever man, Yves Couette, to run Ben & Jerry's, he was given the license to be a 'grain of sand in the eye' of Unilever. He abandoned his suit and tie, and followed a deliberate policy of empowerment and delegation. Tough profit targets were set, but Couette pointed out to staff that this would mean that more money would be donated to charity through the Ben & Jerry Foundation, which would continue to have a free hand to support any charity or movement which it chose (including the anti-globalisation movement).

An unacceptable strategy – Marconi

Throughout the 1980s and 1990s, GEC was seen as a safe, rather stolid company, dominated by the safety-first philosophy of its long-time chairman, Arnold (Lord) Weinstock. The company prospered in household electrical goods and defence electronics, and built up a bank balance of several billion pounds. It appealed to risk-averse shareholders.

In the late 1990s new management, headed by George Simpson, decided on a radical new strategy. The defence electronics business was sold to British Aerospace, most of the domestic electric businesses (Hotpoint etc) were sold, and the company, now renamed Marconi, began a dash for growth in the exciting new world of Internet electronics. The rationale was that Marconi would benefit from the dot.com boom which was raging at the time. The bank balances, plus several billions more, were used to buy up American Internet companies.

Unfortunately, the purchases were made right at the peak of the dot.com bubble, and when the bubble burst, many of the new acquisitions were effectively worthless. Marconi's share price plummeted, and when the company eventually went through a financial restructuring, shareholders effectively lost all their money.

Like all shareholders, the Marconi shareholders should have realised that any share investment is by its very nature risky, but they could legitimately argue that they had originally bought their shares in GEC precisely because it was seen as a low-risk company.

Strategy A scores 50 out of 70 for profitability, but only 10 out of 30 for stakeholder acceptability. Strategy B scores less well on profitability, 30 out of 70, but it scores 20 out of 30 for stakeholder acceptability.

This gives a total score for strategy A of 60/100 (50 + 10), and a total score for strategy B of 50/100 (30 + 20). Strategy A is thus the preferred option.

Decision trees

Here options are progressively eliminated by testing them against various criteria. For example, a company has two decision criteria, high growth (most important) and low cost (less important). It is considering four strategies:

Strategy W   high growth, high cost

Strategy X   high growth, low cost

Strategy Y   low growth, low cost

Strategy Z   low growth, high cost.

The first decision step would eliminate strategies Y and Z, because they are low growth, leaving W and X. The next decision step would eliminate W, leaving X as the preferred strategy.

Scenario planning

Here the options are evaluated against various scenarios for the future. For example, if the organisation thinks that the most likely future for the UK exchange rate is stability, this would favour a policy of manufacturing in the United Kingdom. If the most likely scenario is seen as a rising pound, this would favour manufacturing overseas.

 ACTIVITY

10.6 STRATEGIC EVALUATION

A risk-averse firm with a strong current financial position, but little access to long-term capital, has decided that it must adopt a policy of unrelated diversification, in order to reduce its dependence on a declining industry. It has evaluated a number of areas for diversification, and decided on the appropriate industry to enter. It is now considering the best way to enter the new market.

Its options are:

A   Develop and manufacture a new product.

B   Manufacture an existing product under licence.

C   Set up a joint venture with a firm that already has expertise in this field.

D   Buy out a firm already in the industry.

E   Market under its brand name an existing Taiwanese product not currently imported into the United Kingdom.

It has established the following criteria, and weighted them as follows:

		Weighting
a	Low risk	40
b	Speedy entry into the market	20
c	Low capital cost	20
d	Profitability	15
e	Short payback period	5

Activity

a. Discuss the advantages and disadvantages of each method of entry.

b. Using your own judgement, assign scores to each strategy and rank them.

STRATEGIC IMPLEMENTATION

The final stage in the strategy process is implementation – having decided on the chosen strategy, how is it put into practice? Frequently this will be the most difficult phase of the whole process. It involves a key competency of all managers – the ability to manage change.

INCREMENTAL AND TRANSFORMATIONAL CHANGE

Most of the writers on strategic implementation distinguish between incremental and transformational change, although their terminology varies. Johnson, Scholes and Whittington (2004) see strategic change on a two-by-two matrix, type of change and extent of change. A small change is incremental, a large change transformational. Each is of two types, dependent on whether the change is proactive or reactive. Proactive incremental change is tuning, reactive incremental change adaptation, while transformational change is divided into planned and forced change.

Walton (1999) defines transformational change as change which results in entirely new behaviour on the part of organisational members. He sees transformational change as in its very nature strategic. However, drawing on the work of Quinn on logical incrementalism, he sees incremental change as a possible route to strategic change. He also identifies transitional change, the process of carrying out change.

Porter (1999) concentrates on the outcome rather than the process. Changes such as the introduction of re-engineering or Total Quality Management are transformational, but they are not strategic. He sees them as improving operational effectiveness rather than changing the strategic position of the organisation. They are about doing better the same things as the competition are doing. Operational effectiveness is about running the same race faster, strategy is about running a different race.

MODELS OF CHANGE

The classic model of change was identified by Lewin in the 1950s and developed by Schein in the 1980s (Armstrong 1999; Walton 1999). They identified three stages in change management:

- Unfreezing – creating a readiness for change, through creation of a sense of anxiety about the present situation. The sequence here is to enable those involved to be convinced of the need for change.
- Movement – taking action that will encourage the desired new behaviour patterns. This involves doing things differently, based on access to new information, and identifying with new role models.
- Refreezing – embedding the new ways of working into the organisation.

Lewin also developed the concept of force field analysis – analysing the restraining and driving forces within the organisation which oppose or support the proposed change, and then taking steps to encourage the driving forces and decrease the restraining forces.

Beer took a different approach. He argued that the approach that tries to change attitudes in order to change behaviour is flawed. He argued that change should be approached in an opposite way – put people in new roles which require new behaviours, and this will change their attitudes. This is similar to the theory of cognitive dissonance. Beer proposed a six-stage model of change (CIPD 2004):

1. Mobilise commitment to change through joint analysis of problems.

2. Develop a shared vision.

3. Foster consensus and commitment to the shared vision.

4. Spread the word about the change.

5. Institutionalise the change through formal policies.

6. Monitor and adjust as needed.

The Lewin and Beer models both come out of relatively placid environments. They have been criticised for their assumption that it is possible to plan an orderly transition from one static state to another static state (Burnes 1996). In a more dynamic and chaotic environment like that experienced at present, a more continuous and open-ended change process is more appropriate. They also assume that a 'one size fits all' model of change is appropriate, whereas a more modern perspective would be to take a contingency approach and to argue that each organisation has a unique relationship with its environment. Its approach to change should reflect this.

The emergent approach to change as put forward by Burnes and Shaw (CIPD 2004) stresses that change is not linear. It is not a movement from state A to state B, it is continuous and messy. Just like its environment, an organisation is in a continuous state of flux, and the forces for change emerge as the organisation engages with its environment. Change in this model is bottom-up rather than top-down, and it emerges through experimentation. What is important is to ensure that the organisation is responsive to change, and the best way of doing this is to ensure that the organisation is a learning organisation.

MANAGING CHANGE

Kotter (1995) proposes an eight-step plan for transformation:

1. Establishing a sense of urgency – realising that change is needed.

2. Forming a powerful guiding coalition – a powerful and influential group of change leaders is needed.

3. Creating a vision – what will things be like after the change is achieved?

4. Communicating the vision.

5. Empowering others to act on the vision.

6. Planning for and creating short-term wins – a long change process that

appears to be getting nowhere can be demotivating. Building in some short-term wins can improve morale.

7. Consolidating improvements and producing still more change.

8. Institutionalising new approaches – similar to Lewin's refreezing process.

Bridges and Bridges (2000) identify three stages in a change programme:

1. Saying goodbye – letting go of the way that things used to be.

2. Shifting into neutral – the in-between stage when nothing seems to be happening, but everyone is in a stressful state of limbo. In the case of a major merger, this phase might take two years.

3. Moving forward – when people have to behave in a new way.

They describe seven steps in managing transition:

1. Describe the change and why it must happen – in one minute or less.

2. Make sure that the details of the change are planned carefully and that someone is responsible for each detail.

3. Understand who is going to have to let go of what.

4. Make sure that people are helped to let go of the past.

5. Help people through the neutral zone with communication, stressing the 'four Ps':

 MOSES IN THE WILDERNESS

CASE STUDY 10.10

Bridges and Bridges discuss the change management techniques used by Moses on his way to the Promised Land:

- **Magnify the plagues.** Moses had to convince a key stakeholder (Pharaoh) that change was needed – that he had to let the Jews go. He did this through creating problems for Pharaoh – the seven plagues. The worse the current situation seems, the greater the impetus for change.

- **Mark the ending.** After the Jews crossed the Red Sea, there was (literally) no going back.

- **Deal with the 'murmuring'.** Don't be surprised when people lose confidence in the neutral zone. Moses faced lots of whingeing. He dealt with it by talking to people about their concerns.

- **Build up change champions.** Moses and his lieutenant Joshua appointed a new cadre of judges to champion the change.

- **Capitalise on creative opportunities.** It was in the Wilderness, not in the Promised Land, that the Ten Commandments were handed down.

- **Resist the urge to rush ahead.** Not much seems to be happening in the neutral zone, but it is where the true transformation takes place. Moses was in the Wilderness for 40 years!

Different stages need different leadership styles. Moses was an ideal leader for the neutral zone, but the Promised Land required a new type of leadership, provided by the conqueror of Jericho, Joshua.

the purpose – why we have to do this

the picture – what it will look and feel like when we get there

the plan – how we will get there

the part – what each person needs to do.

6. Create temporary solutions to the temporary problems found in the neutral zone.

7. Help people launch the new beginning.

RESISTANCE TO CHANGE

Resistance to change can be of two types: resistance to the content of change – ie opposition to the specific nature of the change – and resistance to the process of change – ie opposition to how to the change is introduced. Each might be a perfectly rational response to change, however inconvenient to management.

Armstrong (1999) identifies eight reasons that individuals might resist change:

- The shock of the new – people tend to be conservative, and they do not want to move too far from their comfort zones. To this we would add regret for the passing of the old.

- Economic fears – threats to wages or job security.

- Inconvenience.

- Uncertainty.

- Symbolic fears – the loss of a symbol, like a car parking space, may suggest that bigger and more threatening changes are on the way.

- Threats to interpersonal relationships.

- Threat to status or skill – a change may be seen as deskilling.

- Competence fears – concern about the ability to cope or acquire new skills.

THE ROLE OF HR IN CHANGE MANAGEMENT

The crucial role of HR in change management can be clearly identified using Beer's model of change. HR intervention is crucial at each stage of the model, as follows:

1. Mobilise commitment to change through joint analysis of problems. HR should play a leading role in benchmarking and other environment-scanning techniques, and so help to spot the need for change. HR staff are likely to be the organisers of the teams and workshops who are involved in problem identification and analysis. Underpinning this should be a learning organisation, in which HR should be a prime driver.

2. Develop a shared vision. This involves an understanding of the culture of the organisation, and the ability to support and direct the visions which underpin the culture.

3. Foster consensus and commitment to the shared vision. It is essential that those affected by the change should feel that they have ownership of it. Developing and supporting ownership is a key HR skill, as is the fostering and supporting of change champions.

4. Spread the word about the change. Here, as noted by McCarthy (2004), communication is key. McCarthy stresses that this should involve communication with, rather than communication at, those involved. He suggests the concept of 'conversation' as being appropriate here.

5. Institutionalise the change through formal policies. This may well include the development of new HR policies on recruitment, reward and development. It is crucial that the reward system supports the new ways of doing things, for example.

6. Monitor and adjust as needed. HR policy will need to be proactive after the change process is apparently completed. Development policies should be responsive to the need for any new competencies which become apparent.

Armstrong (1999) identifies a number of 'guidelines for change management', in most of which the role of HR is key. These include:

- commitment and visionary leadership from the top
- understanding the culture
- development of temperament and leadership skills at all levels which support change
- an environment conducive to change – a learning organisation
- full participation of those involved, so that they can own the change
- the reward system should recognise success in achieving change
- a willingness to learn from failure – a support culture rather than a blame culture
- support for change agents
- protection of those adversely affected by change.

Ridgeway and Wallace (1994) discuss the role of HR in managing a common strategic change – a takeover. Here matching the culture of the predator and the target are key. They quote from Furnham and Gunter (1993) on how such a match should be identified. It would involve:

- identifying the culture of the acquiring company
- deciding on any changes needed to ensure that culture supports the proposed strategy
- identifying potential acquisitions and their cultures
- isolating likely changes to those cultures
- designing a format for assessing other cultures
- establishing criteria by which to identify suitable acquisitions.

Crucial here is establishing how the senior management of the target company will fit with the acquirer's culture, and what senior staff gaps will be exposed.

The HR department of the acquiring company will also be responsible for ensuring that the procedures and systems of the two companies are compatible, or can be made compatible, including any industrial relations implications. During the takeover process, the HR department also needs to manage communication. This will involve close liaison with PR, as employees of the target company will get a lot of their information about the takeover via the media.

 THE MORRISONS TAKEOVER OF SAFEWAY

CASE STUDY 10.11

The takeover of the supermarket chain Safeway by its rival Morrisons is an example of the most difficult type of takeover to manage – a takeover of a bigger company by its smaller rival. Safeway had three times as many stores as Morrisons, and a bigger turnover, when it was taken over in March 2004.

The cultures of the two companies were totally different. Morrisons was run as a family firm, dominated by the larger than life personality of Sir Ken Morrison, the son of the founder. It was aggressively northern, and prided itself on its 'call a spade a spade' philosophy – nothing subtle, pile it high and sell it cheap. Sir Ken even personally recorded all the store announcements used by the company. Safeway was very different. It had been formed from a number of mergers over the years, was impersonal and bureaucratic, and very southern. Although its stores were smaller than Morrisons it stocked a lot more lines. Its pricing policy was to draw customers in with a few drastic headline price reductions, but it had higher 'background' prices.

The merger also took a long time. Not only did Morrisons bid for Safeway, so did Tesco, Sainsbury and Asda. Because of a Competition Commission investigation, the whole process took 14 months, long enough for gloom and despondency to

spread throughout Safeway. Perhaps reflecting this, or even a subconscious desire to sabotage Morrisons, Safeway introduced a totally new accounting system, incompatible with Morrisons, weeks before the takeover was completed.

Once the takeover was finalised, Morrisons did not handle things in the most tactful of ways. Except for one very small previous takeover, its managers had no experience of managing this kind of situation. The attitude was very much 'we know best', and surviving Safeway management was expected to adopt the Morrisons ways of doing things. The Safeway head office in Surrey was closed, and Morrisons was surprised when only 200 of its 1,600 staff wanted to transfer to Bradford. On the other hand, staffing in the old Safeway stores was increased, as although it stocked fewer lines, Morrisons did more activities in-store (bakeries etc). Although sales rose in the Safeway stores that were converted, they fell in those Safeway stores that were not yet converted, leading Morrisons to issue a profits warning in July 2004.

Morrisons also tended to alienate another important stakeholder, the City. The company was notoriously media-shy, and reluctant to talk to City analysts. This was tolerated before the takeover, as Morrisons was relatively small (a FTSE250 firm), and also very successful. As it was now in the FTSE100, it was much more in the media spotlight, and the City expected a much higher standard of communication.

The Morrisons share price has under-performed the market. From a peak of 256p in March, at the time of the takeover, it had fallen to a low of 171p in September, and had only recovered to 225p (on a rising market)

by the end of November 2004. In 2007, however, it did achieve a high of 345p, although this was still a smaller rise than for the stock market as a whole.

The verdict: a takeover performance which illustrates Morrisons' lack of experience, failure to take the HR needs of ex-Safeway staff into consideration, and perhaps over-confidence.

 ACTIVITY

10.7 PEARMOUNT COLLEGE

Pearmount College is a medium-sized further education (FE) college in the town of Hetherleigh (population 75,000). In many ways it is a typical FE college. In its Ofsted inspections, most aspects are rated as satisfactory (grade 3, the middle of the five grades available). A third of its courses are rated as above average, a third as below average. However, Pearmount is not typical in that it is a tertiary college. Unlike most FE colleges, it is responsible for all post-16 education in Hetherleigh. Except for a Catholic comprehensive, the secondary schools in Hetherleigh do not have sixth forms.

This gives the college a particular social responsibility. As the only post-16 provider, it cannot be selective in its recruitment policy. It is expected to provide educational opportunities for all of the post-16 population in the town.

There are four main types of post-16 providers, all of which compete to score highly in government league tables. These are school sixth forms, which are often selective, sixth form colleges, which are almost always selective, tertiary colleges, which are normally non-selective, and ordinary FE colleges, which tend to offer mainly vocational courses rather than A levels. The main league table competition is between sixth forms, sixth form colleges and

tertiary colleges, and concentrates on A level results. Sixth form colleges tend to score more highly than school sixth forms and tertiary colleges. A recent Ofsted inspection of Pearmount noted that its A level results were at the FE college average, but below the average for sixth form colleges. It also criticised teaching as unimaginative, although it said that some vocational provision was excellent.

Post-16 education is funded by the Learning and Skills Council (LSC), under government guidance. Government funding policy is to concentrate on three main target areas – full time 16–19 education, adult basic literacy and numeracy skills, and adult level 2 qualifications (broadly GCSE grade A–C level). FE and tertiary colleges have responded to this by withdrawing from adult education, unless it fits into the funding priorities, or is fully funded by employers. Pearmount is typical in this. Over the last decade it has withdrawn from many advanced vocational and professional part-time programmes, and concentrated much more on full-time 16–19 programmes. The other continuing pressure from the LSC is to drive up the quality of further education provision, with the threat of withdrawing funding from courses within the priority areas that are deemed to be of low quality.

Jim Merryweather was appointed as the new

principal of Pearmount College in September 2006, following the retirement of his predecessor, who had taken an active role in the town. Within a month of taking up his post, he produced a new teaching and learning strategy for the college. This stressed individual daily targets for students, with daily assessment and measurement of achievement; all assignment work to be completed in college; and fortnightly reports to parents on progress and attendance. His aim was to make the college one of the best sixth forms in the country.

Although there was some concern that the new strategy seemed to focus solely on full-time 16–19 students, it was broadly welcomed by teaching staff, and rapid progress was made in its implementation.

However, Jim also faced the problem that many of his staff were ageing, while others, who mainly taught vocational programmes for adults, were seeing much of their workload disappear. Clearly the college staffing needed to be restructured. One way to do this could have been an early retirement programme, but what often happens in these programmes is that the people opting to take early retirement are the very people you do not want to lose. Another option could have been a programme of retraining and redeployment.

Jim's solution was to propose a radical restructuring, which was announced just before the Easter holidays in April 2007. A new staffing structure was proposed, with more higher-paid posts, but also some low-level posts with a salary ceiling well below that previously available to lecturers. All members of staff were expected to reapply for posts under the new structure, with the clear expectation that some would be unsuccessful.

In addition, holidays were reduced, and the normal working week was increased to 37 hours, all of which could in theory be spent teaching. The working week was also extended to five and a half days, and staff could be requested to work on Saturdays. Staff would no longer be entitled to overtime or time off in lieu.

The reaction of staff was one of horror, particularly as the new posts were immediately advertised internally, although the proposals came under the 90-day consultation period for major redundancies. Teaching staff held a number of one-day strikes, were fully supported by their union and the students union, and also attracted a lot of support within the town.

There was criticism that Jim had failed to consult adequately with stakeholders, and he seemed to have underestimated the affection the town held for the college. As Pearmount had been a tertiary college for over 20 years, virtually every family in Hetherleigh contained someone who had either attended the college themselves, or was the parent of someone who had been a college student.

By the end of the summer term in 2007, half the teaching staff had been made redundant, had found new posts or had taken early retirement. There was severe concern that college staffing would be inadequate to meet demand in 2007–8, and also that the adverse publicity would dissuade many potential students from attending the college.

Questions

1. Critically evaluate Jim's strategy for implementing change at Pearmount College.

2. What techniques do you think can be used to overcome resistance to change?

CHANGE LEADERSHIP

Ridgeway and Wallace (1994) identify a number of competencies required for effective change leadership. These are:

- intellectual skills: intellectually curious and able to handle ambiguity

- influencing skills: assertive, proactive and energetic

- counselling and people skills: sensitive, flexible and adaptable, with a high tolerance of pressure.

While this list is solid, we think that it misses the true essence of change leadership. A good change leader must above all be driven by a vision of the future, and be able to inspire others with that vision. This involves a high sense of values, exceptional communication abilities, a sense of inspiration, and the ability to empower others with the vision. All of these qualities are illustrated in our last case study.

CASE STUDY 10.12

NELSON MANDELA

Nelson Mandela is almost universally recognised as the last, and one of the greatest, inspirational leaders of the twentieth century. His career illustrates the characteristics of a brilliant change leader.

Mandela was born in 1918, a member of a chiefly clan in the Xhosa tribe. He trained as a lawyer, and was drawn at an early age into the struggle against white domination through his membership of the African National Congress (ANC). The political struggle intensified in the 1950s after the election of the white supremacist National Party government, and the establishment of the apartheid system of racial segregation.

In the early 1960s, Mandela was on trial for his life. His statement from the dock in his trial put forward his vision:

> I have fought against white domination. I have fought against black domination. I have cherished the ideal of a democratic and free society in which all persons live together in harmony and with equal opportunities. It is an ideal which I hope to live for and to achieve. But, if needs be, it is an ideal for which I am prepared to die.

Mandela was sentenced to life imprisonment on Robben Island, where he was to remain for 27 years. For much of this he was under a hard labour regime. A telling incident from his imprisonment throws more light on his vision. A particularly tough prison governor imposed a brutal regime on the prisoners, but when he was transferred, he wished Mandela and the other ANC leaders the best for the future. To Mandela, this illustrated the possibility of redemption. The man was brutal not because he had a brutal nature, but because he was conditioned by a brutal system. Like the Catholic Church, Mandela distinguished between the sin and the sinner. From this came his concept of redemption and reconciliation, which was to be a driving force of his presidency.

By the mid-1980s, another key player had entered the scene – F W de Klerk, the new National party leader. De Klerk recognised that the apartheid system must go, and that a settlement must be negotiated with the ANC. In Bridge's terms, this marked the end of the old system, and a move into the neutral transition zone. After lengthy negotiations, Mandela was released from prison in 1990. A new constitution was negotiated, leading to democratic elections in 1994, and the election of Mandela as the first democratic president of South Africa.

Mandela now faced his most severe test as a leader – how to hold the new South Africa together, and forge a new multiracial democratic state. He faced threats on all sides. A right-wing Afrikaner element was threatening civil war, and there was also an undeclared civil war between the ANC and the Zulu Inkatha Freedom Party. The Zulus were the largest tribe in South Africa, and resented the power held by the Xhosa Mandela.

Mandela's approach was to use symbolic acts of reconciliation. He visited the widow of the architect of apartheid, Hendrik Verwoerd. He also presented the rugby world cup to the victorious South African team wearing a South African rugby shirt. Rugby is an Afrikaner sport in South Africa, with almost totally white support. This action helped to reconcile the Afrikaner community to the new South Africa. He also pursued reconciliation with the Zulus. The Inkatha Freedom Party leader, Mangosuthu Buthelezi, was made minister for home affairs, and number three in the government, after Mandela and the vice-president Thabo Mbeki.

Mandela also used the idea of redemption through the Truth and Reconciliation Commission, which he launched with Archbishop Desmond Tutu. The idea here was that perpetrators of political crime could confess their involvement, and receive public absolution. Mandela insisted that this should apply as much to members of the ANC as to the agents of the apartheid regime.

Mandela's last great act of leadership was to recognise that by the end of his term as president in 1999, the transition phase had ended, and that South Africa was into the new beginning. Even his greatest admirers would not call Mandela a great administrator, and he recognised that a new type of more structured leadership was now needed. He therefore retired, leaving the way for Thabo Mbeki, a less charismatic but more structured politician, to succeed him.

When the sculptor Rodin was asked how he would sculpt an elephant, his reply was that he would start with a very large block of stone, and then remove everything which was not elephant. Mandela had a similar vision. Everything which was not part of his vision of a democratic, multicultural South Africa was irrelevant, including bitterness, revenge and recriminations.

CONCLUSIONS

This chapter has discussed the nature of strategy, and its transition from a corporate planning to a strategic management perspective, with a greater emphasis on contingency, experimentation and learning. We have identified the crucial role of change management and of the change leader in ensuring that strategy is implemented as planned.

- Quinn identifies three elements of strategy – goals, policies and programmes.

- Strategy can be analysed at several levels – corporate, business unit and operational.

- Approaches to strategy are connected with the nature of the environment. In the 1950s and 1960s, a placid environment encouraged the rational, logical corporate planning approach, while a more turbulent environment since the 1970s encouraged the more contingent, experimental strategic management approach.

- The leading exponent of the corporate planning approach was Igor Ansoff, while the leading exponents of the strategic management approach are Tom Peters, Michael Porter, Ralph Stacey, Gary Hamel and C K Prahalad, James Quinn and Henry Mintzberg.

- It is important to distinguish between intended strategy and realised strategy.

- Strategic analysis is concerned with the strategic position of the organisation. What are the key characteristics of the organisation, what changes are going on in the environment, and how will these affect the organisation and its activities? This involves an analysis of the expectations of stakeholders, the culture of the organisation, the organisation's vision and values; the environment, as identified through a STEEPLE analysis; and the key resource areas of the business.

- The extent to which there is a mismatch (a gap) between current strategy and the future environment is a measure of the strategic problem facing the organisation.

- Vision, mission, values and objectives are closely linked, and often confused.

- The mission and objectives of the organisation are constrained by corporate governance, stakeholders, business ethics and culture.

- The mission statement provides a benchmark against which policies can be evaluated.

- Resource analysis is internal to the organisation. It is concerned with the strengths and weaknesses parts of SWOT analysis, and measures the efficiency and effectiveness of an organisation's resources.

- Prahalad and Hamel identify the concept of the core competences of the organisation – those factors that give the organisation its key competitive advantages.

- The concept of generic strategy was introduced by Michael Porter, and developed by Cliff Bowman.

- Possible strategies should be evaluated on three levels: suitability, acceptability and feasibility.

- Transformational change is change that results in entirely new behaviour on the part of organisational members, and is in its very nature strategic.

- Bridges and Mitchell identify three stages in a change programme: saying goodbye, shifting into neutral and moving forward.

- Resistance to change can be rational, and must be managed. This is one of the key functions of HR in change management.

- The critical role of a change leader is to be inspirational and visionary.

1. Explain what Quinn means by his three elements of strategy.

2. Why is the corporate planning approach inappropriate for a turbulent environment?

3. What is the role of gap analysis in strategic planning?

4. What are the differences between vision, mission, values and objectives?

5. What do you understand by the expression 'core competence'?

6. Explain the concept of generic strategy as developed by Michael Porter.

7. How can a proposed strategy be evaluated?

8. Why might individuals resist change?

9. What are the six stages in Beer's change model?

10. What are the key requirements for transformational leadership?

TRENDS TO WATCH

- The economic environment seems to be entering into an uneven more turbulent phase, with the surge in the oil price leading to a risk of stagflation – simultaneous rises in inflation and unemployment. Is this leading to a greater emphasis on flexibility and incrementalism in strategic decision making?

- In a more turbulent environment, leadership and change management skills are likely to become even more important. Watch out for examples of inspired leadership.

The leading UK text on strategic management is Gerry Johnson and Kevan Scholes, *Exploring corporate strategy*. A new edition (the seventh) was published in November 2004 (with Richard Whittington). Other valuable strategic management texts are John Thompson with Frank Martin, *Strategic management: awareness and change* (5th edn, 2005), Robert Clark, *Contemporary strategy analysis* (5th edn, 2005) and Bernard Burnes, *Managing change: a strategic approach to organisational dynamics* (4th edn, 2004). John Walton's *Strategic human resource development* (1999) is useful for the HR contribution to strategic management. Also useful is a CIPD factsheet on *Change management* (December 2004), available on the CIPD website.

SEMINAR ACTIVITY

THE SECOND WORLD WAR

Each major participant in the war had a different strategic approach to the war, which reflected their resource situation.

The United Kingdom

- Avoid war if possible.

- If war was inevitable, plan for a long war, and to involve the United States (UK resources were limited, but the United Kingdom could draw on the human and technological resources of the Empire, and hopefully the United States).

- Use the navy to keep supply routes open.

- Build up the defensive capacity of the RAF (fighter planes).

Germany

- Blitzkreig – go for quick, knock-out blows, exploiting the superior fighting ability of the German army.

- Avoid a long war, because of Germany's limited supply of raw materials, particularly oil.

- Avoid a war on two fronts – this made it essential that the USSR was knocked out of the war in 1941–2.

USSR

- Buy space and time (through the pact with Germany in 1939 which gained the USSR half of Poland and the Baltic States).

- Retreat into the interior of Russia to stretch the German lines of communication (just as in 1812).

- Exploit the USSR's vast reserves of manpower.

- Avoid war on two fronts – hence no declaration of war on Japan until August 1945.

- Press the western Allies to open a second front in Europe.

United States

- Avoid war.

- Exploit the mass production capacity of American industry to out-produce the Axis powers.

Japan

- Pre-emptive strike – to destroy the US navy at Pearl Harbour.

- Blitzkrieg.

- Seize oil supplies in Indonesia to make up for Japan's shortage of oil.

- Avoid war on two fronts – hence no declaration of war on the USSR.

France

- Avoid war if possible.

- Fight a defensive war, relying on the Maginot line to repel a German invasion.

Italy

- Initially avoid war, as Italy was militarily weak.

- Once the Germans appeared to have won in 1940, attack France and Britain to gain territory (Nice in France, which had been Italian until 1860, Egypt from Britain, to link up the Italian empire in North Africa).

Spain

- Avoid war with Britain and France, which could easily attack and/or blockade Spain.

- Resist German pressure to enter the war, but if this became impossible, only commit troops to the Eastern Front.

Once the United States had entered the war in 1941, the Anglo–American allies made the crucial corporate-level strategic decision that the war in Europe was to have first priority. In Asia, Japan was to be contained, particularly at sea.

Another corporate-level (but unsuccessful) strategic decision was to attempt to knock Germany out of the war through strategic bombing, exploiting the West's technological and material advantages, while leaving the USSR to defeat the German armies, using its manpower advantage.

Examples of business-unit-level decisions were the decisions to invade Sicily rather than the Balkans in 1943, and Normandy rather than Calais in 1944.

Operational tactical decisions were those to deploy particular national allied armies to particular beaches in the Normandy landings.

Questions

1. How far do the strategic decisions and approaches used in the war fit the characteristics of strategic decisions listed earlier?

2. How far do the strategic approaches taken by the war's participants reflect the core competencies of each country?

CHAPTER 11

Managing in a strategic business context – integrative case studies

LEARNING OUTCOMES

By the end of this chapter, readers should be able to:

- apply their knowledge and understanding of the external business environment to complex situations

- appreciate how the business environment has an impact in real-life situations

- understand how business pressures interact at the levels of an industry and individual firms.

INTRODUCTION

In this final chapter, we examine a major case study of an industry which has been in a state of constant flux for the last 15 years – the beer industry. We examine changes in the industry as a whole, and then analyse case studies of four major players in the industry, which have adopted different strategies in the face of rapid change – Scottish & Newcastle (S&N), Greene King, J D Wetherspoon and Whitbread.

THE BEER INDUSTRY

The UK beer industry forms a fascinating case study. The structure of the industry is unlike that of the rest of British industry. Until the late 1990s, it was also very insular, with little contact with either European or world trends in the beer industry. In the last 10 years it has changed from almost exclusively UK ownership to a situation where more than half of the industry is owned by European or American companies. It is also an industry which has experienced enormous changes in its structure and product range over the last quarter-century, and which was thrown into turmoil by government-inspired change since 1989.

In the rest of Europe (with the exception of the Irish Republic and Belgium) beer means lager – a pasteurised product which is light in texture and colour, and drunk cold. In the United Kingdom, lager has a large and growing share of the market, but beer in the United Kingdom also means ale and stout.

The beer industry in the United Kingdom was unusual before 1989 in being heavily vertically integrated. Some brewers controlled their own sources of raw materials, including malt and hops, and in some cases water, but much more important was forward integration. Much beer is draught beer, sold through pubs and clubs, known as the on-trade. The remainder is sold in bottles or cans through off-licences and increasingly supermarkets, known as the off-trade. The off-trade, particularly beer sold through supermarkets, has increased its share of the market considerably in recent years.

Of approximately 78,000 public houses in the United Kingdom in 1989, 46,000 were owned by brewers, including 34,000 owned by the big six companies. These were known as tied houses, because they were tied to the brewer, and obliged to sell its products, which might include spirits, wines and soft drinks as well as beer.

About 70 per cent of tied houses were tenanted, with the other 30 per cent being managed by employees of the brewery. Tenants pay rent, and take a margin on all goods and services sold. Traditionally, rents were pegged below market levels, but in return the tenant was obliged to buy beer from the brewer at a price set by it.

Other public houses were free houses, which were owner-occupied, and normally could buy their beer from wherever they chose. However, in some cases a loan tie system operated. Here the brewer made a low-interest loan to the publican, who in turn was obliged to sell the brewer's products.

The industry has been marked by a very considerable number of mergers, which reduced the number of companies from around 350 in 1950 to 64 in 1989. The structure of the industry was firmly established by the mid-1960s, when the Big Six brewers (Bass, Allied, Whitbread, Watney, S&N and Courage) controlled 67 per cent of production. By 1989 that had increased to 75 per cent. In addition, as noted above, they owned nearly half the public houses.

Trends in the industry

Beer production in the United Kingdom peaked in the late 1970s, and has declined gently thereafter. Consumption has followed the same pattern. Average beer consumption per head in 1979 was 23 pints a month, and this has now fallen to 18 pints. Over the same period, wine consumption has risen from 9 litres a year to 24 litres (BBC 2004).

Both imports and exports are historically of minor importance in the industry, mainly because of the cost of transporting a product which is mainly water. Beer that appears to be foreign is usually brewed in the United Kingdom under licence. However, in recent years the most rapidly growing segment of the market has been premium lager, much of which is imported from Europe.

The product mix shifted decisively in the period from 1960 to 1990. In 1960, 99 per cent of all beer consumed was ale, while by 1990 lager had overtaken ale, and made up 51 per cent of all sales. This has now risen to 69 per cent. The main forces behind this seem to have been that the British acquired a taste for lager on European holidays; lager was seen as a young persons' drink, and also as a drink that was acceptable to both sexes; its taste and quality were totally predictable; and national brands of lager were heavily promoted by the brewers.

Another long-term trend in the market has been the success of real ale. By the early 1970s, although most beer sold was still ale, it was overwhelmingly a pasteurised 'dead' product. Real ale, or cask-conditioned ale, is by contrast a 'live' product, with the result that although its quality is much higher, it is more difficult to serve and does not keep as long as pasteurised beer. In the early 1970s, it appeared that real ale was likely to disappear from the market. It was then rescued by the activities of the Campaign for Real Ale (CAMRA), a classic example of an interest pressure group. Thanks to CAMRA's efforts, real ale revived and thrived. It is relatively easy to set up a real micro-brewery. Many free houses have done this, and you can more or less do it in your garden shed. Micro-breweries also have favourable tax treatment. As you will see later, real ale is central to the strategy of one of our case study companies, Greene King.

The Big Six brewers consolidated their dominant market position during the 1970s and 1980s through takeovers. They were also themselves in some cases the victims of takeovers. Watney was taken over by Grand Metropolitan, at the time predominantly a hotels group, but later a component of the wine and spirits conglomerate Diageo, while Courage passed to the Australian brewer Fosters. The third member of the Big Six to be involved in a merger was Allied, which merged with the food group J Lyons to form Allied Lyons.

A major strategic move taken by the major companies was to diversify into other areas of the leisure industry. Bass acquired Holiday Inns, Whitbread acquired Beefeater and Pizza Hut, and S&N acquired Pontins Holidays and later Center Parcs.

The overall structure of the industry was analysed by the Monopolies and Mergers Commission in 1989. It identified over 200 brewing companies, classified as:

- Six national brewers (Allied, Bass, Courage, Grand Met, S&N and Whitbread). They had 75 per cent of UK beer production, 74 per cent of the brewer-owned retail estate (pubs), and 86 per cent of loan ties.

- Eleven regional brewers, including Greene King. They had 11 per cent of beer production, 15 per cent of the brewer-owned retail estate and 8 per cent of loan ties.

- Forty-one local brewers. They had 6 per cent of beer production, 10 per cent of the tied estate and 4 per cent of loan ties.

- Three brewers without tied estate (Carlsberg, Guinness and Northern Clubs Federation). They had 8 per cent of beer production, and 1 per cent of loan ties.

- 160 other brewers, mainly very small and local, with less than 1 per cent of beer production.

One key trend of the 1980s and 1990s was the growing internationalisation and homogenisation of the drinks industry. Throughout Europe, including the United Kingdom, the trend was towards lighter drinks, including lager rather than ale, light spirits like Malibu and Baileys rather than traditional spirits like gin or rum, wine, fruit juices, mineral water and colas.

Pubs became less of a male beer-drinking stronghold. More pub drinking was done by women, who were more likely to drink lighter, less alcoholic drinks, and pubs became more of a family place to eat as well as to drink, although to some extent this trend was inhibited in the United Kingdom by the restrictive licensing laws. These in theory prohibited children under the age of 14 from entering bars. Increasingly the traditional pub was replaced by theme pubs (Irish-style bars, etc) and pub-restaurants.

An impact of the recessions at the beginning of the 1980s and 1990s was to encourage a trend towards drinking at home, rather than in pubs. This was assisted by a trend towards canned lagers rather than bottled beers, increasingly sold through supermarkets, usually at a price considerably below that charged in pubs.

The on-trade was also hit by demographic trends. The key pub drinking segment is the 18–25 age group, but from a peak of 23 per cent of the adult population in the early 1980s, this age group fell to a trough of 14 per cent in 1995.

The Monopolies and Mergers Commission Report of 1989 and the Beer Orders

In 1987, the Office of Fair Trading referred the brewing industry to the Monopolies and Mergers Commission (MMC) for investigation as a potential complex monopoly. This was legally possible although the biggest firm in the industry, Bass, only had a 22 per cent share of the market, below the single firm monopoly threshold of 25 per cent. Of particular concern was the way in which the price of beer was rising more rapidly than the general rate of inflation, and the potentially anti-competitive effects of the tied house system. The MMC carried out a painstaking investigation of the industry, and reported in 1989.

The MMC found that a complex monopoly did indeed exist, and that it acted against the public interest in three main ways:

- prices had been rising too rapidly

- consumer choice was restricted because one brewer usually did not allow another brewer's beer to be sold in its pubs

- the tenant's bargaining position was critically weaker than the landlord's (the brewer's).

The MMC's particular concern was with the Big Six national brewers, and their recommendations were mainly aimed at this group. After negotiation these recommendations became the Beer Orders.

The Beer Orders specified that:

- No brewer should own more than 2,000 pubs, plus 50 per cent of the excess number owned over 2,000. This meant that the Big Six brewers had to dispose of 11,000 pubs. None of the regional brewers owned more than 2,000 pubs.

- Tenants of pubs owned by brewers with more than 2,000 pubs (but not managers) were to be allowed to stock a 'guest' beer (a beer brewed by a third party).

- The loan tie was to be abolished.

The clear intention was that competition in the industry should be increased considerably, by limiting the impact of the tied-house system, and by opening up opportunities for smaller brewers to get a foothold in the tied houses through the guest beer concept. The hope was that many, if not most, of the pubs sold by the Big Six would be sold to their tenants, and become free houses. Events were to show, however, that the brewers were ingenious in circumventing the spirit of the Beer Orders, while obeying its letter.

Trends in the industry since 1989

Production and consumption in the United Kingdom has continued to decline since 1989. In the 1990s, overall sales fell by 9 per cent, with sales of real ale falling by 7 per cent in 2002 alone, although they picked up again in 2003. Two major factors influencing the level of sales are the weather, with the hot summer of 2003 boosting sales, and major sporting events, particularly the football World Cup. Within this overall declining market, the trend towards lager has continued, with the biggest growth coming in imported premium continental lager. The share of lager in the market is now around 70 per cent.

When interviewed by the BBC in 2004, Steve Cahillane, the CEO of Interbrew UK and Ireland, saw the future hope of beer in heavy promotion of the company's continental premium lagers, including Stella Artois, Hoegarten and Leffe, each with its own designer glass (BBC 2004). Little hope for traditional English beer there!

The trend towards a growth in the off-trade at the expense of the on-trade (pubs and clubs) has continued. The off-trade grew from 20 per cent in 1989 to around a third in 2000, and 40 per cent by 2006. This trend has been assisted by technological developments which have enabled canned beer to be served with a head similar to that of draught beer – the so-called 'widget', a miniature nitrogen gas cartridge built into the can. The purchasing power of the big supermarkets is as significant in beer as in other grocery products. It was reported in the summer of 1993 that Tesco was able to import Stella Artois lager from Belgium at a price which undercut Whitbread, then the UK distributor, by 25 per cent. The supermarkets also followed an aggressive pricing policy on beer, which saw its store price halve between 1998 and 2002. This policy was financed by a cut in the price paid to the brewers, described by S&N as 'a blood bath'.

A further trend has come about as a result of the introduction of the European Single Market in January 1993. UK residents can now import alcoholic drinks from EU countries without limit, as long duty has been paid on the article in an EU country, and it is to be consumed by the importer him or herself. Importing for resale is a criminal offence, but very difficult to prove. The result has been a stream of vans coming back from Calais full of beer and other drinks, because the duty on beer in France is about a seventh of that in the United Kingdom. Estimates vary of the size of the cross-Channel trade, but it could be up to the equivalent of a million barrels a year, or around 3 per cent of the UK market, equivalent to the output of a medium-sized brewery.

Licensing laws are being liberalised. Already all-day opening is possible, between the hours of 11 am and 11 pm. A children's certificate scheme, allowing under-14s to be admitted, came into force in January 1995. The Licensing Act of 2003 allows pubs to alter their opening hours to suit local demand. This means that some pubs choose to operate on a 24-hour basis.

The reaction of the brewing industry to the Beer Orders and other changes in the environment has been a massive restructuring. This started in October 1990 with a merger of the brewing interests of Courage and Grand Metropolitan. Under the deal, Courage acquired Grand Met's breweries, which it had originally obtained when it took over Watneys, and Grand Met ceased brewing entirely. In return Courage and Grand Met set up a joint company called Inntrepreneur, managed by Grand Met, which took over nearly all Courage's pubs and many of Grand Met's. This was the first appearance of the phenomenon which was to dominate the industry, the giant pubco, a company that ran pubs but did not brew.

In January 1993 came the launch of Carlsberg-Tetley, a joint venture of Allied Lyons, the European seventh biggest brewer, and the Danish company Carlsberg, the European number three. Carlsberg already brewed lager in the United Kingdom, and because it had no tied estate, had built up its strength in the off-trade. Allied was strong on the on-trade, but weak on the off-trade. The deal was investigated and cleared by the MMC. Allied Lyons then merged with the wine and spirits company Domecq, and became Allied Domecq. The new company took the strategic decision to pull out of brewing. In 1996, Bass tried to acquire Allied's interest in Carlsberg-Tetley, but was blocked by the MMC. Carlsberg then bought out the Allied interest, but maintained the Carlsberg-Tetley name. Its Tetley Bitter is the best-selling cask ale in the United Kingdom.

Bass, the market leader, pursued a consolidation strategy, rationalising its production by closing three of its 12 breweries. The company sold 2,700 pubs to comply with the Beer Orders, many of them to new pubcos which agreed to take their beer from Bass. Whitbread, the long-standing number three in the industry, steadily lost ground, and fell to number five. In 1995, S&N acquired Courage, immediately taking it to number one in the market.

By the late 1990s, the Big Six had shrunk to four – Bass, S&N, Carlsberg-Tetley and Whitbread. They were soon to shrink further when in quick succession the Belgian brewer Interbrew, maker of Stella Artois, acquired the brewing interests of first Whitbread and then Bass.

In addition, S&N moved into a leading position in Europe with the acquisition of Brasseries Kronenbourg, the number one beer brand in France, from the French food conglomerate Danone. Interbrew was then forced to sell off many of the brewing interests it had acquired from Bass. These were purchased by the American number two, Molson Coors. The American number one, and the biggest brewer in the world, Anheuser-Busch, brews a small amount of Budweiser in the United Kingdom, but is not a leading player in the UK market. The series of mergers resulted in a market dominated by S&N, InBev (formed by the merger of Interbrew and the Brazilian company AmBev in 2004) and Molson Coors. S&N had a UK market share of 27 per cent in 2006, Molson Coors 20 per cent, and InBev 19 per cent. Bass renamed itself Six Continents, and later demerged into two companies, Intercontinental Hotels, which concentrated on hotels, and Mitchells & Butlers, a pubco, while Whitbread concentrated on its restaurant and leisure businesses (see Whitbread case study).

In 2006, the overall beer market was worth £15.9 billion. This represented a growth of around 1 per cent by value in 2006, but a fall in volume of 0.2 per cent. This very slow volume decline is expected to continue. Premium lager made up 42 per cent of the market by value, with ales, stouts and bitters a further 31 per cent, and standard lager 26 per cent. The United Kingdom is the biggest beer consumer in Europe, with 24 per cent of the European market by value, followed by Germany with 23 per cent.

Of the 60,000 surviving pubs in the United Kingdom, 17,000 are free houses, over 10,000 are owned by brewers, while over 30,000 are owned by pubcos. The first pubco, Inntrepreneur, was bought by the Japanese bank Nomura, and eventually sold to the market leader, Enterprise, which now has 9,000 pubs. The Punch group now operates 8,300 pubs after its takeover of Pubmaster's 3,100 pubs in 2003, and Innspired's 1,000 pubs in 2004. Both Enterprise and Punch are thought to be aiming for 10,000 pubs. Mitchells & Butlers owns over 2,000. The biggest of the old-style integrated brewing and pub-owning companies is Greene King, which owns 2,100 pubs (see Greene King case study).

There is of course no limit under the Beer Orders on the number of pubs which a pubco can own, and the Beer Orders themselves were abolished in 2002 (*Publican* 2002). The news was condemned by CAMRA, which saw it as restricting market opportunities for small brewers, but welcomed by Greene King, the only brewer which was anywhere near being forced to divest pubs under the Orders.

The tied house system had returned with a vengeance, with the difference that rather than being forced to buy their beer from the brewers, tenants were forced to buy from the pubcos. This led to a parliamentary enquiry in 2004 by the Commons Trade and Industry Select Committee, but John Vickers, chairman of the Office of Fair Trading, in evidence to the committee, said that he saw 'nothing intrinsically problematic' in the beer tie, and that he felt there were 'no competition or consumer law issues'.

The total turnover of the pub sector is around £14 billion (2002 figures). Of this around £8 billion is beer, £3 billion other alcohol, and £2.5 billion food. The proportion of food in total takings is rising steadily. About 85 per cent of the population visit a pub at least occasionally, but a third of all sales are to 18–25 year olds. This age group is declining as a proportion of the population. Other long-term trends include:

- The decline of the hard-drinking, teenage

orientated pub chains which were popular in the 1980s, and a movement towards pub-restaurants which are more popular with women and families.

- The decline of the theme pubs (Irish, etc) popular in the 1990s.

- Pubs as a venue to watch big-screen sporting events.

- The impact of the ban on smoking in public places, introduced in England in 2007. Rather as expected, the initial impact seems to have been negative but at the same time seasonal. Beer sales in August 2007, immediately after the ban, were down by 2.5 per cent, but this had increased to 9.7 per cent by November. Clearly smokers are much more prepared to go into the beer garden for a cigarette in the summer than in the winter (Bowers 2008). Many pubs, of course, will have made up for a decline in beer sales with a growth in food sales.

- The growth in wine drinking. In 2004 a BBC *Money Programme* on beer carried out some informal market research, which involved showing people in the street a picture of a pint of beer or a glass of wine and asking their reactions. Reactions to beer included 'binge drinking', 'aggressive', 'old fashioned', 'Northerners' and 'old men', while to wine they were 'business lunches', 'delicious', 'genteel' and 'sophisticated'. This is of course not scientific evidence, as we do not know how the tape was edited, but it might be interesting to carry out a similar experiment with your own friends and relatives.

ACTIVITY

11.1 THE BEER INDUSTRY

Carry out a STEEPLE analysis on the beer industry, analysing key drivers of change, and identifying opportunities and threats facing the industry.

CASE STUDY 11.2

SCOTTISH & NEWCASTLE PLC

Introduction and history

The William Younger Brewery was established in Leith, Scotland in 1749, while the Newcastle Breweries were set up in 1890. The two merged to form Scottish & Newcastle in 1960. In 1995, S&N acquired the brewing interests of Courage, and become the leading brewer in the United Kingdom. In 2000, it acquired Brasseries Kronenbourg and Alken Maes of Belgium from Danone, thereby becoming number two in Europe, just behind Heineken. Also in 2000 it started disposal of its retail estate, a total of 2,700 pubs, restaurants, bars, hotels and nightclubs, a process which was completed in 2003.

Business activities

S&N is a specialist beer brewer, with few other interests. Through a 50:50 joint venture with Carlsberg, Baltic Brewery Holdings (BBH), it has a leading position in the former Soviet Union, a rapidly growing market for beer. S&N sees its future as a leading European brand, although it also has major interests in India and China. Europe is the world's leading market with one third of global volumes, home to five of the world's 10 biggest brewers, and generates 40 per cent of the industry's world profits. The European market is forecast to grow at 2 per cent per annum (volume) and 5 per cent per annum (profit) over the next decade.

S&N is number one in three of Europe's top six national markets – the United Kingdom, France and Russia – and is also number one in Estonia, Latvia and Lithuania, and number two in Belgium, Portugal, Greece, Finland and the Ukraine. It has three of the top 10 European brands – Fosters, Kronenbourg and Baltika.

Financial performance

The company recorded revenues of £3,328 million during the fiscal year ended December 2006, an increase of 2.1 per cent over 2005. The operating profit of the company was £266 million during fiscal year 2006, a decrease of 11.3 per cent over 2005. The net profit was £303 million in fiscal year 2006, an increase of 22.2 per cent over 2005.

Scottish & Newcastle generates revenues through three business divisions: UK (44.9 per cent of the total revenues during fiscal year 2006), International (37.7 per cent), BBH (17.4 per cent).

In 2006, the United Kingdom accounted for 45 per cent of total revenue. UK turnover was up by 5.3 per cent over 2006. The company has lost market share in the United Kingdom. Its UK market share has fallen from over 30 per cent to 27 per cent. It has closed two of its major breweries, the Fountains brewery in Edinburgh and the Newcastle brewery. The International division recorded revenues of £1,567 million in fiscal year 2006, an increase of 1 per cent over 2005, while the BBH division recorded revenues of £724 million in fiscal year 2006, an increase of 19.9 per cent over 2005, and 17 per cent of turnover (Datamonitor 2007c).

Strategic objectives

The company has four strategic objectives:

- brands and innovation
- operational efficiency and driving down costs
- organisational capability
- investing for growth in existing and new markets.

Stakeholders

S&N is proud of its employee communications programme. This includes presentations from the chief executive and dialogue with staff across the group, to put across the message that change today ensures a long-term, successful sustainable future for S&N. New targets have been established with support from all levels of staff.

During 2004, a Technical Safety Group developed a long-term strategy for safety management across the group, with the aim of securing 'incremental improvement through behavioural change'.

The group is aware of the harm done to individuals and society by irresponsible drinking, and through consultation with pressure groups, politicians and other interested parties, has developed a Responsible Marketing Strategy.

The group is also committed to sustainable development and is working on the delivery of a group-wide environmental strategy which will involve the sharing of best practice.

Stop press: On 26 January 2008, the S&N board reluctantly recommended a £7.8 billion takeover bid from Heineken, under which Carlsberg gained BBH and Heineken acquired all S&N's other assets (Wiggins 2008).

ACTIVITY

11.2 SCOTTISH & NEWCASTLE

Carry out a SWOT analysis of Scottish & Newcastle.

GREENE KING PLC

Introduction and history

Benjamin Greene set up Greene's brewery in Bury St Edmunds, Suffolk, still the company's headquarters, in 1799. The company expanded rapidly in East Anglia during the nineteenth century. In 1868, Frederick King set up a rival brewery in Bury St Edmunds to compete with Greene's. This proved difficult, and the two companies merged to form Greene, King and Sons in 1887. The new company quickly established a regional reputation for the quality of its beer.

By the time of the Beer Orders in 1989, Greene King was one of the leading regional brewers, with over 900 pubs, well below the limit at which it would have to dispose of pubs. Since 1989 it has acquired two other regional brewers, Ruddles and Morland, and also several pub chains. As a result of these acquisitions, by 2004 it was the biggest of the regional companies, a super-regional, with 2,100 pubs, and 11.4 per cent of the national on-trade real ale market, as well as 14.1 per cent of the premium bottled ale off-trade. In June 2005, Greene King acquired the 73 pubs of Essex-based TJ Ridley & Sons. Two months later, the company agreed to acquire Belhaven, an independent Scotland-based brewer, for £187 million. In 2006 it acquired Hardys & Hansons plc, a leading integrated pub company and brewer concentrated in the Midlands, bringing a further 83 managed and 185 tenanted/leased pubs. In August 2007 Greene King took over the upmarket seafood restaurant chain Loch Fyne for £68 million. Loch Fyne's outlets are much more profitable than the average Greene King pub, at £278,000 compared with £177,000 (CAMRA 2007).

Business activities

Before its takeover of Laurel Inns in the summer of 2004, Greene King had 601 managed pubs, including the Hungry Horse branded chain, and 1,090 tenanted and leased pubs, designed to be traditional in style and aimed at the more affluent segments of the population. It is also popular in the free house segment of the market. The leading brands are Greene Abbot and IPA, Ruddles County and Old Speckled Hen. Volume sales of all its leading brands are growing at a time of general decline in the real ale market.

Financial performance (£ million)

	2002–3	2005–6
Turnover	536	818
Operating profit	103	191

Seventy-eight per cent of the company's beer sales are external (ie not to the group's own pubs).

Strategic objectives

The strategy is to operate three focused, different but closely related divisions in the drinks and leisure sector – brewing, managed pubs and tenanted pubs. Each runs semi-autonomously, and is not excessively dependent on the others. However, the company does achieve synergy benefits through the close links between the three divisions.

Overall strategy is to differentiate the company from its competitors through:

- concentrating on those market sectors where competition is less intense, barriers to entry are high, and returns more stable

- focusing on traditional drinks and pubs

- developing brands which can stand alone without excessive levels of marketing.

Stakeholders

The company is proud of its relationships with its tenants and licensees. In a national poll of licensees, it came first in each of the last two years in answers to the question 'How would you rate your pub company or brewer as a fair business partner?'

Many of the 650 brewery workers are fourth or fifth-generation Greene King employees, and Greene King is still seen as a family company in Bury St Edmunds, where it is one of the biggest employers.

However, when the new managing director of the brewing company, Rooney Anand, arrived in 2001, he found a company which was over-focused on production, with a very traditional approach to management. Considerable effort has since been put into standardising quality, a difficult task for a real ale brewer, as the product is still live and maturing when it leaves the brewery. It is the first regional brewer to gain the ISO 9001:2000 quality standard across the whole company. He has also introduced the concept of a beer specially designed to be drunk with food – the 'beer to dine for'.

More than 500 of the brewing staff have completed tasting courses, which not only boosts quality but gives them a sense of ownership for the product. Training extends to delivery staff and publicans, and Greene King is the only brewer to paste handling instructions on every cask. This new emphasis on quality helped Greene King to win second place in the Champion Beer of Britain competition organised by CAMRA in 2004 with its IPA brand.

ACTIVITY

11.3 GREENE KING

Carry out a SWOT analysis of Greene King.

JD WETHERSPOON PLC

CASE STUDY 11.4

Introduction and history

JD Wetherspoon was founded in 1979 when a 24-year-old law student Tim Martin acquired his first pub in North London, mainly because he did not like the local pubs. His strategy was to offer a range of real ales and value for money. This strategy proved successful, and the company went public in 1994, with Martin, now chairman, retaining a significant shareholding. The company has continued to grow and now owns 657 pubs throughout the United Kingdom.

Business activities

The core business of J D Wetherspoon is pub operation. Company policy is to manage rather than tenant pubs, thereby retaining total control. The pubs are larger than average, and the company specialises in converting unconventional sites – churches, post offices, banks – into pubs. All the pubs offer low prices, and all-day food, a non-smoking area (offered before the ban on smoking came into effect) and no television or music (except for major sporting events in a few pubs). Approximately three-quarters of turnover comes from bar sales, and one-quarter from food. The company also operates a chain of bars, Lloyd No 1, which is aimed at the young cocktail-drinking market, and JD Wetherspoon Lodges, a chain of budget hotels.

Financial performance (£ million)

	2002–3	2003–4	2005–6
Turnover	731	787	847
Operating profit	75	78	83

Although operating profits were slightly up in 2003–4, this was more than offset by a considerable increase in interest payable, leading to a fall in profits before exceptional items and taxation from £56.2 million to £54.0 million. Operating margins fell slightly from 10.3 to 9.9 per cent, and fell again to 7.9 per cent in 2004–5, before recovering to 9.9 per cent in 2005–6. Operating profit dipped significantly in 2004–5 to £64 million, probably because this year did not include a major televised football event.

Strategic objectives

The strategy of the company is to operate large, low-price pubs, which appeal to the whole family. Further growth is planned, to a maximum of about 1,200 outlets. This is to be achieved through organic growth rather than takeovers, although in the three years from 2004 a net total of only 17 new pubs were opened.

Stakeholders

Tim Martin has firm views on what his customers want – low prices, food constantly available, no music, normally no television, and no smoking. He called for a total ban on smoking in pubs, although he said it would be 'commercial suicide' for Wetherspoons to bring in its own blanket unilateral ban. Nine pubs were converted to non-smoking in 2005–6, and the group was therefore better placed than most for the national ban on smoking in public places introduced in 2007. The company has strong views on responsible drinking, and feels that its policy on food inhibits binge drinking.

Martin has also criticised the general attitude to staff in the hospitality industry, which he regards as 'stone age'. The company has an extensive programme for training pub managers, including in some cases sponsoring them through university. It insists that all managers work no more than a 48-hour week, and all pub managers must ensure that all staff receive two consecutive days off a week and work no more than four late nights in each week. There is a bonus scheme for all staff.

 ACTIVITY

11.4 JD WETHERSPOON
Carry out a SWOT analysis of JD Wetherspoon

 WHITBREAD PLC

CASE STUDY 11.5

Introduction and history

In 1742 Samuel Whitbread set up his first brewery in London. His company expanded steadily throughout the nineteenth century, pioneering bottled beer and branded beer. It went public in 1948. During the 1950s and 1960s it followed a strategy of takeovers of small regional brewers, and it was also a pioneer of lager, acquiring the licences to brew Heineken and Stella Artois. It also diversified, into wines and spirits in the 1970s and 1980s (sold to Allied Lyons in 1989), and into restaurants, setting up

Beefeater, and forming Pizza Hut as a joint venture with PepsiCo. In 1995 it purchased Costa Coffee, and in 1996 the Pelican Group (Café Rouge) and BrightReasons (Bella Pasta).

Other diversifications were into hotels, with the acquisition of 16 Marriott hotels, and a licence to develop the Marriott brand in the United Kingdom. The group also operated Swallow Hotels, and the budget chain Travel Inn. The final prong of diversification was into leisure clubs, with the acquisition in 1996 of the David Lloyd leisure business, the leading operator of health and fitness clubs.

All this diversification left the company as a rather sprawling conglomerate, and the beer business was somewhat neglected. As a result, Whitbread's share of the UK beer market fell steadily, and in 2000 the decision was taken to exit from brewing, with the sale of the brewing company to Interbrew. Pubs and bars followed in 2001. The group has completed the transition from one of the UK's oldest brewers to a leisure conglomerate.

Business activities

Whitbread operates in three main areas. In 2004, hotels contributed 50 per cent of the company's profits. Marriott is now the second-largest four-star hotel business in the United Kingdom, with 62 hotels and 10,000 bedrooms. In October 2004 the company sold a number of its Marriott hotels, but with a 'manage-back' agreement, whereby Whitbread would continue to operate the hotels. This released £800 million, part to be returned to shareholders, part to reduce debt, and part to boost the pension fund. At the same time the company sold its chain of three-star Marriott Courtyard hotels. In 2005 it sold its interest in Marriott to Royal Bank of Scotland, in order to concentrate on Premier Travel Inn, its budget hotel chain, which has 31,000 bedrooms and 430 outlets, making it the biggest hotel chain in the United Kingdom, twice the size of its nearest rival, Travelodge. In 2006 it signed an agreement with Emirates Group to develop Premier Travel Inns in the Gulf region.

The company's pub restaurant brands include Beefeater, with 187 outlets, which unveiled new formats in 2003, the pub restaurant chain Brewers' Fayre, with 246 outlets, aimed at relaxed family eating in an individual setting, and Brewsters, with 149 outlets, aimed at young families with children. However in October 2004 the company decided to abandon the Brewsters concept, and to convert the outlets to Brewers' Fayre, as the emphasis on children had put off adult diners. TGI Fridays, the US-style fast food chain, has 41 outlets, and again updated its image in 2003. Pizza Hut has 578 units, and offers a home delivery as well as an eat-in service. Costa Coffee has 346 outlets, has developed in-store outlets with major names such as Waitrose, Ottakar's and Waterstone's, and plans to increase the number of outlets to 500. Bella Pasta and Café Rouge were sold in 2001.

In July 2006 the company agreed to sell 239 of its freestanding pub restaurant sites (the Disposal Estate) to Mitchells & Butlers for £497 million. In the same month, the company signed an agreement to sell its 50 per cent shareholding in Pizza Hut UK to Yum! Restaurants Holdings.

David Lloyds Leisure is the brand leader in sports and leisure clubs, with 375,000 members, and about a 10 per cent share of the market. The total market is estimated to grow by 50 per cent by 2007.

Financial performance (£ million)

	2002–3	2005–6
Turnover	1788	1692
Operating profit	270	214
Earnings per share (pence)	52	56

In the six months to September 2004, the restaurant division saw comparative sales growth of only 0.7 per cent, while profits there dropped 9.2 per cent.

Strategic objectives

Whitbread's vision is 'to create leisure and hospitality experiences that make people feel better – every time they visit us'. The aim is to grow the business and deliver value to shareholders. The strategy has four elements:

- operate in markets with high growth potential

- be the market leader in these markets

- organic growth

- targets of 5 per cent like-for-like sales growth, double-digit profit growth and 1 per cent improvement in return on capital employed each year.

Stakeholders

Whitbread has a high reputation for the quality of its HR. It has won many training awards, and is involved in a Modern Apprenticeship scheme for chefs. In 2004, Travel Inn was placed 72nd in a list of the 100 best UK companies to work for. The Whitbread HR director is a member of the main board. The company aims to become the employer of choice in the UK leisure industry.

Its website sets out its people management philosophy, which is to treat people according to three basic principles:

- it cares for them

- it makes clear what is required from them

- it treats people as individuals.

All employees receive a copy of the company's comprehensive code of ethics, which is also available on the company website. The company has an extensive community involvement programme, with the overall aim of 'helping young people achieve their potential'.

 ACTIVITY

11.5 WHITBREAD

Carry out a SWOT analysis of Whitbread.

STRATEGY IN THE BEER INDUSTRY

The beer case studies illustrate a number of different approaches to strategy. The Beer Orders forced strategic change on the industry, as the old model of large brewers with large tied estates was no longer legally possible.

For S&N, a change of strategy was essential. At the time of the Beer Orders, it was a large brewer, although not the market leader, and its tied estate, and most of its beer market, were concentrated in Scotland and the North of England. It had two strategic imperatives: to cope with the Beer Orders, and to break out of its regional market and develop nationally. The strategy chosen was that of market leadership, achieved through the takeover of Courage. This gave it national coverage, while the takeover of Kronenbourg gave it international coverage. As the market leader, it enjoyed economies of scale and could pursue a low-cost, efficiency strategy. It also pursued an aggressive programme of overseas expansion, especially through its share in the BBH joint venture. It reasoned that the beer industry was increasingly being globalised, and that it would not be viable in the long term as a purely UK producer.

Under the Beer Orders, leadership in brewing necessitated a drastic cut-back in pub holdings, and it was logical for S&N to sell off the whole of its retail estate. It could have kept a small retail state, but this would not have added to its strategic profile.

Greene King was in a very different position. As a medium-sized regional brewer, it had no chance of competing on cost with the market leaders. Some regional brewers decided to follow the pubco strategy, and abandoned brewing. In most cases this was a mistake, as they were quickly gobbled up by the much bigger specialist pubcos (Gibbs Mew, Boddingtons, Morrells). Greene King opted for focused differentiation, building up both its real-ale portfolio and its traditional-style pub estate, with the aim in each case of offering a premium-quality product. This strategy had the great merit that it involved differentiation into niches which were of no interest to the big brewers and pubcos, but which were potentially very profitable.

In many ways JD Wetherspoon pursued a very similar strategy, focused differentiation. Its chosen niche was large, low-price but quality pubs, building on the quirky personality of its chairman Tim Martin, the Richard Branson of beer. By opting for organic growth it avoided entering into expensive pub auctions with the big pubcos. To date the strategy has been a successful one, but it may now be reaching its limits. Its rate of growth has slowed considerably since 2003, and it has suffered increasing problems with rising costs, which have squeezed its operating margins. The company may be increasingly vulnerable to takeover.

Whitbread is different again. In the 1990s it was a big brewer with a big pub estate, but in neither case was its position dominant. As number three or four, it was very vulnerable to being squeezed by the more efficient, low-cost market leaders. It opted for a radical strategy of diversification away from beer and into the general leisure industry. This enabled it to achieve two strategic objectives: a move into a growth rather than a gently declining industry, and the opportunity to become the market leader in its chosen segments.

Again the strategy has been successful, but it does have weaknesses. The most important is that its three-pronged portfolio, of hotels, restaurants and leisure centres, is probably at least one prong too many. Conglomerates are out of fashion, and the stock market is all in favour of focus. The sale of Marriott and the concentration on the mid market Premier Travel range may lessen this problem, but Whitbread still gives the impression of a company that does not really know where it is going.

Bibliography

CHAPTER 1

ANSOFF, I. (1987) *Corporate strategy*. London: Penguin.

BBC2 (2007) *Working Lunch: Independent cost*, 18 June.

CLOVER, C. (2003) Members 'suspect voting system in National Trust'. *Daily Telegraph*, 24 April.

DAILY MAIL (2007) Internet kills the video store. 4 May.

DAILY TELEGRAPH (2006) 2600 travel jobs axed as consumers book flights on Internet. 16 December.

EDGECLIFFE-JOHNSON, A. (2006) How upstarts continue to upset. *Financial Times*, 15 August.

FINANCIAL TIMES (2007) Video rentals. 8 January.

FIRST CHOICE (2007) Website: www.firstchoiceholidaysplc.com [accessed 3 August 1997].

GIMENEZ, F. (1999) Miles and Snow's strategy model in the context of small firms. Online version available at; www.baer.uca.edu/research/icbs/1999 [accessed 7 September 2007].

HATCH, M. J. (1997) *Organisation theory: modern symbolic and postmodern perspectives*. Oxford: Oxford University Press.

HF HOLIDAYS (2007) Website: www.hfholidays.co.uk [accessed 14 July 2007].

HOLIDAYBREAK (2007) Website: www.holidaybreak.co.uk [accessed 14 July 2007].

HOULDER, V. (2003) Dark cloud of suspicion hangs over National Trust. *Financial Times*, 26 April.

JOHNSON, G., SCHOLES, K. and WHITTINGTON, R. (2004) *Exploring corporate strategy*, 7th edn. Harlow: Financial Times/Prentice Hall.

JOYCE, P. and WOODS, A. (1996) *Essential strategic management: from modernism to pragmatism*. Oxford: Butterworth-Heinemann.

KEYNOTE (2006) *Activity holidays*. Report, February.

LEGG, R. (2005) Breach of trust. *Guardian*, 14 September.

MARKETING (2004) Trouble strikes the travel agent. 23 June.

MILES, R. E. and SNOW, C. C. (1978) *Organizational strategy, structure and process*. Maidenhead: McGraw-Hill.

NATHAN, M. (2000) The paradoxical nature of crisis. *Review of Business*, Vol. 21, Issue 3.4.

NATIONAL TRUST. (2006) *Annual report and financial statements 2005–6*.

PAGE, R. (2005) The sorry tale of Peter Rabbit. *Daily Mail*, 14 October.

PAYNE, S. (2005) Dog owners savage the National Trust. *Daily Telegraph*, 5 December.

PENG, M. W., TAN, J. and TONG, T. W. (2004) Ownership types and strategic groups in emerging economies. *Journal of Management Studies*, Vol. 41, Issue 7, November.

PORTER, M. E. (1980) *Competitive strategy*. New York: Free Press.

PROBY, W. (2005) Out of the country house and into the back to back. *Guardian,* 15 September.

RAMBLERS HOLIDAYS. (2007) Website: www.ramblersholidays.co.uk [accessed 14 July 2007].

SCHWARTZ, P. (2003) *Inevitable surprises: think ahead in times of turbulence.* New York: Gotham Books.

SHORTELL, S. M. and ZAJAC, E. (1990) Perceptual and archival measures of Miles and Snow's strategic types: the role of strategic orientation. *Academy of Management Journal,* Vol. 33, Issue 4, December.

THOMPSON, J. with MARTIN, F. (2005) *Strategic management: awareness and change.* London: Thomson.

TRAVEL WEEKLY. (2004) Waymark still clients' choice. 3 January.

VIDAL, J. (2007) Broader horizons. *Guardian,* 25 July.

WALLOP, H. (2007) Retail video rental chain in liquidation. *Daily Telegraph,* 7 April.

WEIHRICH, H. (1982) The TOWS matrix: a tool for situational analysis. *Journal of Long Range Planning*, Vol. 15, Issue 2.

CHAPTER 2

AKERLOF, G. (1970) The market for lemons: quality uncertainty and the market mechanism. *Quarterly Journal of Economics*, Vol. 84, August.

ALDEN, E. (2006) Former Fed chief warns on oil supply. *Financial Times,* 8 June.

BUCHAN, J. (2006) Oil – we're all addicted. *New Statesman,* 17 July.

BUSINESS MONITOR. (1992) PA1002. Report of the Census of Production, London: Central Statistic Office.

CHOMKA, S. (2006) The season to be generous. *Grocer,* 7 October.

COHEN, N. (1993) Thurrock, Essex, USA. *Independent on Sunday*, 31 October.

COMPETITION COMMISSION. (2007) *Groceries market investigation: emerging thinking.* 23 January.

CROOKS, E. (2006) Oil price rides to economic rescue. *Financial Times,* 27 September.

DOWNES, L. (1997) Technosynthesis: beyond Porter. *Context.* Online version available at: www.contextmag.com/archives/199712/technosynthesis.asp [accessed 8 September 2007].

EAGLESHAM, J. (2004) OFT plans probe of superstore practices. *Financial Times,* 28 June.

EASYJET. (2007) Website: www.easyjet.com [accessed June–July 2007].

ECONOMIST. (2005) *The Big Easy.* 31 May.

FINANCIAL TIMES. (2007) Leader: Unconventional oil. 22 February.

FINANCIAL TIMES. (2006) Leader: Oil pressure puts heat on the economy. 26 August.

FINCH, J. (2004) Tesco takes more business off rivals. *Guardian,* 26 August.

FINCH, J. (2007) Supermarkets wage Easter egg price war. *Guardian*, 5 April.

GHOSHAL, S. (2000) Value creation. *Executive Excellence*, Vol. 17, Issue 11, November.

GILLAN, A. (2001) US air crews bitter at 'downsizing'. *Guardian*, 3 October.

HARPER, K. (2000) Bob Ayling's fall from grace. *Guardian,* 23 May.

HISCOTT, G. (2004) Big chains strengthen hold on Britain's shoppers. *Independent*, 10 August.

HODGKIN, P. (2007) Gift rap. *Guardian*, 5 September.

HOYOS, C. (2006) Opec vows to defend minimum $60 for oil. *Financial Times*, 20 October.

JOYCE, P. and WOODS, A. (1996) *Essential strategic management: from modernism to pragmatism.* Oxford: Butterworth-Heinemann.

KAY, J. (2003) *The truth about markets.* London: Allen Lane/Penguin Press.

KIM, C. and MAUBORGNE, R. (2001) How to earn commitment. *Financial Times*, 22 October.

LAWTON, A. and ROSE, A. (1994) *Organisation and management in the public sector*, 2nd edn. London: Pitman.

LIPSEY, R. and CHRYSTAL, A. (1999) *Principles of economics,* 9th edn. Oxford: Oxford University Press.

LYNCH, R. (2006) *Corporate strategy*, 4th edn. Harlow: FT Prentice Hall.

MCAFEE, R. and TE VELDE, V. (2005) *Dynamic pricing in the airline industry.* California Institute of Technology. Online version available at: www.caltech.edu/mcafee [accessed 11 July 2007].

MCKILLOP, A. (2004a) *Oil price trends through 2004–2010.* Online version available at: www.feasta.org/documents/energy/oilpricetrends [accessed 8 August 2007].

MCKILLOP, A. (2004b) *Oil demand – why so strong?* Online version available at: www.oilcrash.com/articles/mckill-4 [accessed 8 August 2007].

MARKETING. (2006) Seasonal chocolate – quantity makes way for quality. 20 December.

MORTISHED, C. (2003) Private cars fuel oil imports. *The Times,* 12 April.

PATON, N. (2002) Store wars. *Personnel Today,* 12 March.

PORTER, M. (1980) *Competitive strategy: techniques for analyzing indistries and competition*. London: Macmillan.

PURVIS, A. (2004) Why supermarkets are getting richer and richer. *Observer*, 25 June.

SCHUMPETER, J .(1950) *Capitalism, socialism and democracy*, 3rd edn. New York: Harper & Row.

WALKER, R. (1990) Analysing the business portfolio in Black and Decker Europe. In B. Taylor and J. Harrison, *The manager's casebook of business strategy.* Oxford: Butterworth-Heinemann.

WALSH, F. (2006) Chocolate eggs: ethical shoppers storm the shelves for natural and Fairtrade products. *Guardian,* 15 April.

WARD, L. (2001) Charities warn Blair about 'cheap service'. *Guardian,* 22 October.

WEAVER, M. (2001) Labour chooses third way to improve failing services. *Guardian*, 22 October.

WEISS, R. and MEHROTRA, A. (2001) Dynamic pricing and the future of e-commerce; an economic and legal analysis. *Virginia Journal of Law and Technology*, Vol. 11, Summer.

WHEATCROFT, P. (2004) Supermarkets take a convenient route. *The Times,* 17 August.

WINTOUR, P. (2004a) Unions win 'two-tier' victory. *Guardian,* 16 July.

WINTOUR, P. (2004b) Unions bury hatchet with Labour. *Guardian,* 26 July.

CHAPTER 3

ACTIONAID (2006) *Confronting the contradictions: time for action on education*. London.

AISBETT, E. (2003) Globalization, poverty and inequality: are the criticisms vague, vested or valid? NBER Pre-conference on Globalization, Poverty and Inequality, October.

AKCAPAR, B. and CHAIBI, D. (2006) Turkey EU accession: the long road from Ankara to Brussels. *Yale Journal of International Affairs*, Winter–Spring.

BARRELL, R., GUILLEMINEAU, C. and LIADZE, I. (2006) Migration in Europe. *National Institute Economic Review*, No. 198, pp36–39. October.

BOONE, P. (2005) Effective intervention: making aid work. *CentrePiece,* Winter.

BBC. (nd) Born abroad, immigration map of the UK. Online: www.news.bbc.co.uk [accessed 17 April 2007].

BBC. (2005a) BBC news website: www.news.bbc.co.uk [accessed 24 April 2007].

BBC. (2005b) Q&A: Common Agricultural Policy. BBC news website, 2 February: www.news.bbc.co.uk [accessed 30 April 2007].

BBC. (2007) At-a-glance: EU treaty proposals. BBC news website, 23 June: www.news.bbc.co.uk [accessed 24 June 2007].

CIA. (2007) *CIA World Factbook*. Online version at: https://www.cia.gov/library/publications/the-world-factbook [accessed 18 April 2007].

CIPD. (2006) *Offshoring and the role of HR*. January. London: CIPD.

CHURCH, C. and PHINNEMORE, D. (2007) The rise and fall of the constitutional treaty. In M. Cini (ed), *European Union politics*, 2nd edn. Oxford: Oxford University Press.

CINI, M. (ed) (2007) *European Union politics*, 2nd edn. Oxford: Oxford University Press.

CLARK, R. (2005) *Contemporary strategy analysis,* 5th edn. Oxford: Blackwell.

CLENNELL, A. (2004) Call centre switches jobs back from India to Britain. *Independent*, 23 January.

CRANE, A. and MATTEN, D. (2007) *Business ethics: managing corporate citizenship and sustainability in the age of globalization*, 2nd edn. Oxford: Oxford University Press.

DATAMONITOR. (2006) *Tesco plc company profile*. May.

DE JONQUIERES, H. (2003) How enlightened international co-operation turned into a show case for indecision. *Financial Times*, 31 March.

DOWARD, J. and MCKENNA, H. (2007) Immigration figures 'are false'. *Observer*, 29 April.

ECONOMIST. (2003) The Doha squabble. *Economist* (US), 29 March.

ECONOMIST. (2006a) In the twilight of Doha. *Economist* (US), 29 July.

ECONOMIST. (2006b) Trouble at till. *Economist* (US), 4 November.

ECONOMIST. (2007a) Rebranding Thaksinomics. *Economist* (US), 13 January.

ECONOMIST. (2007b) Home and abroad. *Economist* (US), 10 February.

ELLIOTT, L. (2004). What the WTO needs is a new reformation. *Guardian*, 2 August.

ELLIOTT, L. and CONNOLLY, K. (2007) In 2005, G8 pledged $50bn for Africa. Now the reality. *Guardian*, 25 April.

EMMOTT, B., CROOK, C. and MICKLETHWAIT, J. (2002) *Globalisation: making sense of an integrating world*. London: Economist/Profile Books.

FISCHLER, F. and LAMY, P. (2003) 'Free farm trade means an unfair advantage. *Financial Times*, 1 April.

FLETCHER, R. (2006) Thailand junta warns Tesco over expansion. *Daily Telegraph,* 28 September.

FORTUNE. (2006) *Fortune Global 500 2006*. Online: www.money.cnn.com/magazines/fortune/global 500 [accessed 8 May 2007].

FUKUYAMA, F. (1992) *The end of history and the last man*. New York: Free Press.

FUKUYAMA, F. (2004). Bring back the state. *Observer*, 4 July.

GARVIE, G. (2006) Global sport, myth, reality and issues. Online version available at: www.sports.stir.ac.uk [accessed 18 May 2007].

GHEMAWAT, P. (2003) The forgotten strategy. *Harvard Business Review,* Vol. 81, No. 11, November.

GRAY, J. (1995) *False dawn*. London: Granta, p6.

GUARDIAN. (2004) Leading article: Trade talks: get rid of subsidies now. 21 June.

IGLICKA, K. (2005) *The impact of the EU enlargement on migratory movements in Poland*. Centrum Stosunkow Miedzynarodowych (Center for International Relations, Warsaw), October. Online version available at: www.csm.org.pl [accessed 30 May 2007].

INTERBRAND. (2006) *Interbrand Best Global Brands 2006*. Online version available at: www.interbrand.com [accessed 18 June 2007].

INTERNATIONAL LABOUR REVIEW. (2006) The internationalization of employment: a challenge to fair globalisation? Spring-Summer.

JACOBS, M. (2001) Bridging the global divide. *Observer*, 11 November.

JITPLEECHEEP, S. (2001) Boots expansion is on hold in Thailand; to sell its wares in Tops supermarkets. *Bangkok Post*, 2 August.

JITPLEECHEEP, S. (2002a) Less is more for Boots in Asia. *Bangkok Post*, 8 December.

JITPLEECHEEP, S. (2002b) Boots slimming down. *Bangkok Post*, 6 March.

JITPLEECHEEP, S. (2002c) Superstore: saturation foreseen in big-store sector. *Bangkok Post*, 12 June.

KIRISCI, K. (2007) Turkey in the EU: a win-win scenario. In M. Fraser (ed), *European Union: the next fifty years*. Harlow: FT Business.

LEGRAIN, P. (2003) *Open world: the truth about globalisation*, new edn. London: Abacus.

LOEBIS, L. and SCHMITZ, H. (2003) *Java furniture makers – winners or losers from globalisation?* Institute of Development Studies, September.

LUCAS, C. (2001) Doha spells disaster for development. *Observer,* 18 November.

LUNGESEN, D. (2004) Turkey's unrequited EU love. BBC News website: www.news.bbc.co.uk [accessed 30 June 2007].

MACMULLAN, J. (2004) A sweet deal: sugar in Mozambique. In *Taking liberties: poor people, free trade and trade justice*. London: Christian Aid.

MACSHANE, D. (2006) Immigration: don't close our borders. *Economist* (US), 30 October.

MADELEY, J. (2001). No end to shackles. *Observer*, 21 January.

MATHIASON, N. (2003) Debt duties. *Observer*, 20 April.

MICKLETHWAIT, J. and WOOLDRIDGE, A. (2000) *A future perfect: the challenge and hidden promise of globalization*. London: Heinemann, p7.

MIGRATION WATCH. (2007) *Outline of the problem. 2* January. Online: www.migrationwatch.org.uk [accessed 27 May 2007].

MILLERS, T. (2006) *Sporting globalisation*. ABC Radio Network, Australia, transcript of programme broadcast 7 July Online: www.abc.net.au [accessed 18 May 2007].

MONBIOT, G. (2007) If Britain wants to help Africa's poor, it must stop acting like an emperor. *Guardian*, 17 April.

MORRIS, H. and WILLEY, B. (1996). *The corporate environment*. London: Pitman, pp 197–9.

MULVEY, S. (2004) The EU's eastward drift. BBC News online, 5 March: news.bbc.co.uk [accessed 24 June 2007].

MULVEY, S. (2007) Deal paves way for EU to move on. BBC News online, 23 June: news.bbc.co.uk [accessed 24 June 2007].

NUGENT, N. (2006) *The government and politics of the European Union*, 6th edn. Basingstoke: Palgrave Macmillan.

OHMAE, K. (1990) *The borderless world*. Glasgow: Collins.

PHILPOTT, J. and DAVIES, G. (2006) No turning back? *People Management*, 14 September.

PHILPOTT, J. (2007) Britain's eastern European migrant workforce, *Impact*, Issue 19, May.

RYLE, S. (2002) Banana war leaves the Caribbean a casualty. *Observer*, 24 November.

SASSEN, S. (2001) A message from the global south. *Guardian*, 12 September.

SEAGER, A. (2007) Court cuts vulture fund's claim. *Guardian*, 25 April.

SCHOLTE, J. A. (2000) *Globalization: a critical introduction*. Basingstoke: Palgrave.

SEGAL-HORN, S. (2002) Global firms – heroes or villains? How and why companies globalise'. *European Business Journal*, Vol. 14, Issue 1.

SHAH, S. (2004) 'India 'losing ground to UK in battle of the call centres'. *Independent*, 10 April.

SIEMENS. (2007) Website: www.siemens.com

SIMPSON, D. and WOODLEY, T. (2007) Organisation and solidarity across frontiers are the future. *Guardian*, 1 May.

SPENCER, S., RUHS, M., ANDERSON, B. and ROGALY, B. (2007) *Migrants' lives beyond the workplace: the experiences of Central and East Europeans in the UK*. York: Joseph Rowntree Foundation.

STEWART, H. (2002) Africa reinforces debt relief case. *Guardian*, 2 September.

STIGLITZ, J. (2003) *Globalization and its discontents*, new edn. London: Penguin.

SWANN, C. (2004) Sixty years on, and still contentious. *Financial Times*, 29 May.

SWYNGEDOUW E. (2004) Globalisation or glocalisation? Networks, territories and rescaling. *Cambridge Review of International Affairs*, Vol. 17, No. 1, April.

TESCO LOTUS. (2007) *Tesco Lotus key facts*, February 2007. Online: www.tescolotus.net/company/keyfacts.asp [accessed 27 April 2007].

THUROW, L. (1999) *Creating wealth*. London: Nicholas Brealey, p xv.

TISDALL, S. (2007) Confident Turkey looks east, not west. *Guardian*, 26 March.

TRANSPARENCY INTERNATIONAL. (2006) Corruption Perceptions Index. Online: www.transparency.org/policy_research [accessed 30 April 2007].

UNITED NATIONS CONFERENCE ON TRADE AND DEVELOPMENT (UNCTAD). (2001) *World investment report*. New York and Geneva: United Nations.

UNITED NATIONS DEVELOPMENT PROGRAMME (UNDP). (2006) *Human development report.* New York: Oxford University Press.

VENABLES, T. (2005) Multinationals: heroes or villains of the global economy? *CentrePiece*, Spring.

WARREN, E. (2007) Stars of India. *People Management*, 22 February.

WILLIAMS, F. (2001) Global foreign investment flows 'set to fall to 40%'. *Financial Times*, 19 September.

WOLF, M. (2005) *Why globalization works.* New Haven: Yale Nota Bene.

WOODS, N. (2000) *The political economy of globalisation.* Basingstoke: Macmillan, pp3–7.

WOODS, N. (2007) *Power shift: do we need better global economic institutions?* Institute of Public Policy Research, January.

CHAPTER 4

ARTICLE 13 and CBI (2007) *Dwr Cymru Welsh Water.* CBI-CSR Case Studies, September.

ASSOCIATION OF BRITISH DRIVERS. (nd) *The con charge.* Online: www.abd.org.uk/london_congestion_charge [accessed 17 June 2007].

BANK OF ENGLAND. (2003) *Remit for the Monetary Policy Committee of the Bank of England and the New Inflation Target.* Online: www.bankofengland.co.uk [accessed 8 July 2007].

BANK OF ENGLAND. (2004a) *The labour market.* Online: www.bankof england.co.uk/targettwopointzero [accessed 30 October 2004].

BANK OF ENGLAND. (2004b) How do interest rates affect inflation? Online: www.bankof england.co.uk/targettwopointzero [accessed 30 October 2004].

BANK OF ENGLAND. (2007a) *Treasury Committee Inquiry into the Monetary Policy Committee of the Bank of England: ten years on. The Bank of England's submission regarding the economic context.* Online: www.bankofengland.co.uk [accessed 8 July 2007].

BANK OF ENGLAND. (2007b) Governor's open letter to the Chancellor of the Exchequer, 16 April. Online: www.bankofengland.co.uk [accessed 8 July 2007].

BATTY, D. and WEAVER, M. (2006) Q&A: private finance initiative. *Guardian,* 3 May.

BENATI, L. (2006) UK monetary regimes and stylised macroeconomic facts. Bank of England Working Paper no. 290. Online version available at: www.bankofengland.co.uk [accessed 8 July 2007].

BOYCOTT, O. (2004) Transcript reveals doctor's pleas for dying teenager. *Guardian,* 18 October.

BRINER, R. (2001) Why family-friendly practices can also be performance-friendly. *People Management*, 8 November.

BROWN, K. (2001) Standard that has delivered. *Financial Times,* 30 October.

CAULKIN, S. (2003) Wanted: one kick in the pants. *Observer*, 18 May.

CARVEL, J. (2003) Blair puts NHS out to tender. *Guardian*, 14 May.

DANESHKHU, S. (2007a) The quest for improved productivity. *Financial Times*, 22 May.

DANESHKHU, S. (2007b) Output still trails other large countries. *Financial Times*, 26 June.

DAVIES, M. (2004) Troubled waters? The economic implications of higher oil prices. *HSBC Economic Review*, Issue 33, July.

DE GRAUWE, P. (2001) Competitiveness and compassion. *Financial Times*, 8 November.

DEPARTMENT OF TRADE AND INDUSTRY. (1998) *Building the knowledge driven economy.* Online: www.dti.gov.uk/competitive [accessed 29 August 2004].

DEPARTMENT OF TRADE AND INDUSTRY. (2001) *Opportunity for all in a world of change.* Online: www.dti.gov.uk/opportunity for all [accessed 28 August 2004].

DONE, K. (2001) UK sector to gain expertise. *Financial Times,* 11 May.

DONE, K. (2002) MPs attack failure to test air traffic financial model. *Financial Times,* 19 November.

DONE, K. (2006) Nats records second profit. *Financial Times,* 1 July.

ECONOMIST. (2005a) From Lisbon to Brussels. 19 March.

ECONOMIST. (2005b) Jam yesterday. 11 June.

ECONOMIST. (2006a) Britain isn't moving. 2 December.

ECONOMIST. (2006b) Running out of road. 2 December.

ECONOMIST. (2007) A capital idea, 24 February

ELLIOTT, L. (2004) The outlook is not so nice when hidden hazards are exposed. *Guardian,* 18 October.

EUROPEAN CENTRAL BANK (ECB). (2004) *Objective of monetary policy.* Online: www.ecb.int [accessed 18 September 2004].

EUROPEAN UNION. (2004) *European performance in competitiveness and innovation.* Online: www.europa.eu.int [accessed 18 September 2004].

FARNHAM, D. (1999) *Managing in a business context.* London: CIPD.

FEDERAL RESERVE. (2004) *Frequently asked questions: monetary policy.* Online: www.federalreserve.gov [accessed   ].

FORMAN, F. N. and BALDWIN, N. D. J. (1999) *Mastering British politics,* 4th edn. Basingstoke: Macmillan.

GILES, C. (2007) Productivity loses steam under Labour. *Financial Times,* 23 January.

GLAISTER, D. (2007) New York to follow London's example with congestion charge. *Guardian,* 23 April.

GOYAL, A. and JHA, A. (2004) Dictatorship, democracy and institutions: macro policy in China and India. *Economic and Political Weekly (India),* 16 October.

GRAYLING, T. (2000) Winging it. *Guardian,* 16 November.

GROCER. (2004) One year on, blow from Ken's charge revealed. 24 February.

GUARDIAN. (2003a) Duisenberg decorated but still dithering. 10 May.

GUARDIAN. (2003b) Leading article: Accountability vacuum. 3 May.

HALL, S. and HENRY, S. (2006) An independent Bank of England: is that enough? *National Institute Economic Review,* April.

HELLOWELL, M. (2006) Alive and kicking. *Public Finance,* 17 November.

HENCKE, D. (2004) Big players lobbying for piece of the action. *Guardian,* 27 October.

HENCKE, D. (2007) Tories call for auditor to investigate PPP after Metronet collapse. *Guardian,* 20 July.

HM TREASURY. (2006) *PFI: strengthening long-term partnerships.* HM Treasury, May.

HM TREASURY. (2007) Chancellor of the Exchequer's reply to the Governor of the Bank of England. 17 April. Online: hm-treasury.gov.uk [accessed 8 July 2007].

HILTON, I. (2004) A rampaging market, but a long way from global power. *Guardian*, 13 November.

HIRST, J. (2005) The awkward age. *Public Finance*, 14 January.

HUTTON, W. (2004) We must dare to be dynamic. *Observer*, 7 November.

HUTTON, W. (2007) *The writing on the wall*. London: Little Brown.

IPPR. (2001) *Building better partnerships*. Institute for Public Policy Research, June.

JOHN LEWIS PARTNERSHIP. (2007) *John Lewis gazette*, 23 February Online: johnlewispartnership.com [accessed 17 June 2007].

KAY, J. (2002) The balance sheet. *Prospect*, July.

KAY, J. (2003) *The truth about markets – their genius, their limits, their follies*. London: Allen Lane.

KEEGAN, W. (2001) The high cost of falling prices. *Guardian*, 14 November.

KEEGAN, W. (2004a) Erm, there's a danger in paradise. *Observer*, 17 October

KEEGAN, W. (2004b) Keeping an eye on the competition. *Observer*, 31 October.

KING, M. (2007) The MPC ten years on: a speech to the Society of Business Economists, 2 May. Online: www.bankofengland.co.uk [accessed 18 July 2007].

LENNAN, D. (2001) Cartel crooks belong in jail. *Financial Times*, 2 November.

LIPSEY, R. G. and CHRYSTAL, K. A. (1999) *Principles of economics*, 9th edn. Oxford: Oxford University Press.

MALTBY, P. (2003) *Public interest companies: fad or permanent fixture?* Institute for Public Policy Research.

MATHIASON, N. (2004) Casino bill derailed by bitter split in Cabinet. *Observer*, 24 October.

MAYOR OF LONDON (2004) *Transport strategy revision document*. London: Mayor's Office.

MCVEIGH, K. (2007) Manchester to charge drivers for travelling at peak times. *Guardian*, 26 May.

MEREDITH, R. (2007) *The elephant and the dragon: the rise of India and China and what it means for all of us*. New York: Norton.

MERRICK, N. (2001) Minority interest. *People Management*, 8 November.

MILMO, D. (2007) Fate of the tube: who pays? *Guardian*, 17 July.

MILNE, S. (2000) Stuck down the tube. *Guardian*, 15 November.

MULVEY, S. (2003) The EU law that rules our lives. BBC News Online: www.news.bbc.co.uk [accessed 18 October 2004].

NELSON, P. (2001) Does IIP still make the grade? *Personnel Today*, 13 November.

NEW STATESMAN. (2005) Addressing the car pandemic.13 June.

OSBORN, A. (2003) State's golden share in BAA is illegal. *Guardian*, 14 May.

PALMÅS, K. (2005) *The UK public interest company: the idea, its origins, and its relevance for Sweden*. CbiS discussion paper 1, Göteborg University, Sweden.

PHILPOTT, J. (2002) Productivity and people management. *CIPDPerspectives*, Spring.

PHILPOTT, J. (2003) Europe. *CIPD Perspectives*, Summer.

PORTER, M. and KETELS, C. (2003) *UK competitiveness: moving to the next stage.* DTI Economics Paper No. 3, DTI/ESRC, May,

SEARJEANT, G. (2007) Bank Governor hits back at criticism over inflation. *The Times*, 25 April.

SMITH, D. (2007a) We still have a grip on inflation, says Bank. *Sunday Times*, 22 April.

SMITH, D. (2007b) *The dragon and the elephant: China, India and the new world order.* London: Profile.

STEELE, J. (2001) Food for thought: Amartya Sen. *Guardian,* 31 March.

WARD, S. (2000) Brown to gamble on 'spend more' call. *Guardian*, 10 November.

WARNER, J. (2003) Network Rail spends away, but is it really value for money? *Independent*, 8 May.

WARNER, J. (2007) Governor's letter should not be seen as a non-event. Rather, it highlights policy failings. *Independent*, 18 April.

WILEMAN, A. (2007) India rising. *Management Today*, July.

WOLMAR, C. (2007) Congestion cowardice and the capital. *New Statesman,* 5 March.

WOODWARD, W. (2003) School firms' forte is 'lobbying for work'. *Guardian,* 5 May.

WORLD BANK. (2000) Beyond economic growth: meeting the challenges of global development. Online version available at: www.worldbank/depweb/beyond/global./chapter4

WRIGHT, R. (2007a) Cost rises in the first three years. *Financial Times*, 16 July.

WRIGHT, R. (2007b) Working relationship proved dear. *Financial Times*, 18 July.

CHAPTER 5

CARTWRIGHT, S. and COOPER, S. (1997) *Managing workplace stress.* London: Sage.

CURWEN, P. (1997) *Restructuring telecommunications: a study of Europe in a global context.* Basingstoke: Macmillan.

EARNSHAW, J. and COOPER, C. (1996) *Stress and employer liability.* London: IPD.

ELECTRICITY ASSOCIATION. (1998) *Electricity industry review.* London: HMSO.

FREIDMAN, M. (1970) *The counter-revolution in monetary theory.* New York: Institute of Economic Affairs.

HEALTH AND SAFETY EXECUTIVE (HSE). (2006) *2005/6 Survey of self-reported work-related illnesses.*

HEALTH AND SAFETY EXECUTIVE (HSE). (2008) Website: www.hse.gov.uk/statistics (accessed February 2008).

IRS (2002) Court of Appeal guidelines for stress at work cases. *Employment Law Review*, 748, 25 March.

MARTIN, S. and PARKER, D. (1997) *The impact of privatisation: ownership and corporate performance in the UK.* London: Routledge.

MILLER, S. (1999) Council pays £67,000 for stress injury. *Guardian*, 6 July, p4.

PALMER, B. and QUINN, P. (2004) Protracted agony. *People Management,* 6 May, p17.

POLLACK, C. (1997) European Union policies. In I. Lewington (ed), *Utility regulation 1997.* London: Centre for the Study of Regulated Industries and Privatisation International.

RICK, J., MORRIS, S., ATKINSON, J. and WILLIAMS, M. (1997) *Stress: big issue, but what are the problems?* Institute of Employment Studies Report 311, July.

TEHRANI, N. (2002) *Managing organisational stress: a CIPD guide to improving and maintaining well-being*. London: CIPD.

WAINWRIGHT, M. (1994) Mistakes led to chemical plant deaths. *Guardian*, 21 June, p8.

WATKINS, J. (2003) Wellness beats output slump. *People Management*, 18 December, p12.

YARKER, J. and LEWIS, R. (2007) *Management competencies for preventing and reducing stress at work*. London: HSE.

CHAPTER 6

BAIRD, R. (2001) Britain's immigrants overstep line as numbers surge to 135,000 a year. Daily *Express*, 16 November.

BARTLETT, H. and PEEL, N. (2005) Healthy ageing in the community. In G. Andrews and D. Phillips (eds), *Ageing and place*. London: Routledge.

BLANCHFLOWER, D., SALAHEEN, J. and SHADFORTH, C. (2007) The impact of the recent migration from Eastern Europe on the UK Economy. Bank of England Working Paper.

BRINDLE, D. (1999) Northerners heed south's siren call. *Guardian*, 27 August, p3.

BUSINESS WEEK. (2004) America's Bebe boom. 15 March, pp50–52.

CHAMPION, A. (1993) *Population matters: the local dimension*. London: Paul Chapman.

CHARTERED INSTITUTE OF PERSONNEL AND DEVELOPMENT (CIPD). (2007) *Age and recruitment*. London: CIPD.

CIPD/KPMG (2005) *Quarterly labour market outlook, summer/autumn survey*.

CHIU, W., CHAN, A., SNAPE, E. and REDMAN, T. (2001) Age stereotypes and discriminatory attitudes towards older workers: an East-West comparison. *Human Relations*, Vol. 54, No. 5, pp629–661.

DICKEN, P. (2003) *Global shift*. London: Sage.

DOWARD, J. (2003) Future imperfect as longer lifespan looms. *Observer*, 28 December, p9.

ECONOMIST. (2004) Return of the wrinklies, 17 January, p24.

ECONOMIST. (2006) Now we are 300,000,000. 14 October, pp57–58.

ECONOMIST. (2007a) From cheque books to checking pulses. 14 April, p85.

ECONOMIST (2007b). 26 July, p24.

HASKEY, J. (1993) Trends in the number of one-parent families in Great Britain. *Population Trends*, No. 71, pp26–33.

HOME OFFICE. (2007) *Accession monitoring report*. February.

ITEM CLUB. (2006) *Spring forecast*. London: Ernst & Young.

JACKSON, S. (1998) *Britain's population*. London: Routledge.

KYSER, J. (2007) 60 million Californians by mid-century. *Los Angeles Times*, 10 July.

KURTZ, S. (2004) The end of marriage in Scandinavia, *Weekly Standard*, pp9, 20.

LUCAS, E. (2006) Red fades to grey. *Economist*, 27 May, p46.

MARTIN, P. and WIDGREN, J. (1996) International migration: a global challenge, *Population Bulletin*, 51.

MASSEY, D. (1984) *Spatial divisions of labour: social structures and the geography of production*. Basingstoke: Macmillan.

MCCRONE, A. (1999) The pounds and pence of an ageing Britain. *Business Day*, 21 September.

MCSMITH, A. (2007) Figures show number of eastern Europeans in Britain exaggerated. *Independent*, 20 January, p24.

MULLAN, P. (2002) *The imaginary time bomb*. London: Tauris.

NATIONAL STATISTICAL OFFICE. (2007) Website: www.statistics.gov.uk [accessed 26 October 2007].

NICHIPORUK, B. (2000) *The security dynamics of demographic factors.* Cape Town: Rand Publishing.

NORTON, C. (2002) Japan bribes mothers in bid for baby boom. *Sunday Times,* 15 September.

OFFICE FOR NATIONAL STATISTICS (ONS). (2006a) Office for National Statistics.

ONS. (2006b) *Social trends*. London: HMSO.

ONS. (2006c) *Labour market trends*, December, ppS32–33

ONS. (2007) Office for National Statistics.

PEARCE, F. (2002) We need more babies. *Sunday Times*, 17 March.

PERSAUD, J. (2004) Carry on working. *People Management*, 29 July, pp36–37.

PHILPOTT, J. (2007) Britain's Eastern European migrant workforce. *Impact*, No. 19, May, pp24–27.

POLSKA. (2006) Economic Ministry, Poland. Website: www.poland.gov.pl [accessed 12 November 2006].

ROBERTS, I. (2006) Taking age out of the workforce. *Work, Employment and Society,* Vol. 20, No. 1, pp67–86.

SALT, J. (2006) *Current trends in internal migration in Europe.* Migrant Research Unit, University College London.

SMALLWOOD, C. (2003) People power rings changes. *Sunday Times*, 10 August.

SMALLWOOD, C. (2006) 'Reserve army' can defuse demographic time bomb. *Sunday Times*, 20 August.

SMEDLEY, T. (2008) And now for the good news. *People Management*, 6 March, pp. 25–30.

SUNDAY TIMES (2007) Russians told: have a baby and win a fridge. 19 August, p23.

STILLWELL, J., REES, P. and BODEN, P. (1992) *Migration processes and patterns*, Vol. 2: *Population redistribution in the UK*. London: Belhaven.

TARVER, J. (1996) *The demography of Africa*. Cape Town: Praegar Publishing.

UNITED NATIONS. (2005) *Report on world fertility rates at 2003*. New York: United Nations.

UNITED NATIONS. (2006) *World population prospects*. New York: Department of Economics and Social Affairs.

WALLACE, P. (1999) *Agequake*. London: Nicholas Brealey.

WOODHEAD, M. (2004) Exodus heralds end of Schoder's IT dream. *Sunday Times*, 28 March.

WORONOFF, T. (1996) *Japan as anything but Number 1*. Basingstoke: Macmillan.

CHAPTER 7

ABERCROMBIE, N. and WARDE, A. (2000) *Contemporary British society*, 3rd edn. Cambridge: Polity Press.

ADAMSON, L. (2001) It's time to clock off. *Guardian*, 1 December

ALDRIDGE, S. (2001) *Social mobility: a discussion paper.* London: Cabinet Office, Performance and Innovation Unit.

ALDRIDGE, S. (2004) *Life chances and social mobility: an overview of the evidence.* London: Cabinet Office, Prime Minister's Strategy Unit.

ANDERSON, T. and METCALFE, H. (2003) *Diversity: stacking up the evidence.* London: CIPD.

ATKINSON, J. (1984) Manpower strategies for the flexible organisation. *Personnel Management,* August.

BARBER, B. (1998) Speech to the New Labour and the Labour Movement conference, 19/20 June.

BARNARD, H. and GOULDEN, C. (2006) *What will it take to end child poverty? Firing on all cylinders.* York: Joseph Rowntree Foundation.

BILTON, T., BONNETT, K., JONES, P., SKINNER, D., STANWORTH, M. and WEBSTER, A. (1996) *Introductory sociology*, 3rd edn. Basingstoke: Macmillan.

BLANDEN, J. and GIBBONS, S. (2006) Cycles of disadvantage. *CentrePiece*, Summer.

BLANDEN, J., GREGG, P. and MACHIN, S. (2005) Social mobility in Britain: low and falling. *CentrePiece*, Spring.

BRINER, R. 2001, 'Why family-friendly practices can also be performance-friendly. *People Management*, 8 November.

BRINER, R. and CONWAY, N. (2001) Promises, promises. *People Management*, 25 November.

CARVEL, J. (2003) Marriage and family divorced as 41% of children reared in alternative ways. *Guardian*, 8 May.

CARVEL, J. (2007) The figure that shows it pays to be a man. *Guardian*, 5 September.

CHARTERED INSTITUTE OF PERSONNEL AND DEVELOPMENT (CIPD). (2003a) Factsheet: *Managing the psychological contract.* London: CIPD, May.

CIPD. (2003b) Factsheet: *Work–life balance.* London: CIPD, April.

CIPD. (2004a) Trade union learning representatives. *The Change Agenda,* London: CIPD.

CIPD. (2004b) Frequently asked questions: *Parental rights and other family-friendly provisions.* London: CIPD.

CIPD. (2005) *Managing change: the role of the psychological contract.* London: CIPD, November.

CHARTERED MANAGEMENT INSTITUTE (CMI). (2006) *National Management Salary Survey 2005.* Corby: CMI.

CMI. (2007) *National Management Salary Survey 2006.* Corby: CMI.

CLARK, D. (2004) Unto him that hath. *Guardian*, 6 August.

CLEMENT, B. (2001) Honda workers vote for union recognition. *Independent*, 11 December.

COWAN, R. (2004) Met harnesses its diversity in the war against crime. *Guardian*, 2 December.

DORLING, D., RIGBY, J., WHEELER, B., BALLAS, D., THOMAS, B., FAHMY, E., GORDON, D. and

LUPTON, R. (2007) *Poverty, wealth and place in Britain 1968 to 2005.* Policy Press for Joseph Rowntree Foundation.

DUNCAN, G. (2001) Pay of business chiefs soars. *The Times,* 26 July.

FIELDING, T. (1995) Migration and middle class formation in England and Wales 1981–91. In T. Butler and M. Savage (eds), *Social change and the middle classes.* London: UCL Press.

FURLONG, A. and CARTMEL, F. (2001) 'Capitalism without classes. In A. Giddens (ed), *Sociology: introductory readings*, rev. edn. Cambridge: Polity.

GALL, G. (2001) ISTC wins in recognition vote. *People Management,* 22 November.

GALLIE, D. (2000) The labour force. In A. Halsey and J. Webb (eds), *Twentieth century British social trends.* Basingstoke: Macmillan.

GEORGE, V. and WILDING, P. (1999) *British society and social welfare: towards a sustainable society.* Basingstoke: Macmillan.

GIDDENS, A, (2006) *Sociology*, 5th edn. Cambridge: Polity.

GOLDTHORPE, J. (1968–9) *The affluent worker in the class structure*, 3 vols. Cambridge: CUP.

GREEN, A. (2003) Labour market trends, skill needs and the ageing of the workforce: a challenge for employability? *Local Economy*, November.

GUEST, D. and CONWAY, N. (2002) *Pressure at work and the psychological contract.* London: CIPD.

HANDY, C. (1991) *Inside organisations: 21 ideas for managers.* London: BBC Books.

HARLOW DISTRICT COUNCIL. (1993) *Harlow 2000 initiative.*

HARLOW DISTRICT COUNCIL. (2002) *Harlow baseline study 2002.*

HARLOW RENAISSANCE (2007) *Harlow Renaissance Business Plan 2007–2009.*

INSTITUTE FOR SOCIAL AND ECONOMIC RESEARCH (ISER) (2002) Class matters. *ISER Newsletter*, October.

KANDOLA, R. and FULLERTON, J. (1994) *Managing the mosaic.* London: IPD.

KIMBERLY, J. and CRAIG, E. (2001) Work as a life experience. *Financial Times,* 5 November.

MARCHINGTON, M. and WILKINSON, A. (2000) *Core personnel and development.* London, CIPD.

MCKNIGHT, A. (2000) *Earnings inequality and earnings mobility 1977–1996: the impact of mobility on long term inequality,* Employment Relations Research Series No. 8. London: DTI.

MERRICK, N. (2001) Minority interest. *People Management*, 8 November.

MILBURN, A. (2004) Inequality, mobility and opportunity: the politics of aspiration, speech to the Institute for Public Policy Research, 9 November.

MILNE, S. (2007) You can't say it's a problem and then do nothing about it. *Guardian,* 16 August.

MOYNAGH, M. and WORSLEY, R. (2001) Prophet sharing. *People Management*, 27 December.

MULHOLLAND, G., ÖZBILGIN, M. and WORMAN, D. (2005) *Managing diversity: linking theory and practice to business performance.* London: CIPD.

MULLINS, L. (1996) *Management and organisational behaviour*, 4th edn. London: Pitman.

OFFICE FOR NATIONAL STATISTICS (ONS). (2003) *A century of labour market change.* London: ONS.

ONS. (2004a) Flexible working 2003. *Social trends* Table 4.18. London: ONS.

ONS. (2004b) Trade union membership 2002. *Social trends* Table 4.25. London: ONS.

ORTON, M. and ROWLINGSON, K. (2007) *Public attitudes to economic inequality.* York: Joseph Rowntree Foundation.

PARKER, M.(2006) Global scramble to jump aboard the bandwagon. *The Times,* 26 April.

PEOPLE MANAGEMENT. (2004) Royal Mail recruits excluded groups. 28 October.

PETERS, T. J. and WATERMAN, R. H. (1982) *In search of excellence: lessons from America's best-run companies.* New York: Harper & Row.

PHILPOTT, J. (2002) HRH – a work audit. *CIPD Perspectives*, Summer.

PROFESSIONAL MANAGER. (2001) Focused females forge ahead. November.

RAKE, K. (ed) (2000) *Women's incomes over the lifetime.* London: HMSO.

ROBERTS, K. (2001) *Class in modern Britain.* Basingstoke: Palgrave.

ROSS, R. and SCHNEIDER, R. (1992) *From equality to diversity – a business case for equal opportunities.* London: Pitman.

ROUSSEAU, D. (2004) Psychological contracts in the workplace: understanding the ties that motivate. *Academy of Management Executive*, Vol. 18, No. 1, February.

RUNCIMAN, W. G. (1990) How many classes are there in contemporary British society? *Sociology*, Vol. 24, No. 2.

SUTTON TRUST. (2007) *The educational backgrounds of 500 leading figures.* Sutton Trust.

TATLI, A., ÖZBILGIN, M., WORMAN, D. and MULHOLLAND, G. (2005) *Managing diversity: measuring success.* London: CIPD.

TAYLOR, W., PIASECKA, A. and WORMAN, D. (2005) *Managing diversity: learning by doing.* London: CIPD.

TOYNBEE, P. (2004) Going nowhere. *Guardian*, 2 April.

TOYNBEE, P. (2007) Babies who need big money and unflagging commitment. *Guardian,* 12 June.

WALSH, J. (2001) A happy reunion. *People Management*, 8 November.

WILSON, R. M. S., GILLIGAN, C. and PEARSON, D. J. (1992) *Strategic marketing management: planning, implementation and control.* Oxford: Butterworth-Heinemann.

YOUNG, M. (1958) *The rise of the meritocracy.* Harmondsworth: Penguin.

CHAPTER 8

ARKIN, A. (2002) The package to India. *People Management*, 24 January, pp34–36.

BUSINESS WEEK. (2004) Wireless, 21 June, pp62–65.

COYLE, D. and QUAH, D. (2004) *Getting the measure of the new economy.* London: Work Foundation.

DICKEN, P. (2003) *Global shift*, 4th edn. London: Sage.

ECONOMIST. (2000) Communication advances. 23 September.

ECONOMIST. (2004) Salad days. 6 November, pp38–39.

ECONOMIST. (2007) Easy on the eyes. 7 April, pp85–86.

ELIAS, P. (2006) Robot birth simulator used in med schools, Associated Press. Online version available at: www.Livescience.com/robots [accessed 24 October 2007].

FLEXIBLE WORKING (2000) Case: teleworking at Baxter International. October, pp11–14.

FREEMAN, C. (1987) *Technology policy and economic performance: lessons from Japan*. London: Pinter.

GLOVER, C. (2004) Tomorrow's world. *People Management*, 26 February, pp40–41.

GREEN, F. (2002) *Why has work effort become more intense? Conjectures and evidence about effort-based technical change and other stories*. University of Kent Discussion Papers in Economics, July.

HALL, P. and PRESTON, P. (1988) *The carrier wave: new information technology and the geography of innovation, 1846–2003*. London: Unwin Hyman.

HANSEN, N., NOHRIA, N. and TIERNEY, T. (1999) What's your strategy for managing knowledge? *Harvard Business Review*, March-April, pp106–116.

JENSEN, R. (2007) The digital provide: information technology, market performance and welfare in the south Indian fisheries sector. *Quarterly Journal of Economics*, August.

KAHN, H. (1967) *The year 2000*. Basingstoke: Macmillan.

MARTIN, G. (2005) *Technology and people management*. London: CIPD.

NATHAN, M.,CARPENTER, G. and ROBERTS, S. (2003) *Getting by, not getting on technology in UK workplaces*. London: Work Foundation.

PARRY, E., TYSON, S., SELBIE, D. and LEIGHTON, R. (2007) *HR and technology: impact and advantages*. London: CIPD.

PEACOCK, L. (2007) Location beats pay as a top factor in attracting people to work in UK call centres. *Personnel Today*, 14 May.

PEOPLE MANAGEMENT. (1998) Telephone screening at Standard Life. 28 May, p11.

PETHOKOUKIS, J. (2004) Meet your new co-worker. M*oney and Business,* 3 July.

PRICEWATERHOUSECOOPERS (2000) *HR in e-commerce survey*. London: PricewaterhouseCoopers.

PRUSACK, L. (1997) *Knowledge in organisations*. London: Butterworth-Heinemann

REDDINGTON, M., WILLIAMSON, M. and WITHERS, M. (2005) *Transforming HR: creating value through people*. Oxford: Elsevier.

REILLY, P. (2000) *HR shared services and the realignment of HR*. Institute of Employment Studies Report 368, IES.

SCARBOROUGH, H. and CARTER, C. (2007) *Investigating knowledge management*. London: CIPD.

SCARBOROUGH, H., SWAN, J. and PRESTON, J. (1999) *Knowledge management and the learning organisation: a review of the literature*. London: CIPD.

SMITH, D. (2004) Prophet warning. *People Management*, 23 December, pp24–29.

SPARROW, P., BREWSTER, C. and HARRIS, H. (2004) *Globalizing human resource management*. London: Routledge.

STEWART, T. (2001) *The wealth of knowledge: intellectual capital in the 21st century organisation*. London: Nicholas Brearley.

STOREY, J. and QUINTAS, P. (2001) Knowledge management and HRM. In J. Storey (ed), *Human resource management: a critical text*. London: Thomson Learning.

STREDWICK, J. and ELLIS, S. (2005) *Flexible working practice*. London: CIPD.

SUBRAMANIAN, S. (2004) Biotechnology and society. Online version available at: www.chennaionline [accessed 24 November 2007].

TAYLOR, R. (2004) *Skills and innovation in modern Britain*. ESRC Future of Work Programme Seminar Series. Economic and Social Research Council.

ULRICH, D. (1998) *Human Resource champions*. Boston, Mass.: Harvard Business School Press.

CHAPTER 9

ASSOCIATION OF BRITISH DRIVERS. (nd) *The con charge*. Online: www.abd.org.uk/london_congestion_charge [accessed 17 July 2007].

ACCOUNTABILITY. (nd) Primer: sustainability. Online: www.accountability.org.uk [accessed 18 August 2007].

ALDRED, J. (2007) Q&A: plastic bags. *Guardian,* 13 November.

ARGENTI, J. (1993) *Your organisation, what is it for? Challenging traditional organizational aims.* Maidenhead: McGraw Hill.

ARTICLE 13 AND CBI (2007) *SABMiller.* CBI case study series, June.

BARKHAM, P. (2007) World asks town that banned the plastic bag: how can we do it too? *Guardian,* 12 May.

BILLINGTON, R. (2003) *Living philosophy: an introduction to moral thought*, 3rd edn, London: Routledge, p19.

BUSINESS IN THE COMMUNITY (BITC) (2000) *Putting your heart into it: purpose and values.* Report of the Business Impact Task Force 2000. Online: www.bitc.org.uk [accessed 27 September 2004].

BITC (2002) *The public's views of corporate responsibility*. Online: www.bitc.org.uk [accessed 27 September 2004].

BITC (2003) *The business case for corporate responsibility.* Online: www.bitc.org.uk [accessed 27 September 2004].

BITC (2004) *Awards for Excellence 2004*. Online: www.bitc.org.uk/resources/case_studies [accessed 27 September 2004].

BRINKMANN, J. and IMS, K. (2003) Good intentions aside: drafting a functionalist look at codes of ethics. *Business Ethics: A European Review*, Vol. 12, No. 3.

BUTLER, S. (2006) Would you like a bag with that, Madam? *The Times*, 7 October.

CARROLL, A. B. (1979) A three dimensional model of corporate social performance. *Academy of Management Review*, 4.

CARROLL, A. B. (1990) Principles of business ethics: their role in decision making and an initial consensus. *Management Review*, Vol. 28, No. 8.

CARROLL, A. B. (1991) The pyramid of corporate social responsibility: towards the moral management of organizational stakeholders. *Business Horizons*, July-August.

CAULKIN, S. (2003) Ethics and profits do mix. *Observer,* 20 April.

CAULKIN, S. (2004) Unacceptable face of regulation. *Observer,* 28 November.

CHARKHAM, J. (1994) *Keeping good company: a study of corporate governance in five countries*. Oxford: Oxford University Press.

CHARTERED INSTITUTE OF PERSONNEL AND DEVELOPMENT (CIPD). (2003a) *Code of professional conduct and disciplinary procedures*. London: CIPD.

CIPD (2003b) *Corporate responsibility and HR's role*. London: CIPD.

COLLINS, C. and PORRAS, J. (2000) *Built to last: successful habits of visionary companies*, 3rd edn. London: Random House.

CONNOCK, S. and JOHNS, T. (1995) *Ethical leadership*. London: CIPD.

COOKE, J. (2007) Green light for long-haul scampi? BBC News, 19 December. Online: www.news.bbc.co.uk [accessed 20 December 2007].

COWE, R. (2004) Commanding heights. *Guardian,* 8 November.

CRANE, A. and MATTEN, D. (2007) *Business ethics: managing corporate citizenship and sustainability in the age of globalisation,* 2nd edn. Oxford: Oxford University Press.

CURTIS, P. (2004) Market graders. *Guardian,* 17 August.

DE GEORGE, R. T. (1999) *Business ethics,* 5th edn. New Jersey: Prentice Hall.

DEAL, T. and KENNEDY, A. (1990) Values; the core of the culture. In A. Campbell and K. Tawadey (eds), *Mission and business philosophy*, Oxford: Butterworth-Heinemann.

DEPARTMENT OF TRADE AND INDUSTRY (DTI) (2002) *Business and society: corporate social responsibility.* London: DTI.

DRUCKER, P. (1990) What is 'business ethics'? In A. Campbell and K. Tawadey (eds), *Mission and business philosophy*, Oxford: Butterworth-Heinemann.

ECONOMIST (US). (2006) Voting with your trolley. 9 December.

ECONOMIST (US). (2007) Plastics of evil. 31 March.

EUROPEAN COMMISSION. (2001) *Promoting a European framework for corporate social responsibility*. Brussels: European Commission.

EXPLORE WORLDWIDE. (2004) 2004–2005 brochure.

FARNHAM, D. (1999) *Managing in a business context*. London: CIPD.

FINCH, J. (2007) Alliance Boots directors will make more than £10 million from sale of company. *Guardian,* 10 May.

FINCH, J. and ALLEN, K. (2006) Tesco offers carrot to reduce use of plastic carrier bags. *Guardian*, 5 August.

FISHER, C .and LOVELL, A. (2006) *Business ethics and values: individual, corporate and international perspectives*, 2nd edn. Harlow: FT/Prentice Hall.

FRIEDMAN, M. (1970) The social responsibility of business is to increase its profits. *New York Times Magazine*, 13 September.

GOLZEN, G. (2001) What's the big idea? *Global HR,* September.

HARRISON, R. (2002) *Learning and development*, 3rd edn. London: CIPD.

HASTINGS, M. (2007) Binge-flying culture is just beginning. *Guardian*. 7 May.

HENCKE, D. and INMAN, P. (2007) Private equity deals threaten capitalism, warns head of TUC. *Guardian*, 23 May.

HENDERSON, D. (2001) *Misguided virtue: false notions of corporate social responsibility*. Institute of Economic Affairs. Online version available at: www.iea.org.uk.

HOFFMAN, M. (1990) What is necessary for corporate moral excellence? In A. Campbell and K. Tawadey (eds), *Mission and business philosophy*, Oxford: Butterworth-Heinemann.

HOFSTEDE, G. (1980) *Culture's consequences: international differences in work-related values*. London: Sage.

HOME OFFICE (1999) *The Stephen Lawrence Inquiry: report of an inquiry by Sir William Macpherson of Cluny*. London: The Stationery Office.

INDUSTRIAL RELATIONS SERVICES (IRS) (1999) *IRS Employment Trends 675*, March.

JOHNSON, G. and SCHOLES, K. (1997) *Exploring corporate strategy*, 4th edn. Hemel Hempstead: Prentice Hall.

JOHNSON, G., SCHOLES, K. and WHITTINGTON, R. (2006) *Exploring corporate strategy*, 7th edn. London: Financial Times/Prentice Hall.

KEARNS, P. and INGATE, K. (2001) Should the CIPD strike off poor practitioners? *Personnel Today*, 23 October.

KELLY, E. (1999) Corporate citizenship costs more than cash. *Professional Manager,* January.

KOLLEWE, J. (2007) Britain's smoking ban sends brewers east as western markets go flat. *Guardian*, 27 June.

LAWTON, A. (1998). *Ethical management for the public services*. Buckingham: Open University Press.

LEWIS, J. (2002) Testing time. *Personnel Today*, 9 April.

MAHONY, C. (2007) Under new ownership. *People Management,* 12 July.

MAITLAND, A. (2003) Profits from the righteous path. *Financial Times*, 3 April.

MATHIASON, N. (2007) Private equity comes clean. *Observer,* 6 May.

MATHIASON, N. and STEWART, H. (2007) No firm is safe from private equity. *Observer*, 20 May.

MCKEE, G. (2003) Managing human nature: leadership lessons from Venice. *Leader to Leader*, April.

MILNER, M. (2007) Private equity is the workers' friend, CBI told. *Guardian*, 27 November.

MONBIOT, G. (2001) Superstores brand us to ensure we belong to them. *Guardian*, 31 July.

MURRAY, S. (2006) Confusion reigns over labelling. *Financial Times*, 13 June.

PERSONNEL TODAY. (2004) CSR help is at hand. 27 July.

PLENDER, J. (2007) Private equity cannot escape the public eye. *Financial Times,* 24 April.

PROSSER, D. (2007) Fairtrade is booming – but it is still a fair deal. *The Independent*, 24 February.

REITZ, J., WALL, J. and LOVE, M. S. (1998) Ethics in negotiation: oil and water or good lubrication? *Business Horizons*, May-June.

RICHARDS, D. and GLADWIN, T. (1999) Sustainability metrics for the business enterprise. *Environmental Quality Management*, Spring.

SCHWARTZ, M. S. (2001) A code of ethics for corporate codes of ethics. *Journal of Business Ethics,* 41.

SNELL, R. (1999) Managing ethically. In L. Fulop and S. Linstead (eds), *Management: a critical text*. Basingstoke: Macmillan.

TAIT, N. (2003) A line between protest and persecution. *Financial Times*, 8 September.

TARGETT, S. (2004). Is good governance good value? *Financial Times*, 17 April.

THORNTON, P. (2007) Inside the dark box: shedding light on private equity. *Work Foundation*, March.

TREANOR, J. (2007) Banks sound alarm over debt-laden buy-out firms. *Guardian*, 6 June.

TURNER, B. (2006) Plastic bags are much the lesser evil. *Grocer*, 11 February.

WELDON, S. (2003) Communicating corporate social responsibility at Go-Ahead. *Strategic Communications Management*, Vol. 7, Issue 3, April-May.

WILLIAMS, R. (2001) Under pressure, under pressure, under pressure. *Business Review*, September.

WINTOUR, P. (2007) Brown sets tough targets for reducing carbon. *Guardian,* 20 November.

CHAPTER 10

AIR TRANSPORT WORLD. (2006a) Ryanair: ryanair.com. July.

AIR TRANSPORT WORLD. (2006b) The world's top 25 airlines. July.

ALBERGE, D. (2007) Independent booksellers are queuing up to buy *Harry Potter* from Tesco. *The Times*, 17 July.

ANSOFF, H. I. (1965) *Corporate strategy.* Harmondsworth: Penguin.

ARMSTRONG, M. (1999) *Managing activities*. London: CIPD.

BAGNALL, S. (1995) Kwik Save slips as price war bites. *The Times*, 3 November.

BATTERSBY, J. (1999) Nelson Mandela's moral legacy. *Christian Science Monitor,* 10 May.

BLOOMSBURY. (2007a) Summary of corporate milestones. Online: www.bloomsbury-ir.co.uk.

BLOOMSBURY. (2007b) Financial results. Online: www.bloomsbury-ir.co.uk [accessed 8 August 2007].

BLOOMSBURY. (2007c) Press release – record breaking first 24 hours of *Harry Potter and the Deathly Hallows*, 23 July. Online: www.bloomsbury-ir.co.uk [accessed 8 August 2007].

BOROUGHS, D. (1999) Proving that one man can make a difference. *US News and World Report*, 24 May.

BOWMAN, C. and FAULKNER, D. (1996) *Competitive and corporate strategy.* Homewood, Ill.: Irwin.

BRIDGES, W. (1995) Breaking with the past. *Human Resources*, September-October.

BRIDGES, W. and BRIDGES, S.M. (2000) Leading transition: a new model for change. *Leader to Leader*, 16, Spring.

BBC2. (2007) *Working lunch*, 19 September.

BRUCE, A. (2001) This M&S is Simply Food. *Grocer*, 21 July.

BRUCE, A. (2003) Simply Food set to grow fast. *Grocer*, 24 May.

BURNES, B. (1996) *Managing change: a strategic approach to organisational dynamics*, 2nd edn. London: Pitman.

BUSINESS WEEK. (2006) Walmart with wings. 27 November.

CADBURY. (2007) Website: www.Cadbury.co.uk [accessed 18 June 2007].

CHARTERED INSTITUTE OF PERSONNEL AND DEVELOPMENT (CIPD). (2004) Factsheet: *Change management*. Online version available at: www.cipd.co.uk [accessed 28 August 2007].

CLARK, R. (2005) *Contemporary strategy analysis,* 5th edn. Oxford: Blackwell.

COLLINSON, P. and SEAGER, A. (2007) Northern Rock crisis: call to City grandees that threw lifeline to drowning bank. *Guardian*, 15 September.

COMPETITION COMMISSION. (2006) *HMV Group plc and Ottakar's plc: proposed acquisition of Ottakar's plc by HMV Group plc through Waterstone's Booksellers Ltd.* May.

COPE, N. (1996) Pile 'em high, sell 'em cheap, take £1bn. *Independent*, 19 August.

COPE, N. (1999) Somerfield back on the discount shelf. *Independent*, 26 July.

CROGGON, P, (2007) Letter to the editor. *The Times*, 17 September.

DAVIES, G, (2007) The roots of moral hazard. *Guardian*, 15 September.

DILBERT [nd] Website: www.dilbert.com [accessed 8 July 2004].

DONE, K. (2007) Ryanair orders 27 Boeing jets. *Financial Times*, 31 May.

DUNCAN, G. and WEBSTER, P. (2007) MPC founding member comes out swinging against Bank's bailout decision. *The Times*, 15 September.

DURSTON, J. (2006) Food sales drive group recovery at upbeat M&S. *Grocer,* 27 May.

ELLIOTT, V. (2007) Cadbury fined £1m for selling contaminated chocolate bars. *The Times*, 17 July.

FENTON, B. (2007) Potter sets another Bloomsbury record. *Financial Times*, 29 June.

FINCH, J. (2000) No one wants to buy Kwik Save. *Guardian*, 19 April.

FINCH, J. (2004) Morrisons' duo determined to deliver. *Guardian*, 8 September.

FINCH, J. (2005) £1.1bn Somerfield takeover agreed. *Guardian,* 15 October.

FINCH, J. (2007) Integration hasn't gone as well as we'd have hoped. *Guardian,* 6 July.

FURNHAM, A. and GUNTER, B. (1993) *Corporate assessment.* London: Routledge.

GILCHRIST, S. (1993a) Supermarkets face cut-price threats. *The Times*, 26 January.

GILCHRIST, S. (1993b) Kwik Save warns price war will hit profit growth. *The Times*, 25 November.

GROCER. (2003) Flexible ranging for Simply Food. 8 November.

GROCER. (2006a) Fitting right in to the locality. 11 February.

GROCER. (2006b) BP trial with M&S said to be driving spend, footfall. 1 April.

GROCER. (2007) Simply Food roars in forecourt drive. 26 May.

HAMEL, G. (1996) Strategy as revolution. *Harvard Business Review*, July-August.

HAMEL, G. and PRAHALAD, C. K. (1994) *Competing for the future.* Boston, Mass.: Harvard Business School Press.

HAMSON, L. (2004). Marks's quality is its key advantage. *Grocer*, 6 November.

HAMSON, L. (2005) Simply ideal food for UK travel hubs. *Grocer,* 30 April.

HUGHES, C. and TIGHE, C. (2007) Impregnable self-belief takes a battering. *Financial Times*, 15 September.

HOLLINGER, P. (1998) Somerfield, Kwik Save hope that size will matter. *Financial Times*, 17 February.

JOHNSON, G., SCHOLES, K. and WHITTINGTON, R. (2004) *Exploring corporate strategy*, 7th edn. Harlow: Pearson.

JORDAN, D. (2007) Time comes for Harry to fly to the rescue, *The Times*, 4 April.

KEYNOTE. (2007) *Market report: bookselling*. London: Keynote.

KOTTER, J. (1995) Leading change – why transformation efforts fail. *Harvard Business Review*, March-April.

LORD, R. (1990) A measure of corporate success. *The Times*, 30 July.

MCCARTHY, B. (2004) How to manage organisational change. *People Management*, 9 December.

MESURE, S. (2004) Morrisons keen to show it hasn't lost its magic touch. *Independent*, 8 September.

MESURE, S. (2007) Bloomsbury looks for new media to replace Potter. *Independent,* 4 April.

MILMO, D. (2007a) After Harry Potter and the prophets of doom. *Guardian,* 30 July.

MILMO, D. (2007b) Ryanair introduces £4 check in fee as latest surcharge to slash costs. *Guardian*, 25 August.

MINTZBERG, H. (1994) *The rise and fall of strategic planning*. Hemel Hempstead, Prentice Hall.

MINTZBERG, H. (1998) Five Ps for strategy. In H. Mintzberg, J. B. Quinn and S.Ghoshal, *The strategy process*, rev. European edn. Hemel Hempstead: Prentice Hall.

PETERS, T. (1985) *Thriving on chaos*. New York: Macmillan.

PETERS, T. and WATERMAN, R. (1982) *In search of excellence*. New York: Harper & Row.

PORTER, M. (1980) *Competitive strategy: techniques for analysing industries and competition*. New York: Free Press.

PORTER M. (1985) *Competitive advantage: creating and sustaining superior performance*. New York: Free Press.

PORTER, M. (1999) *On competition*. New York: Free Press.

PRAHALAD, C. K. and HAMEL, G. (1990) The core competence of the corporation. *Harvard Business Review*, May-June.

QUINN, J. (1980) *Strategies for change: logical incrementalism*. Homewood, Ill.: Irwin.

RIDGEWAY, C. and WALLACE, B. (1994) *Empowering change: the role of people management*. London: IPD.

RIGBY, E. (2006) Somerfield makes a Kwik sale. *Financial Times,* 25 February.

RYANAIR. (2003) Economy and mobility: the Ryanair business model. Online: www.ryanair.com [accessed 18 July 2007].

RYANAIR. (2007) About Ryanair. Online: www.eyanair.com/site/EN/about [accessed 18 July 2007].

SEBAG-MONTEFIORE, H. (1993) Who's who at the Zoo? *Management Today*, July.

SENGE, P. (1990) *The fifth discipline*. London: Century Business.

SHELLEY, T. (2007) Bloomsbury looks for magic after Potter. *Financial Times*, 4 April.

SIVELL, G. and DOLAN, L. (1995) Supermarkets shape up food price fighters. *The Times*, 10 January.

STACEY, R. (1991) *The chaos frontier: creative strategic control for business*. Oxford: Butterworth-Heinemann.

STACEY, R. (1993) *Strategic management and organisational dynamics*. London.

STARMER-SMITH, C. (2006) Disabled groups attack 33p Ryanair levy. *Daily Telegraph*, 13 May.

STEVENSON, H. H. (1989) Defining corporate strengths and weaknesses. In C. Bowman and D. Asch (eds), *Readings in strategic management*. Basingstoke: Macmillan.

STEVENSON, T. (1996) Kwik Save losing the bean war. *Independent*, 3 May.

TAIT, N. and WIGGINS, J. (2007) Cadbury in record £1m fine for unsafe chocolate. *Financial Times*, 17 July.

TEATHER, D. (2007) Model executive puts Hornby back on track. *Guardian*, 21 December.

TEMPUS. (1993) Kwik Save. *The Times*, 30 April.

THOMPSON, J. and MARTIN, F. (2005) *Strategic management: awareness and change*, 5th edn. London: Thomson.

TOMLINSON, H, (2001) Stop me and buy a Ben & Jerry's. *Independent on Sunday*, 9 December.

TOWNSEND, A and WEBB, T, (2004) A City memo to Morrisons: you're not a little firm up north now. *Independent on Sunday*, 12 September.

WALTON, J. (1999) *Strategic human resource development*. London: FT/Prentice Hall.

WATSON, E (2004) Food standalones will continue. *Grocer*, 17 July.

WILLIAMS, R. (2007) Cadbury fined £1m for salmonella offences. *Guardian*, 17 July.

WORKERS' EDUCATIONAL ASSOCIATION (WEA) IN NORTHERN IRELAND. (nd) Mission Statement and WEA Values. Online: www.wea-ni.com [accessed 18 July 2004].

WRAY, R. (2006) Bloomsbury's profits drop without Potter's magic this year. *Guardian*, 12 December.

ZOOLOGICAL SOCIETY OF LONDON. (nd) ZSL mission statement. Online: www.zsl.org [accessed 28 August 2004].

ZOOLOGICAL SOCIETY OF LONDON. (2003) *Annual review*.

CHAPTER 11

BOWERS, S. (2008) Smoking ban hits beer sales. *Guardian*, 4 January.

BBC. (2004) *The Money Programme: The booze business: trouble brewing*. 3 November.

CAMRA. (2007) *Hertfordshire's pints of view*. October/November.

CAULKIN, S. (2003) Brewing up taste for success. *Observer*, 26 October.

GREENE KING PLC. (2004) Report and accounts 2003–2004.

DATAMONITOR (2004a) Greene King company profile, 2004.

DATAMONITOR (2004b) J D Wetherspoon company profile, 2004.

DATAMONITOR (2004c) Scottish & Newcastle company profile, 2004.

DATAMONITOR (2004d) Whitbread company profile, 2004.

DATAMONITOR (2006) Whitbread company profile, 2006.

DATAMONITOR (2007a) Greene King company profile, 2007.

DATAMONITOR (2007b) J D Wetherspoon company profile, 2007.

DATAMONITOR (2007c) Scottish & Newcastle company profile, 2007.

GWYTHER, M. (2001) Whitbread on the wagon. *Management Today*, September.

JACOBS T. and STEELE M. (1997) The European brewing industry. In G. Johnson and K. Scholes (eds), *Exploring corporate strategy: text and cases*, 4th edn. Hemel Hempstead: Prentice Hall.

J D WETHERSPOON. (nd) Website: www.jdwetherspoon.co.uk [accessed 28 September 2007].

JOHN, P. (2004) Tradition that goes back to the mash tun. *Financial Times*, 10 July.

MILLAR, M, (2004) Whitbread gets HR on board to drive agenda. *Personnel Today*, 4 May.

PROTZ, R. (ed) (2004) *Good Beer Guide 2004*. St Albans: CAMRA.

PUBLICAN. (2002) Beer Orders to be revoked. 20 February.

SCOTTISH & NEWCASTLE. (nd) Website: www.scottish-newcastle.com [accessed 28 September 2007].

STEVENSON, R. (2004) S&N cheers end of supermarket bloodbath. *Independent*, 24 June.

WHITBREAD. (nd) Website: www.whitbread.co.uk [accessed 28 September 2007].

WIGGINS, J. (2008) S&N keeps door open for rival bids. *Financial Times*, 26 January.

WRAY, R. (2004) Whitbread seeks £800m in series of sell-offs. *Guardian*, 29 October.

Index

9/11, 77, 94, 111

A
A8 countries, and EU enlargement, 100–1
AA, and private equity, 291–3
activity holidays, 22–4
advertisements, 157
Africa, 186, 189
    family planning programme, 189
    tripling of population, 186
age distribution UK, 198
ageing population, 205
agricultural subsidies, 66–7, 77–8
AIDS, 205
Aisbett, E., 89–90
Akerlof G., 33
Aldridge, S., 244
Alliance Boots plc, and private equity, 291–3
Al-Qaeda, 3, 37
Amazon plc, 328–9
Anglo-Saxon model of corporate
    governance, 290
Ansoff, I., 8
artificial intelligence, 253
ASDA plc, employment of older workers, 206
Asian Tigers, 71, 90
Association of South East Asian Nations
    (ASEAN), 70
asylum seekers, 193
Atkinson, J., 239
atypical employment, 200
Audit Commission, 180

B
BAA plc, 122
balance of payments, 110
bananas, 74–6
    and banana war, 76
    and comparative advantage, 74–5
Bank of England, 112, 116–19, 120
    and 9/11, 120
    and inflation, 117–19
    and Monetary Policy Committee, 117–19
Barroso, J. M. D., 61, 62
Baxter International inc, teleworking, 260
Beacon Press, 305
beer industry, 357–70
    Beer Orders, 360
    pubcos, 362
    and strategy, 369–70
Belarus, 186
Ben & Jerry's, 341
Bentham, J., 275
Bernanke, B., 119
bilateral monopoly, 40
Billington, R., 274–5
biotechnology, 252
birth rate, 187
birth simulator, 256
Blair, T., 127
Bloomsbury Publishing plc, and *Harry
    Potter*, 327
Boston Dynamics plc, 254
Boston Matrix, 45–7
Bowman, C., 337
Brazil, 93, 204
    declining birth rate, 204
    footballers from, 93
Bretton Woods Conference, 70
Bridgend Borough Council, demographics
    case study, 207
British Airways plc, 35, 51
Brown, G., 111, 113, 116, 125, 127, 128–9,
    130, 225
    and competitiveness, 130
    and London Underground, 128–9
    and Metronet, 128–9
    and Monetary Policy Committee, 116
    and National Air Traffic Services, 125
    and privatisation, 125
Bulgaria, 186
Burnes, B., 344, 354

business cycles, 109
Business in the Community, 286, 294–5, 298

C
Cadbury, A., 291
Cadbury report 1992, 291
Cadbury-Schweppes plc, and failure of values, 321–2
Cairns group, 77–8
call centres, 81, 95, 97
    and India, 97
    and offshoring, 97
Carillion plc, 298
Carpetright plc, 158
Carroll, A., 275–7, 293, 300
cell production systems, 256
central banks, 116–21
    and interest rates, 116–20
    and 9/11, 121
Centrica plc, 194
change, 344–51
    change leadership, 351
    managing change, 344–50
    models of change, 343–4
    resistance to change, 346
    and the role of Human Resources, 346–8
chaos theory, 315
child labour, 285–6
child poverty, 228
China, 81, 83, 118, 138–41
    and Communist party, 139–41
    and economic development, 138–41
    and India, 138–41
    and Opium Wars, 81
    and Philips, 83
    and Siemens, 83
    and world demand, 118
Chrystal, A., 36, 53
CIPD, 235, 237, 238, 244, 280–1, 282, 308, 344, 354
Citizens Advice Bureau, 150
civil law, 145
claimant count, unemployment, 109
Clark, R., 354
Clarke, K., 116, 130
    and Ken and Eddie show, 116

class, 218–21, 230
    death of, 221
Coco de Mer, 281
codes of practice, 147
collective bargaining and the law, 164–7
collusion, 37
command economy, 9
Common Agricultural Policy (CAP), 66–7, 77–8
common law, 147
Commonwealth Immigration Act 1956, 192
communications technology, 250
comparative advantage, 74–5, 95
    and globalisation, 95
Competition Act 1998, 154
Competition Commission, 56, 155, 329
competiveness policy, 112, 129–33
congestion charge, 133–5
Connock, S., 308
consideration, 152
Consumer Credit Act 1974, 159
consumer protection, 153–9
Consumer Protection Act 1987, 157
containerisation, 251
contestable markets, 36
contraception, 189
contract law, 151
Co-operative Bank plc, 294
core competencies, 325–6
corporate governance, 273, 289–92
    and Germany, 289
    and Japan, 289–90
    and Venetian Republic, 289
corporate manslaughter, 303
corporate social responsibility, 273, 293–7, 300–6
    case studies, 294–5, 296
    definitions, 293–4
    and government, 302–4
    and Human Resources, 300–1
    and profitability, 304–6
COSHH Regulations 1988, 170
cost leadership, 330–33
    and KwikSave, 332–3
    and Ryanair, 330–1
courts system (UK), 147
CPI (inflation measure), 110, 116

Crane, A., 308
criminal law, 146
Crown Prosecution Service, 146
culture, 49, 127, 314, 322
    and public sector, 49
    and strategic management, 314, 322

D
De George, R. T., 278
death rate, 189
debt relief, Third World, 78–80
deflation, 114
demand curve, 29
demography, 185–205, 206, 209, 213
    implications for government, 209
    implications for international
        society, 213
    implications for organisations, 206
    statistics, 185–205
Deng Xiaoping, 140
dependency ratio, 210
deregulation, 45
D'Estaing, G., 67
differentiation, 330, 334–6
    and Marks & Spencer, 334–5
    and Northern Rock, 335–6
digitisation, 44–5
Dilbert, 324
discrimination, protection from, 161
Distance Selling Regulations 2000, 159
diversification, 55
diversity, 238–9
    and police, 239
    and sharia mortgages, 239
Doha Round (WTO), 77–8, 91
Donaghue v Stevenson 1930, 153
doorstep selling, 156
Drucker, P., 281
duty of care (health and safety), 168–9
    on employees, 169
    on employers, 168
Dwr Cymru Welsh Water plc, 123
dynamic pricing, 31–2
    and easyJet, 31–2

E
Easter eggs, 39–40
Eastern Europe, demography case
    study, 194–5

easyJet plc, 31–2, 38
eBay, 33, 132
e-commerce, 55, 132
economic growth, 110, 138–41
    China, 138–41
    India, 138–41
economic objectives, 110–11
Economic and Monetary Union,
    112–13
    and euro, 112–13
    and European Central Bank, 119
economies of scale, 35, 41
Edexcel, 284
education, 73–4
Egg McMuffin, 317
Electronic Commerce Regulations
    2002, 159
Electronic Funds Transfer at Point of
    Sale (EFTPOS), 13, 55
Ellingham, M., 30
embourgeoisement, 221
Employment Act 2002, 165
employment contracts, sources of, 160
employment law, 159–67
Employment Relations Act 1999, 167
employment rights, 161–5
Employment Rights Act 1996, 165
employment trends, 228–31
    by sector, 228–9
    feminisation of the workforce,
        229–81
    older workers, 199–200
Enron Inc, 291, 306
environment
    placid, dynamic, turbulent analysis,
        7–9
equal opportunities, 238–9
Equal Pay Act 1970, 162
ethics, 273, 274–8, 279–82, 287–8
    absolutism, 274
    business ethics, 281–8
    codes of ethics, 287–8
    definitions, 274
    ethical dilemmas, 277–8, 285–6
    ethical principles, 274–7
    golden rule, 275
    professional ethics, 279–81
    relativism, 276
    utilitarianism, 276

ethnicity of UK population, 195
euro, 112–13
European Central Bank, 63, 119, 120
    and 9/11, 120
European Commission, 60–1, 63, 68
European Council of Ministers, 61–2,
    63, 68
    and Qualified Majority Voting, 62,
    68
European Court of Justice, 62, 63
European Economic and Social
    Committee, 62–3
European Parliament, 62–8
European Union, 57, 58–69, 59, 63,
    64–7, 67–9, 77–8, 105–6, 112–13,
    119, 131
    aims of, 58–9
    Charter of Fundamental Rights, 68,
    69
    Common Agricultural Policy, 66–7,
    77–8
    and competitiveness, 131
    constitution of, 67–9
    and Doha Round, 77–8
    enlargement of, 64–7
    and euro, 112–13
    and European Central Bank, 119
    federalist model of, 59
    historical background to, 58
    integrationist model of, 59–60
    legislative process in, 105–6
    and Reform Treaty, 57, 69
    single market model of, 59
    Stability and Growth Pact, 63
E-V-R congruence, 14–19
    and National Trust, 19
exchange rates, 112
Exodus Ltd, 23
Explore Worldwide Ltd, 23–4, 308–9

F
Fair Trading Act 1973, 154
Fairtrade, 296–7
Federal Reserve, 119, 120
    and 9/11, 120
female forfeit, 230
fertility rate, 188
Financial Services Authority (FSA),
    179–80

fiscal policy, 111–12
Five Firm Concentration Ratio, 36–7
Five Forces Model (Porter), 40–5
flexibility, and productivity, 132
flexible organisation, 232–3
flexible working, 233
focus, 330
food miles, 300
France, Second World War strategy,
    355
Friedman, M., 94, 112
    and monetarism, 112
Friends Provident plc, 305
Fukuyama, F., 82, 94
full employment, 110
further education, 349–50
future workplace, 234

G
G8, 79
game theory, 38
Gandhi, M., 139
Geldof, B., 79
General Agreement on Tariffs and
    Trade (GATT), 70, 75
gene therapy, 253, 268
General Electric Inc, 26
genetically modified organisms
    (GMOs), 252
George, E., 116
    and Ken and Eddie show, 116
George, V., 244
Georgia, 186
Germany, Second World War strategy,
    365–6
Giddens, A., 221
Gini coefficient, 225
Gladwin, T., 308
global brands, 84
global warming, 298
globalisation, 80–97
    case studies of, 86–9
    debates on, 89–91
    definitions of 80–1
    drivers of, 82
    and labour market, 94–7
    and outsourcing, 95–7
    and poverty, 90–1
    and profits, 96

and sport, 93
and Third World, 90–1
see also multinational corporations, transnational corporations
golden rule, 111, 118
golden shares, 122
Goldthorpe, J., 221
Greene King plc, 365–7
Gresham's law, 33
Gross Domestic Product (GDP), 108

H
Hamel, G., 315, 325–6
and core competences, 325–6
Handy, C., 233
Harlow (Essex), and social structure, 231–2
Harry Potter, 56, 319, 327
health and safety, 168–77
regulation, 168–77
role of Human Resources, 175–6
Health and Safety at Work Act 1974, 168–70
Health and Safety Commission, 170
Health and Safety Executive, 170
Henderson, D., 306
Hewlett-Packard Inc and H-P Way, 316
HF Holidays Ltd, 24
Higgs Report 2003, 291
High Court, 148
Hoffman, M., 282
holidays, employee right to, 165
Honda, 318
Hong Kong, business ethics in, 276–7
Hornby plc, 319
House of Lords, 105, 149
Huntingdon Life Sciences, 285
Hutton, W., 141

I
IBM, 253
imperfect information, 33
Improvement Notice (Health and Safety), 172
incremental change, 343
India, 81, 95–6, 96–7, 97–8, 138–41, 204
and call centres, 81, 96–7
and China, 138–41
dealing with birth rate, 204
and Doha Round, 97–8
and economic development, 138–41
and offshoring, 95–6
indictable offences, 146
industrial structure, 228–9
inflation, 109–10, 112, 113–14, 114–15, 116, 117–19
and interest rates, 113–14
and unemployment, 114–15
Information and Consultation Regulations 2004, 167
information technology, 250
injunction, 146
institutional racism, 302
interest rates, 113–14, 116–19
and central banks, 116–19
and inflation, 113–14, 116–19
International Labour Office (ILO), unemployment definition of, 109
International Monetary Fund (IMF), 70–2, 73–4
international trade, 74–5
and comparative advantage, 74–5
and free trade, 74–5
Internet, 252
Investors in People, 136
Iraq, 2–4, 37
US war policy in, 2–4, 37
Ireland, 187
Italy, Second World War strategy, 355

J
J D Wetherspoon plc, 366–7
Japan, 189, 190–1
corporate governance in, 289–90
death rate, 189
demography case study, 190–1
keiretsu, 232, 289–90
Second World War strategy, 355
Java, furniture industry in, 86
Johns, T., 308
Johnson, G., 11, 283–4, 290, 322, 337–8, 354
Joseph Rowntree Foundation, 227
Jubilee 2000, 79

K

Kay, J., 26, 121
Keegan, W., 133
Kerala, fishermen and technology, 251
Ketels, C., 133
Keynes, J. M., 111
Kiley, B., 128–9
Kimberly-Clark, health and safety case
    study, 177
King, M., 118–19
knowledge management, 265
Komatsu, 324
Kotter. J., 344–5
K-waves, 248
KwikSave plc, and cost leadership,
    332–3
Kyoto Treaty, 298, 308

L

Labour Force Survey, 109
labour market, 198, 206, 258
    and technology, 258
    in UK, 198, 206
Latinos, demography case study, 196
Lawton, A., 49, 280
legislative process, 104–6
    in the EU, 105–6
    in the UK, 104–5
Legrain, P., 90–1, 92, 94–5
Lewin, K., 343–4
life-cycle analysis, 338
Lipsey, R., 36, 53
Lisbon Programme, 131
Livingstone, K., 128–9, 133–5
London, 128–9, 133–5
London Underground, 49, 128–9
London Zoo, 323
Lovell, A., 308

M

Macmillan, H., 122
Macpherson report, 302
Major, J., 106, 230
Make Poverty History, 79
Malawi, education in, 73–4
Maltby, P., 123
Mandela, N., 351–2
Manual Handling and Operations
    Regulations 1992, 171

manufacturing employment, decline
    of, 203
Mao Zedong, 139
Marconi plc, 341
market economy, 26, 28–38
market structure, 27–8
markets, and demography, 206
Marks & Spencer plc, 295, 334–5
    and diversification, 334–5
    and Simply Food, 334–5
marriage, decline of, 204
Marx, K., 218
Maternity and Parental Leave
    Regulations 1999, 165
Matten, D., 308
McDonald's plc, 317
Meredith, R., 141
meritocracy, 245
Metronet Ltd, 128–9
Metropolitan Police, 239, 302
    and diversity, 239
    and institutional racism, 302
Mexico, declining birth rate, 204
MFI plc, 157
Micklethwait, J., 99
migration, 192–7
    discouraging, 197
    encouraging, 196
Miles, R. E., 19–20
minimum efficient scale, 41
Mintzberg, H., 316–17
mission, 320–4
mission statements, 323–4
Mitchell, S., 345
mixed economy, 27
Modbury (Devon), and plastic bags,
    299
Monbiot, G., 73–4
monetary policy, 112, 116–20, 121
    and 9/11, 121
    and central banks, 116–20, 121
monopolistic competition, 34
monopoly, 34–6
monopsony, 40
moral hazard, and Northern Rock, 336
Morris, H., 59–60
Morrisons plc, 291, 348–9
    and takeover of Safeway, 348–9
Moses, 345

Moynagh, M., 234
Mozambique, sugar industry in, 86–7
Multigenome, 288
multinational corporations, 84–5, 90–2

N
National Air Traffic Services (NATS),
    privatisation of, 124–5
National Health Service, 28, 121, 211
    implications of demographic
        change, 211
    and markets, 28
    and nationalisation, 121
National Minimum Wage Act 1998,
    165
National Trust, 18–19, 107
    and E-V-R congruence, 19
National Union of Mineworkers, 143
Nationwide Building Society, 126
Nehru, P., 139–40
Network Rail, 123
new economic paradigm, 132
new unionism, 239–40
non-accelerating inflation rate of
    unemployment (NAIRU), 112,
    114–15
non-price competition, 38
Nortel, Human Resources and
    technology case study, 266
North American Free Trade Agreement
    (NAFTA), 69–70
Northern Rock plc, 293, 335–6
    and differentiation, 335–6

O
obiter dicta, 144
objectives, 3, 320–2
    SMART objectives, 321
Office for Communication (OFCOM),
    179
Office of Fair Trading (OFT), 154–8
    doorstep selling case study, 156
    extended warranties case study, 155
    unfair contract terms case study,
        158
offshoring, 95–7
    and call centres, 97
oil prices, 30
oligopoly, 36–9, 54–6

ombudsman, 150
Opec, 30, 37
Opium Wars, 81
opportunity analysis, 12–13
optical character recognition, 259
optical fibre technology, 148
Ottakar's plc, 328–9
outsourcing, 95–7, 214, 264
    and call centres, 95–7
    of Human Resources, 264
    of work internationally, 214
Oxford Bus Company, and
    stakeholders, 283

P
Pakistan, and child labour, 275, 285–6
participation rate, 199
paternity leave, 165
Pearmount College, and change
    management, 349–50
pensions, implication of demographic
    changes, 211
perfect competition, 28–33
PEST analysis, 5–6
Peters, T., 232, 314
Philips AG, 83
Phillips, A. W., 114–15
Phillips curve, 114–15
Philpott, J., 138, 244
plastic bags, and sustainability, 299–300
Poland, 64, 66–7, 69, 100–1
    and CAP, 66–7
    and EU membership, 64
    and EU Reform Treaty, 69
    and immigration from, 100–1
political parties, influence of, 106, 107
population, 187–212
    age distribution, 210–12
    drivers of change, 187–93
    ethnicity of, 195–6
    future predictions, 204–8
    geographical distribution, 204–8
    growth, 186–7
    working, 197
    and world resources, 215
Porter, M. E., 11, 40–5, 133, 315, 319,
    330, 337, 339, 343
    and competitiveness, 133
    and Five Forces model, 11, 40–5

and generic strategy, 330, 337
and value chain, 339
Porter's Five Forces Model, 11, 40–5
portfolio analysis, 45–8, 319, 338–9
poverty, 225–8
child poverty, 228
Prahalad, C. K., 315, 325–6
precedent, 144
pressure groups, 106–8
attitude groups, 107
functions of, 107–8
interest groups, 107
price determination, 30
price discrimination, 31–2
price war, 37–8, 39, 55–6
private equity, 291–3
and corporate governance, 291–2
private finance initiative (PFI), 49,
125–9
and London Underground, 128–9
and NHS, 126–7
privatisation, 121–3, 124–5
and NATS, 124–5
Prodi, R., 61
productivity, 130–3
Prohibition Notice, health and safety,
172
Prusack, L., 171
psychological contract, 234–6
public interest companies, 123–4
Public Interest Disclosure Act 1998,
279
public ownership, 120–1
public–private partnerships, 126–7,
128–9
and London Underground, 128–9
and NHS, 126–7
public sector, and strategy, 48–50

Q
qualified majority voting, 62, 68
Queen's Bench Division, 148
Quinn, J., 312, 316

R
Railtrack plc, 123–4
Rake, K., 230
Ramblers Worldwide Holidays Ltd, 24
recession, definition of, 109

recruitment, and technology, 259
redundancy, 166
regulation, 143–84
regulators, 177–81
responsibilities, 178
Reilly, P., 171
Reporting of Diseases and Dangerous
Occurrences Regulations
(RIDDOR) 1995, 171
resource analysis, 324–6
restrictive practices, 132
Rhine model of corporate governance,
290
Ridgeway, C., 347–8
Richards, D., 308
risk, and Northern Rock, 335–6
risk assessment (health and safety),
172
road pricing, 133–5
robotics, 254–6
Romania, 186
Rose, A., 49
RPI (inflation measure), 109–10
RPIX (inflation measure), 110, 116
Runciman, W. G., 218–19
Russia, 186
Ryanair plc, 38, 330–1
and cost leadership, 330–1

S
safety representatives, 172
Safeway plc, 348–9
Sainsbury's plc, 54–6, 291
and private equity, 291
Sale of Goods Act 1979, 158
scenario planning, 314
Scholes, K., 11, 283–4, 290
Scotland, demography, 187
Scottish & Newcastle plc, 363–4
Second World War, national strategies,
355–6
sectoral employment, UK, 201
service sector employment growth, 201
shared services, Human Resources,
263, 269
Shell Directional Policy Matrix, 47
Shell plc, and scenario planning, 314
Siemens, 83
Sierra Leone, life expectancy in, 189

Singapore, death rate, 189
Singh, M., 140
Single European Act, 1986 59, 61–2
Small Claims Court, 147
Smith, D., 141
Snell, R., 276, 277
Snow, C. C., 19–20
social inequality, 223–5
social mobility, 220–3
    absolute mobility, 222
    intergenerational mobility, 222
    intragenerational mobility, 222
    relative mobility, 222
social partnership, 239
social stratification, 221–2
socio-economic classifications, 221–2
    JICNARS classification, 220
    NS-NEC classification, 221–2
Somerfield plc, 333
Spain, Second World War strategy, 355
specific perfomance, 146
sport, and globalisation, 93
Stability and Growth Pact, 63, 138, 211
    and demography, 211
Stacey, R., 315
stakeholders, 282–3, 284, 285, 292, 319,
    339–42
    acceptability, 319, 339–42
    definition, 282
    mapping, 282–3
    and private equity, 292
Standard Chartered Bank plc, shared
    services, 265
Standard Life Ltd, selection, 260
standard of living, 108, 137
Statutory Sick Pay, 166
STEEPLE analysis, 6–7, 11, 319
strategy, 312–24, 330, 337–48
    generic strategy, 330, 337
    intended strategy, 316–17
    models of strategy, 313–17
        chaos theory, 315
        corporate planning, 313–14, 316
        strategic management, 314–18
    realised strategy, 316–7
    strategic analysis, 318–24
    strategic decisions, 312–13, 330,
        337–42
        acceptability, 339–42

strategic evaluation, 337–42
    suitability, 338–9
strategic implementation, 324,
    343–8
strategic levels, 313
strategic management, 314–18
strategic option screening, 340–2
tactical management, 313
stress, 173–5
    case studies, 174
    causes, 173–4
    cost of, 173
summary offences, 146
supermarkets, 54–6
superstores, 54
supply curve, 29
Supply of Goods and Services Act
    1982, 158
surveillance technology and
    employment, 270
sustainability, 298–300
Sutherland v Hatton 2002, 174
SWOT analysis, 11–14, 319, 324–5

T
tax havens, 84
technology, 247–72
    change, types of, 249
teleworking, 260–1
Tesco plc, 39, 54–6
Thailand, 87–9, 300
    and globalisation, 87–9
    and food miles, 300
Thatcher, M., 106, 112, 221, 224, 230
Third World, 71–4, 77–8, 78–80
    and debt relief, 78–80
    and Doha Round, 77–8
    and IMF, 71–4
    and WTO, 77–8
Thompson, J., 14–18, 354
threat analysis, 12–13
Tiger economies, 71
tools of economic policy, 111–13
tort, 145
TOWS analysis, 13
Trade Descriptions Act 1968, 157
trade unions, 92, 240–2
    global unions, 92
    and social partnership, 239

union recognition, 242
Trades Union Congress (TUC), 240–1
Transfer of Undertakings Regulations
    (TUPE) 1981, 49, 50, 165
transformational change, 343
transnational corporations, 84–5
Transport for London, 128–9
travel and tourism industry, 207
Treaty of Amsterdam, 63
Treaty of Maastricht, 61
Treaty of Nice, 61, 67
Treaty of Paris, 58
Treaty of Rome, 58, 61, 66
tribunals, 149
Turkey, 65–6
    and EU membership, 65–6
    and human rights, 66
    and Islam, 65
two–tier workforce, 50

U
Ukraine, demography, 186
unemployment, 109, 114–15
    and inflation, 114–5
Unfair Contract Terms Act 1977, 158
unfair dismissal, protection from, 162
Unilever plc, 341
union recognition, 241–2
Uruguay Round (WTO), 76
USA
    and Doha Round, 77–8
    financial advice for the elderly, 208
    and second world war strategy, 355
    war policy in Iraq, 1–4, 37
    war policy in Vietnam, 1–4
USSR, Second World War strategy, 355

V
values, 3, 286–7, 320–1
    and Cadbury-Schweppes plc, 320–1
value-chain analysis, 339
Vertex Ltd, 241

video rental, decline of, 9–10
Vietnam, 1–4, 205
    declining fertility rate, 205
    US war policy in, 1–4
vision, 320–1
Volkswagen, outsourcing to Eastern
    Europe, 215
voluntary sector, 48–50
vulture funds, 80

W
Walker v Northumberland County
    Council 1995, 144
Wallace, C., 347–8
Walton, J., 343, 354
war on terror, 94
Waterman, R. H., 23, 232
Waterstone's plc, and takeover of
    Ottakar's, 328–9
Weber, M., 218–19
whistleblowing, 278–9
Whitbread plc, 367–9
W H Smith plc, 328
Wilding, P., 244
Willey, B., 59–60
Wolf, M., 90
Wooldridge, A., 99
work–life balance, 236–7
work organisation, 232–7
Workers' Educational Association
    (Northern Ireland), 325
World Bank, 57, 72–3
World Trade Organisation (WTO),
    75–8, 91
    and Doha Round, 77–8, 91
    and Uruguay Round, 76
Worsley, R., 234
Wyplosz, C., 72

Y
Youngs plc, and food miles, 300